The LAFAYETTE ESCADRILLE

The LAFAYETTE ESCADRILLE

Herbert Molloy Mason, Jr.

This edition published in 1995 by SMITHMARK Publishers, Inc.
16 East 32nd Street, New York, NY 10016.

SMITHMARK books are available for bulk purchase for sales
promotion and premium use. For details write or call the
manager of special sales, SMITHMARK Publishers, Inc.,
16 East 32nd Street, New York, NY 10016; (212) 532-6600.

This edition published by arrangement with John Hawkins
& Associates, Inc., New York and with W. S. Konecky
Associates, Inc.

ISBN: 0-8317-5712-4

Printed In the United States of America

10 9 8 7 6 5 4 3 2 1

Special thanks and acknowledgment are given to:
KENNIKAT Press, Inc., for permission to quote from the *Lafayette Flying Corps*, edited by James Hall and CharlesNordhoff. Copyright 1920 by J.N. Hall & C. B. Nordhoff. Copyright renewed 1948 by J. N. Hall & Laura Nordhoff.
David Wooster King, for permission to quote from L.M. 8046.
James McConnell Truitt, for permission to quote from the letters of James McConnell.
Paul A. Rockwell, for permission to quote from his book, *American Fighters in the Foreign Legion*, as well as from *War Letters of Kiffin Yates Rockwell*.
Albert K. Pavelka, for permission to quote from the letters of Paul Pavelka.
Sarah Spencer Thénault, for permission to quote from *L'Escadrille Lafayette* by Lieutenant Colenel Georges Thénault.
Dorothea E. Bridgman, for permission to quote from the letters of Ray C. Bridgman.

To

RIGMOR

CONTENTS

MAPS

The LAFAYETTE ESCADRILLE

The Rumpler Taube

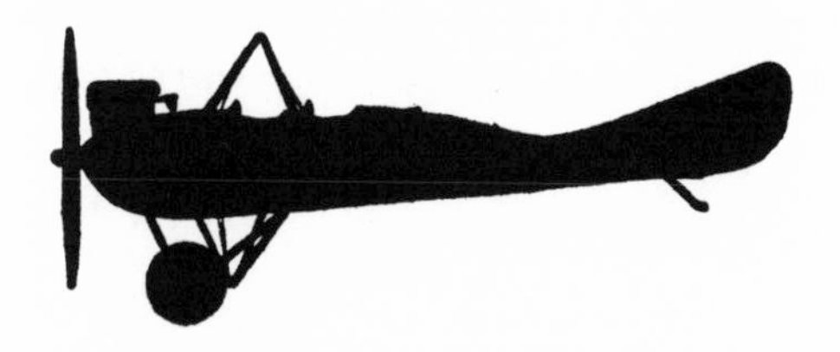

CHAPTER 1

CLASH OF ARMS

No person within the territory and jurisdiction of the United States shall take part, directly or indirectly, in the war, but shall maintain a strict and impartial neutrality.

—WOODROW WILSON, August 3, 1914

Late in the morning of July 31, 1914, two statesmen were proceeding by car to the Morgan-Harjes Bank in Paris. Despite the stifling heat, the occupants were sealed from view by curtains drawn tightly across the opened windows. Only brief gusts of warm air penetrated the darkened interior of the car where the men sat in silence. When the automobile glided smoothly to a stop in front of the bank, the chauffeur got out and opened the door for Myron Herrick, the American Ambassador. Then the door was closed, leaving Herrick's counterpart from Germany, Wilhelm von Schoen, sitting alone on the hot leather seat.

Von Schoen was perspiring, and it was not only from the summer's heat. On the eve of the worst crisis in Europe in nearly fifty years, he was short of ready cash. He had received orders from Berlin only that morning to return the German Embassy staff of ninety men and women, together with everything they had brought with them to France. The thirty-first was a Friday, and von Schoen had only that weekend to crate and ship embassy property. He had desperately racked his brains all that morning before deciding to ask Herrick for the money. After all, the United States was three thousand miles away from the catastrophe that was about to engulf Europe, and the Americans seemed to be not only neutral, but isolationist.

Herrick shortly returned to the waiting automobile and climbed into the oven-like interior. Smiling sympathetically, he handed von Schoen a manila envelope containing five thousand dollars in cash. On the following Monday, August 3, the German Ambassador and his staff departed for Germany—the trip financed with American funds. One of the few things von Schoen left behind was a declaration of war, which became effective at six forty-five that same evening.

Those first few days in August were among the loveliest of the year; the sun was warm in a cloudless sky and a gentle breeze washed over all of Paris. But the glory of the weather went unheeded and a vast silence descended upon the great city, a silence broken only by the blare of trumpets and the sounds of regiments on the move.

Long columns of infantry marched in a solid press up the wide boulevards lined with a sea of civilians watching them go. The infantrymen sweated mightily in their red woolen trousers, dark blue greatcoats and red woolen *képis*, but they marched with an easy swing and a confident air, for they were the regulars. Behind them loomed the sleekly groomed cavalry horses whose hooves clopped hollowly on the cobblestones. The riders were splendidly uniformed in gleaming steel breastplates, shining copper helmets topped with horsehair plumes and high, mirror-like boots. They could have been riding off to Waterloo—but behind them rolled the caissons and horse-drawn artillery pieces, the new and terrible 75s. The sight of those lean, quick-firing guns dulled somewhat the illusion that this would be a war in the old style. Here and there in the crowd, men raised their straw boaters and cheered, but for the most part the people stood silent, except for the women who wept at the sight of sons, husbands and lovers moving off to war.

The rush to the colors included an astonishing number of foreigners whose motivation was summed up by an Italian writer named Canudo who published a dramatic explanation in a Paris newspaper:

"Foreigners, friends of France, who during their sojourn here have learned to love and cherish her as a second country, feel an imperious need to offer her their arms.

"Intellectuals, students, workmen, able-bodied men of all sorts —born elsewhere, domiciled here—we who have found spiritual nourishment or material food, we grouped ourselves together in a solid band of volunteers . . ."

More than three thousand Italians living in Paris gathered together and voted to offer themselves in a body to the French Army. They would call themselves, they said, the Legion of Garibaldi. Then groups of men from dozens of nations—including eight hundred Germans and Austrians—clamored to form national volunteer corps to fight for France.

The war was hardly forty-eight hours old before a body of Americans trooped into Ambassador Herrick's office and asked "if it was legal to fight." Herrick got out French and American books that dealt with laws governing neutrals and carefully explained that enlistment in the French Army would cost them their citizenship, but added that if they joined the Foreign Legion the risk of loss of citizenship was slight. Herrick slammed his fist down on his desk and concluded, "That is the law, boys, but if I were young and in your shoes I know mighty well what I would do!"

"At this," Herrick later wrote, "they set up a regular shout and each gripped my hand and then went rushing down the stairs as though every minute was too precious to be lost."

As flattered as the French were to have so many foreign volunteers demanding to serve, they were swamped with their own mobilization problems: more than four thousand trains with their arrival and departure times clocked to the minute were rolling through the country, each loaded with troops bound for various rendezvous points. Then, on August 8, *Le Journal Officiel* advised: "The Minister of War has authorized the acceptance of foreign volunteers for the duration of the war only. However, no enlistments of foreigners can be received until 21 August, 1914."

The technicality that allowed Americans to enlist in the *Légion Étrangère* without forfeiting their U. S. citizenship lay in the wording of the enlistment contract itself. Legion volunteers were not required to swear an oath of allegiance to France; the contract required only that the Legionnaire promise "to serve with faithfulness and honor," and to "follow the corps, or any fraction of the corps, wherever the government wishes to send it."

Impatient for the arrival of the enlistment date, the Americans gathered each morning in the garden of the Palais-Royal to learn the rudiments of close-order drill. They were trooped around the square by a onetime West Point cadet named Charles Sweeney, thirty-two, from Spokane, Washington. At first Sweeney's marchers numbered about twenty Americans who had been living in Paris at the outbreak of war; but the straggling ranks began to fill with countrymen who had been traveling on vacation in different parts of Europe, and by others arriving from the States on almost every boat that reached harbor. After nearly three weeks Sweeney had worn himself hoarse, but by then his ragtag platoon executed facing and flanking movements so well they were actually applauded by the French who gathered daily to watch the fun.

On August 21, the swearing-in ceremony was held in the great courtyard of the Hôtel des Invalides, repository of so much of France's military history. The huge golden dome that sheltered the remains of Napoleon Bonaparte looked down on the blinding white yard filled with colorfully uniformed army officers, silk-hatted diplomats and the hodgepodge of Americans, Englishmen, Poles, Spaniards, Russians, Italians, Greeks, South Americans, Serbs, Croats, Arabs, Sicilians, Norwegians, Swedes, Danes and others whose nationality could only be guessed at. The yard rang with patriotic speeches defying Germany and promising revenge for the humiliation of 1870; they praised the "selfless act of so many foreigners who wished to contribute their part of courage and blood to the history of France." When the last paper had been signed, forty-three Americans were accepted as privates in the *Légion Étrangère*. Their pay would be thirty cents a month.

The next day, Count Albert de Mun rose to his feet in the Chamber of Deputies and exclaimed, "France has foreign volunteers! But Germany, *she* has deserters!" This kind of optimistic nonsense concerning the nature of the enemy was to persist for nearly two years in the face of repeated and bloody demonstrations that one French soldier was indeed not worth two of the German. Even as de Mun spoke, the initial clash of armies along the frontiers had claimed more than 300,000 Frenchmen—dead, wounded or prisoners of war—victims of inferior strategy and tactical shortcomings.

French strategy had been planned well in advance. In essence, the plan was simple: muster three-quarters of a million men in the eastern corner of France and plunge straight forward through Alsace and Lorraine and drive on to the Rhine. *Grand Quartier Général* (General Headquarters) depended upon the élan and sublime courage of the French infantryman, led by the magnificently trained St. Cyr officers, to sweep all before them. But the French armies were woefully short of heavy guns ("not needed") and the staff at G.Q.G. failed to take into consideration what machine guns ("of little account") might do against advancing infantry in the open.

To the blare of bugles, the masses of French infantry charged ahead, their long bayonets glinting in the bright sunshine. German machine guns cut them to pieces. Again and again the French hurled themselves with almost inhuman valor against the guns, but the slaughter was beyond belief and the projected advance to the Rhine turned into a near rout instead.

Disaster piled upon disaster as the Germans moved swiftly and ruthlessly in the north, rushing downward in the execution of their own war plan, devised by Count Alfred von Schlieffen nearly ten years before. German strategy was based on a mammoth wheeling movement through neutral Belgium that would carry their armies through Paris and, similar to the slamming of a heavy door, swing behind the French rear, pinning their enemies against the Swiss frontier. In the early stages, von Schlieffen's strategy worked as its creator had intended, punching large holes in the French defenses in the west; with the mercilessly thinned forces reeling back from the frontier in the east, the politicians in Paris were verging on panic. Barely three weeks after the war had begun with high hopes of a quick victory that would erase the shame of 1870, they were faced with the unbearable prospect of a second and even worse humiliation.

Thus it is not surprising that the recently sworn-in foreign volunteers were quickly sent off to training centers as fast as they could be loaded aboard trains. The first group left the Gare St. Lazare at 9 A.M. on August 25, and within the next seventy-two hours 1600 recruits were installed in barracks at Rouen. To their surprise, a large number of the volunteers found themselves quartered in what had once been a school for young ladies.

"Rouen," wrote one of the Americans, "was teeming with a marvelous, heterogeneous collection: wounded from the British army, stragglers from the Belgian Army, refugees, French reservists, British Army Service Corps units—all wandering around the streets aimlessly, some terribly depressed, others hilarious and singing, and a good portion of them drunk."

The volunteers were bedded down on compressed bales of straw that covered almost every square foot of the barracks floors. They lay down to sleep fully dressed in the civilian clothes they had worn from Paris, to be roused from a heavy slumber at four the next morning by a cursing sergeant. The noncom called for two volunteers. A cherubic-looking onetime Harvard undergrad from Rhode Island, David Wooster King, and one other stepped smartly forward. "My imagination ran wild," said King. "I saw myself as the last man in a desperate rearguard action. Or perhaps the Germans were advancing on Rouen and I would be chosen to light the fuse to blow the bridge." But the sergeant led them off to a large, foul-smelling shed where they were handed swabs and told to clean the latrines. This, the first military detail performed by the Legionnaires, taught them a cardinal rule of intelligent soldiering: never volunteer for anything.

With a floodtide of Germans pouring down toward Paris, the government panicked. Training depots in the north were ordered evacuated, their personnel to be transported to the interior. Thus only six days after the Legion recruits had arrived at Rouen, orders came, transferring them to Toulouse, 150 miles to the south. The volunteers were as carefully shielded by press censorship of the chaotic situation along the battlefront as were the civilians, and the sudden shift meant to them one thing only: the government believed that Rouen, a full seventy miles from the nearest German military unit, was doomed. Then came the shocking news that the cabinet ministers and deputies had precipitously fled the capital and bolted for Bordeaux, 120 miles away. The French Army in the field, getting ready to fight the battle of the Marne that would decide the nation's fate, never forgave the politicians for this seeming act of cowardice that was an open admission of a lack of confidence in the stubbornly resisting soldiers and in the officers who led them.

The Legionnaires were herded aboard small wooden railway cars that reeked of manure. They were still wearing their civilian clothes, by now crumpled and filthy, and they carried only an army blanket and a one-liter canteen. The cars were designed to accommodate either eight horses or forty men, but into each were jammed fifty-six sweating recruits. Shortly before the train pulled out of Rouen, the Legionnaires were issued a large can of bully beef apiece and told that each can would keep one man alive for four days. Then the door banged shut and the train started jolting its way out of the station for the long journey south.

The men were packed together so tightly that there was room for only about half of them to sit at a time; lying down to sleep was out of the question. In such close confinement, sharing a common misery, the Americans got to know each other's background in detail.

William Thaw II, a heavy-framed man with black hair combed straight back from a high forehead, was one of two sons of one of Pittsburgh's oldest and wealthiest families. At twenty-one, Thaw had already made a name for himself in aviation in America and in Europe. He left Yale in 1913 in the middle of his sophomore year to devote his time to flying—learned by taking weekend hydroplane lessons while still a freshman. Newspaper columnists reported that during the summer Thaw "initiated Newport society leaders into the mysteries of the air," and in the winters he lived in Palm Beach where he "took passengers as high as they wanted to go for $20." In New York, Thaw made headlines by becoming the first man to fly up the East River passing underneath all four bridges—a feat his contemporaries believed suicidal. Anticipating longer ranges in aircraft, Thaw tried to interest backers in a scheme to deliver mail to inbound ships before they reached port. To prove that it could be done, he flew over the approaches to New York Harbor and accurately dropped a bundle of newspapers on the deck of the *Imperator* as the ship nosed into the channel. Nobody but Thaw saw merit in the scheme, however, so he turned his attention to an invention just completed by his younger brother, Alexander. It was a stabilizing device and the brothers believed it would win a $100,000 award offered by the French for a significant mechanical contribution to flight safety. Bill Thaw installed the device on a 100 h.p. Curtiss pusher and took it to France in the spring of 1914. He entered the Schneider Trophy Race, held in the Bay of Monaco in April, and although his airplane qualified, Thaw failed to place. With the war imminent, the French abandoned the safety competition. The day the conflict began Thaw offered his services as a pilot in the French *Service Aéronautique*, but was turned down. Then he joined the Legion.

There was one other in that tightly packed car who claimed to be an aviator. To those who believed him, Weston Bert Hall was adventure personified. He had, he said, been a famous racing car driver before a Turkish sultan, Abdul Hamid, offered him payment in gold to fly spotting missions against the Bulgarians in the Balkan Wars of 1912. But his love for France, Hall said, tore him away from the lofty world of automotive competition and freelance combat flying.

The facts were somewhat different. Hall had come to France in 1912 as the chauffeur of a Fort Worth, Texas, cotton broker. Fired from the job almost immediately, he drove a taxi in Paris until the outbreak of war. At various times, Hall gave his birthplace as Higginsville, Missouri; El Paso, Texas; and Kentucky. Nobody ever learned just where Hall was born or, indeed, if Hall was his right name. He was, however, "genial, charming and probably the biggest liar in the Legion."

At the opposite end of the pole from Bert Hall were the

Rockwell brothers, Kiffin and Paul, twenty-two and twenty-six respectively. They were born in Newport, Tennessee, and they had lived in Asheville, North Carolina, and in Atlanta, Georgia, where they were sharing an apartment on West Peachtree Street when the war broke out. They were well over six feet tall, looked at the world through clear blue eyes and had rather prominent, stubborn chins. But where Paul was easygoing and good-natured, Kiffin was quick to anger and visibly intolerant of those whose standards of conduct he felt did not measure up. To Kiffin Yates Rockwell, there were no shades of gray; the world and everything in it was white, or it was black.

Both Rockwells were Southerners to the marrow, but it was Kiffin who had been fired the most by tales told the two boys by their maternal grandfather, Enoch Shaw Ayres, who had fought for the Confederacy from the opening shot of the Civil War until Lee's formal surrender at Appomattox Court House. The more Kiffin listened to his grandfather and the other white-haired old men of the town, the more it seemed to him that a man's real worth could only be determined on the battlefield.

In 1909 Kiffin became a "Brother Rat" at Virginia Military Institute, partly because it was the alma mater of Stonewall Jackson. He was beaten "regularly and religiously" with bed slats, tin dippers, bayonets and broomsticks. On Saturdays he would walk the few hundred yards to the campus of Washington and Lee University and eat lunch with his brother. With some pride Kiffin showed Paul his "wound stripes." Paul "fairly frothed at the mouth with rage and indignation," but Kiffin only laughed drily and said that it was all in the game and was the only way to make men.

A year later Kiffin received an appointment to Annapolis, but turned it down and entered the same school as his brother. When he graduated, Kiffin left the South and toured the East and parts of Canada, looking for a place to settle down. Then he went to San Francisco and got a job in an advertising agency. But a year after he had left Virginia, he was back in the South. He moved in with his brother in the Peachtree Street apartment and went to work for another advertising agency.

Kiffin finally found what he was seeking in the war clouds gathering over Europe. At about the same time von Schoen was leaving Paris, Rockwell mailed off a letter to the French Consul in New Orleans offering both his services and his brother's. The next day, with war a reality, the two brothers packed their suitcases and took the train to New York, where they sailed for France aboard the *St. Paul.*

When the Rockwells' distraught mother asked her sons why they were going off to France, perhaps to get killed, Kiffin replied: "You know I have always been a great dreamer and I just couldn't keep myself from this trip. If I should be killed in this war I will at least die as a man should and would not consider myself a complete failure . . . I think if anything will make a man of me, it is this giving of one's best for an ideal."

Another unabashed idealist was Alan Seeger, a tall, square-jawed man of twenty-six who had spent his childhood in New York City, part of his impressionable youth in Mexico and his maturing years at Harvard and in Paris. Classmates at Harvard knew him as a passionate worker and an "obstinately silent man" who spoke only when aroused and then only on such matters as love and death, heroism and sacrifice. Seeger made many friends in the Latin Quarter, despite his reticence, and it was there he wrote his first book of poems. Seeger watched his French literary and artistic friends vanish suddenly from the Quarter the day war was declared, and then he enlisted in the Legion. "I could not," he said, "go on enjoying the pleasant things in life, for the defense of which my friends were shedding their blood. How could I," he added, "leave millions of other men to experience an emotion of which I should be unaware?"

When it was pointed out to him that in sharing this emotion he might easily be killed by German bullets, Seeger replied: "Life and death have equal value, provided each be glorious." Whatever the rationalization, Seeger saw the war as an unparalleled opportunity to live life to the hilt.

There was one professional killer among the American volunteers, René Phélizot. Born in Chicago, Phélizot ran away from home when he was thirteen and got a job as cabin boy on a Mississippi River passenger boat. When he was fifteen he worked his way across the Atlantic. For ten years before the war Phélizot had earned great sums of money as an elephant hunter and dealer in ivory, and he was one of the best-known big-game killers in the Lake Tchad region. He had taken a holiday to France in July 1914 and was in Paris the day his father's country was invaded by the Germans. Ten years in Africa had rubbed away much of Phélizot's American exterior, and with his fluent command of French he could easily have passed as a *colon*—a colonist. But it was Phélizot who had carried an oversize Stars and Stripes at the van of the Americans who marched down the Avenue de l'Opéra on the day they hiked over to the Gare St. Lazare for the trip to Rouen.

As the troop train rattled and jolted its way south, the heat grew worse and the still-undisciplined recruits thoughtlessly took long pulls from their canteens of lukewarm water, canteens that had seemed so heavy at the beginning of the journey. By the morning of the second day the water was gone and the solitary diet of salted meat aggravated the men's already raging thirst. There was no other water on the train, and in a futile attempt to gain a measure of relief from the heat and the growing smell of unwashed bodies packed tightly together, some of the men risked broken necks by pulling themselves through the windows at the tops of the coaches to reach the feeble current of air pouring over the slowly moving train. When the train stopped for water at the small pumping stations along the route, the dehydrated Legionnaires leaped from the roofs of the cars and poured from the doors seeking water spigots from which to fill their canteens. There were never enough spigots, and politeness gave way to frenzy as men jostled, shoved and pulled one another this way and that in an effort to get the narrow mouths of their canteens under the slow trickle of water from the few taps available. The few old Legion noncoms and officers on the train cursed and pleaded, but the recruits were insensible to any thought save that of slaking their thirsts, and only the shrill whistle of the narrow-gage locomotive as it prepared to pull away from the pumping station was able to stampede the men back aboard the cars.

The Russians, with a Slavic distrust of others, went against the orders of the noncoms to open only one tin a day for four men, and instead each Russian opened his can of bully beef, eating some and hoarding the rest under his jacket. In the intense heat the meat went bad and one by one the Russians fell violently ill. By the morning of the fourth day they were being taken from the cars dead.

The seemingly interminable ride came to an end on the evening of September 4 after nearly ninety hours. The distance from Rouen to Toulouse was covered at an average speed of approximately 2 m.p.h., about the pace of an elderly couple out for a Sunday stroll.

When the train pulled to a stop at the station, noncoms barked orders and the disheveled, unshaven, soot-covered recruits staggered stiffly from the cars and lined up by companies on the station platform. They were to march through the streets of Toulouse in full view of the evening crowds; and they were told to smarten up, but were not told how this miracle might be accomplished. Here and there national flags were unfurled, and battered felts and crushed straw boaters were straightened in a futile effort to present a military appearance. Finally the noncoms gave it up and ordered the march to begin.

"We were filled with a certain amount of pride as we marched out," said Dave King, "for surely the good citizens of Toulouse would appreciate our *beau geste* and would realize we were there of our own volition." Word of the arrival of the train had spread through the town, and as the ragged band of marchers turned into the main street their pride turned to astonishment and then outrage as the crush of people lining both sides of the narrow street greeted them with invective followed by a barrage of ripe tomatoes, apples and rotten vegetables. Through the din certain of the screamed insults could be made out.

"Ah, les brigands!"

"Sales boches!"

"En voilà des prisoniers!"

Then it dawned on the bewildered recruits they were being mistaken for German prisoners of war. Shouted explanations by the few officers and noncoms were drowned by the howling of the mob, so the detachment double-timed up the street through a rain of garbage to reach the sanctuary of Pérignon Barracks.

The barracks at Toulouse, former home of the 183rd Infantry Regiment, were large enough so that only thirty-two men shared the same room. Each man had a low wooden bed, and above that, a shelf on which to stack clothing. After supper, the recruits threw themselves down on the straw-filled pallets that served as mattresses and fell into deep sleep. But despite the bone-weariness that affected them all, they pitched and tossed for most of the night. When a rafale of bugle calls jolted them awake at four the next morning, they were covered with red welts. Suspicious, one of the Americans raised one end of the bed, then let it fall with a thump. "You could actually hear them," he said, "as they plopped on the floor and scuttled for cover." Old-timers told them what to do: burn the straw and paint the beds with kerosene. Still scratching furiously, the men marched off to breakfast. They were given steaming mugs of coffee, but no bread, and afterward were formed into sections of sixty men each to draw uniforms.

Each man was issued a heavy blue greatcoat, coarse white duck fatigue uniforms, a red *képi,* laced field shoes apparently made of iron, wool shirts, a blue sash nine feet long, two blankets and a suit of long underwear. The rifle each man carried was the 1868 Lebel, an 8-shot, 8mm-caliber, bolt-action piece that weighed over 9 pounds and was 51 inches long. With the long, thin French bayonet attached, the Lebel reached the ungainly length of just over 6 feet from butt plate to bayonet tip. Bayonet scabbard, harness and two large leather cartridge boxes completed the issue, except for a tin-plated bowl with a cover and a knife and fork. There was no issue of socks in the Legion; instead, for those who asked, there were small squares of cheap muslin that must be placed with care around the foot, one piece overlapping another in a precise pattern, before the hobnailed shoe was carefully slipped on.

The complete Legion issue of uniforms, mess gear, rifle and cartridges, plus the emergency ration of twenty pieces of hardtack and two cans of "monkey meat," tipped the scales at just over a hundred pounds, and all of it went on the Legionnaire's back when on the march. When stacked on the shelves above each man's cot, the basic uniform issue made a pile three feet high.

Almost daily, fresh recruits arrived until there were nearly three full battalions of them. Then, on the fifth day, the volunteers were called out to watch a splendid sight: the arrival from North Africa of a battalion of regulars of the Second Regiment.

They came swinging through the gates preceded by the blare of bugles and the staccato beating of snare drums. The veterans of *le Deuxième* were baked almost black by the desert sun and almost all wore short, neatly trimmed black beards. They were from nearly every nation on earth and they wore their uniforms with the unconscious air of men who have never worn anything else. "They were soldiers, by God," said an American, "and we felt proud to be numbered among them."

The regulars were divided among the recruits so that there was in each section at least one veteran for each two rookies. The *anciens* soon taught the new volunteers what it meant to soldier in the Legion. Forced marches along the Garonne River were a special agony to Bill Thaw, who hated to walk ten feet to get a glass of water if it could be avoided, but by the end of two weeks even Thaw was making it back to the barracks after hikes of twenty miles burdened with a killing load. More than one man, however, had his shoes filled with blood after one of those excursions. Trench-digging and accuracy with a rifle were almost forgotten in the instructors' enthusiasm for the bayonet. The Legionnaires spent weary hours charging across the training ground under a broiling sun, running hard for practice trenches a full half-mile distant, there, gasping and panting, to plunge their knitting-needle-like bayonets into yielding bags of straw.

The use of the bayonet to terrify the enemy was promulgated in a handbook issued to every recruit. One sentence read: "From the moment of action every soldier must passionately desire the assault by bayonet as the supreme means of imposing his will on the enemy." Legion recruits were given only cursory instruction in the use of the complicated St. Étienne machine gun, and it was hinted that habitual use of deep trenches was tantamount to hiding from the Germans. Machine guns and trenches, they were told, belonged to defensive-minded troops; only the spirit of the offense could bring victory to France.

The French General Staff obviously had learned nothing from the American Civil War, when entrenched marksmen and well-laid field guns had shot to pieces time and again masses of advancing infantry charging across open fields with bayonets.

To sustain the men, who were putting in a grueling twelve hours a day in the field, the Legion provided two meals a day in addition to the cup of coffee given out first thing in the morning. At eleven each man received a bowl of soup containing bits of bread and meat, plus a cup of coffee and a cup of *pinard,* the standard army red wine. At five in the afternoon, when the training day was at an end, goulash and the same ration of coffee and *pinard* were doled out. With the evening meal was issued half a loaf of coarse peasant bread heavily flavored with saltpeter. The loaves were stamped with the date of baking on the top, and after the tenth day the bread could be refused. But as one Legionnaire pointed out, refusal only meant self-denial. Every ten days three ounces of tobacco, called *Scafarlati des Troupes,* was issued, but it tasted so vile, most of the new men sold their shares to the veterans.

Since the arrival at Toulouse, news of the heavy fighting above Paris had been as ominous as it was scarce. But by September 15 the papers were filled with glowing accounts of what was called the Miracle of the Marne.

General Alexander von Kluck, with Paris only a tempting twenty miles away, had wheeled his divisions inward, south and east, thereby breaking the solid phalanx that was inexorably pushing back the French all along the line. Seeing his chance, General Joseph Simon Galliéni launched a violent attack on the German right wing, using the newly created *Armée de la Défense de Paris,* most of which was rushed to the combat zone in the city's taxicabs. Three German army corps, totaling nearly 50,000 men, were pulled from the easterly part of the line to meet Galliéni's sudden offensive, thus weakening the German front northeast of the capital. French and British forces moved forward, threatening to sever contact between two entire German armies, which would have left the invader open to attack from the rear. Robbed of its impetus, the back of the von Schlieffen plan was broken and the Germans began a steady retreat. Within five days they had fallen back twenty-five miles. Then, like crabs, the opposing armies moved sideways trying to outflank each other, stopping only when they reached the sea. Exhausted, both sides started digging in.

Incredibly, French casualties during the first six weeks of

the war reached nearly 750,000, a figure that included 200,000 dead.

G.Q.G. began combing the training centers for replacements. At Toulouse the call was for 500 veteran Legionnaires and 500 trainees with previous military experience, both groups to form a battalion for immediate transfer to the combat zone. The recruits who stepped forward were faced with a tough-looking noncom barking questions and writing down the answers in a notebook. He first approached a gangling Brooklynite named Herman Chatkoff, whose last job had been washing cars in Montmartre. "Previous service?" the sergeant asked.

"Five years," Chatkoff replied, "with the Salvation Army." Thaw, Seeger and the Rockwell brothers claimed to have spent months campaigning with the Mexican Army. The noncom raised a skeptical eyebrow and commented that men who drilled so poorly could have served in no army that he was acquainted with. Thaw glibly explained that the fighting in Mexico was all guerrilla warfare needing little knowledge of close-order drill.

Dave King satisfied the sergeant with a recital of his outstanding record while at the Columbia Institute Military Academy in New York. King later admitted: "I was only seven at the time, but the words *école militaire* work wonders in France."

In the end, all of the Americans were taken into Battalion C of the Second Regiment and told to draw 120 rounds of ammunition per man, and to turn in their white fatigue pants for the regulation red of the French Army. With barely four weeks of training behind them, the recruits who had volunteered entrained for the Front on September 30.

The battalion, one thousand strong, swung out through the gates behind the regimental flag snapping in the early morning breeze. And even after they had disappeared down the street, those who had stayed behind could hear them singing, their voices raised high in a bouncing melody known to half the world:

Nous sommes soldats de la Légion,
La Légion Étrangère;
N'ayant pas de Patrie,
La France est nôtre mère!

Morane Parasol

CHAPTER 2

ENNUI

There is no romance to the infantry. It is only a matter of being a good day laborer.

—KIFFIN ROCKWELL

Mailly-le-Camp sprawled across 27,000 acres of rolling hill country covered with sparse growths of scrub pines. Eighty-five miles east of Paris, Mailly was only a little less than thirty miles from the Front at its closest point; when the wind was blowing from the north the constant rumble of the guns reached the ears like the sound of distant thunder.

Mailly was the largest staging area in France during the early days of the war, and it was there the train carrying Battalion C finally stopped after three days and nights on the rails from Toulouse. The iron curtains at the station windows were riddled with shrapnel, and the narrow streets were littered with rubble and broken glass. Looking up, the Legionnaires could see gaping holes in the walls and roofs of the buildings, put there by the furious shelling during the Battle of the Marne only two and a half weeks before.

In the pine groves some distance from the station the Legionnaires went through the same spirited bayonet exercises they had performed day after day at Toulouse. The area was strewn with the debris of battle left there by Germans and French alike: spiked helmets covered with gray-green wool, smashed rifles, haversacks whose contents were scattered in the pine needles, rusting bayonets, red *képis*, spent brass cartridge cases, boots, hobnailed shoes, crushed mess kits, empty canteens. In the denser sections of the groves, Legionnaires sent out to gather dry wood for cooking fires occasionally stumbled across swollen corpses covered with bluebottle flies that buzzed insistently, oblivious to the presence of anything living. One squad searching for pine branches returned with a prisoner, a gaunt, sullen Uhlan who had been hiding from patrols for more than twenty days, waiting for the Germans to return. Living on the iron rations stolen from the bodies of his dead comrades, he had refused in the face of gnawing hunger and thirst to give himself up "because we were told the French shoot every man they take prisoner."

There was only one branch line from Châlons-sur-Marne, the nearest supply depot, to Mailly, and it had been torn up by the recent shelling. Foraging parties often walked miles to buy vegetables from outlying farms, returning furious at the outrageous prices they had to pay. The older hands learned that Mailly housed a veterinary hospital for field treatment of wounded horses, and every day they stood hopefully outside the compound, waiting. As the days passed, even the new men looked forward to a helping of freshly roasted *filet de cheval.*

Less than a week after the arrival at Mailly almost every man in the battalion was crawling with lice. "By an irony of fate," said King, "it was our poet who first complained of the roughness of army underwear. He scratched in forced aloofness, never smiling; he took them as seriously as he did everything else." The Americans strongly suspected the Arab Legionnaires as the hosts for "Monsieur Toto" (as lice were called in the Legion) because the Koran forbids the killing of any living thing without special sanction. Germans, yes; vermin, no. Since only thorough fumigation will rid clothing of lice, the practice of "shirt-reading" was

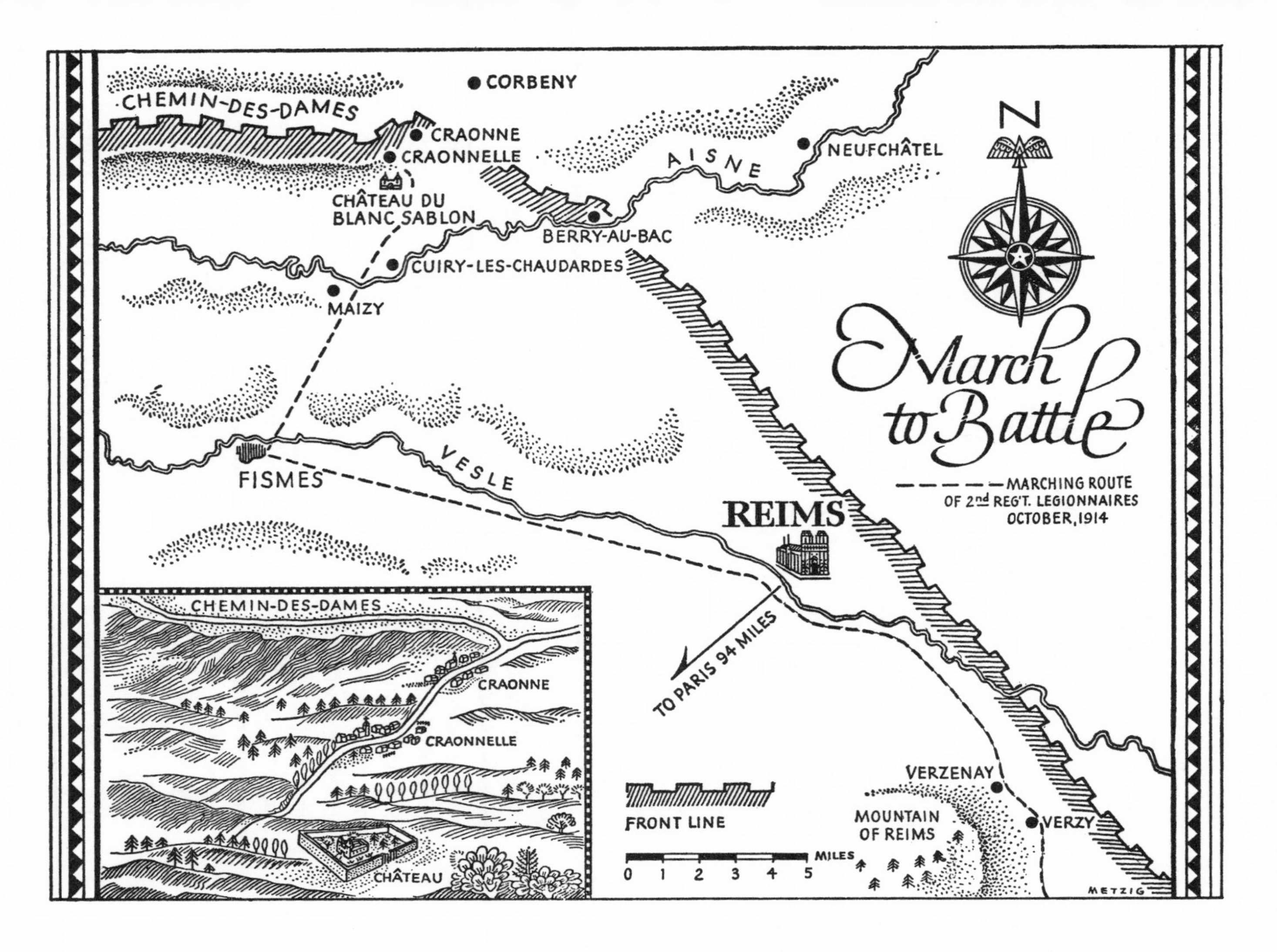
March to Battle
MARCHING ROUTE OF 2nd REG'T. LEGIONNAIRES OCTOBER, 1914
N
CORBENY
CHEMIN-DES-DAMES
CRAONNE
CRAONNELLE
CHÂTEAU DU BLANC SABLON
AISNE
NEUFCHÂTEL
BERRY-AU-BAC
CUIRY-LES-CHAUDARDES
MAIZY
FISMES
VESLE
REIMS
TO PARIS 94 MILES
VERZENAY
VERZY
MOUNTAIN OF REIMS
FRONT LINE
0 1 2 3 4 5 MILES
CHEMIN-DES-DAMES
CRAONNE
CRAONNELLE
CHÂTEAU
METZIG

done more to pass the time than anything else, and like soldiers everywhere the Legionnaires grew to accept being lousy with the same equanimity with which they accepted everything else.

The battalion, with three others gathered from distant training areas, left Mailly before sunrise on October 18, when the officers put them on the road to Reims, more than fifty miles distant. Two weeks of route marching and practice charges across hilly ground had worked wonders with the new volunteers, and they reached Fère-Champenoise, fifteen miles along the road, the same afternoon without a single man falling out. Vertus was reached the next day, and on the twentieth the footsore Legionnaires passed through Épernay, thirty-seven miles from the starting point, and began toiling up the slopes on the western side of the mountain of Reims. In columns of fours the 4000 Legionnaires, who coiled gently around the slopes and through the yellow-green Champagne vineyards, resembled, from a distance, a mammoth blue-and-red caterpillar working its way up the side of the mountain. But three days' relentless hiking under a suddenly hot sun began to take its toll.

The hundred pounds of equipment on their backs dragged them down; straps cut cruelly through their heavy wool uniforms, now soaked with sweat, and the 9-pound rifles grew heavier by the mile. Neck muscles ached unbearably from straining against the brutal load and leg muscles knotted into painful bunches, causing some of the men to stamp along like stiff-kneed cripples. Every step on the unyielding road sent a jarring shock through spines that were taut as bowstrings. Heads throbbed with the constant pounding, and a dull ache settled behind the eyes. But worst of all were the feet of the new men who had chosen to wear the Legion issue of "Russian Socks," which took months of practice to wrap properly; otherwise the muslin shifted, forming ridges that rubbed unmercifully against the tender skin, causing painful blisters and scraping raw sores on the sides of the feet and the tops of the toes.

Thaw and King fell out of the marching column and sat down heavily by the side of the road, gingerly slipping their boots from their burning feet, which had been turned into "a sort of painful

IN THE FOREIGN LEGION

A sniper fires from shattered steeple toward the Chemin-des-Dames.

Alan Seeger

Outpost: David King and Fred Zinn.

VERDUN

Escadrille pilots hunted the enemy over these hills in front of Verdun.

Nieuports rolled from Bessaneau hangars, were mounts for de Laage, Johnson, Rumsey, McConnell, Thaw, Lufbery, Rockwell, Masson, Prince and Bert Hall. Behonne, July 1916.

Lufberry *(above)* in his cockpit ready to attack. Downing German two-seaters *(like the plane shown at left)* became his specialty.

Ted Parsons was grateful for Lufbery's skill. Parsons was being chased by the Germans until Lufbery showed up and achieved his seventh confirmed kill.

Walter Lovell standing beside Spad VII.

Sgt. Campbell's Nieuport lost its lower left wing while in full flight at 3,000 feet. Maneuvering with unusual skill, he landed the plane in a beet field. Standing *(left to right)* Sgt. Soubiren, Sgt. Rockwell, Lieut. Chicomski, Capt. Thénault, Sgt. Campbell, Lieut. Thaw.

German observation ballons faced fiery destruction from such bizarre weapons as Le Prieur rockets *(below)* launched by Norman Prince.

Veteran Charles Johnson *(above)* relaxes over *Pinard*. Crippled Charles Nungesser, who brought luck to No. 124 at Verdun, poses beside his Nieuport 17 *(right)*.

Fokker E-IIIst.

Chapman gambled . . . and lost.

Balsley challenged . . . and survived.

Kiffin Rockwell test-fires Lewis gun.

German Gotha loading up bombs

TARGET: OBERNDORF

World's first strategic air strike was led by visionary Captain Felix Happe.

Raymond Collishaw flew Sopwith 1½ strutter for first of sixty kills.

The ungainly Farman bomber.

GALLERY 1

Chaudun, 1917. *(Back row, left to right)* Bridgman, Doc Rockwell, Jones, Peterson, Dugan, MacMonagle, Lovell, Arnoux de Maison-Rouge.
(Bottom row) (unknown), Masson, Bigelow, Johnson, Thaw, Thénault, Parsons, Hewitt, Willis, Haviland.

Thénault and Fram.

Féquant

Thaw

Lufbery

GALLERY 2

Bigelow

Lovell

Genêt

Marr

Jim Hall

Pavelka

Willis

Johnson, Fred Prince

Marshall

"Doc" Rockwell and his Spad Fighter

Nieuport 17 at liftoff.

Da Laage in Morane Monocoque in which he was killed.

Ronald Hoskier

Nearly unrecognizable, the wreckage of this plane closely resembles that of Hoskier's downed Morane Monocoque.

Thénault and de Laage (between white crosses) at funeral of Hoskier and Dressy.

THE BOCHES

Handsome German Albatros planes like these, and the planes shown on top of opposite page, became a particular nemesis to N. 124

Dud Hill just before the beginning of a patrol.

Bill Thaw taxis his Spad VII into position for takeoff.

A trip to the trenches to confirm Escadrille kill. (Left to right) Infantry officer, Thénault, Fred Prince with camera, Didier Masson.

Lufbery's Spad (with Hank Jones in cockpit). Note personal good-luck symbol — a swastika in black.

This is how Ken Marr wrecked Ted Parson's Nieuport when he overshot the landing field.

Bill Thaw holds the American flag, presented to N. 124 by the famous *Chasseurs Alpins* regiment. Chaudun, 1917.

marmalade." Looking at the blisters and the blood, the new Legionnaires decided they were fit cases for the ambulance.

"This illusion, however," said King, "was rudely shattered by the bull voice coming from the top of a horse." The two Americans looked up and saw the regimental commander, Colonel Passard, glaring down at them. "What are you doing there?" he roared.

"Our feet are cut to ribbons, my colonel. We cannot march any more."

Passard slid his hand to the holster at his side and pulled out his heavy French service revolver, which he leveled at the Americans. "March all the same!" he shouted. Thaw and King painfully put their shoes back on, helped each other from the ground and hobbled back up the road to rejoin the section.

That night the regiment reached Hautevilliers, where the men were quartered in and around an eighteenth-century Benedictine abbey. The men flung themselves down and took off their shoes, wondering how they would be able to keep going the next day. Corporal Weidemann, a seventeen-year veteran of the Foreign Legion and a former noncom in the Prussian Guards, walked among the prostrate men looking at their feet. Then he knelt down by one man and showed them what to do.

He extracted a needle and a length of heavy thread from his pocket and rubbed the thread with grease. Then he slipped the needle and thread through a large blister, cutting off each end of the thread, which would act as a drain. He smeared tallow over the inflamed area, and on the inside of the man's socks. More tallow was spread around the inside of the shoe, which was put back on before the foot had a chance to swell. The process was painful, but efficient.

The Legionnaires were on the road again at sunrise, and by two that afternoon they struck Verzy, where they were quartered in long, concrete-floored sheds used for grape storage. The older soldiers found a cask of wine, which they refused to share with the others, "and the night was made hideous by song, drunken laughter and squabbles." The next morning the column hiked a mile and a half around the side of the mountain to Verzenay, which was just behind the line of battle. From across the valley the popping of rifles and the heavier cracking of field artillery reached the town, and the Legionnaires realized they were practically at the Front.

The Americans were quartered in a stable at the far end of the town and considered themselves lucky; the Germans methodically shelled Verzenay once in the morning and once in the afternoon, but their pieces were laid so that the shells burst in the upper end of the village, away from the stables. The Legionnaires stayed at Verzenay two days; on the morning of the twenty-fifth they greeted with cheers the sight of a long convoy of empty busses that were to take part of them to Fismes, sixteen miles to the east. The Legionnaires of the 1st Regiment were detailed to stay near Verzenay, while the 2nd Regiment was to move eastward and take over another part of the line. Happily the American section climbed aboard the busses, which began rolling down the undamaged road. All of the Americans, that is, except the members of Ninth Squad.

This squad was made up of the tallest men in the battalion and included Thaw, the Rockwells and Seeger, four other Americans, two Englishmen, a Norwegian, a Swede, a Serb and one Frenchmen—all under the command of Corporal Weidemann, the blister expert. Ninth Squad was particularly unfortunate in that Weidemann was disliked by Sergeant Térésien, the section leader, and every unpleasant job handed to his section was passed on to the Ninth. Térésien is described by King as "an irascible little Breton, a onetime naval lieutenant who had been cashiered for striking a superior. He had joined the Legion to regain his rank, and he made life hell for everybody who stood in his way."

Ninth Squad was to follow the long line of mule-drawn wagons carrying the reserve ammunition and rations for the battalion that had just left by bus. The wagons and the sixteen men of the *garde de convoi* left Verzenay at four-thirty the next morning; the Legionnaires started down the road angered almost to tears, and with nothing in their stomachs except cold coffee.

Fismes that night was a madhouse of milling troops, but there was no sign of the 2nd Regiment; Weidemann had all the supplies for two thousand men, but he didn't know where they were. A motorcycle rider finally tracked him down in the crowded streets and handed him a message that ordered him to get the wagons across the Vesle to a place called Cuiry-les-Chaudardes. Looking at the map, Weidemann cursed: they still had another fifteen miles to go.

Weidemann pushed the flagging animals and the exhausted men forward through the darkness until eleven that night, when they could go no farther. The men dropped to earth on the top of a plateau that was swept by chilling winds. After a while, rain began drumming down, but nobody moved.

The convoy reached Cuiry at ten the next morning during desultory shelling. The shots were wide of the town, falling mostly in the adjacent sugar-beet fields. The utterly fatigued men of Ninth Squad staggered off to the barn where their section was quartered, hardly bothering to lift their heads as the 77s whined overhead.

The 2nd Regiment rested in Cuiry for forty-eight hours. When darkness fell on the evening of October 29, the Legionnaires formed columns of twos outside the town and started walking down a graveled road toward the lines.

The road ended abruptly, turning into a narrow path that led through trees so closely planted that the tops laced together, shutting out even the pale rays of the autumn moon. The column dissolved into a lurching line of men walking in single file, groping their way forward with their hands. "It was here," said one of the Americans, "that we struck one of the real horrors of war—mud. Liquid mud, full of treacherous roots. Mud like chewing gum, squelching our boots off. Mud with a stench obscene and putrid. Somebody down . . . up again, cursing foully. Hours and hours we floundered through the pit-black night. Then we were through the woods."

Shadowy forms rose from the ground and slipped to the rear. By ones and twos, the Legionnaires eased themselves into the rifle pits and awaited the coming of the dawn.

The 2nd Regiment was attached to the 36th Division, which held part of the line below the Craonne plateau, almost dead center of the battlefront. The position was important because it was less than twenty miles from Reims, where the Aisne-Champagne fronts hinged—a juncture then known as "the cornerstone of the defense of Paris."

The day following the Legion occupation of the hill broke clear and warm, with sunshine flooding the peaceful-looking countryside. Five of the new men (wearing the bright red trousers of the French Army) rose from cramped positions in the shallow trenches and got up to explore the area and to stretch their leg muscles. Almost immediately a 77 cracked across the gentle valley, and a shell screamed through the air, landing almost in the middle of the upright Legionnaires. Three were killed outright, and two others were badly mangled. With the range established, the Germans raked the area for an hour. No one else was killed, but the harrowing incident demonstrated the danger of walking around in the daytime wearing uniforms better suited for an opera stage than a battlefield.

The defense works occupied by the troops of Battalion C were little more than a series of shallow rifle pits originally dug by the British. They were later connected by irregular lines of crude ditches scraped into the earth by the French 218th Regiment, which the Legion had relieved. After the fury of the German bombardment had spent itself, the Legionnaires put aside their rifles and were issued picks and shovels. All that day, they slammed picks into the hard ground, tearing up the earth, which was then shoveled over the lip of the trench and patted smooth to form a low breastwork. By late afternoon the trench was deep enough to stand in. At five the Legionnaires were told to quit work for the day and to stand by for hot food. They put their jackets and greatcoats back on and sat on the cold trench floor to wait for the *soupe corvée* to come up from the field kitchens that had been installed 300 yards down the reverse slope in a patch of woods.

The sound of a droning engine jerked their attention upward, where a lone German airplane flew overhead. The plane slowly circled the woods for a few minutes, then flew back across the lines. Its pilot dropped a map on which were marked the coordinates of the wood. A few minutes later the now-familiar sound of incoming 77s filled the air again and the earth shook with the detonation of dozens of 25-pound rounds of high explosive. When the shelling stopped, the kitchen was scattered over half an acre of landscape. Fourteen men lay dead and another thirty were badly wounded. There was no hot food that night, nor on any night thereafter. The new kitchen was set up two miles to the rear in the middle of a swamp. The route ran up and downhill through a quagmire and the going was slippery and maddeningly slow. The stew was ladled into kettles scalding hot, but by the time it was carried back through the mud to the line, a layer of cold grease had formed on the top and the stew was lukewarm.

Barbed wire had not come into general use as a tactical defense measure and covering patrols had to be sent out each night to maintain the integrity of the line. During the first week at Craonnelle, one of these scouting expeditions was led by the Company *Adjudant* (Sergeant Major), "a thick-set, coarse little swine with homosexual tendencies named Pasqualaggi," a man detested by every man in the battalion. He and six others crawled out into no man's land; Pasqualaggi stopped, telling the others to go ahead, that he would wait where he was. Some time later, the patrol returned carrying Pasqualaggi by his arms and legs and he was dripping blood. The other members of the patrol told the officer conducting the questioning that they had lost their bearings on the way back and had mistaken the *Adjudant* for a German outpost and had opened fire. "That was their story," said King, "and they stuck to it." Pasqualaggi lived to be sent to the rear.

It was rare that a patrol encountered Germans, other than those who lay dead between the lines along with hundreds of British and French killed during the first weeks of the war; but lying on the cold earth while on outpost duty, ears straining to catch the slightest noise, stimulated imaginations to the point where anything that moved seemed to be the enemy.

Shortly after the Pasqualaggi episode, King and two other Americans, Dennis Dowd and Edward Morlae, were prone on the earth in no man's land, listening for sounds of approaching Germans. They had lain there motionless for nearly two hours under a cloudy sky that threatened rain. Suddenly the clouds parted and King made out twelve shadowy forms advancing on the skyline just in front of them. "Christ, here they come!" he said. The three men hastened back to their lines and reported to Sergeant Térésien that the Germans were coming.

"Independent firing!" yelled Térésien. "Keep your shots low until you can pick your target." Within seconds the night became alive with the crash of rifles firing as fast as excited fingers could pull triggers and reload the tubular magazines. To the left of Térésien's section came answering flashes and roars, sending bullets whistling dangerously close overhead. The angry exchange lasted a half hour, then gradually died down. Silence. Somebody volunteered to go out and investigate. He returned a few minutes later bent double with laughter. The enemy had been a dozen homeless cows, wandering around in search of grass, "nine of whom paid the full penalty." The answering fire had come from another section of the line that bent away to the left, forming a V, occupied by Legionnaires who thought they were being taken from the flank. A lucky few fed on fresh beef the next day, cooked over low fires in the dugouts, the slabs of meat skewered on the hitherto-virgin bayonets.

According to a schedule laid out by staff officers at G.Q.G., troops were supposed to spend only four days in the front line before pulling back to second-line trenches, a few hundred yards to the rear, where, it was assumed, the risk to life was less. After six days in this reserve line the men were then allowed to spend four days in a rest area designated by regimental commanders.

It was not uncommon, however, for the men of the 2nd Regiment to spend twelve straight days in the first line; and when they were sent back to the reserve trenches they usually found a large pile of picks, shovels and saws waiting. After stacking arms, the Legionnaires picked up the rusting tools and hacked at the sodden trench floors and the walls, which crumbled with every jab. Those with saws sloshed their way to nearby woods to cut down trees to use as roof supports for the dugouts, which were constantly being deepened. The back-breaking work was usually done under heavy shelling, for the Germans had the area under constant observation. There was little French counterbattery work, due to the discouraging fact that at the beginning of the war the Germans had ten guns for every one the French could field, and the famous 75, with an effective range of 8000 yards, could not always be brought to bear on the heavier German guns placed far behind their own lines.

The Legionnaires worked eight to ten hours a day digging,

chopping, hauling heavy logs through swamps made almost impassable by cold autumn rains. When work stopped, usually at six in the evening, the exhausted Legionnaires splashed wearily down the widening trenches to their dugouts, where they dined on the usual tepid soup before falling asleep on lice-infested straw. From one of these damp, fetid holes Kiffin Rockwell was moved to write: "There is no romance or anything in the infantry. It is not a question of bravery, but a question of being a good day laborer." He might have added that day laborers slept in warm beds and earned eighty times as much money for the same amount of work.

Cuiry-les-Chaudardes, the regimental rest area, was little better. A ramshackle village set in a sea of mud, Cuiry was populated by "forty surly inhabitants, six of whom were later shot for conveying information to the enemy." The stagnant village was hardly pleased to have a battalion of Legionnaires quartered in their homes, attics and haylofts, and gouged the troops unmercifully from behind makeshift counters in their homes where they sold tinned jam, sweet biscuits and *vin mousseaux.*

The attitude of the people of Cuiry toward the Legionnaires changed from an indifferent surliness to open hostility the day the troops tore down the church steeple. Colonel Passard noted that the steeple, which was the tallest structure still standing in the area, provided an ideal regulating point for German artillery. He ordered it pulled down.

A Legionnaire climbed to the top of the church with one end of a heavy rope, which he fastened to the steeple. Below, nearly a hundred men of Battalion C dug in their heels and began to pull. The *curé,* his black skirts dragging in the mud and manure, hastened up the street with the villagers following closely behind. They pleaded with Gallic earnestness, then threatened the colonel and his men with a vengeance that properly belongs to God; but Passard was unmoved, and a few minutes later the steeple toppled to the ground in a heap of lath and masonry.

When the battalion moved back up to the line, Third Section was sent to relieve troops occupying a once-magnificent château on a hill south of Craonnelle, whicn lay a thousand yards down the gentle slope. The Château de Blanc Sablon, a gutted ruin, stood in the center of a large wooded park that was entirely surrounded by a thick stone wall some eight feet high. The top floor of the château had been shot away by German shelling and the high windows on both remaining floors were only gaping windows; but the vaulted ceiling that covered the basement remained, providing shelter for sixty men. The gatekeeper's lodge, by a quirk of fate, had not been hit. Exploring, David King found the interior filthy.

"The Hun had evidently had one last banquet here. A long table in the main room was piled high with dirty dishes, glasses and wine bottles, and the enemy had left his usual trademark, excrement, everywhere. In the middle of this debris of debauch lay a small white satin slipper. Evidently Fritz had been true to his traditions of the *Kurfürstendamm.* Had the owner escaped? My mind went back to my mother's place—in France—not so far from the tide of invasion, and I was damned glad I was in the show."

The wall that surrounded the château and its wooded park was just over two miles in circumference; the stretch of mortised stone facing northward toward the enemy measured 500 yards in length, and was about 100 yards from the château itself. For perhaps a hundred yards on the other side of this wall the ground ran level before dropping off toward Craonnelle; thus no really unobstructed view of the village could be had. However, past Craonnelle and across the valley rose the menacing heights of the Craonne plateau, a large barrow that dominated the valley and the rolling hills beyond for miles in every direction. Here the Germans were solidly dug in, with an unexcelled view of the park where the Legionnaires lay hidden in dugouts scattered throughout the woods. Along the heights of the plateau ran the Chemin-des-Dames, a centuries-old road, which was the mainstay of the German defensive works. Across from the château, the Chemin-des-Dames angled slightly to the east. Thus the entire park was in enfilade. None of this was apparent to the men of the Third Section, who moved onto the premises late at night in a drizzling rain . . . the walled-in château seemed to them at the time a sanctuary.

Ninth Squad was ticked off to stand guard along the northern wall, but despite its great length and the fact it was nearest the enemy, Sergeant Térésien delegated only six men for the job. Corporal Weidemann posted three of his squad at the far left of the wall, where they stood on planks supported by barrels, peering across the darkened valley toward the plateau. Kiffin Rockwell and Alan Seeger were stationed at midpoint, in front of a large hole that had been torn in the wall by a shell. They propped a door and a ladder against the hole, looking occasionally around the sides for German patrols. The rest of the squad was taken by Weidemann to the far right of the wall, where they took shelter in a corner dugout roofed over with logs and earth.

The night passed without incident, adding weight to the belief that the park was a safe, cozy place to be. At seven Rockwell left his post and walked back to the château, where he picked up the morning rations for the guard detail. The sun was over the horizon, bathing the valley in diffused light. From the château, Rockwell could see over the wall to the Chemin-des-Dames beyond; it seemed that the Germans were frighteningly near, that they must be looking straight at him. Gripping the handles of the ration cans, he began walking quickly back toward the wall. *Crack!* The first shot whined overhead, followed by a dozen others that seemed to come from three different directions—which indeed they were. Rockwell crouched and ran to the safety of the wall, where he and the others spent all that day under desultory rifle and machine gun fire from the plateau. The range, at nearly two miles, was great, but not so great that a man could not be killed if struck.

At ten-thirty that night, Rockwell and Seeger were crouched against the wall waiting for the relief to come up. Something hissed softly through the air and thudded at Rockwell's feet. Startled, the two men looked at each other and whispered simultaneously: "What's that?" Rockwell reached down and picked up a heavy metal object and idly turned it over in his hands, trying to see in the dark.

"Good God," Seeger suddenly said in a loud voice, "it's a hand grenade!" Rockwell heaved it over the wall, where it failed to explode. Seeger ran off to the post at the right to get the corporal, who came running back just as a second grenade sailed over the wall, again almost hitting Rockwell. He jumped across the ladder into Weidemann's arms just as the grenade exploded with a deafening roar. A squad of Germans burst through the door, catching the two Legionnaires in the open. Shouting "*Aux armes!*" the two men turned and ran for the safety of the woods. Rifles cracked behind them, and Rockwell heard Weidemann fall heavily to the ground. Rockwell bent low and ran into the woods with bullets whistling around him.

With Weidemann dead, the Americans at the post on the left were without anyone to tell them what to do, so they flopped to the earth. The Germans were now between them and expected reinforcements and they held their fire for fear of hitting the other men of the section. They lay there under heavy rifle fire, fear and indecision rendering them incapable of action. A Mauser bullet creased one man's neck; another's rifle was smashed; a third felt a burning jolt as a slug passed between his fingers.

The other Legionnaires, lying in the woods with their long rifles shoved out in front of them, also refused to fire at the Germans for fear of hitting their own men along the wall. Sergeant Térésien dashed from cover with two men, but they were stopped by Rockwell and Seeger. Seconds later, the firing stopped and the five Legionnaires cautiously made their way to the hole in the wall and boarded it back up. By this time the entire section had come up from the cellar of the château and they fanned out through the park seeking Germans. They found none; the only evidence of the raid was the body of Corporal Weidemann, with his head bashed in and his pockets turned inside out. The Germans had also cut off his tunic buttons and regimental badges and broken the stock of his rifle.

This incident pointed up several things about the men of Battalion C. To Rockwell, the raid was "rather a disgrace for us all . . . impressed us more like a murder than warfare. The Germans," he concluded, "had no military point to gain by doing what they did; it was done as an act of individualism and a desire to kill."

In this last, Rockwell was mistaken: the obvious purpose of the raid was to establish the identity of the French regiment that had moved into their sector; Weidemann's lapel badges with the green 2 embroidered into the cloth would tell them all they needed to know. Rifling pockets for possible important papers was standard procedure, and the killing of the corporal should have come as no surprise. But the instructors at Toulouse, while extolling the virtues of the bayonet and the exhilaration of grand sweeps across the open countryside, had neglected to mention that war is essentially like a back-alley gang brawl.

The Americans posted along the wall felt betrayed by the older Legionnaires, especially the officers and noncoms, who were accused by one American of "stupidity and neglect for putting us in such a deathtrap without more men and telling us the real situation." The truth is, the older Legionnaires knew little more about Western Front tactics than did the men they led. Quelling tribal revolts in the desert was a world away from the situation at Craonnelle, or anywhere else in France for that matter. Six men to guard a half-mile stretch of wall were about thirty too few, especially since the sergeant had not seen fit to post a man on the *German* side of the wall, where an alarm could have been sounded before it was too late. The makeshift way in which the hole in the wall had been sealed was a further enticement to an alert enemy. The Germans learned far more quickly than the French the value of sudden raids, and were more rapid to seek and exploit tactical advantages.

It was clear that the new men and the veterans from Africa would have to learn together, but after the incident at the wall the relations between the two groups became strained. The Americans called the older Legionnaires an ignorant lot of mercenaries; they were accused in turn of having enlisted only for free food. "There isn't one among you," sneered a noncom, "who wouldn't sell his rifle for a pot of jam."

The seed of bitterness bore tragic results when the battalion next was sent down from the lines to Cuiry. A coffee wagon had been set up in the middle of a courtyard where a hundred-odd Legionnaires gathered seeking shelter from a cold wind. Herman Chatkoff stepped up to the wagon and asked for a second cup, saying he had had none before. The cook, an *ancien* from Morocco, told Chatkoff he was a cheat and a liar like all the other Americans, and that he and one other Arab could make the entire American section eat the dunghills in the courtyard. René Phélizot, who had been listening, stepped forward laughing, at the same time a second Arab, from the machine gun section, walked over to stand beside the cook. Phélizot suggested he and Chatkoff take them on, but the cook declined. The machine gunner was eager, however, so he and Phélizot squared off. The Arab butted Phélizot in the face, and the American went down, pulling the Arab with him. They scrambled to their feet and fought in the center of a ring of shouting Legionnaires. The Arab was getting the worst of it when another *ancien,* an Alsatian, broke through the ring swinging his heavy, wine-filled canteen at the end of a leather strap. The 5-pound weight struck Phélizot in the head and he went down unconscious.

The ring of Legionnaires disintegrated into a mêlée of cursing combatants, Americans versus the machine gunners. The brawl was broken up by an armed guard, but only after five Americans and six others were knocked cold. It took three men to pull Chatkoff away from the Alsatian, whom he had been kicking with his heavy, hobnailed shoes.

When Phélizot came to, he complained of a splitting headache and difficulty in focusing his eyes. In a daze he wandered off to the dispensary, but the doctor accused him of malingering and marked him fit for service. The next day Phélizot collapsed on the road and rolled unconscious into a ditch. A passing officer found him there several hours later, already partially paralyzed from a skull fracture. Phélizot was loaded into an ambulance and taken to the base hospital at Fismes. He lay unmoving in his bed until late that afternoon. A doctor saw him struggling to rise and went over to the bed, where Phélizot clumsily unwound a battered, dirty American flag from his waist. Holding it in front of him, Phélizot gasped through clenched teeth, "*Je suis américain!*" then he fell back against the bed. The doctor bent over, but Phélizot was dead.

When the news reached Phélizot's section, the free-for-all began all over again. The fight was broken up at the point of bayonets, but not before the Alsatian had been kicked to death by an unknown number of boots. The entire American section was placed under open arrest—for their own protection, an officer later admitted.

The cold that winter was intense and unrelenting. The American section was moved to the other side of Craonnelle to guard a smaller château, where the first job that awaited them was the clearing of a cellar knee-deep in freezing water in which floated the bodies of French and German soldiers. This done, Ninth Squad was posted outside the château, where they crouched for fourteen hours in shallow holes in a driving snowstorm, with only intermittent relief.

As the winter wore on, the Legionnaires learned the meaning of frontline attrition—and not all of it was due to enemy action. Constant exposure to the elements crippled no fewer than seven Americans in Battalion C; Paul Rockwell was nicked in the right shoulder, then developed inflammatory rheumatism. The pain increased until he was no longer able to lift a rifle. He was sent to hospital, where treatment proved futile, and was put out of the fighting for good. Fred Zinn, a spare, studious-looking engineering graduate from the University of Michigan, suffered agonies with swollen adenoids. Comrades found his snoring unbearable, so Zinn forced himself to stay awake at nights, hoping to catch some sleep in the daytime. But twice he was caught dozing while on guard, and only intervention by King, whose eloquence in French clearly stated Zinn's case, saved him from the firing squad. Zinn was sent to the rear for surgery.

Although Bill Thaw was an infantryman in fact, he was a flyer at heart and had come to the conclusion that there was little to be gained by staying with the regiment until he either died of pneumonia or was blown up by impersonal shelling. The next time the battalion went into bivouac at Cuiry, Thaw learned that a prewar friend named Félix Brocard was stationed at an airdrome nineteen miles away. Thaw and two other Americans—Bert Hall and James Bach, an engineer from St. Louis—hiked through the snow to the flying field, where Thaw explained to Lieutenant Brocard that all three infantrymen wanted to switch to aviation. Brocard, who had great respect for Thaw's reputation as a pilot, promised to do what he could. Late in December, not long afterward, transfer orders came through. Thaw and the others struggled into their burdensome packs for the last time, picked up their rifles, shook hands with their envious section mates, then began slogging down the communication trench that led away from the misery at Craonnelle.

Thus far, the Americans had been spared serious casualties

from the almost daily sniping and artillery fire that issued spasmodically from the Chemin-des-Dames. Then, on February 17, 1915, the Germans unleashed a furious bombardment that blanketed a two-mile stretch of the line at Craonnelle. The machine gun section was dug in to the left of the town. One of the gunners, Edward Mandell Stone, twenty-seven, refused to take cover, believing the Germans would be pouring down from the plateau the moment the fire lifted. A few minutes later Stone was knocked backward away from his gun by a piece of shrapnel that struck his chest, penetrating the left lung. Stone, a Chicagoan who had graduated from Harvard in 1908, died ten days later in the hospital at Romilly-sur-Seine. He was the first American citizen killed in World War I.

With nearly all of his friends gone, and with a new sergeant in charge of Third Section—an American he called "a notoriety-seeking sonofabitch"—Kiffin Rockwell applied for transfer. On March 18 he shifted to the 1st Regiment, then in the line east of Reims. He was agreeably surprised to find the regiment living "in a sort of wonderful underground city, with trenches eight feet deep and three feet wide. They wind around everywhere, all of them leading to the front combat trench, which has loopholes every two feet and a firing step." The 1st Regiment had been in this sector since it came up to the line, and with the exception of a minor push toward Prunay that gained them almost a mile of country as flat as a billiard table, the Legionnaires fought the same kind of war that was being fought everywhere else on the Western Front—patrol actions in no man's land that achieved little but always managed to up the day's total of killed and wounded.

In the first week of May, the Moroccan Division and its 1st Regiment Legionnaires pulled out of Reims and entrained for the Artois, ninety miles to the northeast. Here, the first major Allied offensive of the war was to take place in an effort to break the stalemate that had prevailed for eight months.

This attack across the red clay of the rolling Artois plain was under the command of Marshal Ferdinand Foch, who hoped for a breakthrough using eighteen divisions. The 1st Regiment moved into position on May 5, and was put to work digging trenches leading to the German line, only a hundred yards away. Four days later, at daybreak, the French batteries in front of Arras opened up on the German line "where you could see nothing but smoke and debris." Crouched against the parapets, the men of the 1st Regiment waited to go over. Above them, the sky was a brilliant blue, paling as the sun climbed higher. There was a ragged metallic clicking sound that ran all along the 12-mile line as bayonets were slid home, locking into place on nearly 150,000 rifles. Shells whined and roared overhead, the sharp smell of cordite wafting back into the French lines from the explosions across the way. The agonized waiting lasted until 10 A.M., when blasts from whistles pierced through the sound of the guns. Here and there officers stood up on the lips of the trenches screaming, "*En avant!*"

"Then," said Rockwell, "I saw the finest sight I have ever seen—men from the *Premier Étrangère* crawling out of our trenches with their bayonets glittering against the sun, advancing on the Boches."

Seven minutes later, Rockwell's battalion moved from the reserve trench and began running through the communication trenches to the first line. German shells were falling in and around the communication trenches, but the Legionnaires stepped over their own dead to get into the first line. One shell crashed into the forward trench just as Rockwell's section arrived. The company commander's face turned scarlet, but he wiped the blood from his eyes, yelled an oath at the Germans and crawled out into the open, waving for his men to follow. Like many another officer that day, the captain wore spotless white gloves and carried a varnished mahogany swagger stick.

After the deep shadow of the trenches, the men blinked their eyes at the brilliant sunshine that flooded the Artois plain that spring day. The Legionnaires started forward at a steady trot, yelling and cheering into the din of battle that surrounded them. The earth shook under their feet from exploding German shells; the air over their heads hummed and cracked from passing Mauser slugs and in front of them came the relentless *chug-chug-chugging* of the machine guns. The brief furious bombardment by the French batteries had been laid on by too few guns of too small caliber; the Maxim gun positions were almost all intact. Rockwell, jogging along over the uneven ground, saw an entire section of sixty men cut down in front of him like wheat before a scythe. But there was no hesitation and "as fast as men fell it seemed new men sprang from the ground to take their places. To think of the horror of the thing was impossible. All I could think of was what a wonderful advance it was and how everyone was going against that stream of lead as if he loved it."

The German trenches were taken after a bitter hand-to-hand struggle. The Legionnaires leaned up against the trench walls gasping for breath, oblivious of the dead and dying that lay all around them. Then they scrambled up in the open and continued the steady dogtrotting advance, holding their light combat packs in front of them to act as a shield. The 1st Regiment swept through the small villages of La Targette and Neuville-St.-Vaast; the regimental commander, Colonel Pein, was caught up in the spirit of exultation manifest in his Legionnaires and he crawled from his command post, picked up a rifle from the battlefield and joined the charge. He was killed a few minutes later. Just outside Neuville-St.-Vaast, a bugler named Theissen climbed up to the top of a haystack, where he sounded the charge until a German bullet toppled him to the ground.

By three that afternoon the Moroccan Division had driven a hole nearly three miles deep in the German lines. But the decimated battalions were running into increasing German resistance and the advance had been reduced to a painful crawl. Rockwell's company, now whittled thin, was under the command of a *sous-lieutenant* who had seen the captain and his second-in-command shot dead. Rockwell, the officer and an American named Paul Pavelka were lying together in a shell hole where they had been pinned down for thirty minutes by heavy machine-gunning from the front and the flanks.

When the fire slackened, the lieutenant stood up and ran forward through the smoke that drifted over the battlefield, waving his arm for the survivors to follow. "Well," Rockwell said, "we might as well get it over with." He grabbed his rifle and pack and jumped out of the hole, trotting after the lieutenant. He went forward only twenty yards, when a machine gun slug ripped into his thigh, spun him around and slammed him to the ground. Pavelka ran up and started fumbling with his first-aid packet, but

Rockwell waved him on. Pavelka stood for a moment, then ran forward without looking back.

Rockwell dragged himself to a shell hole and flopped over the rim to the bottom, where a man lay gasping his life away. Rockwell first turned his attention to his own wound. The bullet had left a neat, bluish hole on the inside of his upper right thigh, passing through the fleshy part without touching the bone. He bandaged the wound, then turned his attention to the man lying beside him, a rifleman from the 156th Regiment shot through the stomach and beyond aid. After a while the man died, and Rockwell crawled from the hole and began dragging himself to the rear.

The field was a charnel house of the dead and the dying. Of the 4000 men of the 1st Regiment who had gone against the enemy, only 1700 escaped death or wounds; Rockwell passed most of the others as he made his way painfully over the ground he so recently had covered. The lightly wounded asked him for water, but he had none; the horribly mutilated asked him to put them out of their misery, but his rifle was back in the shell hole. As the blood-red sun disappeared from the warm spring sky, Rockwell pulled himself up against a haystack a half mile from where he had been hit, there to wait the coming of the *brancardiers* to take him to the rear. When the stretcher-bearers finally came, they passed him by, saying they had orders to pick up only those very badly wounded. Rockwell struggled to his feet and, with the aid of a stick, hobbled nearly two miles to the rear, there to collapse in the courtyard of a farm where lay hundreds more. The next day, by walking and hitching rides on artillery wagons, he made it to an evacuation center, where he was ticketed and put aboard a train filled with wounded. The train passed through Paris at midnight, rolling on until it reached Rennes, where the wounded were taken off and put in the hospital.

Rockwell's gunshot wound had gone untreated for four days, but through great fortune it did not become infected with deadly gas gangrene. The doctors told him he would be walking again within a month.

On the battlefield north of Arras, stretcher-bearers came across the shrapnel-riddled body of a French *adjudant* who had used his last moments to pen a message. *Adjudant* Sedley's two-sentence legacy was jerkily traced out on a message blank with a wooden splinter which the dying man had dipped in his own blood. "I die content," he wrote, "because we are victorious. *Vive la France!*" What Legionnaire Sedley would have written had he been in possession of the facts is a matter for conjecture.

The first Battle of Artois ended after forty-eight hours with more than 100,000 casualties; worse, the French had not anticipated the initial gains of up to four miles and no reserves were on hand to exploit the breakthrough. After murderous losses, what was left of the French divisions pulled back under heavy counter-attack, keeping only 10,000 yards of raddled earth. The cost, at ten men per yard, was frightful; the gain, inconsequential.

General Headquarters could look back on May 9, 1915, as the day it staged its first grand assault across open country with the bayonet, but it was no victory.

Rockwell spent six weeks in the hospital at Rennes, and when he left for Paris on convalescent leave his leg was completely healed. He stayed with his brother, Paul, who had signed on with the Chicago *Daily News* as a correspondent. Wounded American volunteers were still a great rarity in the capital, and the brothers were invited almost nightly to dine at richly set tables that still offered generous portions of *haute cuisine*.

One night the Rockwells dined with Bill Thaw, who was in Paris on a 24-hour pass. Thaw began his tour with the *Service Aéronautique* as an aerial gunner, but now he wore the wreathed wings of a pilot, having successfully managed to short-circuit the long training period.

After a month with Deperdussin Squadron 6, Thaw got permission to go to St. Cyr, where he was to demonstrate his ability to pilot any aircraft that happened to be handy. The chief instructor ordered a Caudron G2 rolled from the hangar. The G2 was a maze of wires and struts and, like all Caudrons, had a four-wheeled undercarriage and twin rudders set on long booms running aft from the main planes. The G2's 80 h.p. Gnôme rotary engine allowed a maximum speed of 70 m.p.h., and since the top wing rested almost on the pilot's head, upward visibility was extremely poor.

With the eyes of every man on the field watching, Thaw successfully got the airplane off the ground and safely into the air, where he frantically searched the unfamiliar cockpit for gauges and dials and gingerly tested the controls. He later admitted he was scared witless for the first few minutes of flight, since he had never taken off from anything except salt water and had never seen a G2 except from a distance. After ten minutes Thaw brought the Caudron down for a smooth landing on the grass and was warmly congratulated by the chief instructor. After only five weeks of advanced combat tactics, Thaw was posted to Caudron Squadron 42 (abbreviated C.42), an observation unit based at Nancy, in the northeastern part of France. His was the distinction of becoming the first American pilot to fly against the Germans during World War I.

Thaw's new squadron was equipped with Caudron G3s, two-seater versions of the G2. Although the G3 had the same low performance figures, it could stay aloft four hours and was strutted and braced and tail-boomed in such fashion that it was remarkably sturdy and capable of absorbing much punishment. Although armed only with a Winchester carbine, the G3's endurance and hardiness made it the finest artillery-liaison aircraft the French had.

Early in May, on one of those beautiful spring days that are perfect for flying—when the air is cool and the bright sky above is dotted only with cirrus clouds 20,000 or 30,000 feet above the earth—Thaw and his observer, Lieutenant Félix, were sent nearly twenty miles behind the lines to photograph a German long-range 380mm gun that was lobbing shells into Nancy. Silhouetted as they were against the clear blue sky, they offered an inviting target to enemy antiaircraft guns, which picked them up at the line and started a barrage that continued all the way to Hampont, where the big gun was secreted in a wood.

The sky around the Caudron grew black with the bursting of 8-pound shrapnel shells, but Thaw calmly flew back and forth over the woods while Félix stood over his huge camera, tripping the shutter at precise intervals, laboring in the wind to change the flat, heavy plate-holders. Small pieces of sky appeared in the long, narrow wings of the Caudron. Bracing wires snapped and sang, whipping in the wind. One, then another, strut was shot away by hot jagged steel that punctured dozens of holes everywhere, but never struck Félix or Thaw or the whirling cylinders of the smoothly running engine. A half hour later, his mission completed, Thaw turned for home.

The flapping of the shredded fabric, the snapping of the shot-apart bracing wires, the absence of four interplane struts, the sickening sight of the rudder cables hanging together by single strands—these were worse to Thaw and his passenger than the ringing detonations of 77mm shells that bounced the plane around the sky all the way back to the lines; craft less badly damaged had simply folded in the air, plummeting the crews to earth like falling stones. But the Caudron held together, and Thaw nursed it safely to the ground at Nancy. The mechanics who gathered around the tattered G3 shrugged their shoulders in eloquent gestures that indicated the plane had flown its last sortie. Only the engine was salvaged.

The *sang-froid* displayed by Thaw and Félix that day earned them a citation from the general commanding the Army of Lorraine, and with the citation Thaw was elevated to sergeant.

Although Thaw had created a favorable impression on his superiors from the moment of his entry into the "Fifth Arm," Bert Hall had immediately gotten himself into trouble. Reporting to St. Cyr, Hall was interviewed by the commandant, who listened while the American told him of his aerial missions behind enemy lines during the recent Balkan troubles. Hall was going to try to bluff his way into a pilot's rating without benefit of training. He asked which airplane he might borrow in order to prove his skill, and was directed to a Blériot.

He climbed into the cockpit, strapped himself in and signaled for the mechanic to pull the propeller through. The engine roared into life and the Blériot rolled down the field, weaving an erratic course. The plane lurched uncertainly into the air, then plunged through the side of a canvas hangar. When Hall climbed unhurt from the wreckage, the commandant yelled, "Why, why—you know nothing at all about flying!"

"No," Hall sheepishly admitted, "but I thought I might be able to get the hang of it." Luckily the authorities decided that such brashness might be turned to good account, so Hall was sent to Pau where he would learn piloting from the beginning.

At Pau, Bert Hall continued to boast about the valuable services he had performed as a pilot for Abd el Krim, and he graphically described "furious bayonet charges" he had taken part in at Craonnelle. These lies, told for the benefit of his barrack mates, eventually reached the ears of the camp commandant, who began a search for Hall's records. Outside of his enlistment contract with the *Légion Étrangère*, no papers could be found—not even a birth certificate. Agents who questioned Hall's Montmartre acquaintances learned that he had often bragged that he was the object of a three-year search by the Boston police to answer charges of a Mann Act violation, and that Hall had said more than once, "The warden of the Rhode Island State Penitentiary badly wants to get his hands on me." French authorities began to wonder if they had another F. C. Hild on their hands.

Hild was an American bicycle racer who had managed to enlist in the French Air Service during the first month of the war. After a few weeks in pilot school, he deserted and returned to the United States. He gave out a number of newspaper interviews in which he criticized the equipment, discipline and training of the *Service Aéronautique*—but what was worse was the fact that the French had strong reason to believe Hild had sold military information to the German Embassy in Washington.

The report on Hall cast suspicion on his character and his reliability. In fact, the authorities vaguely suspected him of being a German spy. Two *sûreté* agents, posing as student pilots, slept on either side of Hall while he was in training and he was closely watched wherever he went. Hall was kept at Pau for six months while futile efforts to link him with German agents continued.

James Bach, however, completed his training and was sent to the Front early that summer. Bach's squadron, MS.38, flew two-seater Morane-Saulnier reconnaissance planes known as Parasols, due to the elevation of the single wing above the cockpit, which afforded unobstructed visibility downward. With its high rate of climb and slow landing speed, the Parasol was ideally suited for the mission Bach volunteered for on the morning of September 23, 1915.

Bach and another MS.38 pilot, Sergeant Mangeot, were called

into the captain's office for briefing, where they saw two men in civilian clothes sitting in chairs near the desk. Bach had never seen the men before, but he knew they were saboteurs. He and Mangeot had flown such men behind enemy lines before. The agents were to blow a section of railway between Hirson and Mezières, up near the Belgian frontier; Bach and Mangeot were to fly the saboteurs and their explosives to the area, land them, and come home alone.

Bach asked if there was a suitable field where they could land safely and take off again. Yes, the agents said, they knew of a splendid field not far from Rocroi, only a mile from the border. Both men explained that they had lived all their lives near Rocroi and knew the area as well as a man knows his own backyard.

Rocroi was nearly fifty miles behind the German lines, but despite that fact the mission was made in broad daylight. The flight proceeded without incident, and the planes began letting down for a landing only a little more than an hour after takeoff. The landing field chosen by the saboteurs could hardly have been worse—bordered by heavy woods on all sides, its uneven surface strewn with rocks, overgrown with scrub brush and dotted with tree stumps. Bach and Mangeot had no choice but to land. They got down roughly, waited until their passengers were out of the planes and running to the woods, then lost no time in taking off.

Bach lifted cleanly from the earth, then looked over his shoulder for Mangeot's plane, just in time to witness a spectacular ground loop of the second Parasol, which spun around in a half circle and ended up on one smashed wing, the undercarriage dangling in a twisted mess of wood and wire. Bach saw Mangeot stagger from the wreckage. He turned into the wind for his second landing.

The Parasol bumped down and Mangeot ran over and threw himself into the empty rear cockpit. Bach had no sooner lifted the tail than the propeller struck a tree stump and shattered. The forward momentum of the plane carried it to the end of the field where it thudded nose-on into a large tree. Following the not inconsiderable noise of the crash, there was dead silence. With both Parasols wrecked, they faced a long walk home.

They hid in a tree until dark, then started walking south

through the woods. At dawn they entered a clearing where a farmhouse stood, apparently deserted. Hearing no sounds, they boldly approached the buildings, turned a corner and stepped into a courtyard filled with Germans.

Charged with espionage, they were thrown in jail to await trial. Although the two saboteurs had successfully blown the railway, they evaded capture, and the German prosecution could not link Bach and Mangeot with the demolition. The pilots avoided the firing squad, but spent three years—less a month—in captivity. Bach was the first American prisoner of the war.

Besides Thaw, Bach and Hall, at least one other American had, by March 1915, entered the French *Service Aéronautique*. He entered the gates of the flying schools without the purgatory of the trenches, but he faced a grim and discouraging battle nonetheless. In pursuit of his dream to create an all-American air squadron, he voluntarily engaged the sticky might of French bureaucracy.

The Greeks had their Thermopylae, Texas had its Alamo, and Norman Prince had the Quai d'Orsay.

Blériot XI

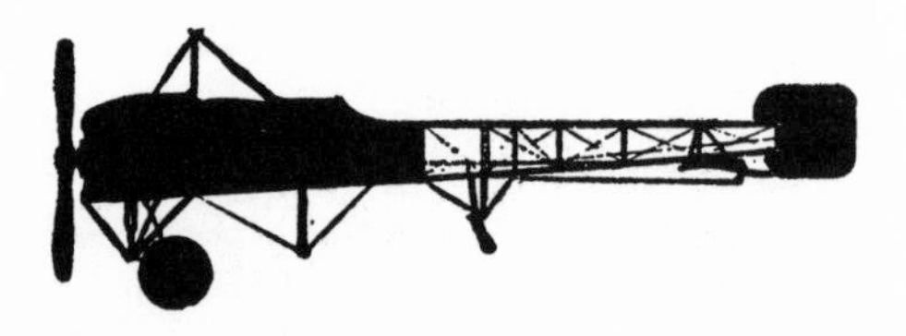

CHAPTER 3

PER ARDUA AD ASTRA

It is the cause, it is the cause, my soul! Let me not name it to you, you chaste stars! It is the cause.

Norman Prince was the ideal Quixote to battle the windmills of bureaucracy that lay in the path of creating an all-American squadron within the existing framework of the French *Service Aéronautique*. At twenty-eight he was young enough to maintain unquenchable enthusiasm, but not too young to be taken seriously. From his early childhood he had spent the summers at Pau at the family's large estate where he learned to speak fluent, voluble French. Moreover, Prince was already a licensed pilot, having learned to fly at Marblehead in 1911.[1] Money was the least

[1] But against his father's violent objections. Prince used the pseudonym of George W. Manor, which appeared on his *Fédération Aéronautique Internationale* license No. 55.

of his worries; he was the scion of Frederick H. Prince who was reputed to be the wealthiest man in New England, which would make him rich indeed. The older Prince (he was fifty-six at the time) was a lavish entertainer. One guest at the Prince mansion remembered: "Fred serves champagne at luncheon, tea and dinner. It is hard to say why he discriminates against breakfast." Norman grew up in the company of the top half of the Four Hundred and was competent at the subtle infighting of high society drawing-room conversations. He was equally at home outdoors on horseback, graduating from Shetland ponies to spirited French geldings which he rode while hunting wild boar in the rugged chain of hills below the Pyrénées.

He had inherited all of his father's hard-driving qualities: ebulliency, cockiness, aggressiveness, physical hardiness and irascibility when matters failed to go as planned.[2] With such similar and volatile temperaments, it is not to be wondered at that the two men were often at odds. Norman's filial rebellion reached a climax when he sailed, against his father's wishes, for France on January 20, 1915. The coming of the war, coupled with his ambition to create *"une escadrille américaine,"* provided Prince with the opportunity to make his name as well known as his father's, while lending a hand to a country he admired at least as well as he did his own.

Lastly, Prince was a Harvard lawyer (Class of '08)—a qualification not to be underestimated when confronting Gallic evasiveness.

To be close to the scene of operations, Prince obtained a suite at the Hôtel Palais d'Orsay, from where he would wage his campaign. He started by looking up influential Americans residing in Paris, but many of them said the idea was neither feasible nor in keeping with Woodrow Wilson's overwhelming desire for Americans to remain neutral. Two of his countrymen, however, Robert Bliss and Robert Chanler, were greatly interested in the idea and provided letters of introduction to various functionaries of the *Ministre de la Guerre*. Prince was courteously received, but there

[2] At seventy-three Frederick Prince was still playing polo. During a match at the Myopia Hunt Club in 1933, Prince brought his mallet down on the head of another player "with malice, prepense and aforethought." Prince's defense in court: "Merely a rub of the game."

was little enthusiasm and no promises of help. Prince then wrote a long letter directly to Étienne Alexandre Millerand, the War Minister himself. The reply when it came was discouraging—and contradictory. Millerand wrote Prince that no American volunteers could be accepted into French aviation because of the popularity of this branch with French soldiers, "hundreds of whom—far more than can be used—are applying for training as pilots." The response implies Millerand's ignorance of the fact that at the time he wrote the letter Thaw, Bach and Hall were already in flying school.

Although Millerand had shut the door in Prince's face, Prince manifested his stubbornness by again approaching Robert Bliss for help. This time Bliss provided Prince with an entrée to the War Ministry through Jarousse de Sillac, an aviation enthusiast with a post high up in the Ministry of Foreign Affairs. De Sillac, although about the same age as Prince, had a keen sense of propaganda and foresaw the potential value an American squadron would have in the efforts of the French to sway American opinion. De Sillac put his feelings on paper in a letter which he addressed to a Colonel Paul Victor Bouttieaux at the *Ministère de la Guerre,* a man de Sillac apparently believed could exert more influence than the Minister himself.

"It appears to me," wrote de Sillac, "that there might be great advantages in creating an American squadron. The United States would be proud of the fact that certain of her young men, acting as did Lafayette, have come to fight for France and civilization. The resulting sentiment of enthusiasm could have but one effect: to turn the Americans in the direction of the Allies. There is a precedent in the Legion of Garibaldi, which has had an undeniably good influence on Franco-Italian relations . . ."

Four days later, on February 24, 1915, Bouttieaux sent back a brief but encouraging reply:

"I think your candidates will be welcomed. They should contract an engagement with the French Army for the duration of the war, and should agree to fly only the aircraft customarily used in the French Air Service."

Bouttieaux, apparently writing in haste, overlooked the fact that Americans enlisting in the French Army stood to forfeit their citizenship; the way around this problem of course had already been solved by enlistment in the Foreign Legion, which—in the case of aspirants to the Air Service—would be no more than a formality and would not require infantry service in the trenches. But the last sentence in Bouttieaux's letter is puzzling. While it is true that both Thaw and Prince could have afforded to purchase their own aircraft, no such plan was contemplated and one wonders what Colonel Bouttieaux had in mind.

During the weeks Prince was conducting his door-to-door campaign, two more Americans arrived in Paris who were potential recruits. One of them Prince knew quite well.

Frazier Curtis, a thirty-six-year-old Bostonian, was considered somewhat old to take up combat aviation, but he and Prince had flown together at Marblehead the year before, and Prince welcomed Curtis as a supporter. Curtis had just returned from England after unsuccessfully attempting to join the Royal Flying Corps without having to give up his citizenship.

Elliot Christopher Cowdin, the son of a Tuxedo Park silk-ribbon manufacturer, had been only a year behind Prince at Harvard and grew up (although on a lesser scale) in a similar environment. Cowdin's father, John, was another of the well-known Long Island polo players.

Prince could now total six possible American pilots for the projected escadrille—all that were needed for a squadron in those days. With Bouttieaux's scant endorsement, Prince believed his crusade in Paris was at an end. He, Curtis and Cowdin signed their enlistment papers during the first week in March and left the capital for Pau.

But there the project stalled; the letters were pigeonholed in the bureaucratic maze at the Ministry of War, which was more concerned with the problem of arming, feeding and clothing more than two million soldiers of all branches; moreover, its energies were being expended in preparation for the offensive in the Artois, as well as dealing with thorny questions of budget, infantry replacement drafts, production problems created by too-few factories converted to the manufacture of war material and the training of women workers to take the places of skilled machinists who had been called up with their regiments. Measured against these massive problems it is small wonder that the matter of a half dozen American pilots had little priority. And as

Millerand had pointed out, there were hundreds of French youths on the waiting list for pilot training, hoping to fill vacancies that did not yet exist.

Two months rolled by. Prince and Cowdin finished the course at Pau and were sent to VB.108, a bombardment squadron, where they piloted two-seater Voisins—ungainly craft that could do only 65 m.p.h. but could carry a good load of bombs and were armed with a free-firing Lewis gun for defense. Frazier Curtis, however, proved that he really wasn't cut out to be a pilot. After three successive crashes he was given a month's convalescent leave before final discharge from the service.

Despite the silence from the Ministry, Curtis went doggedly ahead seeking possible volunteers for the projected American squadron. During this search he learned that one of the directors of the American Ambulance Corps, an American society physician named Edmund Gros, was actively at work on parallel lines. Curtis went to see Gros and offered to join forces.

Gros, a longtime resident of Paris, was an imposing figure. An excess of vanity gave him the stance of a field marshal, and his face was set off by a large, arrow-straight nose under which bristled a heavy black moustache. Those who knew him well described him as pompous and self-important, but his bedside manner was one of warm geniality. The doctor's knowledge of aviation was slight, but he was a good organizer and did know how to get things done.

Curtis introduced Gros to de Sillac and they decided to try a direct approach to the Chief of French Military Aeronautics, General Auguste Edouard Hirschauer, who had been in his post since 1912. The approach to Hirschauer would be no ordinary office call. De Sillac arranged for an informal luncheon at the home of Senator Menier where, under the influence of a leisurely meal followed by brandy and cigars, Gros and de Sillac hoped to be able to present an impressive case. Hirschauer was convinced except for one point: bringing up the subject of the deserter Hild, he asked who would guarantee the integrity of every American who wished to join the French Air Service? De Sillac unhesitatingly put his career and his reputation on the line by offering to vouch for each American accepted. When the luncheon broke up, Gros and de Sillac had Hirschauer's guarantee that the squadron, to be known as *l'Escadrille Américaine,* would be created in the near future.

With this promise in hand, the Franco-American Committee was formed as an administrative unit, with de Sillac acting as President. The next problem to be solved was a financial one. Gros called on William K. Vanderbilt, whose wealth, interest in aviation and opposition to American neutrality were well known. When Gros had finished explaining the purpose of the call, Mrs. Vanderbilt walked over to her desk and sat down and wrote out a check for $5000 which she handed to Gros. "Now, K.," she said to her husband, "what will you do?"

The graying multimillionaire produced his checkbook and quickly wrote out a check for $15,000. Vanderbilt's gift was more than an impetuous gesture; he had been urging American help to France since August 1914, and on his own had equipped entire hospital trains and paid for tons of medical supplies. The money given to Gros was the beginning of a constant flow of dollars that Vanderbilt provided during the Escadrille's existence.

The summer dragged on into fall, but still there was no action taken by the Ministry to form the Escadrille. However, one significant fact did emerge during the weeks of waiting: the French were beginning to accept enlistments for aviation from American volunteers, who had been denied admittance since the acceptance of Prince, Cowdin and Curtis in March. By October 18 there were seventeen Americans either flying in French squadrons or in training. Among them was Kiffin Rockwell. During this same period Gros continued beating the countryside for applicants. He made repeated visits to ambulance units in which Americans were serving, and he scanned the dossiers of the ninety U. S. citizens still dodging German shells with the Legion.

Gros, it turned out, had far greater ambitions than Prince. He was working on plans to sprinkle Americans throughout regular French squadrons over and above those who would be concentrated in the original Escadrille. Prince was voluble in his opposition to the doctor's expansion of his own idea, which he thought diluted the original. But he was alone in his protests, and Gros proceeded.

In December, five months after the lunch with Hirschauer, Thaw, Prince and Cowdin were suddenly given leave to visit the United States. They arrived in time for Christmas with eight days at their disposal. Hardly had they stepped from the gangway in the freezing Manhattan winds when praise and controversy erupted in the nation's press. Although the three aviators were inconspicuously turned out in Chesterfield toppers and bowler hats they were recognized from news photographs taken in France which frequently appeared in the big city dailies. During their leave they grew used to flash powder exploding in their faces and they gave out interviews in which they extolled the fighting qualities of the French while giving modest accounts of their own activities in the air.

Thaw was singled out for particular attention by reporters, partly because of his cousin Harry's notoriety following the fatal shooting of architect Stanford White in Madison Square Garden nine years before.

Reaction to the wave of adulation that swept over the three men was not long in coming. George Sylvester Viereck, then editor of the pro-German *Fatherland*, demanded that Secretary of State Robert Lansing intern the trio of pilots. He fired off a thousand-word telegram to Lansing that said, in part:

"I call your attention to the urgent necessity of taking action in the case of Thaw, Cowdin and Prince, of the French Army Flying Corps. All three men have stated that it is their intention to return to the battlefront. Their escape would constitute a grave international scandal.

"The argument has been advanced by an eminent American lawyer that if these three French officers (sic) are interned all the German reservists in this country ought to be interned likewise. This however is not in accord with established precedent in such cases.

"Inasmuch as these three officers are embodied in the armed forces of a belligerent power a German submarine meeting them on the high seas would be entitled to capture them. Their American citizenship would not protect them. The United States cannot, without violating the letter and the spirit of neutrality, permit these young men to rejoin the enemies of a country with which we are still at peace."

Viereck's hypocritical bombast required no answer; more serious were similar demands made by the German Ambassador, Johann von Bernstorff, whose own campaign to intern the pilots began in the men's barbershop of the Ritz-Carlton Hotel in New York City.

On the first morning after his arrival, Thaw stepped into the barbershop for a shave. Sitting in the chair next to him was von Bernstorff, whom Thaw had met several times before at prewar diplomatic functions. The German was pleasant at first, chiding Thaw for his breach of the law; then, more seriously, he suggested that Thaw and his companions voluntarily intern themselves to avoid what well could amount to an international incident. Thaw, his face covered with lather, remained silent. The shave finished, Thaw rose from the chair and smiled. Putting on his black bowler, he turned to von Bernstorff and said, "Excellency, war is hell." He nodded and walked through the revolving door to the street outside, letting in a sharp gust of cold air.

Von Bernstorff took up the matter with Secretary Lansing, this time formally demanding internment. But before the State Department was forced to act on the demand, the three pilots slipped aboard a French liner and sailed for Le Havre. They had brought the war a little closer to America's isolated shores, leaving behind a vivid impression of the romantic life led by a new breed of fighting man actively abetting the avowed French cause of preserving the civilized world.

It is difficult to ascertain the full impact at the Ministry of War and upon G.Q.G. of the tumult created by the appearance of the three volunteer airmen in neutral America, but the facts are clear enough. Shortly after the pilots returned to France, Hirschauer was replaced by Colonel Henri Jacques Regnier, and on March 14 Regnier informed de Sillac and Gros that G.Q.G. had formally approved the plan of grouping existing American pilots in one squadron. Moreover, the German onslaught against Verdun that began on February 21 had shown with painful clarity the eventual necessity of bringing American resources into the war if the Allies were to succeed in crushing Germany.

On April 20, 1916, *l'Escadrille Américaine*—officially on the rolls as N.124—was formed at an airfield outside an ancient town in the Department of the Haute-Saône. Chosen to command was a twenty-nine-year-old St. Cyr graduate, Captain Georges Thénault, who had applied for the job months before. His executive officer, Lieutenant Alfred de Laage de Meux, was selected from an observation squadron where he had earned a reputation for reckless bravery.

Thaw, Prince, Cowdin, Rockwell and Bert Hall—now free of suspicion—were joined by a former ambulance driver named James Rogers McConnell, and a recent transfer from the infantry, Victor Emmanuel Chapman.

Nieuport 11

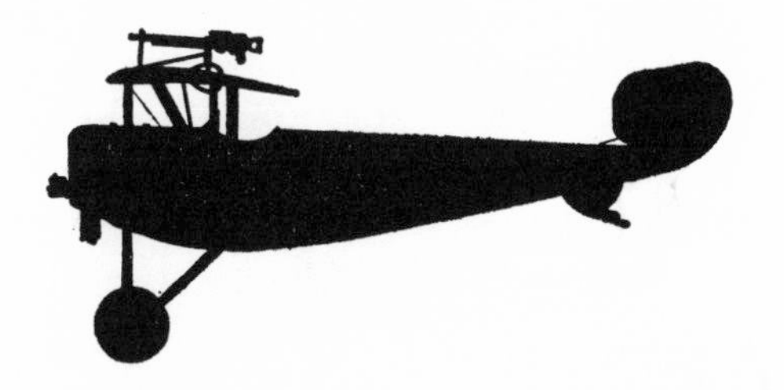

CHAPTER 4

IDYLL

I began to wonder whether I was a summer resorter or a soldier.

—JAMES MCCONNELL

The Escadrille began its operational career at Luxeuil-les-Bains, a small resort town in the northeastern corner of France, only thirty-five miles from the Swiss frontier. Seldom have men had such peaceful surroundings from which to wage war; the Front was forty miles away, and even when the wind was from the north, no sound of distant guns came to alter the pleasant feeling that the war no longer existed. Warm spring sunshine flooded the verdant hills, bathing the lilac-scented meadows in a purple glow. The scent of pine was carried down from the mountains by fresh breezes that shook the aspens in silvery-green ripples of color. Fresh-running streams, fed by distant torrents, wandered down from the hills above, streams filled with leaping trout grown to succulence in the absence of fishermen from the Haute-

Saône—men who had been gone from the valley since that hot August day nearly two years before.

Luxeuil, in peacetime, was a spa. Roman soldiers serving their time in Gaul centuries before had discovered the warm-water springs bubbling to the surface of the earth, and there had made camp. Sited on the vestiges of these camps, Luxeuil grew popular but never very large. It was Francis I who established Luxeuil as a playground for kings in the early part of the sixteenth century, and the town really came into its own during the reign of Louis XV when the Queen (née Marie Leszczynska) and the dandies at court made of Luxeuil a royal romping ground.

In 1916 Luxeuil numbered less than three thousand inhabitants, most of whom were women. Physically untouched by the war, far removed from the anger of the guns, Luxeuil was safe, unspoiled and—in the eyes of the arriving Americans—a soldier's paradise.

The pilots moved into a small stone villa adjoining the Roman baths. Each had a private room with a feather bed and a window overlooking the hills beyond. Five minutes' walk down the shaded cobblestone street brought them to the dining room of the Hôtel Pomme d'Or, a hostelry that had been in the Groscolas family for many generations. "Our motto," Auguste Groscolas told them, "has always been not to make money but to maintain the good name of the house and, above all, its cuisine." The pilots dined on white tablecloths covered with steaming dishes of such delicacies as fat trout, baked hare, roasted grouse and chicken en casserole—all washed down with bottles of Bourgogne, a wine of such exquisite vintage the bouquet alone "could turn one's head." After each meal came trays filled with oven-fresh pastry, and individual aluminum pots of filtered coffee. For all its great quantity and indisputable quality, a meal at the Pomme d'Or never cost more than four francs—less than one American dollar.

Ostensibly the Escadrille was sent to Luxeuil to provide fighter escort for a bombardment squadron based on the airfield a mile outside town. The squadron was under the command of the most famous bomber pilot in France, Captain Félix Louis Maurice Happe—known throughout the Air Service as the Red Corsair. Happe's trademark was a thick, well-trimmed beard, and he had earned his reputation as a guerrilla fighter of the skies who took fantastic chances. He flew a 1914 Maurice Farman pusher, a plane obsolete by 1916 standards but preferred by Happe because the factory had installed extra fuel tanks on his plane, enabling him to range deep inside enemy territory. On four separate occasions Happe and his mechanic flew to Friedrichshafen, 110 miles behind the lines, to bomb the Zeppelin sheds. Returning from one of these solo raids Happe dived his Farman at a German troop train again and again while his mechanic raked the cars with machine gun fire. For this outrage the Germans placed a price on Happe's head of 25,000 marks (over $6000), a price most Frenchmen thought conservative.

Happe's daring was his downfall as an independent operator. He had sent through a request to G.Q.G. for permission to land behind the German lines next to a rail center, capture the station master at pistol point and bring him back to France where information could be pried out. Headquarters, in some alarm, vetoed the idea and instead promoted Happe to command of a Farman squadron of his own. But Happe's good fortune failed to rub off on the others, and losses had been heavy.

When Thénault took the others into Happe's office to introduce them, the bearded terror was sitting at his desk writing letters. In front of him were eight oblong, red leather boxes. Happe explained the boxes contained *Croix de Guerres* that he was sending to the families of the men killed in a raid on Habsheim a few days previously. Happe referred to the Americans as "saviors," and urged them quickly to prepare themselves for action.

Happe's urging was in vain: the French had supplied everything a squadron needed for operations except aircraft. There were fifteen new Fiat trucks, rest tents, workshops, an office for Thénault, a switchboard and seventy ground crewmen—nearly ten men for each pilot and plane. Nieuports were slow in coming through because of the constant demand for replacement aircraft made by the overworked squadrons at Verdun.

Thénault was not content to sit and wait. He motored to the

neighboring field at Fontaine where he managed to secure the loan of a training Nieuport that belonged to N.49. Prince made himself thoroughly unpopular by flying the borrowed machine through a hangar wall on his first flight. Prince was uninjured, but the plane was a total write-off.

To break the monotony of being grounded, Thénault loaded the big open touring sedan with pilots and took them for long trips in the mountains. These all-day excursions introduced the Americans to the wild beauty of the Vosges and to the gentle loveliness of Alsace, where the cherry trees lining the highways were in full blossom. They motored to the emerald-like twin lakes at Gérardmer, northeast of Luxeuil, and they wound their way through the lush Val d'Ajol that impressed McConnell as "ravishingly beautiful, with steep mountainsides bristling with a solid mass of giant pines and myriads of glittering cascades tumbling downward through faireylike avenues of verdure." There was a practical side to these trips as well. Thénault pointed out every possible piece of flat ground where a forced landing might be attempted; some of these fields were no larger than 150 feet square, but they were carefully marked on maps for future reference.

The Escadrille hadn't been at Luxeuil more than a week when German reconnaissance planes began flying high over the field two and three at a time. Wheeling overhead, glinting in the sun, they taunted the Americans, who could only curse impotently from the ground. "Great big slow things," Rockwell said bitterly, "one man with a Nieuport could have gotten them all."

Thénault sent off one exasperated telegram after another asking for planes, but it wasn't until the first week in May that they arrived—six of them, hauled up in vans from the Nieuport factory at Issy-les-Moulinaux. They arrived disassembled, and the pilots pitched in to help the fitters and riggers from Issy with the complicated and painstaking job of putting them together. Armed with plumb bobs, spirit-level protractors, 50-foot lengths of steel tape graduated in millimeters, balls of light twine, vernier gauges, hexagonal wrenches, screwdrivers and sheets of detailed assembly instructions, the riggers tackled the dismembered airplanes with scientific dedication. With the fuselage placed on sawhorses, the tailskid, landing gear, center-section struts, lower and upper planes, V-struts and tail assembly were critically aligned a section at a time, then bolted on. When the last plane was put together the Nieuport workers packed their tools and went home, leaving the job of tuning the engines and fitting the machine guns to the squadron mechanics and armorers.

The Nieuport 11—known affectionately to the pilots as the *Bébé*—was the latest in French single-seater fighter aircraft. Its raked-back top wing spanned only 24 feet 6 inches and its gross loaded weight was only a little more than 1100 pounds. Blessed with an initial high rate of climb of 650 feet per minute, a top speed of nearly 100 m.p.h. and a hummingbird-like maneuverability, the *Bébé* Nieuport had in a short time wrested aerial supremacy from the enemy Fokker E-III that had ruled the sky since the summer before.

Nieuports were powered with 80 or 110 h.p., nine-cylinder rotary engines manufactured by Le Rhône. On a rotary, the propeller was bolted directly to the engine crankcase and everything, including the cylinders, revolved around a stationary crankshaft. This gyrating mass of wood and machined steel imparted a noticeable degree of torque when in flight—a relentless motion that could be put to advantage by the pilot when executing turns to the right. There was no carburetor; the fuel, a mixture of gasoline and high-grade castor oil, was sucked from a hollow portion of the crankshaft and fed directly into the combustion chambers of the cylinders. Thus, rotary engines either ran full out, or not at all. A degree of control of the r.p.m. was provided by an ignition cutout switch located on the control column. The engine was cut in and out manually with great frequency—a procedure that kept the plugs from fouling, and imparted to the speeding airplane a high-pitched, intermittent buzzing like that of a hornet flying past a series of widely spaced baffle boards.

Highly rated though it was, the *Bébé* Nieuport suffered a major handicap in its armament. The French and British lagged behind the Germans in the development of a synchronizing gear that allowed a fixed, belt-fed machine gun to be fired through the propeller arc. As a consequence, the Nieuports that reached the Front in the spring of 1916 were fitted with a drum-fed .303 caliber Lewis gun mounted on the top wing where the fire would clear the whirling propeller blades. A Lewis drum of forty-seven rounds could be emptied in only five seconds of continuous firing, necessitating frequent reloading in combat. Changing drums in the air was a feat for a contortionist. The pilot first pulled the gun down on its pivot so that the barrel was pointing straight up. Then he half stood in the cockpit and strained forward in the vicious blast of the prop wash to grasp the empty drum and replace it with a fresh one. Since a loaded drum weighed nearly five pounds and presented a flat surface to the wind, it required both strength and finesse to get the drum seated squarely on the spindle on the first attempt. More often than not, the pilot was forced to relinquish his grip on the control column with his left hand and—grasping the stick between his knees—use both heavily gloved hands to get the drum firmly seated. In the middle of combat, with a German firing on one's tail, this cumbersome procedure was a frantic business.

Now that he had six factory-fresh aircraft at his disposal, Captain Thénault meticulously planned for the Escadrille's first patrol. He traced the proposed route on a large-scale topographical map, and he drew diagrams showing each pilot's place in the formation. Rockwell would lead, flanked on either side by Chapman and McConnell, while Thénault and Thaw held station behind and above to act as guards over those Thénault called "my young eagles." But intermittent rainsqualls, gusting winds and overcast skies postponed N.124's maiden voyage over the lines for another week.

The morning of May 13 broke warm and clear, and the five-plane formation left the ground shortly after six. Climbing steadily, the Nieuports kept a loose V formation until at 7000 feet they nosed into a developing overcast. Flying through the cold, moist opaqueness, McConnell began losing sight of Rockwell and Chapman and increased his climb, hoping to get above them where he could—he thought—maintain contact. But they were soon swallowed up in the whiteness and when McConnell came out on top he was alone in the sky. He flew on, straight toward Switzerland. Thénault, who had seen the formation scatter in the overcast, kept his eye on McConnell's ship and came out into the clear at the same time. Thénault later admitted he was on the verge of panic at the thought of having one of his men interned on the squadron's first patrol. Thénault was flying a 110 h.p. Nieuport and had little difficulty in closing the gap between himself and the disoriented Carolinian. Using violent, exaggerated hand gestures, Thénault managed to herd McConnell back to the north, where they rejoined the others.

To the south the glittering peaks of the Alps projected through the solid white cloud layers, and to the east the pilots could see sunlight flashing from the surface of the Rhine that curved away into the distance. They crossed the lines southwest of Mulhouse at 13,000 feet in the clear, where they were greeted with ranging shots from an antiaircraft battery located in the forest of Nonnenbruch. The sky quickly filled with splotches of oily black smoke, and Thénault watched in amusement from above as Rockwell led McConnell and Chapman in furious attacks on the harmless-looking puffs. They swooped again and again through the small black clouds hanging motionless in the sky, shredding the smoke in swirling tendrils with their propellers. Tiring of this sport, Rockwell headed for Habsheim in a long slanting dive. He leveled out high over the field where Fokkers were known to be, and flung his tiny plane around in whirling acrobatics, challenging the Germans. But no Germans came and, low on fuel, the Nieuports turned for home, fifty miles away, west across the mountains.

Good formation flying was never a strong point with graduates of French military flying schools, where the emphasis was upon self-reliance. Students started and finished their flight training on a solo basis—under the progressive, hard-headed Blériot system, no instructor ever sat behind a student ready to correct mistakes.

Training was begun in clipped-wing Blériot Penguins, machines incapable of flight, designed only to teach the student how to taxi in a straight line. Next came full-scale Blériots in which crow-hops were made, then circuits of the field at low altitude. After each flight, French *moniteurs*—most of whom had seen combat—held critiques. From flat turns, students graduated to banked turns using the warp-wing system peculiar to 1914–1915 aircraft. Then came spirals, spot landings and an altitude test that required a flight at 6000 feet for an hour. Students were breveted after successful completion of two cross-country trips of 150 miles each. Pilots assigned to *escadrilles de chasse* (literally, "hunting squadrons") were then sent to *l'École Nieuport* to master gunnery and aerobatics.

New pilots usually arrived in the combat zone with seventy or eighty hours' air time [1] and had the utmost confidence in their ability. Lacking, however, was sufficient training in close-formation work—a tactic the Germans were rapidly developing in the skies over Verdun.

German daylight reconnaissance flights over Luxeuil came to an end with the arrival of the Escadrille's Nieuports; the Germans came at night instead, unloading bombs. The first raid caught the field unprepared, and four mechanics standing in the open were blown to bits, six others badly wounded. Night interception was unknown, and the field's only defense was the antiaircraft guns firing at the telltale blue exhaust flames in the darkened sky above.

To a fighter pilot, there are few indignities that match being bombed from the air while sitting helpless in underground shelters. Rockwell, impatient and sensitive to insult, resented these raids more than the other pilots did. On the morning of May 18, just after the bombing, he took off alone to "make a little tour over the lines."

Thirty minutes later he crossed into German territory northwest of Mulhouse, where his engine began acting up. Just as he turned back for his own side of the lines, he caught sight of a German two-seater reconnaissance plane flying some two thousand feet below—in all probability one that had so insouciantly flown over Luxeuil the week before. Forgetting the balky Le Rhône, forgetting everything except the ugly, square-cut plane beneath him, Rockwell dived. The German observer saw him coming and opened fire at long range. Rockwell felt the impact of the slug as it smacked into a wing, but he held his fire, flying straight at the German plane. When he was less than a hundred

[1] In sharp contrast to the British R.F.C. dual system that sent pilots into combat with sometimes fewer than twenty hours in their logbooks.

feet away—so close he could distinguish the features of the observer crouched firing behind his gun—Rockwell clamped down on the trigger and heard the Lewis crack out four shots; then Rockwell swerved violently to the left only a split second before colliding with the Germans. Looking quickly upward, he saw the observer and the pilot slump from sight, the observer's rear gun pointing uselessly up in the air.

Rockwell circled and watched the two-seater sideslip, then head downward out of control in a steep dive. A few minutes later he saw the enemy plane smash into the ground, raising a cloud of smoke and dust just behind the German lines.

A French forward observation post telephoned confirmation to Luxeuil, so the news beat Rockwell to the field. An excited Thénault extravagantly recommended Rockwell for the *Médaille Militaire,* while Paul Rockwell sent from Paris a bottle of eighty-year-old bourbon—a treasure almost beyond price in France. After some debate, it was decided to ration the liquid gold one drink at a time to a pilot whenever he had a confirmed kill. Rockwell drained his two ounces and the bottle was put away.

"All Luxeuil," commented McConnell, "smiled on Kiffin—especially the girls."

Fokker Eindekker Scout

CHAPTER 5

THE KILLING GROUND

Verdun has become a battle of madmen inside a volcano.
—A FRENCH STAFF OFFICER

I am reported killed twice already.
—VICTOR CHAPMAN

At a quarter past seven on the morning of February 21, 1916, thunder roared out of the north and an avalanche of destruction fell upon the French at Verdun. Four-, eight- and seventeen-inch shells howled through the wintry air and crashed with blinding flame along an eight-mile front guarding the approaches to the city. The fire pulverized trench systems, ripped woods to kindling and altered the very shape of the hills. The bombardment was furious, unceasing, devastating. French infantrymen, stunned by the murderous fury of the shelling, huddled against

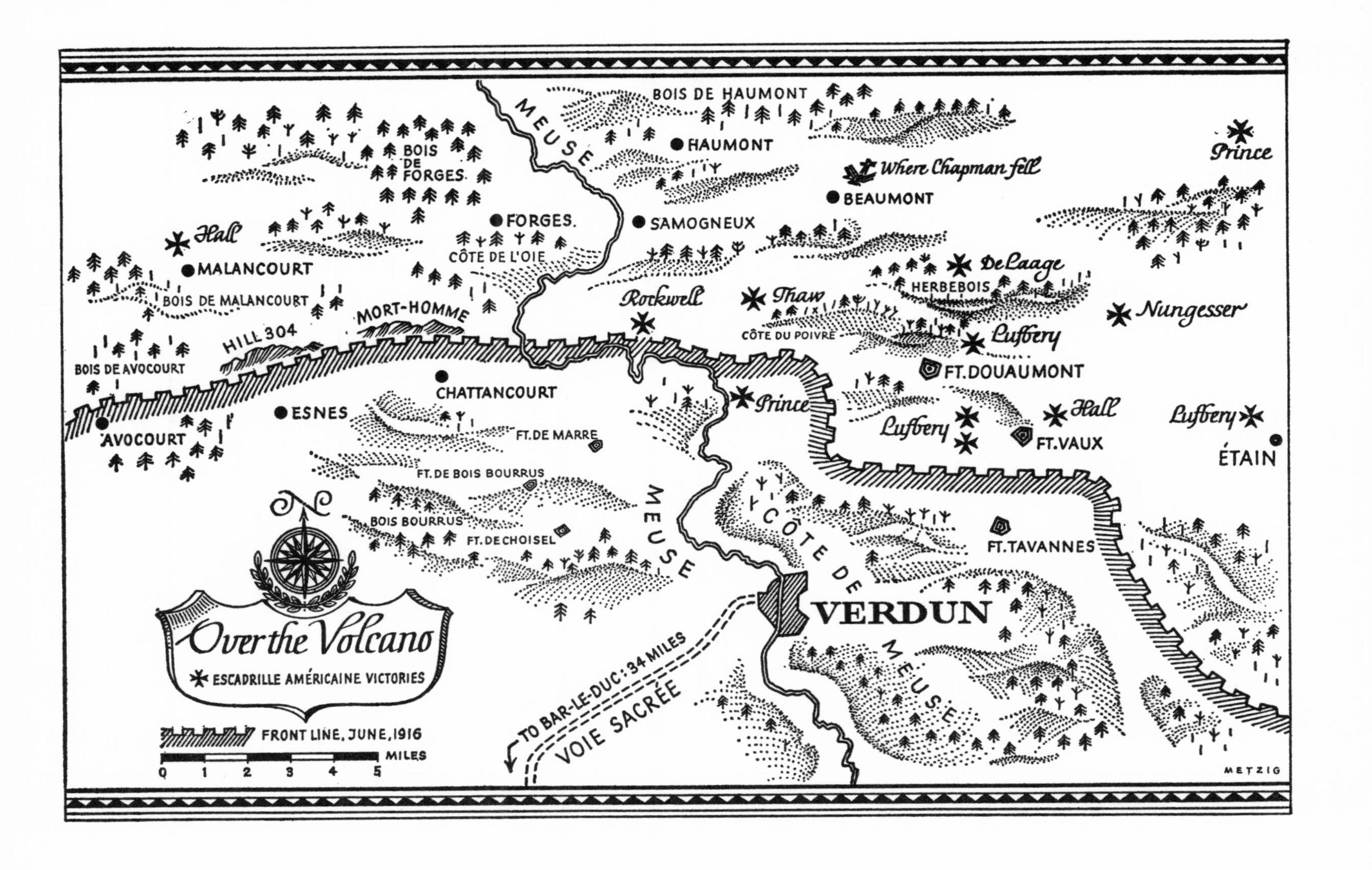
Over the Volcano
ESCADRILLE AMÉRICAINE VICTORIES
FRONT LINE, JUNE, 1916
MILES
0
1
2
3
4
5
BOIS DE HAUMONT
HAUMONT
MEUSE
BOIS DE FORGES
FORGES.
CÔTE DE L'OIE
Hall
MALANCOURT
BOIS DE MALANCOURT
MORT-HOMME
HILL 304
BOIS DE AVOCOURT
AVOCOURT
ESNES
CHATTANCOURT
SAMOGNEUX
Where Chapman fell
BEAUMONT
Prince
Rockwell
Thaw
CÔTE DU POIVRE
DeLaage
HERBEBOIS
Nungesser
Lufbery
FT. DOUAUMONT
Prince
Lufbery
Hall
FT. VAUX
Lufbery
ÉTAIN
FT. DE MARRE
FT. DE BOIS BOURRUS
BOIS BOURRUS
FT. DE CHOISEL
MEUSE
CÔTE DE MEUSE
FT. TAVANNES
VERDUN
TO BAR-LE-DUC: 34 MILES
VOIE SACRÉE
METZIG

the heaving earth and waited. The cannonading continued non-stop through the long morning and into the late afternoon. At four, in the gathering dusk, a gray tide of exultant German storm troops rose from their underground shelters and moved across the battered landscape.

The attack went forward through snow squalls and bitter cold. At the end of four days' bloody fighting, the Germans had punched their way five miles through the crumbled French defenses, capturing mighty Fort Douaumont,[1] only four miles from the northern edge of Verdun.

General Henri Philippe Pétain poured reserves of men and artillery into the battle, and resistance stiffened. Vicious hand-to-hand combat swirled through the shattered woods and across the blasted ground. Positions changed hands once, twice, then changed again. The *Sturmtruppen* and the *poilus* fought themselves to the point of exhaustion; gasping for breath, they sought strength to attack again, and strength to hold.

The air services of both armies quickly assumed a respected status at Verdun. The French, badly outnumbered in artillery, helped make up the deficiency with the *Service Aéronautique*—the indispensable Argus of corps and division artillery commanders. French counterbattery work largely owed its excellence to the slow Caudron and Farman observation planes that ceaselessly roamed over the smoke of the battlefield, pinpointing German batteries for the 155mm guns, whose long range and accuracy were the terror of German gunners. But the price of aerial ascendency was high: of two hundred French pilots sent to Verdun after the battle opened, seventy were killed within a month. When the *Escadrille Américaine* arrived to join the fighting on May 20, the airspace over the approaches to Verdun was as bitterly contested as the churned-up landscape underneath.

The air war over Verdun was fought in an arena measuring approximately twenty miles long, five miles deep and two miles high—almost all of it within enemy lines, for the Germans were

[1] Fort Douaumont, through an almost incredible series of blunders and misunderstandings, was virtually unmanned when the battle opened.

on the defensive in the air. They maintained dawn-to-dusk patrols over their own territory, using fighter and observation aircraft as a protective umbrella for artillery, troop concentrations and supply lines. But there were never enough planes to make this "aerial barrage" effective, so the Farmans and Caudrons always managed to fight their way through this imperfect screen, despite heavy losses.

Thénault secured a villa to quarter his pilots—a two-story stone building halfway between Bar-le-Duc and the airfield at Behonne, twenty miles from Verdun. A cook was installed at the villa, where meals were as succulent as they had been at Luxeuil.

Wrote Kiffin Rockwell to his mother:

"We are certainly living an incongruous life. We live like princes when we are not working. An auto comes to take us to the field; we climb into our machines—which the mechanics have taken care of—they fasten us in and fix us up snugly, put the motor *en route,* and away we go for two or three hours to prowl through the air, looking for an enemy machine to dive on and have it out with."

The Germans had a chance to test the mettle of the Americans over Verdun two days after they arrived. Thénault led a patrol over Étain on the morning of the twenty-second, and as they crossed the lines three German planes crossed by underneath. Without waiting for a signal from Thénault, Bert Hall plunged down alone. To the German observers sitting in the rear cockpits of their stable two-seaters, the diving Nieuport presented a beautiful target. Hall was greeted by accurate fire from three spitting machine guns and his plane was hit repeatedly. Hall dived right past the German formation and wisely decided to leave them alone. That same afternoon, Hall, Rockwell, Prince and Thaw were up guarding a French observation plane hovering over Fort Douaumont. Off to the left, Hall caught sight of a two-seater Aviatik heading for French territory. He peeled away from the others and went after it.

The Aviatik, flying alone, turned northeast for its own territory, but Hall had the advantage of height and speed and caught the German just at the lines at 12,000 feet. The observer swung his gun up at Hall and opened fire. Hall grimly held course, watching the tracers skimming along his right wing, ripping holes in the fabric. Hall opened fire and felt his Nieuport tremble as the Lewis gun rattled off a long burst. The German pilot was killed instantly, and the Aviatik started a lazy spiral toward the earth two miles below. Hall followed the stricken plane down to 3000 feet, from where he saw it slam into the ground outside of Malancourt, two miles inside the German lines.

The Escadrille was on schedule for two patrols a day, sharing the duty with other squadrons based within a twenty-mile radius of the battlefield. These patrols were staggered so that there was always a patrol up at different segments of the Front in three layers: one at 1000 feet, a second at 6000 feet and a high patrol at 12,000. These altitudes and the two-a-day frequency were required; voluntary patrols in between these times, and at altitudes of the pilots' own choosing, were allowed by nearly every fighter-squadron commander, and Thénault was no exception.

On the morning of May 24, Rockwell and Thaw climbed out of bed at three, hurriedly drank some hot, black coffee and drove to the field where they had their planes rolled from the hangars. They left the ground just as the sun was coming up over the eastern ridge of hills that bordered Behonne. They followed the winding course of the Meuse and crossed the lines north of Verdun. Below them, its white fabric clearly visible against the dark smudge of the battlefield, flew a Fokker monoplane. Thaw and Rockwell dived straight down on the unsuspecting German and Thaw's first burst killed the enemy pilot and sent the Fokker plunging into the ground. Elated, the two Americans flew back home to report the kill.

They landed at Behonne in time to have their tanks refilled and for Captain Thénault's briefing on the scheduled morning patrol. Thénault traced the route on the map, then said, "Follow me, and attack *only* if I give the signal."

Thénault took off first, followed by de Laage, Thaw, Rockwell and Chapman. The five Nieuports formed up over Éparges, southeast of Verdun, then turned north for the lines. The sky above them was a brilliant blue, dotted with puffs of cirrocumulus clouds faintly tinged with pink from the rapidly rising sun. In the stable coolness of the early-morning air the formation moved across the face of the battlefield with only a slight bobbling motion as individual pilots jockeyed back and forth, up and down, a foot or so at a time to maintain a V formation that must have warmed Thénault's heart. Then, far to the east, near Étain, Thénault discovered twelve big German two-seaters creeping low in formation over the earth. They reminded Thénault of "sheep passing across a vast green prairie." He had no intention of attacking an enemy that was "too numerous, too low and too far away." He gave the Germans only passing notice, and flew straight ahead.

Then—despite the captain's orders given less than an hour previously, and despite the potentially suicidal tactical situation —one of the pilots nosed down and away from the Nieuport formation and swung steeply toward the Germans. In that moment all air discipline was lost, and Thénault watched his formation split apart into a disorganized rabble as one, two, three Nieuports flung themselves after the self-appointed patrol leader. Thénault's feelings at the usurpation of his prerogative can well be imagined, but he nonetheless followed his men into the fight that was rapidly developing.

As the fierce onslaught fell on them suddenly from the skies, the German formation was at first disrupted; three of the two-seaters made hurried landings where they were—but the others stayed on to fight. They shifted from an echelon of Vs into a vast circle so that each man could protect the tail of the man in front of him. Rockwell arrived during this shift in position and dived on what appeared to be a straggler, but by the time he reached firing range, he was within the arcs of fire of several of the German observers' guns, and his plane was struck again and again. One slug exploded on his windscreen and fragments of glass and steel were driven into the lower part of his face with stunning force. Shocked, numbed with pain, with blood spattered over his goggles, Rockwell dived through the murderous fire and turned for home, skimming low over the ground.

Chapman was put out of action just as quickly; a German observer had put a burst into Chapman's plane, one slug ripping through the sleeve of his flying suit and cutting a shallow but painful furrow on his arm. He, too, turned for home. De Laage and Thénault escaped from the hornet's nest without damage and made their way back to the field without further incident.

Thénault landed only a little before Rockwell, and he stood on the field waiting for the Carolinian to get his long legs out of the cockpit. Mopping blood from his slashed upper lip, Rockwell strode over to Thénault. In a heated Southern drawl he unlashed a broadside of invective against the Germans made up of every foul expletive known to the Foreign Legion. Then he went to the dispensary to have the glass splinters plucked from his face.

De Laage and Chapman landed, but Thaw failed to return. There was no news at Group Headquarters, so they drove back to the villa to have lunch while Thénault got on the telephone seeking information about the missing American. But *central téléphonique* knew nothing, and Thénault dejectedly returned to the table. It wasn't until early afternoon that the telephone in the villa rang with news: Thaw had been shot down, but was alive. Thénault and the others got into the staff car and drove the thirty miles to where Thaw lay in a small hospital at Dieue, on the outskirts of Verdun. They found him sitting up in bed, smiling, his left arm in a cast.

Thaw had suffered the same fate as Rockwell and Chapman; in diving on a two-seater during the mêlée, his plane had been riddled by machine gun fire and a slug had smashed into his arm, just above the elbow. The shock of the hammer-like blow rendered his arm numb and useless from the shoulder down and the wound bled profusely. With his good arm he swung his plane away from the fight and headed for the French lines. He landed roughly near Fort Tavannes and was pulled from the bloody cockpit almost unconscious. *Poilus* put him on a stretcher and took him to a field dressing station, where the flow of blood was stopped; then he was taken in an ambulance to where he now lay. The next day, Thaw was on his way to the American hospital at Neuilly.

The morning's fiasco brought to light several significant facts, not the least of which was that the Escadrille pilots could flaunt the authority of their commanding officer and get away with it. Despite open violation of his orders, with the consequent personnel casualties and aircraft damage, Thénault was powerless to impose punishment. He took command of N.124 under a unique handicap: on written orders from the Foreign Office and the Ministry of War, he was forbidden to apply to the Americans the same strict standard of discipline that prevailed in the rest of the French Air Service.[2] Not only was this policy psychologically unsound, it worked a hardship on Thénault and lessened the effectiveness of the Escadrille as a fighting unit.

As far as the fight itself was concerned, it was clearly demonstrated that an uncoordinated attack from above on a massed formation of two-seaters was as futile as it was dangerous. Moreover, the attack had been delivered without the protection of top cover and without bothering to see whether or not there were Fokkers lurking in the sun. Had there been, all five Nieuports—without altitude to maneuver—would in all likelihood have been shot down. If there was any consolation for Thénault, it was the fact that his men were demonstrably aggressive—the *sine qua non* of a natural fighter pilot.

In June the right bank of the Meuse before Verdun shook with new convulsions as the German assault reached new heights of fury. More than two thousand German guns opened up on the weary French defenders who became the first victims of a new terror weapon: phosgene gas fired by artillery. But through the gas and the rain of high explosive, the muddy *poilus* stood firm; and when the waves of German infantry came across the torn ground they met fiercely stubborn resistance—especially from the terrible, quick-firing 75s. A French staff officer, observing the attack through binoculars, wrote:

"Beyond, in the valley, is German infantry advancing in mass formation. We telephone through to the batteries and the ball begins . . .

"There is a whistle over our heads; it is our first shell on its way. It falls right in the middle of the enemy infantry; their regiments spread out, and as they deploy, fresh troops come pouring in. We

[2] In January 1915 a French pilot named Georges Félix Madon ran out of fuel while trying to reach his field in heavy fog and landed in Switzerland. Twice escaping from internment camp, Madon made his way back to France, where he was handed a sixty-day jail sentence because he was *suspected* of having landed in Switzerland on purpose. Madon went on to score forty-one official kills.

telephone our batteries, shouting encouragement, and the first few ranging shots turn into a deluge of shells that pours on the Boches. The first wave of the assault is decimated—the ground is dotted with heaps of dead; but the second wave is still pressing on. Our shells carve awful gaps in their ranks. Through glasses, we can see men maddened, men covered with earth and blood, falling one upon the other. Nevertheless, like an army of rats, the Boches continue to advance. The whole valley is turned into a volcano—and its exit is blocked by a barrier of the slain."

On June 1, the day the German softening-up began, a wave of bombers flew over Behonne and continued to Bar-le-Duc where they unloaded high explosive on the town, killing forty civilians. Part of the Escadrille was returning from patrol just as the enemy force had finished its work of destruction and was wheeling for home, but the only American who got within firing range was Norman Prince. He fired off a drum of Lewis ammunition without effect, then reached up to reload. His elbow accidentally hit the ignition switch and his engine stopped cold. Prince, not realizing why it had quit, thought he had engine failure and hurriedly landed dead-stick, just making the field.

The raid not only angered the Americans, it embarrassed them. Since its inception the Escadrille had provided a seemingly endless source of exaggerated copy for French and American news media. "The reporters in town," wrote Chapman to his sister in America, "see their chance for news; and they will soon have us bringing down a German a day apiece, and dying gloriously weekly. I am reported killed twice already . . ."

French newspapers, on sale in neutral Switzerland, were thoroughly read by the Germans seeking possible news of military value, and thus the Germans knew a great deal about the squadron of American volunteers. The American pilots assumed the raid was for their benefit, prompting one of them to say: "I am ashamed to be seen in town if our presence has caused death to innocent people." This was not the case, however.

Bar-le-Duc, which had a prewar population of some ten thousand, was the southern end of a vital chain of communication and supply, linked to Verdun thirty-three miles north by a 22-foot-wide road known as *La Voie Sacrée*. Through Bar-le-Duc and up the twisting "Sacred Way" went everything needed to feed and equip more than half a million men; moreover, Bar-le-Duc was a rail center for supplies moving east and west, and housed the Headquarters for the air units operating in the sector. Any one of the reasons was sufficient to risk a force of bombers miles inside enemy territory; certainly a nuisance raid on the town for the dubious honor of the Americans living there was—at the height of the battle—out of the question. Still, the feelings of the pilots are understandable when we take into account their hypersensitivity to newspaper accounts of a prowess they did not yet possess.

The second week in June brought black skies and heavy rains to the parched Verdun battlefield, and for nearly a week aircraft on both sides were grounded. "I sit in an upper window," Chapman complained, "while waves of leaden clouds drift by, and the other heroes play poker while the indefatigable gramophone churns out some vulgar tune below, and the Captain practices scales on the piano. It is disintegrating to mind and body, this inertia." But by the fifteenth the clouds were burned away by a brutally hot sun and Chapman's inertia was converted into the momentum of combat.

Captain Thénault carefully briefed his pilots for the morning patrol of June 17, explaining they had orders to guard the right bank of the Meuse so that no Germans could cross the river on the side where the ground battle was building to a furious climax. Under no circumstances, he stressed, were they to cross over to the left bank; their job was to keep enemy artillery-regulating planes away from the crucial center of the battlefield. This explained, Thénault took off, followed by de Laage, Chapman and a new man named Clyde Balsley.

They had just crossed the lines near Champ—there to swing north to follow the deep bend in the river—when Chapman pulled out of the formation and hurtled across the Meuse, heading straight for a big A.E.G. twin-engine bomber seen approaching in the distance. Once again Thénault watched his closely knit patrol disintegrate as de Laage and Balsley peeled off to follow Chapman. But the German pilot had seen the attack coming, and the bomber wheeled away and dived for safety in the direction of the Bois de Forges, escaping before the Nieuports could get within range. The rest of the patrol time was spent as it was intended, flying monotonously up and down over the right side of the Meuse. When the time was up, everybody turned for Behonne except Chapman, who waved and dived away from the others.

He landed on a small field near Verdun and refueled. Then he took off and flew back over the lines, intending to find the A.E.G. that had frustrated him only a short time before. Chapman did not find the bomber, but five Fokkers found him. The American picked one, and opened fire.

As if by magic the Fokker vanished, to reappear seconds later on Chapman's tail, both machine guns blazing. A bullet ripped up the empennage just behind Chapman's back, tore through his helmet inflicting a nasty gash, then passed on to smash the windscreen. Another slug snapped the right aileron control rod, which passed through the top wing about a foot over the pilot's head. The Nieuport immediately snapped into a vicious spiral toward the earth.[3]

Blood flowed over his goggles and Chapman saw the ground whirling up at him through a red haze. He pushed the goggles up, letting the wind blow the blood back into the slipstream. Then he grabbed the severed control rod with his big right hand, while easing back on the stick with his left. The plane came out in a shallow dive, and Chapman fought it down to a landing at Froids, not far inside the French lines. He left the Nieuport there for salvage and, with a bandage on his head the size of a Sikh turban, was driven back to his own field in the staff car belonging to N.67—whose commanding officer, Captain Saint-Sauver, ordered him not to fly again until the wound had healed.

Back at Behonne, Chapman laughed off Thénault's suggestion that he turn himself in at the hospital. He asked instead that the captain get him another Nieuport as soon as possible—one with a more powerful engine.

During World War I, statisticians worked out the average combat life expectancy of a fighter pilot as approximately two

[3] From Chapman's description, the other pilots believed the Fokker that shot him down was piloted by Captain Oswald Boelcke, a *Pour le Mérite* holder and German national hero.

weeks. This figure included pilots shot down on first patrol and veterans who lasted through several seasons of aerial warfare. Every time a pilot fresh out of replacement pool completed a patrol, he believed—not without justification—that his chances of survival increased. Then, after several months, he began to think he had outlasted his luck and was living on borrowed time. The truly critical period in a pilot's life was during the first few days of combat; sometimes he became a casualty within the first few minutes. The painfully brief career of Clyde Balsley is perhaps typical of green pilots on both sides in mid-1916, a period that witnessed air battles fought by entire formations; single combats were getting rarer as opposing air strengths greatly increased.

Balsley—a slender, jug-eared, hawk-nosed youth of twenty—had worked in his widowed mother's bakery in San Antonio, Texas, before coming to France in 1915 as a volunteer ambulance driver. Balsley's child-like enthusiasm, coupled with his poor-boy capacity for hard work, soon won over grimly serious pilots like Rockwell, who, at twenty-four, reacted to the Texan with barely concealed skepticism because of the latter's "youth and inexperience." Balsley flew a few practice patrols behind the lines, and he was over the Front the day Chapman was wounded. Then, at approximately 5:45 A.M. on June 18, Clyde Balsley engaged the enemy.

Thénault left the field at Behonne that morning with seven pilots trailing in his wake, but when he reached the lines he discovered that only Rockwell, Prince and Balsley were still following his lead, the others apparently having decided to patrol elsewhere. The four remaining Nieuports huddled together and flew on. At 15,000 feet they encountered the uppermost of three layers of an estimated forty German planes, more than any of them had ever seen together in the air.[4] Clustered at the top were fifteen two-seater Aviatiks that quickly demonstrated their truculence by opening fire at the extreme range of 1000 yards. Thénault led his three Americans in a wide sweep to the rear of the Germans, where they circled cautiously for a quarter of an hour, undecided, but out of range. Suddenly one of the Aviatiks

[4] And about 20 percent of the total German air strength at Verdun at the time.

detached itself from the others and slid downward, sailing underneath the circling fighters.

Prince took the bait and nosed steeply down at the Aviatik in a dive that seemed to Rockwell "a regular death-drop." Then Balsley's plane disappeared. Believing both men had been killed, Thénault and Rockwell turned from the suicidal odds and headed for their own lines. Prince had not been killed, but he had been paralyzed with fright when a bullet fired by the German observer creased his helmet, miraculously not touching his scalp. Prince hurtled past the straight-shooting gunner and kept his nose pointed for home.

Balsley, mesmerized by the sight of so many of the enemy, failed to notice he was now alone in the sky with the hostile force. An Aviatik drifted into his field of vision, then: "One second I poised for decision. In that second, lay my future; I would take him!" Balsley pushed his stick forward and dived on the German. Remembering what they had taught him in school, he held his fire until the bulk of the enemy biplane loomed large in front of his engine cowling. He gripped the lever on the stick that actuated the firing mechanism and heard a solitary pop as his Lewis gun fired once, then jammed. When he reached upward for the gun he realized there was no time to clear the stoppage; two German planes were on his right, one on his left, and the one he had attacked was now sitting on his tail firing.

Balsley frantically swung his plane this way and that, but even when he plunged into the wet opaqueness of a cloud the hail of bullets followed. He rolled over on his back, the belly of his Nieuport facing the sky. Then a bullet tore through his hip and exploded against the bone with the force of a hard-swung sledgehammer. The blow jammed his left foot forward against the rudder bar and the plane snapped down and whipped into a sickening spin. Balsley's right leg was numb, paralyzed, and he was unable to shove it forward to swing the rudder around. He placed his hand on his knee and pushed as hard as he could, while drawing his left leg back; since both feet were strapped to the rudder bar, the backward movement of his left leg tended to push the right leg forward. Through great effort Balsley managed to turn the rudder and the gyrating Nieuport came out of the spin and he leveled off, keeping his hand pressed against his knee to hold the rudder straight. *Crack-crack-crack!* Balsley had no need to look over his shoulder. He frantically put the stick forward and dived vertically, watching the altimeter needle unwind. When the screaming plane reached 2500 feet he hauled back on the stick, praying the riddled wings would stay on. The plane groaned and creaked as it came out of the dive not far above the treetops, but the wings held. He flashed by the French first line only fifty feet off the ground and had a brief glimpse of the blue helmets of the infantrymen as they crouched low to avoid the rapidly sinking airplane. His wheels caught up in the tangled, rusted ruins of the barbed wire in front of the reserve trench, and the Nieuport flipped over on its back in a grinding shower of dirt and debris. When the dust settled, Balsley was hanging upside down in the cockpit and a steady stream of gasoline from the ruptured fuel line flowed over his face and the front of his flying suit. Terrified of fire, Balsley undid the catch on the seat belt and dropped heavily to the ground. He dragged himself through the weeds slowly, like a dog with a broken back, but collapsed face down after only ten yards. Then the Germans began shelling the area, and Balsley pressed his face against the earth and waited.

"I felt so little pain," he recalled, "I was sure I was not badly wounded. I would have to let my mother in Texas know that I was all right. Then I would be sent to Paris. I wondered who my nurse would be. Then I would be sent back to the squadron, and the next time I would get my German. But it was more of the good times in Paris that I thought of than my job."

When the shelling stopped, four *poilus* made their way through the barbed wire and crawled to where Balsley lay prostrate in the field. When they learned that he could not walk they grabbed him by his arms and feet and began dragging him across the uneven ground. "Then," Balsley said, "like a beast unleashed, my pain broke from its long stupor. The four men dragged me like a sack of grain through the long grass, over and under and across the web of barbed wire. The pain was such torture that I almost fainted." When the *poilus* reached an advanced field dressing station, they dumped Balsley and went back to the lines. A doctor came along and jabbed a needle filled with antitetanus serum into the pilot's chest and ticketed him for the hospital at Vadelaincourt, five miles behind Verdun. It was there that his real ordeal would begin.

Compassion was a quality in Victor Chapman that rose quickly to the surface. When the news of Balsley reached the Escadrille he was the first to fly to the hospital to see if he could ease the Texan's suffering. He found Balsley in a shed filled with thirty badly wounded French infantry officers. In the stifling heat of mid-June the closely packed shed had "all the stagnant horror of a dream." The heavy air reeked of carbolic acid, the nauseating stench of gangrene and of bodies long unwashed. Flies buzzed insistently in the fetid air, and the chorus of groans was pierced from time to time by forlorn cries of men whose minds were unhinged by pain. Chapman found Balsley lying naked under a woolen blanket on top of a filthy straw-filled mattress placed on three wooden planks. He was in a delirium of thirst, sucking feverishly at a piece of wet muslin; the bullet that had shattered against his hipbone had also perforated his intestines with small holes in a dozen places, and water was denied him. Chapman asked a passing surgeon if his suffering friend could have oranges, and when told that he could, he smiled broadly and promised Balsley he would bring oranges "if he had to fly to Paris to get them."

In the days that followed, Chapman busied himself collecting oranges where he could, while gloating over a brand-new 110 h.p. Nieuport Thénault had obtained for him from the depot—hinting that now he would be able to get back at the Germans for gashing his scalp. At night, in the room they shared, Rockwell would plead with him to exercise a little more caution in the air. But caution had never been a Chapman characteristic.

As a child of ten he had plunged into a lake and rescued a boy who was drowning. Later that same year he risked a horrible mangling when he scooped his younger brother to safety from between two freight cars that were being coupled. When he was twelve he ascended a steep gabled roof and stood silhouetted against the sky. An aunt who was watching him from the lawn below stood horrified as he scrambled from the roof to the gutter, where he began what appeared to be a silent fandango; he had blundered into a hornets' nest and the aroused insects were stinging him viciously, but he carefully worked his way down from the dangerous perch. Through red, swollen lips he laughed at his aunt's fears for his safety.

There was as much poet in Chapman as there was adventurer. When, at age nine, it was learned that he liked to sneak out of bed at dawn to wander the lush green countryside of upstate New York, a lady visitor to the Chapman house asked him why. "Because it is the best time of day," he answered. "The light is muzzy and all the creatures are out." This love of the beauty and wonder of nature had not been tarnished by nearly two years of war. While at Verdun he wrote a letter to his sister in America that revealed his awe of the element in which he waged combat.

"Clouds are not thin pieces of blotting paper, but liquid ceaselessly changing steam. I played hide-and-seek in and out of them yesterday; sometimes flat blankets like melting snow on either side below me, or again, like great ice floes with distant bergs looming up, and open water near at hand, blue as the moonstone cloud, floating full, for all the world like a gigantic jelly fish . . . I was going from below the clouds to above them, circling in some hole; thus I realized the size and thickness of the walls—300 meters sheer from top to base, of dazzling whiteness. Some have many feathery, filmy points and angles; others are rounded and voluminous with cracks and caverns in them—these are all the fair-weather fleecy clouds. Then there are the lower, flatter misty ones, and the speckled or mare's-tail clouds, above which one never reaches. There are a lot of trumpet-shaped and wind-blown clouds this evening and I should like to go out and examine them, but it's a bore for my mechanic . . ."

By June 23 Chapman decided he was again ready for combat; he had test-flown his new fighter, aligned the Lewis gun and had the plane painted a blue-gray color by his devoted mechanic, Louis Bley. Despite the fact his head was still swathed in bandages, making awkward the fitting of a flying helmet, he insisted on making the late-morning patrol with the others. The air that morning was ominously quiet, and by nine the Americans were back at Behonne without having fired a shot.

Chapman, as usual, was the last to land. He came in too high, and over the center of the field he cut the ignition switch and bounced down to a spine-jarring landing. Bley rushed over to inspect the damage and found that Chapman had broken the "Sandows," shock cords made of half-inch-thick bands of rubber and fabric wrapped around the juncture of the axle and landing-gear struts. As Bley got down on the grass to unwrap the severed cords Chapman lifted his eyes to the sky where came the distant and unmistakable sound of unsynchronized engines that heralded the approach of German raiders. Chapman yelled to Bley to get out of the way and started to climb back into the cockpit. Bley scurried from underneath the fuselage and began waving his arms. He pointed at the landing gear and excitedly explained to Chapman that he was certain to turn over if he attempted a landing without new shock cords. Chapman replied that it was all the same to him if he turned over, only he had to get after *les boches*. They stood there—the big American with the bandaged head, and the little Frenchman with a handful of rubber cord—arguing until the sounds of the bombers receded; the Germans weren't going to Bar-le-Duc after all. Chapman grinned at Bley, then went to lunch.

When he learned that Thénault was taking a couple of men over the lines at twelve-thirty, Chapman lost no time in inviting himself to accompany them partway. He told Thénault he would leave them before they reached the lines because he was flying to Vadelaincourt with a package for Balsley, whom none of them expected to live. At a quarter past twelve he walked outside to his airplane, where Bley stood waiting, having just finished replacing the shock cords. Chapman stuffed the package containing oranges and chocolate into the cockpit, then swung himself into the seat. Bley started the engine, and he and Chapman watched Thénault and the other two pilots take off. Chapman reached over the side of the cockpit and shook hands with Bley, yelling: "*Au revoir*, I'll be back soon!" Then Bley pulled the chocks from the wheels and watched the Nieuport roll down the field and rise into the air. He watched until the plane was only a tiny speck against the sky.

From time to time Thénault glanced over his shoulder to see Chapman's Nieuport trailing the formation far to the rear and some distance above. But as he and the others approached the lines the Captain diverted his attention to dodging antiaircraft bursts and to the possibility of combat ahead; on this day the renewed offensive had pushed German infantry closer to Verdun than on any day since the struggle began four months previously and, as the events of the past week had shown, they were not especially idle in the air.

Just past enemy-held Fort Douaumont, Thénault observed a brace of German two-seaters cruising below and he signaled attack. The three Nieuports nosed over, but before they were within firing distance three Fokker monoplanes jumped on them from out of the sun. Attacked from above, outnumbered and more than two miles inside enemy territory, Thénault wisely left the two-seaters alone and led the others to safety. Two of the nice things about the Nieuports was that they could not only outdive Fokker E-IIIs, but also outrun them on the level when emergencies arose—provided a patrol leader acted quickly enough, as Thénault had done. They finished the rest of the tour unmolested and then went home.

When they got out of their planes back at Behonne, Thénault asked if Chapman had returned with news of Balsley. Rockwell, who was on alert duty that afternoon, said no, but that he should be returning soon. They stood around in the heat of the late afternoon sun watching the sky, but no planes came. By four they were beginning to worry, but before anyone could call the hospital for word on the missing American, a Farman pilot rang up from a distant escadrille and over the static-ridden wire Thénault learned what happened to Chapman.

The Farman pilot and his observer had seen Thénault lead the others down on the two-seaters and had seen them attacked in turn by the Fokkers. Then, from above, Chapman's plane had jumped down after the five Germans; the two-seaters dived for safety, but the three Fokkers scattered adroitly and re-formed to catch up Chapman's plane in a withering cross fire. Chapman—probably killed instantly—fell against the stick and the stricken Nieuport dived vertically for the earth from 10,000 feet. The Farman pilot watched the wings tear loose from the splintered struts and sail away into the sky, and saw the fuselage plunge into the ground near the ruins of Beaumont, more than three miles inside German territory. No, the Farman pilot said, there wasn't the slightest chance the pilot could have lived following such a smashup, even had he been alive when the plane struck. With that, he rang off.

It was hard to believe that the vital Chapman was dead; Louis Bley *would* not believe it, and stood by the hangars staring at the empty sky until long after the sun had gone down, waiting for his *patron* to come home. Finally he gave it up and walked morosely back to the barracks.

That night, shortly after eleven, a violent storm blew up out of the north; the sky crackled with jagged streaks of lightning, strong winds rose that battered the wooden shutters of the Escadrille's villa and torrents of rain fell from the blackness of the sky. Kiffin Rockwell was sitting alone in the terribly empty room he had shared with Chapman. Smoking one cigarette after another, he listened dejectedly to the raging of the storm until eleven-thirty, when the telephone downstairs rang. The voice on the other end said somebody should get to the hospital, for Clyde Balsley was dying.

Rockwell, Thénault and McConnell piled outside and got into the squadron staff car and fought their way through the storm to Vadelaincourt. After two maddening breakdowns they managed to reach the hospital at three the next morning. Dripping wet, they entered the humid air of the shed and found Balsley conscious and surprised to see them at that hour. They talked for a few minutes, then left. Nobody mentioned Chapman. On the way out, Thénault questioned the doctor about the call and was told that four hours before Balsley had been taken with a raging fever and was thought to be at the point of death.

The next day Elliot Cowdin flew to the hospital and gave Balsley some oranges. He could not bring himself to tell the still-feverish pilot that Chapman was dead; instead, he told Balsley that "Chapman's machine was busted," but that he would be over as soon as it was fixed. It wasn't until a day later that he learned the truth.

A French officer reading a newspaper in the cot next to Balsley's looked over to the American and asked: *"Connaissez-vous un américain, Victor Chapman?"*

"Oui."

"Eh bien, il est mort."

Balsley's eyes filled with tears, and later, when he tried to eat one of the oranges, it choked him. For a long time afterward oranges were to remind Balsley of "the heavy black hair, the great arms and the sincerest eyes in the world." [5]

June had not been a happy month for the Escadrille; its best-loved pilot was dead, the youngest lay shattered in a hospital and Elliot Cowdin was suddenly stricken with ulcers and unraveled nerves and had to leave the Front for medical care and eventual discharge from the French Air Service. But the squadron received a minor boost to morale on July 1 when a *prise d'armes* was held on the field to award decorations and promotions. Bill Thaw, who had come up from Paris with his arm in a sling, was kissed and given the Legion of Honor; Rockwell and Hall were handed the *Médaille Militaire,* and Prince and Hall were elevated to *adjudant,* while McConnell and Rockwell were raised to sergeant. Thaw wanted to stay, offering to prove to Thénault that he could fly as well with one arm as two, but the Captain sent him back to Paris.

It was on that day, too, that General Sir Douglas Haig launched the Battle of the Somme in an effort to relieve Verdun. After a seven-day bombardment that was supposed to neutralize German defenses, nearly a quarter of a million British and French infantrymen climbed out of their trenches and walked forward into the stuttering of hundreds of intact machine guns. Among those in the assaulting waves were Americans of the Foreign Legion. One of the Legion objectives was the village of Belloy-en-Santerre, a heavily fortified ruin lying beyond a long stretch of open ground. Under the cover of darkness on the night of July 3 the Legionnaires moved up to relieve French Colonial troops who had suffered brutal losses during the first three days of fighting. The Legionnaires lay exposed in an open field until daybreak, then rose from the ground yelling like demons and stormed

[5] Balsley spent six weeks in the charnel house at Vadelaincourt—sleeping one night with a corpse on either side of him—before transfer to the American Hospital at Neuilly. He underwent surgery eight times and was not able to return to the United States until the fall of 1917. The French decorated him with the *Médaille Militaire* and the *Croix de Guerre,* and he finished the war in Washington, D. C., as a captain in the U. S. Air Service.

across two hundred yards of barren plain to get at Belloy.

Alan Seeger, in the first wave, carrying a newly issued *Chauchat* automatic rifle, went down almost at once. Struck in the legs and stomach by six machine gun slugs, he lived long enough to apply dressings to his wounds and to plant his new rifle into the earth to mark the place where he lay. That night, after Belloy was taken, Seeger's body was found and buried with hundreds of others at the foot of Hill 76, just south of the village. Seeger's last line in the last letter he sent home might well have served as his epitaph: "If you are in this thing at all, it is best to be in to the limit. And this is the supreme experience." He died just thirteen days after his twenty-eighth birthday.

Despite almost unbelievable losses (80,000 killed and wounded on the first day) the stubborn Somme offensive continued almost without letup for nearly five months; in the end it was considered by realists to have been another failure. By the time it was set in motion, the Germans had shot their bolt at Verdun, but the unstoppable battle raged on.

To Jim McConnell, the battlefield seen from 10,000 feet was "a strip of murdered Nature. It seems to belong to another world. Every sign of humanity has been swept away. The woods and roads have vanished like chalk wiped from a blackboard; of the villages nothing remains but gray smears where stone walls have tumbled together. The great forts of Vaux and Douaumont are outlined faintly like the tracings of a finger in wet sand.

"Columns of muddy explosions spurt up continually as high explosives tear deeply into the area. During heavy bombardments and attacks I have seen shells falling like rain. The countless towers of smoke remind one of Gustave Doré's pictures of the fiery tombs of the arch-heretics in Dante's Hell. A smoky pall covers this sector under fire, rising so high that at a height of 1000 feet one is enveloped in its mist-like fumes. Now and then, monster projectiles hurtling through the air close by leave one's plane rocking violently in their wake. Airplanes have been cut in two by them.

"For us, the battle passes in silence, the noise of one's engine deadening all other sounds. In the green patches behind the brown belt, myriads of tiny flashes tell where the guns are hidden; and those flashes, and the smoke of bursting shells, are all we see of the fighting. It is a weird combination of stillness and havoc, this Verdun conflict viewed from the sky."

Despite its losses in June, the Escadrille grew fat with pilots. By July 1 the squadron numbered twelve, including Thénault and de Laage. This increase reflected the general strengthening of French *escadrilles de chasse* all along the line to meet the heavy demands imposed by the violence of the fighting along the Somme as well as at Verdun. In addition to the original seven Americans of N.124, thirty others were either in training or were already breveted by the first week of July, and more were coming. Thus there was not only a guaranteed supply of replacement pilots for *l'Escadrille Américaine*, but enough Americans left over to be fed by ones and twos into regular French squadrons at the Front. Doctor Gros's relentless recruiting, abetted by transoceanic press coverage of N.124, was paying off.

On July 5 Thénault and his constant companion—a big German shepherd named Fram—took themselves off to Paris on leave. Lieutenant de Laage assumed command and if the Americans believed Thénault to be overcautious, they found de Laage suicidally heedless of danger. He led his first patrol a full twelve miles behind enemy lines, attacking German formations regardless of number. He led them down on a mixed bag of Fokkers and some new two-seater Aviatiks "that went so fast we looked as if [our Nieuports] were tied." De Laage, maneuvering out of streams of machine gun fire, whipped into a vicious spin at 10,000 feet and whirled violently downward, managing to level out a bare 500 feet above the earth. When the Americans returned to Behonne virtually on the dregs of fuel left in their tanks, McConnell was moved to comment: "De Laage will keep this *Nach Berlin* stuff up once too many times and about half of us will stay over there."

Alfred de Laage de Meux came by his impetuosity and love of attack through his heritage and early experiences in the war. Descended from an old Orléans family that had fielded French warriors for centuries, de Laage, a lieutenant in the 14th Regiment of Dragoons, was at the Front before the war was a week old. Superbly uniformed, superbly mounted, he spent day after day in the saddle, scouting the movements of German infantry and cavalry during the bloody Battle of the Frontiers. Twice he returned from patrol with his uniform pierced with bullets, but he seemed to bear a charmed life. Then, on August 31, 1914, while skirting the flanks of two regiments of German cavalry and a regiment of machine gun supported infantry, his horse was shot out from under him and a rifle ball slammed through the fleshy part of his thigh. Lying helpless on the ground, de Laage awaited capture, but his faithful orderly, Jean Dressy, galloped up and helped him aboard his own horse, and together they rode triumphantly back to Regimental Headquarters with the information de Laage had risked his life to get; and Dressy, his to bring him back. By the time the wound had healed, the cavalry as a scouting force was dead, so de Laage transferred to aviation and became an observer with Farman Squadron 30. So eager was de Laage to come to grips with the enemy, he performed the incredible feat of learning to fly while at the Front; later he was granted his pilot's badge—having never gone through a day of school—and managed to shoot down a German observation machine while piloting a Farman, which had never been designed for an attack role. When Thénault had chosen him as executive officer of N.124, de Laage was delighted—as were the Americans without exception. Witty, urbane, a delightful raconteur speaking flawless English, he was the ideal second to Thénault, who could never quite manage to reach the men under him. If de Laage was quick to lead men into danger, he was just as quick to get them out.

He took Rockwell on a wide sweep of the right bank of the Meuse one morning just at sunrise, and over Étain, twelve miles east of Verdun, they saw a German two-seater flying some distance below. De Laage let Rockwell go down after the German while he stayed above to protect his tail. Rockwell was barely in firing position when two Fokkers dropped on him from the rising sun. The Germans paired up on either side, above and behind him, and opened fire. In the meantime de Laage had been jumped by a third Fokker but had turned and got on the German's tail only to have his Lewis gun jam. When de Laage looked down and saw Rockwell being hounded he broke off with his own adversary and dived headlong for the unequal fight below. Unarmed, de Laage flung himself at the Fokkers, which scattered before the onrushing Frenchman. Rockwell, who had believed his last moment had come, banked and followed de Laage in a hurried flight to the safety of their own lines.

Starved for victories, the pilots spent more and more off-duty hours stalking Germans on both banks of the river. De Laage, Rockwell and Hall caught an observation plane just as it was crossing the lines one morning and they went down line astern. Rockwell dropped within twenty yards of the two-seater and opened fire, holding down on the trigger until an entire Lewis drum was emptied at the Germans; he turned away to avoid colliding, and de Laage swooped down. He fired off one drum, reloaded and shot away a second forty-seven rounds. He pulled up and Bert Hall appeared on the two-seater's tail an instant later and got off an additional twenty rounds; but the Germans flew steadily on, unhurt, unhurried, contemptuous of them all.

Later that afternoon Rockwell and Hall went out alone and found a solitary Aviatik cruising above the clouds at 12,000 feet. Rockwell dived first and the Aviatik put its nose down to get away from the Nieuport. Then two Fokkers leaped on Rockwell's tail, only to be attacked in turn by Hall—who jerked his head around when the familiar *tac-tac-tac* warned him that two Fokkers had fastened themselves on *his* tail. Down they hurtled, seven antagonists linked in combat as though strung together with twine. The deadly game of follow-the-leader continued straight down for 6000 feet filling the air with the popping of machine guns and the angry snarl of engines pushed to maximum r.p.m. When the Aviatik—first in line—plunged into a cloud and disappeared, the carnival-like formation split apart and the nerve-wracking battle was over. Hall's plane was riddled with holes, but he was untouched, and he and Rockwell made it back to the field.

Despite valiant efforts, none of the pilots of N.124 managed to rack up an official kill during the first three weeks of July—a period of exceptionally heavy fighting in the air. Pilots returned from battle sure of a kill, only to have the claim turned down. The day-in, day-out combats that went without recognition was a source of irritation and helpless frustration. The difficulty in obtaining confirmations was due to the French regulation that required a pilot's claim to be corroborated by a witness from the ground or an independent aerial observer not connected with the squadron making the claim. Because the great majority of combats took place well within German-held territory, few of the successes could be witnessed by French observation posts on the ground, or from balloons tethered some distance behind their own front line. One theory advanced for this system is based on the fact that the majority of French pilots were enlisted men, therefore they were not automatically placed in the category of "gentlemen," whose word alone might have been sufficient. Sometimes, well-meaning ground observers only added to the confusion.

"One day," explained Rockwell, "Lieutenant de Laage and I attacked two machines. One of them went straight down and I thought the pilot had been killed, but he re-dressed close to the ground with nothing wrong. However, he was seen going down by a post of observation which did not see him re-dress. The post sent in a report that a German machine had been brought down in German lines; they wanted to give us the credit, but we both knew we had not brought down the machine and told them so, explaining the circumstances. Yet two well-known French pilots claimed it the following day and were given the credit. So, all in all, you can't tell much about what is going on in aviation . . ."

Captain Thénault returned from leave, and Bill Thaw rejoined the Escadrille—his arm now out of the sling—but still the squadron went scoreless. Finally a talisman appeared in the form of Lieutenant Charles Eugène Jules Marie Nungesser, already a living legend to the French because of his daring, coolness in combat and an ability to absorb fantastic punishment at the hands of the enemy and still come back for more.

Nungesser was well known for the bizarre insignia painted on the fuselage of his Nieuport—a skull and crossbones flanked by two burning candles below a coffin, the whole superimposed on a black heart. Stocky, square-jawed, with pale blue eyes and a heavy head of dark blond hair, Nungesser's face was ridged and welted with scar tissue, and his broken jaw and split lips turned a smile into a grimace. Earlier in the year while test-hopping a new Ponnier biplane, he had crashed when the engine cut out on takeoff, the plane spinning into the ground. When Nungesser was pulled from the wreckage, both legs were oddly twisted and blood poured from his mouth; his legs were broken and his jaw was dislocated when the control column rammed between his teeth, puncturing his palate. Eight weeks later he was back with his squadron, N.65, and his injuries kept pace with his victories and citations; he brought down a balloon and a two-seater, but was shot in the mouth; he crashed and broke his jaw again, but returned to shoot down two Fokkers in an hour-long duel, when he was hit again. Following a crash landing in the French forward trenches that dislocated his knee, Nungesser was relieved from duty and sent to a hospital to convalesce. A few days later, on July 12, he was with the Americans, with whom he had decided to spend his sick leave. He climbed from the cockpit carrying a heavy cane and wearing a well-tailored black uniform clinking with medals awarded him by a grateful and awed government for his fantastic devotion to duty and his nine confirmed victories. First-time recipients of the Nungesser smile were astonished: glaring from between the scarred lips were two rows of solid gold teeth, the originals having been scattered across the battlefields and in military hospitals.

On July 21 Nungesser limped to his airplane and took off to look for Germans. He found two, a Fokker and an Aviatik, and after a brief combat shot down the Aviatik and sent the Fokker scurrying for safety. It was Nungesser's tenth kill, the fourth for the Escadrille—its first in nearly two months. The drought was broken.

Two days later Bert Hall went out in mid-afternoon and jumped a solitary Fokker—this time one without any friend lurking above. Hall got on the German's tail and followed him down in a diving turn. The German, apparently a beginner, maneuvered clumsily and "was firing all of the time." Hall had no difficulty in staying on the Fokker's tail, closing in and firing two short bursts. The enemy plane lurched in the sky, then "spun like a bastard for 10,000 feet" to crash between the ruins of Vaux and Damloup in sight of thousands of *poilus*. Hall, who was almost constantly casting admiring glances at an expensive wrist watch taken from an ambulance driver in a poker game a few days before, accurately reported the time of the fight as 3 P.M. and his victory was quickly confirmed.[6]

Four days later, north of Fort Douaumont, Rockwell, de Laage and Prince flushed a two-seater out of the clouds and Rockwell dropped on the German's tail and opened fire. The German nosed down, then pulled up; de Laage flashed in and poured a stream of fire into the hapless craft and it spun down to crash between Ornes and Bezonvaux. Barely fifteen minutes later Rockwell pounced on two more Germans, and one drifted down out of control, but only de Laage received confirmation.

There were any number of recklessly courageous pilots who flung themselves at the enemy with more élan than skill or good sense, but few lived long enough to run up high scores or to pass on their experience as competent patrol leaders. There were others whose natural feel for flying was coupled with a deadly aim and a desire to live long enough to kill as many Germans as possible; these men shone as brilliant stars, but their achievements in creating havoc among the enemy were almost always personal and they had little to give to others. Rarer still was the individual who struggled every step of the way to become a pilot at all, who had to develop instincts that seemed to be lacking, who nursed himself along with dogged patience to become, finally, consummately skilled in his craft—yet who took time to give of himself so the squadron as a whole might benefit. Such a man was Gervais Raoul Lufbery, who had joined N.124 in the last days of May.

Lufbery stood only 5 feet 7 inches tall, but his body was cast solidly on a square frame that was heavily muscled. Deeply set eyes gazed thoughtfully from underneath a broad forehead, the mouth firm over a square jaw. He wore the ordinary heavy wool uniform of a French Army enlisted man, complete to wrap-leggings and heavy hobnailed field shoes—the uniform, like the man underneath, was neatly fitted together, solid, practical

---

[6] The squadron was generally skeptical of Hall's claims. One pilot wrote to a friend in Paris: "As we all know, Hall is an awful liar and hot-air artist who rushes in to report a victory every time he sees something burning on the ground."

and utterly lacking in frills or pretension. At thirty-one he was the oldest pilot in the Escadrille, but it was a taciturnity bordering on aloofness that commanded respect, not his age. Essentially a loner, Lufbery was economical with his words and the story of his fascinating travels only came out in bits and pieces as time went by. When he joined, the others knew little about him other than that he had been born in France, had lived for a while in Wallingford, Connecticut, and had piloted Voisin observation planes with VB.106 for six months before transferring to fighter school.

Lufbery's first weeks at N.124 were, for him, unspectacular; he made no kills, took few chances, said little. But he was learning. Observing that frequent jamming of guns jeopardized success in combat, he painstakingly checked each round of .303 ammunition that went into his gun; any round that bulged slightly here, that was burred a little there, he threw away. Whereas few of the others knew the difference between an intake valve and a rocker arm, Lufbery was a skilled mechanic who could discern trouble before it developed; often he emerged from the workshops with his arms grease-covered from having helped tear down and reassemble his own Le Rhône.[7] Above all, he concentrated on the fundamentals of piloting, working to make his airplane an extension of himself. The weeks rolled by, and Lufbery bided his time.

Monday, July 31, was a suffocatingly hot day. Declining lunch, Lufbery took off alone and cruised toward Étain, twelve miles east of Verdun. He watched not only for an unwary German but also to make sure he was not being stalked from above. Then, over the twisted, blackened stumps that had once been the Étain Forest, he observed a two-seater making its way southward. Clearing the sky above him with a long, sweeping glance, he worked his way carefully around until the sun was at his back, then dived. The German observer wheeled around and began firing; Lufbery held his dive until he was within range, then

---

[7] Prevalent was the attitude held by Rockwell that "an aviator need not know much about the works of his machine. He needs only to know how to fly it; the rest he can leave to his mechanic. Aviators who know too much about their craft are usually nervous—they understand what it means when the motor makes a funny noise. We others go on flying, blissfully ignorant and hoping for the best."

opened up. The German pilot skidded and got away from the bullet stream and tried to get on Lufbery's tail, but the Nieuport easily outturned the bigger two-seater and once again Lufbery was in position, his Lewis gun pounding steadily. Suddenly the German plane slid, rolled on its back and fell straight down, a sliver of flame licking from underneath the cowling. Lufbery circled overhead until the enemy two-seater splashed into the forest in a gush of flame, then he turned and flew back to Behonne. The victory was confirmed and Thénault was so pleased he jumped into the staff car and drove to the Headquarters of Marshal Joffre to put up Lufbery for the *Médaille Militaire.*

Three days later he jumped a flight of observation planes over Fort Vaux and shot two of them down, one right after the other; both were confirmed. Five days after this spectacular double, Lufbery and McConnell set out to protect a brace of French observation machines regulating an artillery shoot near Douaumont. McConnell became separated from Lufbery in a cloud and failing to find him again, remained on station above the Frenchmen. Far above, Lufbery was stalking an Aviatik headed for a mission inside French territory. He climbed unseen above the unwary German and then plunged down. The German pilot was inept and Lufbery had no trouble in getting on his tail, where he bored in close to deliver a stream of bullets into the clumsily maneuvering enemy.

McConnell was far below the fight and ignorant of the drama being enacted above him until he banked and saw the Aviatik falling out of control, Lufbery's Nieuport hovering above. "As the German plane turned over," McConnell reported, "it showed its white belly for an instant, then seemed to straighten out. Then it glided earthward in big zigzags. The pilot must have gripped the controls even in death, for the plane did not tumble as most of them do. Just as I was going down to see where it landed, I saw it skimming across a field. It was outlined against the shell-wracked earth like a tiny insect until, just northwest of Fort Douaumont, it crashed down upon the battlefield. A sheet of flame and smoke shot up from the tangled wreckage. I watched it burn, then I went back to my observation machines."

Over lunch, Lufbery briefly described the fight, said he believed the pilot had been killed, leaving the terror-stricken observer to watch helplessly as the earth rushed up to smash the plane to bits. Lufbery concluded softly, "Those poor fellows."

The Escadrille score now stood at ten, but Norman Prince showed little elation at the creditable showing. In May, nearly three months before, he had shown ill-disguised bad humor when Rockwell bagged the squadron's first German—an honor Prince thought should have gone to him. As N.124's score grew, so did Prince's discomfiture and he determined to accomplish something spectacular. Continued efforts to destroy an enemy airplane met with no success, but he found a method of waging war no other pilot in the Escadrille had tried: attacking German observation balloons with air-to-air rockets!

In June of that year the French evinced great interest in rocket-carrying Nieuports when four German *Drachen* were flamed in less than thirty minutes along the Somme. The weapons system had been developed by naval Lieutenant Yves Le Prieur while incendiary ammunition for machine guns was still in the testing stage. In use, the Le Prieur rockets—the same kind used in American Fourth-of-July celebrations—were mounted in tiers of four on the outer wing struts and fired electrically from the cockpit. Wildly inaccurate, the rockets forced the pilot to fly within 125 yards of the target before discharging the eight fire-spewing projectiles; the uncomfortably close range allowed the pilot less than three seconds to fire and pull up to avoid ramming the corpulent bag he had just attacked.

Prince pleaded for rockets and Thénault—to whom no request of the rich New Englander's was too extreme—agreed to secure them. When the long wooden crates arrived, Prince and his mechanic worked all one day rigging the rockets to the V-struts and hooking up the solenoid. The job done, Prince hounded Group Headquarters seeking map references where German balloons were reported. McConnell usually accompanied Prince on these expeditions, but by the time they arrived at the map coordinates the balloons had either been pulled down, or were not there. Bad luck dogged the hunters until one day they found a balloon where H.Q. said it would be, and Prince went down while McConnell stayed on top for protection. When it seemed that collision was imminent, Prince fired the salvo and zoomed clear with only feet to spare. When he looked back, the big black silk bag had vanished, leaving only a smudge of oily-looking smoke. In his eagerness to report his success, Prince attempted to land at the same time as McConnell and nearly rammed his escort plane as they touched down on the field. Frantically maneuvering to get out of the way Prince ground-looped and nosed over, sliding tailfirst in a cloud of dust down the center of the field. He was uninjured, but the top wing had been ripped loose and the damaged plane had to be towed away.

Nungesser departed on August 15, taking with him, it seemed, the Escadrille's recent good fortune. Prince's accident was followed by a series of disheartening mishaps that grew in seriousness as they increased in frequency.

Returning from patrol, Lufbery misjudged his landing approach and came in too high. He cut the ignition switch, but was unfortunately flying in a nose-down position and the Nieuport bounded heavily against the earth, flipped over and slewed crazily until it smashed up against an embankment. Pilots and mechanics rushed out to the wreckage expecting to find Lufbery dead, but he wasn't even scratched. He hung dazed upside down in the cockpit while a steady stream of fuel from the ruptured tank flowed into his face. He swallowed some of the high-octane gasoline mixed with castor oil and became wretchedly ill. Only after two days of violent nausea was he able to crawl, ashen-faced, from his bed.

In August the Germans—having failed once and for all to take Verdun—were on the defensive, and it was the French who were attacking without letup. Fierce and bloody fighting raged between Thiaumont and Fleury; the guns flamed and roared around the clock, leaving a fantastic harvest of the dead—the infantry may have been the queen of battles, but artillery was king, and the observation planes were its handmaidens. From dawn to dusk the Caudrons hovered over the churned-up ground sending back corrections to the guns so the slaughter could continue. And above the Caudrons, the Nieuports of the Escadrille. "Far below us," wrote McConnell, "the observation and range-finding planes circle like gliding gulls. Sometimes it falls to our lot to guard these machines from Germans eager to swoop down on their backs. Sailing high above them makes one feel like an old mother hen guarding her chicks." It was after one of these protection patrols that McConnell learned what it was like to be inside a Nieuport as it disintegrated around him.

McConnell, Rockwell and Prince had stayed on station above Fleury until twilight. When they started home, McConnell's engine began cutting out and he fell behind the other two, who made it to Behonne just as darkness closed in. But McConnell was still aloft, peering into the gloom searching for a field—any field. He saw one, a small one, lined with trees; beyond the trees was a deep ditch. As his engine spluttered its last, McConnell let down toward the field, but the darkness threw off his perception and he misjudged his height and overshot. The ground blurred as the plane shot down the field, but McConnell had a fleeting glimpse of a large number of French soldiers "who rushed out to be in on the finish." The wheels banged into the ground and McConnell threw his arms up over his face when he saw that his hurtling plane was headed straight for two huge trees. The Nieuport streaked between the trunks, leaving the wings behind in a splitting crash of sound. The naked fuselage bounded across the uneven ground and slammed heavily into the opposite side of the ditch. The tail whipped over and was crudely severed by some low-hanging telephone wires. McConnell came to upside down in the crumpled cockpit, surrounded by the excited, incredulous voices of the *poilus* who were working to free him from the twisted framework of the wrecked airplane.

His back was painfully injured, but he insisted on flying in borrowed machines. But when Thénault saw that it required two men to help the big North Carolinian into the cockpit, he sent him to Paris on short leave. While there, Paul Rockwell helped him dress for the daily rounds of the Chatham Bar, Harry's and other watering places in the capital. McConnell returned to the squadron a week later, but his back was no better. Thénault discovered that it required others to help McConnell into his clothes and that he could not walk without assistance, so he ordered McConnell to the hospital. "Captain," McConnell protested, "not being able to walk doesn't prevent me from flying."

"Jimmy," Thénault said firmly, "go to the hospital."

Rockwell helped him pack and put him aboard the train for the *Hôpital Auxiliaire* at Vitry-le-François.

In mid-August, when Paul "Skipper" Pavelka arrived at Behonne, he failed to comment on the fact that he was the thirteenth pilot on the roster. He sourly observed, however, that Thénault had issued him "a hoodooed machine"—the same one Thaw was flying when shot in the arm, and the one Prince had wrecked only a short time before. Although new wings had been fitted, the rest of the plane looked disreputable: dents marred the cowling, patches were spotted on the worn fabric, the struts had lost their varnished luster, the tires looked thin and the fuselage was drably overlaid with oily grime. Pavelka climbed into the cockpit with distaste, but on the first trial flight he learned that Louis Bley's diligent attention to the engine enabled him to nurse the Nieuport to 13,200 feet, and that it didn't handle badly, after all. Even so, Pavelka figured he would need a lot of luck to override the jinx that came with the airplane. Fortunately, luck was one commodity the tough-looking Pavelka had never been without.

During the charge across the Artois plain in May 1915, Pavelka was one of the few Legionnaires to emerge from the carnage without a scratch. A month later, Pavelka's regiment attacked near Souchez and he saw half his company drop on either side of him before they had advanced a hundred yards. When he reached the German second line a Bavarian lunged at his stomach with a bayoneted rifle, but Pavelka whirled and caught the heavy blade in his leg. The German flung his arms up, yelling "*Kamerad!*" The American blew out the man's brains and then fell bleeding to the ground. Recovering in a hospital far behind the lines, Pavelka was chosen from among hundreds of wounded men to give English lessons to classes of pretty young French girls in the school next door to the convalescent ward. Healed, he left this pleasant duty in time to rejoin the First Regiment in its assault on the Heights of Souain in the Champagne in late September. A shell burst only ten yards in front of Pavelka and he was flung violently to the ground. When he picked himself up he gazed at the rifle shattered in his hands and at the shredded greatcoat that was smoking from the passage of hot steel fragments. His head ached and his ears rang, and when he removed his newly issued steel helmet he discovered that it was dented all over—but he was nowhere wounded. When the regiment had spent itself in the charge and drifted back, Pavelka was one of ninety men out of a battalion of 250 still alive to answer to roll call. After Souain, he decided to switch to aviation. But his worst experience was yet to come.

Pavelka's second flight in the "hoodooed machine" was nearly his last. At 10,000 feet and still inside friendly territory, a valve broke allowing raw fuel to pour out inside the cowling encasing the whirling, red-hot cylinders. Instantly the nose of the plane was engulfed in orange flame and clouds of oily black smoke. Horrified, Pavelka felt a rush of searing heat flood across his face. Not wanting to leap two miles to certain death, he cut his switches and put the burning plane into a violent sideslip. At once the heat lessened, but the sideward motion of the fall whipped the flames up and across the length of the wing, where the highly volatile doped fabric blazed up in a crackling roar, sending charred bits of wood and linen fluttering away in the rush of wind. After an agony of waiting, Pavelka fell far enough to distinguish the nature of the terrain below. He was directly over a marsh. He righted the plane less than a hundred feet above the earth and immediately felt the full force of the inferno of heat that swept back toward his face. Ducking his head under the rim of the cockpit, he hauled the stick back as far as it would go and then felt the terrific bang on his spine as the plane slammed belly-first into the soft slime. He frantically undid the seat belt and went over the side into the mud. He staggered, rolled and crawled through the foul-smelling mud until he was fifty yards away from the blazing airplane, then was knocked flat from concussion as the fuel tank exploded, showering the air with flaming debris. German artillery, using the rising column of smoke as an aiming point, laid down a barrage on the marsh. Exploding shells sent geysers of mud and shattered trees into the air, but Pavelka believed he had lived through the supreme horror, and picked himself up and walked heedlessly through the barrage until he was out of the marsh.

The helmet and goggles had saved his eyes and hair, but his

hands and the lower part of his face were painfully blistered. He had survived, as few men did, the most sickening experience of the 1916 airman—and incidentally was rid of the jinxed Nieuport.

The Escadrille's run of bad luck stopped as suddenly as it had begun. On August 23 Prince, whose appetite had been far from sated by burning the balloon, went out alone and found an Aviatik, apparently unguarded. From an altitude advantage of 2000 feet Prince swooped down and got off a long burst into the unsuspecting two-seater. The observer was killed at once and slumped from sight. The enemy plane was defenseless from the rear and Prince could easily have finished it off. But he was nearly six miles inside the German lines, and what good was a kill so far from any French observation post? Prince pulled up alongside the uncertain German pilot, fired his gun, and pointed violently to the French lines. Reluctantly the German banked to the south, and ten minutes later glided down to a safe landing in a meadow outside of Verdun. Elated, Prince flew back to Behonne, where his story was at first greeted with skepticism. But after checking, Thénault put him in for the *Médaille Militaire*.

Then the first of the autumn rains came, and the squadron had nearly a week's rest—a week made even brighter by news that they were to prepare to move, perhaps to the Somme.

By September 9 the pilots were packed and ready to go, but the orders had not come. The morning was bright and clear and Rockwell went up for the first time in many days. Just across the German lines he found a two-seater sailing beneath him and dived. He killed the observer with his first burst, and followed the diving enemy down to 4000 feet, firing steadily. Two Fokkers came down on him from above, forcing him to break off pursuit, but the ensuing fight with the Fokkers was inconclusive and Rockwell got away. The two-seater he had attacked was finished; French ground observers saw it plunge into the ground just inside German territory, where it was shelled to bits. Thénault was so pleased he immediately began the paper work recommending Rockwell's promotion to *sous-lieutenant*.

And that same afternoon Prince dived on three Fokkers, rattled off a long burst at the hindmost German and swept away before the startled enemy pilots knew what had hit them. Looking back over his shoulder, Prince saw one of the Fokkers lurch from the formation and hurtle downward to crash almost in the German first line. News of the confirmation was waiting for him when he landed.

On September 14, movement orders came and the pilots boarded the train for a 72-hour leave in Paris. They deserved it, having spent 113 days in the line at Verdun, where they ran the Escadrille score to thirteen. As the summer drew to a close, the battle over which the Americans had flown had slowly flickered out. Seven hundred thousand men either lay dead on the battlefield or endured agonies in hospitals.

And the Germans did not pass.

Aviatik C-II

CHAPTER

6

THREE DAYS IN ANOTHER TOWN

The young women, the young girls! Their unknowing eyes threw furtive glances at the medals and the uniforms. These sheep's eyes almost made one believe he was a hero.

—GEORGES THÉNAULT

Captain Thénault had barely time to see the last crate of squadron records carried safely from his office at Behonne when an orderly rushed in, saluted and handed him a telegram. Ripping open the seal, Thénault was shocked to learn that his most valuable pilot had been thrown in jail. The message read: *Suis retenu dans un local disciplinaire place de Chartres. Lufbery.* Thénault could not imagine why Lufbery should be behind bars, but he knew why the pilot had gone to Chartres.

Like nearly everyone else who fought in French uniform

Lufbery had a *marraine,* or godmother. These *marraines* were of all ages and they belonged to no particular strata of society; however, most of them were young and pretty, as was Lufbery's, and soldiers sought them out on leave whenever possible. The institution of the *marraine* as an aid to morale was peculiar to the French, who realized that—next to regular rations and periodic leaves—nothing was so beneficial to the individual soldier as the comforting realization that someone in the rear areas was truly interested in his welfare. Letters from home were often filled with complaints and urgings that the *poilus* come back to put matters right, but letters from *marraines* were always filled with good cheer and encouragement. *Marraines* also found time to knit a seemingly endless stream of woolen mufflers, gloves and *passe-montagnes.* Although pilots had less need by far than the average infantryman for comely sponsors, the newspaper publicity given their exploits made them especially attractive to *marraines.*

A few days before the squadron left Verdun, Lufbery approached Thénault and asked for permission to leave ahead of the others. He explained that his *marraine* lived in Chartres, fifty-six miles south of Paris, and that he would like to see her before rejoining the rest of the pilots in the capital. Thénault agreed, but pointed out he could not grant him official permission. The Escadrille as a whole had been granted only seventy-two hours in Paris, such leave not to begin before the fourteenth. Lufbery departed without papers. Now Thénault stood with the telegram in his hand that told him something had gone haywire. He reached for the telephone and got through to Chartres.

"I found at the other end of the wire," Thénault said, "an old general—very irritated. I learned from him that Lufbery had engaged in combat with a railroad employee, and that the fight had terminated in the first round with the gentleman of the railroad losing six teeth. It seems that the railway man had demanded that Lufbery show him his ticket and leave papers. Lufbery's leave was technically unofficial, so of course he had no papers. The railway employee made the mistake of putting his hand on Lufbery, a gesture which Lufbery—with the cast of mind of those from the Front when facing those at the rear—considered an insult to him and his chestful of decorations. Lufbery promptly cracked the man in the teeth, and was arrested.[1]

"The old general took a grave view of the matter. I explained to him, with some anxiety, that he was dealing with an American volunteer, and that his bravery would be of far more use to France in the cockpit of an airplane than behind prison bars. The old general finally relented and I was able to set the captive free."

That September in Paris was marked by unseasonably chill winds and an unusual amount of depressing fall rains. Mornings that promised a pleasant, sunny stroll had a nasty way of turning foul, and those who ventured out minus umbrella or cape risked a sudden drenching. But the weather—so vital a concern while at the Front—was now of little consequence to the Escadrille pilots. Their most cherished hours were spent inside the Chatham Bar, less than a five-minute walk from the Opéra. Indeed, the rain that pelted down outside added extra charm to the Chatham, whose low-ceilinged interior was jammed corner-to-corner with heavy wooden tables. Here pilots and observers sipped early-morning coffee laced with brandy, vermouth cassis—and with the coming of the Americans, whiskey sours. From their perch on the tall stools at the semicircular zinc bar they watched the crowds of pretty girls hurrying through the rain to meet (or seek) luncheon companions; in the evenings, when the skies were clear, they watched them pass at a more leisurely pace. By 9 P.M. the place was packed, and airmen seeking friends on leave in Paris could almost always find them by elbowing their way into the smoky interior of the Chatham, or at Harry's a few doors up the street on rue Daunau.

The wild Jean Navarre, with twelve German planes to his credit, stormed into the Chatham one night just out of the hospital. Navarre had been badly wounded in a combat near Verdun, and this wound (his second), coupled with the recent

[1] Lufbery had a penchant for punching railwaymen. Some years before the war while working as a ticket-taker in the Bombay railway station, he had knocked down a fat, influential Hindu when the Indian berated him for not saying "sir." Lufbery promptly lost his job, but escaped imprisonment.

death of his brother in combat, had unhinged his mind slightly. Over great quantities of *fine à l'eau* Navarre refought old aerial battles at the table. The conversation triggered a renegade element in the twenty-one-year-old hero. He suddenly got up from the table and made his way through the door to the street outside. Navarre commandeered a taxi from a driver who was awestruck at the number and variety of medals the pilot was wearing pinned to the rear of his tunic. The driver watched in horror and admiration as the ace wheeled the high-riding taxicab up and down the sidewalks.

When arrested, Navarre explained to the *gendarmes* that he was merely demonstrating how it was done at the Front. Then he pulled from his pocket a medical certificate that stated he was not to be held responsible for his actions. The *gendarmes* wanted no part of this highly decorated madman and let him go with a lecture. Navarre returned to the Chatham and thought it all a great joke.

Granville Fortescue, a globe-trotting American reporter, was in the Chatham the first evening the Escadrille pilots arrived, and was on hand to greet Lufbery who had just been sprung from detention in Chartres. After exchanging reminiscenses with Lufbery about the Philippines—where Lufbery had spent a two-year hitch with the U. S. Army—Fortescue managed to draw out the details of his first successful aerial combat.

"The brief story," wrote Fortescue, "as he told it, looks cold in type. Yet his gestures—typical of his French origin, his expression, the short sentences like bursts from his machine gun made the story intensely vivid. Each sentence painted its own picture."

I saw a single German machine and I went for him.

"What were your sensations at the moment?"

Didn't have time for sensations. I began firing at him. Then we both circled, firing all the time. Suddenly, his machine seemed to turn all white. He was upside down. Then he caught fire. He fell, reminding me of a smoking cigarette butt dropping through the air. Then I came home.

"What seemed to worry these fliers more than the chances of aerial combat," remembered Fortescue, "was what would happen to them if they were captured within German lines. From a source supposed to be German, they believed they would be shot immediately. I reassured them this would not be so.

"Studying these aviators," Fortescue concluded, "it was simple to catalogue them as young, reckless, resourceful in the new style of warfare and largely enamored of the romance surrounding aerial battles."

Men like Fortescue and Paul Scott Mowrer of the Chicago *Daily News* were welcome at the knights' round table at the Chatham; both reporters took the trouble to learn first-hand what kind of war was being fought, and they delved into the motivations of the Americans who were helping to fight it. The copy they filed was usually accurate and pared thin of embarrassing adjectives. More often than not, however, the N.124 pilots shied away from reporters and the attendant publicity. As Kiffin Rockwell stated time and again, "The Escadrille isn't doing any more than any other French squadron." In this, Rockwell was correct, but it was a futile argument in the face of American journalistic tradition.

One brash correspondent fresh from the States made his way to the Chatham one night and sat down, uninvited, at the table where some Escadrille pilots were drinking. He broke in the conversation and begged for "some real-life adventure stuff" for his paper. One of the pilots agreed to tell of a hair-raising experience—not on himself, as modesty wouldn't allow it—that Bill Thaw had recently undergone. Since Thaw wasn't in the Chatham at the moment, he would be unable to object to a recounting of his latest heroism. The correspondent, sensing a scoop, got out pad and pencil as the pilot began to talk.

"Bill was flying alone over German territory, about twenty miles behind the lines, when an archie shell almost got him. Bill got mad as hell at the Boche for almost killing him, or what was worse, making him prisoner. Old Bill got so mad in fact that he landed his Nieuport right beside the German battery and took his Lewis gun from the top wing. Then he charged those Germans, spraying hot lead all around him. When Bill had emptied the drum, all the Germans lay dead. That satisfied Bill, so he put the machine gun back on the wing and took off and flew home."

Incredible as it may seem, the correspondent did not realize his leg was being unmercifully pulled; the story was picked up and run in American papers. In Pittsburgh, where Thaw was already a legendary favorite son, he was elevated to the status of a hero of Gothic proportions.[2]

However much the American pilots resented publicity, it had its benefits. "The German papers," reminded Thénault, "occupy themselves with us, and this publicity is perhaps the best propaganda, for it shows which side the youth of America is on. There is no volunteer squadron in Germany!"

Ambassador Herrick pointed out: "The people of the United States owe a special debt to these boys. When the sting of criticism cut into every American soul, they were showing how their countrymen could fight if given the chance. To many of us they seemed saviors of our national honor, giving the lie to current sneers upon the courage of our nation. The influence upon sentiment at home was tremendous. Amid the haggling of notes and the noise of German protestations, here were Americans shedding blood for a cause in which the heart of the American people was already enlisted."

One-armed General Henri Gouraud, of G.Q.G., summed up French sentiments when he said: "When men who have no obligation to fight, who could not possibly be criticized if they did not fight—yet nevertheless decide upon their own individual initiative to risk their lives in defense of a cause they hold dear—then we are in the presence of true heroes. The young Americans who entered the *Légion Étrangère* and the *Escadrille Américaine* are in every sense heroes, and France owes them all the homage that word implies."

Although the delights Paris offered fliers on leave were as exhilarating as they were inexhaustible, there were few places in the city that either medals or money could buy that had the flavor of home. Nothing quite takes the place of home-cooked meals and the chance to drop one's boots on the carpet and sprawl in an overstuffed living-room chair. Few groups of foreigners serving

---

[2] That the reading public believed the outrageous lie is not surprising. In 1914 many Americans were convinced that Germans raped nuns, cut the hands off male Belgian children so they would be unable to handle weapons when grown, and chained their own men to their machine guns so they would be forced to die at their posts.

with the French were as fortunate in having a home away from home as were the Americans, who since the early days of the war had been given the run of a large house at 80 rue Boissière, in the southwestern part of the city.

This house, located in the heart of a quiet residential section, was kept by a Boston society woman named Alice W. Weeks. Her son, Kenneth, who had published half a dozen books, had given up his career to enlist in the First Regiment of the Foreign Legion. Weeks, twenty-seven, was killed during the storming of Carency on June 16, 1915, and thereafter there was no favor too great to ask of Alice Weeks, who became known as *Maman Légionnaire*. She was as hospitable to privates as she was to officers, and she spent enormous sums over the years on such costly items as chocolates, pure wool shirts and whiskey which she sent to soldiers in the line. Any uniformed American who showed up at her door broke could expect a loan or a hot meal, or both. Although coal was scarce and dear by mid-1916, Alice Weeks managed somehow to keep enough on hand so that overnight and weekend visitors could always wake up and have a hot bath and shave with hot water in the mornings. And 80 rue Boissière was the only place in Paris where a man could get a decent cup of coffee and a slice of Boston layer cake served in bed. No soldier ever abused the privileges he enjoyed at the Weeks home, but five of the Escadrille pilots nearly cost *Maman Légionnaire* the services of a first-rate cook.

It started the second day in Paris when one of the new men, Dud Hill, ran across a small item in the classified section of the Paris *Herald*. A man had a baby lion he was willing to part with for five hundred francs. Deciding the squadron was overdue for a mascot, Hill, Thaw, Prince, Hall and Kiffin Rockwell formed a syndicate to buy the lion. Each pilot put up a hundred francs, with the exception of Bert Hall, who said he would pay later. Thaw put up Hall's share, and they all jumped into a taxi and drove to the suburbs of Paris. There, they entered the home of a Brazilian dentist who told them the cub was born on a liner while crossing from Rio and was in perfect health. The pilots paid over the money—worth then about $125—and hailed another taxi and drove to the Chatham for the christening.

"Whiskey," commented one of the pilots, "was a cute, bright-eyed baby who tried to roar in a most threatening manner, but who was blissfully content the moment one gave him one's finger to suck. He got a good view of Paris in the few days the boys were there, for someone was always borrowing him to take him some place. Like most lions in captivity, he became acquainted with bars—but the sort Whiskey saw were not for the purposes of confinement."

The Rockwell brothers took the cub from the Chatham to Alice Weeks's house and sat him down on the floor of the salon. The cub, about the size and color of a cocker spaniel, started waddling across the carpet on its stubby legs, headed for the kitchen. At that moment the door swung open to admit the middle-aged Belgian maid carrying a loaded silver tray. The miniature lord of the jungle looked straight up and emitted a squawk-like roar. The maid's mouth flew open; she retreated into the kitchen where she filled the air with outraged cries. The lion could stay, she said firmly, or she could stay—but not both. When Mrs. Weeks agreed to keep the lion out of the kitchen during the remaining day or two of the pilots' stay, the maid relented. But she gave the harmless Whiskey a wide berth on her rounds of the house.

On the morning of the sixteenth, the last full day of leave in Paris, Bill Thaw dropped around the house and asked if anybody was interested in seeing the new planes promised them by the French. Rockwell, Lufbery, Prince and Hill hurriedly finished their coffee and they all piled into a car Thaw had borrowed for the twenty-minute drive to the Nieuport factory and testing grounds at Issy-les-Moulinaux.

At Issy they were greeted enthusiastically by a Nieuport representative and led down narrow aisles inside a building that reeked with the smell of banana oil. They tramped softly across the flooring covered with sawdust and metal shavings. Workers were bent over long tables, carefully sanding down each small wooden part before fitting them into place inside fuselage or wing section; the work was so beautifully done, one pilot commented that it seemed a shame to cover it up. The workshops reverberated with the sounds of whirring saws, pounding hammers and the soft scratching of the sanders. Women sat patiently sewing Irish linen to the wooden skeletons, using heavy thread and a diagonal stitch for added strength. At the end of the building stood a few of the new machines, covered, doped and assembled.

The new aircraft were Nieuport 17s, which were rapidly replacing the *Bébés* at the Front. Outwardly the two models looked much the same, but they differed mechanically in several significant aspects. "How fast will she climb?" the pilots asked. They were told that with the new 110 h.p. Le Rhône engines, the new model could reach 10,000 feet in approximately nine minutes—or nearly twice as fast as the *Bébé*. Note, said the factory man, that the wing area has been increased to fifteen square meters and that the camber of the airfoil section has been increased, too. He added that the new model weighed 133 pounds more than the *Bébe,* but that it was about 12 m.p.h. faster in level flight.

But by far the most stirring feature of the Nieuport 17 from the pilot's point of view was the installation of a belt-fed Vickers .303-caliber machine gun synchronized to fire through the propeller. This lethal addition, coupled with improved performance characteristics, placed in the hands of French fighter pilots an airplane superior to anything the Imperial German Air Force could put in the air. No more would they be forced to struggle to change Lewis drums in the middle of combat, and no more—they were assured—would they have to watch helplessly as German planes outclimbed them.

The problem of synchronizing the passage of a stream of bullets through the whirling blades of a propeller driven at 1200 r.p.m. had been solved by Tony Fokker in forty-eight hours in April 1915, but the Nieuport 17s were the first operational French single-seaters to carry a synchronized gun.

A French mechanic, Sergeant Alkon, had solved the synchronization problem for his own country. A cam driven by the engine operated a series of push rods and levers which prevented the gun from firing when a propeller blade was in front of the muzzle. Alkon's design called for exacting tolerances in the manufacture of parts and in the installation of the gear, but the French were up to it, and the Alkon gear worked well with the Vickers. With wear, of course, the timing would be thrown off and the pilot risked shooting off his own propeller, but for the next six months the mechanical contrivance, complicated though it was, was counted by French pilots to be the greatest single contribution to the science of aerial combat since the war began. The gun was fed with a linked web belt containing 500 rounds, giving the pilot nearly a full minute of firing time. And since the gun was bolted on top of the fuselage immediately in front of the windscreen, the pilot could reach the breech mechanism to clear simple stoppages.

Back in Paris the pilots asked Thénault when the squadron would receive its complement of these new fighters. Thénault said he didn't know; the combat groups along the Somme were getting priority, the Americans would have to wait their turn. Then he added that the Escadrille was growing larger: new pilots had been promised, and in fact the first one had already been assigned to N.124 and would be going back with them to the Front.

The new man was Robert Lockerbie Rockwell (a distant cousin of Kiffin and Paul Rockwell) from Cincinnati, Ohio. Rockwell, whom everybody soon called Doc, had interned at the Anglo-American Hospital in Paris and was working at an auxiliary hospital in St. Valery-en-Caux when he decided to switch to aviation. Rockwell had deep-set eyes, jet-black hair and wore a brushy moustache. A prewar pilot, he had experienced little difficulty in learning to handle French combat aircraft, but he learned that the capriciousness of rotary engines could betray the mechanically ignorant.

At Pau, Rockwell was aloft in a Caudron, having completed his altitude test. Without warning, his engine began cutting out. Too far from the field to attempt a dead-stick approach, Rockwell let down in a pasture. He examined the power plant, but was unable to locate the difficulty. Anxious to get back to Pau and have his instructor look at the barograph that would prove he had passed the test, Rockwell decided to attempt to restart the engine. He summoned the aid of several farmers who had left their plows to watch the airman tinkering with the strange machine. While the farmers held the wings, Rockwell stepped around to the nose and placed both hands on a propeller blade. Raising one leg in the air, he snapped the blade sharply down, expecting to hear the Le Rhône burst into its song of power. It burst into flames instead.

The farmers scattered, but Rockwell dashed around to try to retrieve the precious barograph. The fuselage was an inferno, and

Rockwell was driven back by the crackling flames. With scorched eyebrows, Rockwell retreated to where the farmers were standing and together they watched while the Caudron collapsed in a smoking heap.

Rockwell, along with the others, assumed that the Escadrille would be moved to the Somme at the expiration of the three-day leave. Haig's futile nonstop offensive was still butting ahead against stubborn German resistance, and the number of fine, sunny days had allowed the war in the air to accelerate to crescendo level. By September, two months after the battle opened, the French and British were employing 780 aircraft of all types against an estimated German strength of 885. The Germans had the cream of their fighter squadrons operating over the Somme battlefields—including Oswald Boelcke's *Jagdstaffel* 2—and many of them were equipped with new-type Albatros D-II and Halberstadt D-II single-seaters, both mounting twin Maxim guns firing through the propeller. The struggle for aerial supremacy had never been so bitter, nor so vital. Sir Douglas Haig, who had come to realize the indispensable role aircraft played in artillery liaison, had likewise been made aware that these valuable, slow-moving planes needed, above all, protection. That month he wrote to London, pleading for more fighters.

Thus it came as a surprise and a disappointment when Thénault broke the news that the Escadrille was ordered back to Luxeuil, where there was little activity in the air and hardly any on the ground. He could not explain this unexpected move.

The Escadrille pilots arrived at the Gare de l'Est at seven the following morning to find the station a bedlam. Everywhere were *poilus* and their families saying tearful farewells; noncoms rushing madly about trying to herd recruits into a semblance of order; sweethearts seeking lovers; wives carrying pathetic bundles of cakes, searching for husbands; harried conductors blowing whistles. The engine stood chuffing under the glass-domed shed, getting up a head of steam, while trainmen scurried through the crowds yelling, so as to be heard above the babel, *En voiture! En voiture!*

Through this surging mass of humanity stepped Bill Thaw

carrying the lion cub under his arm. Thaw and the others got aboard the coach, where Thaw settled down in his seat with Whiskey resting contentedly in his lap. The conductor came along presently demanding tickets. He punched Thaw's ticket, then leaned down for a closer look at the rotund, short-eared furry shape in the pilot's lap. The conductor suspiciously asked Thaw what kind of strange animal he was carrying. "This," replied Thaw with some gravity, "is an African dog."

"*Tiens, tiens!* Quite an interesting dog." Bending even closer, the conductor poked his nose in the cub's muzzle. At this, Whiskey raised his head and muttered an undeveloped roar, at the same time unsheathing his claws from his oversized forepaws. The conductor recoiled. "But it's a lion!" he stammered. "A veritable lion!" Several women who had gathered to coo over the tiny animal shrieked and flew down the aisles. The conductor flew into a rage and ordered Thaw and his "ferocious beast" off the train. During the heated monologue, the other pilots gave silent thanks that it was the even-tempered Thaw and not Lufbery who was taking the abuse from the railwayman. Thaw merely smiled, oblivious to the furor behind him, and got off the train.

He showed up at Luxeuil the next day, with Whiskey safely in a crate. "Imagine," said Thénault, "this high-bred lion, this future lord of the jungle—a fellow used to the finest in Paris—the Savoy, the Ritz, the Chatham—imagine such a one consigned with the luggage. It was a degradation."

Nieuport 17C-1

CHAPTER

7

JEB STUART'S CHARGER

I pay my part for Lafayette and Rochambeau.
—KIFFIN ROCKWELL

The Escadrille pilots standing on the airdrome back at Luxeuil could guess that something big was in the air, for down the field were rows of newly erected hangars and a great number of new bombers of a type none of them had ever seen before. The bombers bore the red-white-blue roundels of the British Royal Naval Air Service, which was now at Luxeuil in force; more than fifty pilots and a thousand enlisted men had come to the Vosges for the mission that lay ahead. The newcomers had energetically encircled the field with sandbagged antiaircraft gun emplacements, thoughtfully adding deep-slit trenches nearby; they had learned of the German hit-and-run raids of the previous spring, and were determined to protect themselves against similar incursions. The well-organized, briskly efficient British force was a heartening addition to Happe's own slender command, whose chief asset was the raw courage of its commander.

Captain Happe only partially cleared up the mystery of the Escadrille's return to the Vosges, the most dormant sector on the Western Front. The bearded commander of *Groupe de Bombardement* 4, his eyes alight with the fire of expectation, told the Americans he knew only that the biggest raid of the 107-week-old war was in the offing. To the questions *Where*? *When*? Happe shrugged; G.Q.G. was maintaining secrecy.

The weather turned cold, and misty rains swept down from the distant mountains. To the Americans, grounded in any case because the coveted Nieuport 17s had not come up from the depot, the disagreeable weather was an added irritation. They stayed cooped up at the Pomme d'Or where they were forced to listen to Captain Thénault's labored efforts at the piano. They drank, wrote letters home and to Paris and read with amusement offerings from the American press. One editorial (from the Chicago *Tribune*), however, aroused the wrath of every man in the squadron. It ran:

> BRING BACK OUR AVIATORS
>
> If active operations are to follow in Mexico, the deficiency of our army in experienced airmen will be felt.
>
> In France, Flanders and perhaps also with the Central Powers, there are American aviators. They ought to return for service under their own flag as soon as possible. If they are not moved to do so in such an emergency, they do not deserve American citizenship.
>
> The War Department should get in touch with these men and facilitate their release from foreign service. They are greatly needed at home.

The ignorance displayed by the *Tribune* was appalling. To begin with, there were more Americans flying for the French than the United States had airplanes. In late 1916 the U. S. Army's Aviation Section, Signal Corps, numbered twenty-three aircraft. Most of these were Curtiss Jennies, utterly worthless for combat, even along the Rio Grande. This force was all that remained of a total of fifty-nine airplanes given to the army by Congress since 1909. If even half the Americans then in France returned home, there wouldn't have been enough airplanes to go around.

And the supposition that Americans were flying for Germany was, in the eyes of the Escadrille pilots, absurd and insulting. "They don't realize," one pilot bitterly exclaimed, "that the French have spent something like $5000 apiece in training Americans—men they have taken out of the ranks for the specific purpose of making pilots of them. America hasn't spent a cent on any of us. To try to take us back now, just when we are beginning to pay dividends, would be a rotten trick. But there isn't the slightest chance any of us will go back."

On the twentieth, five of the new fighting planes arrived from the depot, and the riggers and fitters went to work to get them operational should the weather turn for the better. The pilots, although impressed with the new firing-interrupter gear for the Vickers gun, insisted on mounting the conventional Lewis gun on the top wing as before; the firepower would be doubled, and they liked the added insurance the Lewises would offer should the yet-to-be-proved interrupter gear fail in combat.

The armorers reported that they would have two machines available on the twenty-third, but even if more could have been made ready, there was not enough ammunition for them: through some procurement oversight only a thousand rounds were available for the entire squadron. The night before the planes were to be ready, Thénault allotted the serviceable Nieuports and the ammunition to Rockwell and Lufbery and told them they could go on patrol the following morning if the weather looked promising.

That evening after dinner, Rockwell, Skipper Pavelka and the others were sitting at tables in the bar downstairs at the hotel sipping at cognac and munching from a large box of Swiss chocolates sent to Rockwell the day before. Rockwell, more pensive then usual, looked up suddenly at Pavelka and said, "Paul, if I'm ever shot down make sure I'm buried where I fall." Before Pavelka had time to protest, the tall Southerner drawled out, "And just in case I am killed, I want you all to take whatever money you happen to find on me and drink to the destruction of the damned Boche."

The morning of September 23 broke clear and cool. From the window of his hotel room Rockwell could see only scattered, light clouds in the pinkish sky. A slight breeze ruffled the faded curtains at the window—a breeze that carried with it no smell of rain. It would be a perfect morning for flying. Rockwell hurriedly shaved, put on his flying suit, stuffed his long legs into his fur-lined boots, grabbed up his helmet and goggles and went downstairs to breakfast. He and Lufbery made quick work of the strong black coffee and rolls, paying little attention to the envious remarks made by the others who could not fly that day; to them, Rockwell and Lufbery were "lucky dogs." Lufbery accepted the free cigarette offered from Rockwell's silver case, and the men lighted up as they went out of the door to the waiting staff car for the five-minute drive to the field.

Rockwell began, as he had hundreds of times before, the procedure for getting into the narrow confines of a Nieuport cockpit, running up the engine and taking off. He placed one boot into a step cut into the side of the fuselage, grabbed a cabane strut and hauled himself upward, swinging his right leg inside the cockpit. Then, with both hands placed on the padded rim of the cockpit, he pushed himself slightly upward, weight supported by his arms, then lowered himself deep down inside the cockpit that smelled of gasoline, castor oil and fresh dope. He pulled the wide, webbed belt tight across his lower abdomen and locked it. Placing his boots on the rudder bar, he kicked sharply left-and-right, looking over his shoulder to see the rudder flipping from side to side. Then he pushed the stick all the way forward and hauled it all the way back, checking to see if the elevator was depressing and elevating correctly. He pushed the stick from side to side, watching the ailerons on the top wings describe their narrow, opposed arcs. Each of these motions produced squeaking noises from the friction of the cables working against small metal pulleys, and satisfactory thumps and bangs as the movable panels reached the limits of their intended travel.

With the controls checked out, Rockwell signaled his mechanic, who stepped up to the wooden propeller and placed both hands close together on the thick upper part of the blade. *"Coupe! Plein gaz!"* he barked.

Rockwell checked to see that the ignition switch was turned to *Off* and that the fuel cock was in the full *On* position. *"Coupe! Plein gaz!"* he replied. The mechanic pulled the propeller through once or twice, sucking the fuel through the hollow crankshaft and into the cylinders.

"Contact!" the mechanic bawled.

Rockwell flipped the ignition switch to *On* and yelled *"Contact!"* in return. With one leg raised in the air, the mechanic snapped down hard on the propeller, and the primed Le Rhône exploded into life with a cloud of blue-white smoke belching from the cowling; then the engine settled down to its steady, high-pitched roaring. Satisfied, the mechanic ran around to the side of the vibrating airplane and grabbed at the ends of an oily pair of ropes, jerking the wooden chocks from under the wheels; then the men holding the lower wings ducked away. Freed of all restraint, Rockwell's Nieuport bumped down the grass, headed into the wind. Rockwell's mechanic, and others standing near, turned their backs on the departing airplane, for the prop wash had a way of blowing bits of gravel and dirt into men's faces with stinging force.

Rockwell kept the stick well forward until the tail lifted from the grass; then, as he picked up speed, he eased the control column gently back and watched the horizon drop away underneath his cowling. The plane left the ground, the still-spinning wheels flinging back bits of turf in their wake. With the stick kept back, the Nieuport rose higher and higher, and within a few moments Rockwell's plane, followed closely by Lufbery's, was only a distant speck droning in the vastness of the sky.

Lufbery took up a position slightly above and behind Rockwell, who led the way northeast from Luxeuil toward the rising bulk of the Vosges. They flew on, climbing steadily, until they reached the steeply rising *Hartsmanwillerkopf* mountain, the last important prominence before the terrain sloped gently down toward the valley of the Rhine. Although the *Hartsmanwillerkopf* was inside enemy lines, no bursting shrapnel rose to greet them; looking over their windswept cockpit rims, the Americans saw why: far below were several Fokkers headed west. In unison the American pilots reached forward over the tiny windscreens and pulled back the charging handles of the Vickers guns; as the handles snapped shut sharply forward, a round of ammunition was injected into the breeches. Rockwell pushed the nose of his airplane steeply down and the little fighter hurtled toward the enemy formation.

Rockwell and Lufbery reached the Fokkers at almost the same instant. Lufbery opened the fire first, only to have his Vickers gun jam at the first burst. He grappled with the charging handle, but could not clear the stoppage. He pulled up and away from the Germans, followed by Rockwell who, fortunately, had not gotten himself inextricably involved with the milling Fokkers. Both Americans returned across the lines, where Lufbery set down at Fontaine, home of *escadrille* N.49. Rockwell circled the field and watched Lufbery climb from the cockpit and wave; then he nosed up again and started back to the lines alone.

Rockwell climbed to 10,000 feet in a clear blue sky. By himself, and only twenty minutes from Colmar where so many enemy fighters were based, he nevertheless sought to return to the *Hartsmanwillerkopf* to reflush the game they had been forced to abandon. But before he reached the mountain he found instead a far more tempting target—a solitary German airplane inside French lines. The intended victim was a two-seater Aviatik, the same type that he had vanquished once before—and the same type that had brought so much woe to Escadrille pilots before: Rockwell's first wound over Verdun, Chapman's grazed arm, Thaw's bloody elbow wound the previous May—all caused by diving at the rear of German two-seater observation craft. There had been a repeated lesson in this for all of them, but the attack-minded Rockwell disregarded the manifest danger signals, and in this error lay the seed of his own destruction. He pushed the nose over and dived straight for the rear of the Aviatik.

What happened next was described by a French artillery captain who witnessed Rockwell's attack through a pair of field glasses.

When Rockwell began his precipitous attack the German rear-gunner immediately swung his gun up and opened a withering blast of fire; the artillery captain could see the tracers streaking past the plummeting Nieuport and could hear distinctly the distant popping sound. Only when the captain thought the two airplanes were about to collide did he observe that the machine gun on the French plane was in action. For a mistaken instant the captain caught his breath, for it seemed to him that the Aviatik had lurched in the sky and was heading down. But he was witnessing the German pilot's frantic maneuvering to slip his plane out of the path of the onrushing Nieuport. The fighter nosed steeply down and plunged vertically for the earth. In morbid fascination the artillery captain kept his glasses trained on the streaking plane; he watched horrified as the wings on one side ripped loose and fluttered away in the wake of the fuselage. He kept his glasses on the now madly spinning airplane until it smashed to earth after a two-mile fall. The Nieuport tore into a field of flowers a few hundred yards inside the French lines near the village of Rodern—not two and a half miles from the spot where Rockwell's first kill crashed four months before.

German field guns opened up on the wreckage, and members of a French 75 battery risked their lives to dash through the shelling to drag Rockwell's body from the twisted remains of his airplane. They carried Rockwell to a communication trench and laid him down on the duckboards. While the shelling was still going on, a medical officer hunched over Rockwell's body and opened up the bloody flying suit. A hideous wound gaped in the chest, and the officer knew that Rockwell had been killed instantly. A blanket was drawn over the dead pilot's face, and somebody went down to a dugout to telephone the news to the escadrilles in the area.

At Fontaine, Lufbery's Nieuport had just been refueled and the stoppage cleared in his new Vickers gun when word came through about Rockwell. Lufbery's eyes turned cold. He got in the cockpit and took off in a dangerously steep climbing turn, headed for Rodern. He ranged over the area like an avenging angel, seeking the Aviatik that had claimed the life of his friend, but the skies over the Vosges were empty. Then he banked savagely around and flew east, far inside German lines. He swooped low over the enemy fields at Colmar and at Habsheim, but he could find no Germans. Low on fuel, he was forced to give up the idea of immediate revenge and flew back to Luxeuil. He found the other pilots convened at the Pomme d'Or. Earlier Thénault and de

Laage had driven to Rodern to talk to the witnesses of the fight, and on the way back home de Laage sat in the rear of the squadron car, tears streaming down his face.

In the stilled atmosphere of the Pomme d'Or, Captain Thénault could only say to the wondering pilots: "The best and bravest of us is no more." Stunned, the pilots stood awkwardly in the dining room, then drifted away one by one.

Kiffin Rockwell was buried two days later in the little cemetery two blocks away from Luxeuil's main street. The town's gardens had been stripped of flowers to place on the casket containing the body of the fallen American aviator. The wooden casket was placed aboard a farm wagon that creaked its way through Luxeuil, drawn by a horse ridden by a steel-helmeted *poilu*. Behind the wagon marched in funereal step the pilots of the Escadrille, followed by the British pilots and five hundred of their ground crewmen. Bringing up the rear of the lengthy column slow-marched a full battalion of French infantry. As the procession made its way through the narrow streets, Nieuports from half a dozen French escadrilles flew low overhead, scattering flowers in their wake.

At the graveside, Captain Thénault stood bareheaded to deliver the benediction. The great crowd stood silent in the sunshine as Thénault raised his head and began to speak.

"Here by this tomb so recently closed, we meet to pay our final duty to our comrade . . . He was happy in the midst of danger; the greater the strength of the enemy, the more anxious he was to attack. Never did Rockwell consider that he had done enough. His courage was sublime . . . where Rockwell was, the German could not pass. . . . He was a great soldier with a high sense of duty. He gave himself to France, and for France he sacrificed himself."

Thénault concluded, "To you, our best friend, in the name of France I bid you a last farewell. In the name of your comrades, who have so often proved they know how to keep promises . . . we swear faithfully to guard your memory and to avenge it."

Bert Hall, who often boasted of the close friendship he shared with Rockwell, was not on hand to listen to Thénault's high praise and promises of revenge. Even as Thénault's mellifluous French phrases were rolling over Rockwell's freshly-dug grave, Hall was in Paris trying to peddle the story of Rockwell's last fight to the daily papers.

Rockwell's death drew unprecedented reaction from the press on a worldwide level. Never before had the death of a combat aviator attracted as much attention as did Rockwell's. Thousands of men were dying each day along the tortured length of the Western Front—but Rockwell represented more than an individual who fell in battle; he represented an idea.

Eulogized—and speculated—the Charleston, South Carolina, *News and Courier:* "Kiffin Rockwell had in his veins the blood of some knight-errant of the age of chivalry. Why should this young Southerner have given his gallant life for France? Perhaps because this splendid France of today stirred his imagination so powerfully that he could do nothing less than offer his sword as Lafayette offered us his in our fight for liberty. Perhaps because he was one of those restless spirits to which life without adventure is but a sad and monotonous pilgrimage. He has just ridden to a soldier's death on a steed swifter than the finest charger that ever bore Jeb Stuart to battle."

In Paris, *L'Illustration* commented, "Kiffin ignored danger and fear. He went into combat as to a ball. The name of this young hero (he was only 24) will live always in the memory of France."

And in Berlin, the *Deutsche Tageszeitung* saw in the demise of the American a portent, and threatened editorially: "The news of the death of the famous American aviator, Rockwell, merits the greatest attention. It is not an isolated case. There is an entire squadron of American aviators who have given their service to our enemies. America is not content with fighting us in stealth on the question of submarines, she participates actively in the struggle against us. The United States favors our enemy in a manner contrary to neutrality. America must be made aware of our profound indignation; she must also be aware that we consider this participation by her citizens in a war against us a direct provocation."

Rockwell's death had focused the attention of millions—neutrals and combatants alike—on the handful of American volunteer airmen who were, as Rockwell once stated, "fighting for the cause of humanity, the most noble of all causes."

The most telling, and least high-flown, statements came from the men who had known Rockwell best—those who had fought alongside him. Pavelka wrote the details of Rockwell's last fight with "that Boche bastard" to Jim McConnell, who was still in the hospital. "Everything went fine in the fight, and it was a case of one or the other. The Boche *mitrailleur* hit poor Kiffin in the breast, but the dirty son-of-a-bitch used an explosive bullet, for the poor boy had a hole as big as your fist in him. God almighty, Jim, I feel terribly broken up about Kiffin's death. I am all the wilder because we have no machines, nor no cartridges. Lufbery is the only one who has cartridges, and he has only about 100 for his Vickers. How in hell can we avenge Kiffin under such circumstances? Five machines for twelve pilots, and only a few cartridges. I remain ill at heart . . ."

Alice Weeks's house in Paris was flooded with callers and letters alike offering condolences. From William Thorin, of Canton, South Dakota, came a scrawl written from a hospital behind the lines. "I can't write much," apologized Thorin, "because the news about Kiffin gives me a fever. Even a fellow like me who has seen all kinds of sights and lost plenty of comrades both on land and sea, cannot help feeling sorry, because it ain't every day you meet fellows like Kiffin. At the same time we must remember it is war. Kiffin knew very well what he was doing when he joined this outfit, but like a man he done his duty. Yes, even more than his duty, as he wasn't obliged to serve this country, but being a man and knowing right from wrong, he couldn't stand out of it, so I think you would rather sooner like to see any of us die like men than be cowards and hide behind neutrality."

Paul Rockwell stayed on at Luxeuil for a few days afterward, seeming dazed and somehow expecting that his older brother might return. Didier Masson, sensing that Rockwell's inner grief might be more than he could bear, borrowed a two-seater Nieuport 12 from Captain Happe and took Rockwell aloft for his first airplane ride, hoping perhaps that the initial experience of seeing the earth in perspective from a roaring, vibrating combat airplane might divert the sorrow of the dead man's brother. But the intended therapy was not to be: the oil reservoir sprang a leak, spraying them both with hot castor oil. Masson made a hurried forced landing, and the two men climbed from the cockpit, not exhilarated, but shaken and nauseated.

Then Pavelka borrowed the squadron car and drove Rockwell to the spot where Kiffin's plane had gone in. There wasn't much to see; the bulk of the wreckage had already been removed, leaving only a deep hole in the earth gouged out by the engine, a few fragments of the propeller and pieces of fabric stained with oil and dried blood. Rockwell marked the spot with a white wooden cross and the two men went back to Luxeuil. When Paul Rockwell boarded the train for Paris that afternoon, he clutched a box under his arm that contained everything his brother had carried aloft with him on his final flight: a *Médaille Militaire,* a *Croix de Guerre,* some personal letters, a fountain pen, a wristwatch with the hands stopped at nine-fifty and the silver cigarette case, "crushed and bent fantastically."

To the depressing aftermath of the funeral was added an intriguing mystery. The day following the burial, Pavelka and Dud Hill returned to the cemetery and carefully measured the plot, intending to decorate the grave with ornamental woodwork. Two days later, having gathered the necessary lumber, tools and carpenters, Pavelka returned with Lufbery to oversee the job. They were astonished to discover Rockwell's final resting place already fenced in by a neat wooden enclosure, the mound of earth carefully trimmed and covered with flowers. The two pilots sought out the caretaker who told them the local florist had been out earlier that morning, attended to the work and departed. In town, Pavelka and Lufbery questioned the florist, who would tell them only that the arrangements had been made "by a lady from Paris, a cousin of the brave American aviator." He added that she had paid him well to place fresh cut flowers on the grave once each week, but neither bribes nor threats could induce the Frenchman to say more.

"To us," Pavelka wrote Paul Rockwell, "it is all a mystery." And so it has remained to this day.

Sopwith 1½ Strutter

CHAPTER 8

BOMBS ACROSS THE RHINE

The complete disarming or destruction of the enemy must always be the aim in warfare.

—KARL VON CLAUSEWITZ

For lack of ammunition—then being expended so prodigiously over the Somme—the Escadrille stayed grounded day after day; the disgruntled pilots, with time to kill, turned to the countryside. Bill Thaw went out one morning carrying the expensive tackle purchased months before, and returned beaming with a monster trout at the end of his line. Placed on the scales in the hotel kitchen, the gleaming fish swung the pointer to the 6¾-pound mark. Lufbery and Pavelka spent long hours tramping through the verdant hills, once returning with dew-wet baskets filled with more than ten pounds of succulent mushrooms. When these distractions palled, the Americans visited the airdrome to further friendships with the newcomers. "We get along O.K. with the 'Limeys,' " Pavelka reported. "They are mostly Canadians and are just like Americans."

The Canadians belonged to No. 3 Wing, R.N.A.S., a unit which had been disbanded following the unsuccessful 1915 Dardanelles campaign, and which owed its rebirth to a farsighted concept on the part of Winston Churchill, First Lord of the Admiralty. German Zeppelin raids on the east coast of England and upon London proper had by late 1915 reached such heights that the public outcry for retaliation forced the British Government to act. Churchill was directed to organize a bombing force from R.N.A.S. resources in order to strike at the German homeland. Churchill realized that while retaliation raids might lower the morale of German civilians living in target cities, they could not appreciably affect the outcome of the war. He ordered that when the striking force became operational it was to concentrate its bombs on industrial targets. Thus was born the earliest concept of strategic bombing by an independent air command.

But things went wrong from the start.

Owing in part to failure of the French to fulfill hopelessly large engine contracts for the British, and partly due to problems imposed by the rapid expansion of the Royal Flying Corps at home, the R.F.C. was plagued by a shortage of aircraft with which to aid Haig's offensive on the Somme. This materiel shortage was met by repeated requests to the R.N.A.S. for transfer of their latest one- and two-seater bombers, the Sopwith "1½ Strutter," to R.F.C. squadrons already in the field. Since the need for any and all kinds of aircraft was acute along the Somme, it was decided that strategic bombing would have to wait; accordingly sixty-two Sopwith 1½ Strutters were turned over to the R.F.C., which had the crews to man them.

Woefully short on equipment, the best that No. 3 Wing could manage during the summer of 1916 was to send three 1½ Strutters to accompany six French bombers to raid the German benzine stores at Mulheim in the Ruhr. The raid was carried out without loss on July 30. It wasn't until September that No. 3 Wing was up to strength and ready for full-scale operations. As constituted at Luxeuil, the wing was composed of seven flights of seven

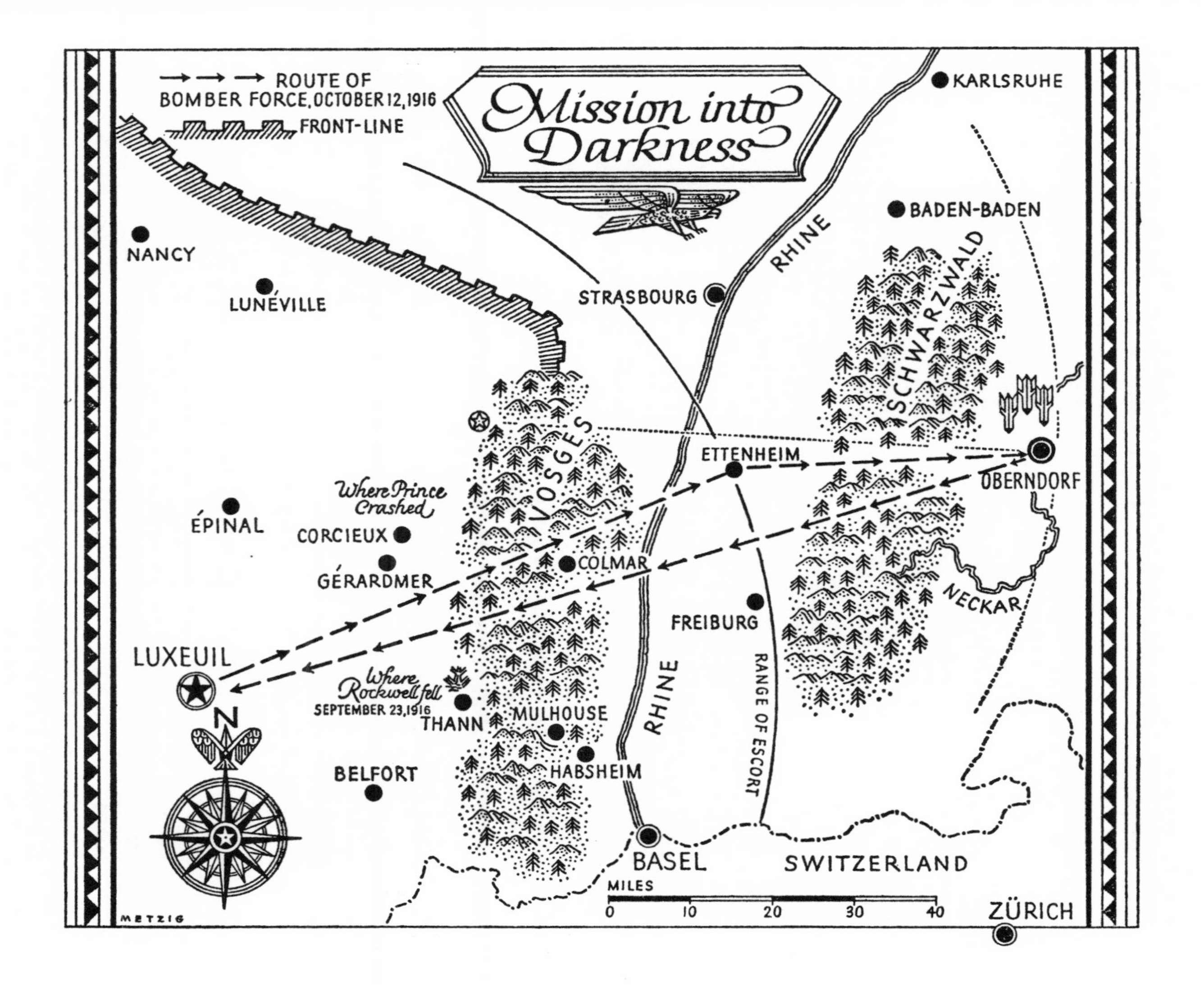
Mission into Darkness
ROUTE OF BOMBER FORCE, OCTOBER 12, 1916
FRONT-LINE
KARLSRUHE
BADEN-BADEN
RHINE
SCHWARZWALD
NANCY
LUNÉVILLE
STRASBOURG
VOSGES
ETTENHEIM
OBERNDORF
Where Prince Crashed
ÉPINAL
CORCIEUX
GÉRARDMER
COLMAR
FREIBURG
NECKAR
LUXEUIL
Where Rockwell fell
SEPTEMBER 23, 1916
THANN
MULHOUSE
RHINE
RANGE OF ESCORT
N
HABSHEIM
BELFORT
BASEL
SWITZERLAND
MILES
0
10
20
30
40
ZÜRICH
METZIG

aircraft each—five single-seater Strutters and two two-seater Strutters—forty-nine aircraft in all.

The 1½ Strutter owed its name to the unusual center-section struts which were splayed outward in a W shape; the inner strut was noticeably shorter that the outer, which gave the illusion of 1½ struts. The Strutter resembled many of the Sopwith designs —broad wings with slight dihedral, a short tail—but was unique in several respects.

This airplane was the first British machine to arrive at the Front in any numbers armed with a Vickers machine gun firing through the propeller. The Vickers' fire was interrupted when a blade was in front of the muzzle by the newly developed Scarff-Dibovsky gear, a mechanical device similar to the one in use by the French. On the two-seaters, the rear compartment was occupied by the observer who was armed with a Lewis gun mounted on a Scarff ring, a new mounting that allowed the gunner to traverse his fire smoothly and quickly to cover attacks from the side, rear and—by guess-aiming—from nearly directly overhead. Thus armed, and powered by a 130 h.p. Clerget rotary engine that pushed it to speeds exceeding 100 m.p.h., the Strutter was, in the words of one of the pilots, "a difficult hornet to contend with."

Additional airspeed and flight-attitude controls were provided the pilot in the form of air brakes—square panels set in the trailing edges of the lower wings that flipped upward at a 90-degree angle—and an adjustable tailplane, which the pilot could shift in inclination by turning a small wheel located on the right side of the cockpit interior. The Strutter's inherent stability, plus the adjustable horizontal stabilizer, allowed it to be flown hands off. The pilot could execute a well-mannered turn by applying pressure on the rudder bar, whereupon the plane would put on its own bank. Landing, the pilot could turn the stabilizing wheel all the way back, shut off the engine, and the plane would pick up its own gliding angle. The Strutter was so stable pilots had to use main force to get the nose down in a dive. "Some of the days," fondly recalled one Strutter pilot, "were very cold and it was rather jolly to be able to fly about with hands in pocket."

A bizarre incident in 1916 graphically illustrated the stability characteristics of T.O.M. Sopwith's latest creation. A British officer was loading his men into a truck in an open field some seventy-five miles behind the lines. Overhead, he heard the sound of an approaching airplane and watched as a Strutter banked gently into the wind and glided slowly down to a near-perfect landing. The crew failed to emerge from the motionless aircraft, so the officer walked over to see if he could render assistance. He climbed up on the wing to greet the crew, only to step back to the ground a moment later, his face registering shock. Both pilot and observer were dead, killed in some aerial battle over the lines an hour or so before. Riddled with bullets, the faithful Strutter had returned home, carrying with it its two lifeless crewmen.

Watching the skilled R.N.A.S. pilots put the Strutters through their paces, the Americans were hopeful as to the outcome of the mission that lay ahead. Day after day, when the weather permitted, the Canadians were aloft practicing tight formation flying—vital to an effective defense against fighter attacks. From twenty to thirty Strutters took part in these exercises, filling the air with the synchronized snarl of rotary engines. One morning the entire field snapped alert at the accelerating whine of an airplane streaking earthward in a power dive.

One of the Strutters from the formation thundering overhead was falling earthward, the engine howling as if to tear itself from the mounts. Horrified watchers on the ground could see the pilot struggling with what were probably hopelessly jammed controls. The airplane smashed into the earth at the far end of the field and disintegrated.

A few days later a French pilot, up for a joyride with a passenger in the *Groupe*'s Nieuport 12, brushed wings with a lone Strutter. The two planes separated and almost immediately the wings of the Nieuport collapsed and folded alongside the fuselage, which dropped like a stone and crashed at the edge of the field in a mushrooming ball of smoke and flame. Then the wings of the Strutter buckled and it plunged to the ground. Four men had been killed within the space of minutes. Luxeuil turned out for another multiple funeral.

Relations between the Americans and the Canadians were warm, especially after hours when in the barracks and on blankets on hangar floors the Escadrille pilots matched skill with the British at gambling.

One Canadian pilot recalled: "We hit it off well, particularly at poker. There were three so-called leagues: the small-fry, with a 5-franc ($1) limit; the small-timers, with a 20-franc limit, and the big-timers with no-limit betting. The Americans, being better heeled, were normally able to sustain the no-limit game. We Canadians seemed to spend our time moving up and down from the knockout blows in the big league, then advancing from the small-fry to try again later at the top.

"In the big league, each man had by his side a roll of toilet paper, and when he made his bets he tore off a sheet upon which he wrote his I.O.U.s—sometimes they ran as high as 5000 francs, worth then at least $1000. Several players were loaded with these paper I.O.U.s, and the heavy losers used to pray that the Lord would bring the wealthy down safely—*on the wrong side of the lines.*"

However well they mixed socially, the men of No. 3 Wing were far from impressed with the command setup that prevailed at N.124. Commented one Canadian pilot: "From the point of view of discipline, the situation was practically impossible for the French. Imagine a body of financially well-off Americans—basking in the knowledge they were volunteers from a neutral country—who habitually played no-limit poker, who imported unlimited booze and food and who comprised a body of men far superior educationally and possessing a far greater experience of the world than their French companions in arms—a French commander would have experienced great difficulty controlling such a body of men if they had been French citizens and fully subject to French army regulations.

"The pilots gave the impression of being very war-like, even amongst themselves . . . there was a tendency to resolve themselves into cliques, wherein individuals of similar tendencies grouped and lambasted the others. Consequently, teamwork suffered. Although the early members of the Escadrille comprised pilots of high potential in every way . . . their French commander seemed helpless to cope with such independent, high-spirited men. Moreover, the French Army Administration, not unnaturally, were very anxious to sustain sympathetic responses in the United States. The general result was that the American pilots enjoyed a wide measure of freedom of action."

The day of the duelist was rapidly drawing to a close, and the Canadians prophesied that anyone who failed to believe that it was concentrated teamwork—not individual heroism—that would win the war in the air, would pay the price.

Days grew into weeks, and still the Escadrille remained idle; to Thénault's repeated telegrams demanding ammunition came only vague promises. And as for more news about the coming raid, only silence. Thénault, due for leave, called on Happe at Group Headquarters to see if he knew anything, but the Red Corsair said there had been no word whatsoever. That afternoon Thénault placed de Laage in command, packed his valise, slipped a lead on his dog and boarded the train for Biarritz.

A few days later, a carload of Vickers ammunition arrived at Luxeuil. Lufbery and Prince were in the air and across the lines a few hours afterward, still burning, they said, to avenge the death of Rockwell. As it turned out, they almost joined him.

They set off for Mulhouse, but got separated in heavy cloud, and Lufbery went on alone. He broke through the overcast directly over the German field near the town and proceeded to circle the field, daring the Fokkers to come up and fight. Finally Lufbery made out the shapes of several E-IIIs being rolled out into takeoff position. He shot a glance at his watch and realized he had barely enough fuel to fly the fifty miles back to Luxeuil. Reluctantly he turned for home.

In the meantime Prince was still dodging in and out of the clouds, seeking Lufbery's Nieuport. Then he, too, broke into the clear over Mulhouse and immediately ran afoul of the Fokkers stirred up by Lufbery's insolence. The Germans boxed him in, and the man on his tail proved to be a crack marksman. One bullet, probably explosive, slammed into the leading edge of the lower right wing and Prince felt the wood split the length of the panel. Another slug, missing his head by inches, carried away the steel cabane strut in front of his face. He felt the shocks as his plane was hit again and again, then he did the only thing possible: he put the nose down and dived, praying the riddled plane would hold together. The extra 30 h.p. counted for a great deal just then, and the Nieuport streaked away from the Fokkers' murderous fire.

While Prince was struggling for his life, Lufbery landed back at Luxeuil with his tank nearly dry. When he asked if the New Englander had returned and learned that he had not, Lufbery quickly refueled and took off again to seek his partner.

Not ten minutes later, watchers on the field saw Prince's Nieuport limping in to land. Prince emerged from the cockpit looking white and drawn, and Pavelka remarked, "Nimmie was greatly shaken up, and stuttered a great deal when explaining things."

Half an hour later Lufbery was once again across the lines, futilely searching for Prince. He found instead a solitary Fokker which, from the markings, he recognized as one he had tangled with once before. Lufbery got on its tail, but before he could open fire the German flashed away. Seconds later came the *tac-tac-tac* from the rear—the German had somehow gotten behind him. A quick climbing turn, a slip to the left and Lufbery brought the Fokker once more in front of his gun; he had time for only a brief rattle of fire before the slippery enemy plane again dropped away and out of the line of fire. Around and around they went, chasing each other across the sky, drifting nearer to the German base at Habsheim.

In the middle of the duel Lufbery caught sight of a flash of white from across the French lines. He recognized the smoke puff as a signal from a forward antiaircraft battery telling him that a German aircraft was penetrating French territory. Lufbery's first duty as a fighter pilot was to halt such violations of French airspace; he broke off the fight with the Fokker, waving at the pilot as he streaked westward. The German returned the salute and, probably low on fuel, headed down for Habsheim.

When Lufbery neared the raveling white smoke of the aerial shell burst he found directly below him a two-seater German reconnaissance plane and—without pausing to clear the sky above him—dived headlong, in Rockwell fashion, at the waiting quarry. Above the roar of his own engine, above the shrieking of the interplane wires singing shrilly in the wind, Lufbery caught the warning sound of the crackle of machine gun fire to his rear. A Fokker, dropping from the sun, was glued to his tail, both Maxim guns working furiously. *Thud, thud, thud* as slugs slammed into the engine; the smell of singed fur as bullets zipped through his lined flying suit; a tug as a solitary missile sliced through his boot—then a drumfire of bullets tattooed his wings and rained on his elevator. Lufbery slipped and skidded, diving frantically away from the hail of fire. Only his exceptional skill as a pilot and an inordinate amount of luck enabled him to escape the bullet stream. He flew home with fabric from the riddled wings flapping in the wind, nursing altitude and praying the damaged craft would stay in the air long enough to get him down on the ground. The engine spluttered and jerked spasmodically, but it ran, and Lufbery managed to ease the plane down at Luxeuil. For the second time that morning, pilots and ground crew ran out to find an ashen-faced pilot sitting in a shredded airplane. Lufbery's Nieuport never flew again; the guns and instruments were stripped from their mountings and the plane hauled to the "boneyard" behind a hangar.

Three days later Prince climbed into his patched Nieuport and set off alone to square accounts with the enemy. He jumped a Fokker returning to base at Habsheim, and after a brief combat shot it down. He came back to Luxeuil jubilant, but the consensus was they would have a hard time in the days ahead if the German pilots were all of the same quality encountered earlier.

Secrecy was not one of the great French military virtues. All too often, ground offensives were marked by a disheartening knowledge on the part of the enemy as to the place and, at times, the exact hour when an assault was due to go in. *Poilus,* having been told surprise would be on their side, left their trenches to charge confidently across broken fields only to find the Germans alert and waiting, safely dug in behind endless thickets of machine guns.

Determined that security would not be breached regarding the mission that G.Q.G. had planned for the waiting airmen at Luxeuil, the planners kept Captain Happe and his R.N.A.S. counterpart, Wing Commander R. Bell Davies, in the dark until the day before the strike was scheduled. On the afternoon of October 11, 1916, Happe received orders to get the force under way on the following day. At last the target was known: Oberndorf-am-Neckar.

The town itself, built on the sides of hills leading directly down to the valley formed by the Neckar River, was of little importance. But located on the western edge of the neat little community was a loose cluster of buildings housing the famous Mauser *Waffenfabrik.* The oldest structure, known as the Lower Works, dated from the eighteenth century and had been converted to arms-making after serving as an Augustinian cloister. Standing four stories high and solidly constructed of brick, stone and masonry, the cloister had been meant to endure for centuries. A few hundred yards to the rear of the cloister building—and separated from it by a narrow-gauge railroad track—sprawled a huge assembly building known as the Outside Works. The third main building, a four-story brick structure known as the Upper Works, was located a half mile from the Outside Works. The space between the plant buildings was filled in tightly with steeply gabled houses, storage buildings and stores of every description. The plant complex was so wedded physically to the town of Oberndorf itself it was difficult to tell where, exactly, the factory area began and the town left off. The target occupied an area roughly the shape of an elongated triangle, 1600 yards long and 500 yards wide.

It was here that the bulk of the standard German infantry arm, the Model 98/K, 7.92mm rifle, was made. These rifles rolled from the Mauser works on an average of four thousand a day, helping to overcome the wastage on the battlefields and filling the hands of replacements being fed into the furnace before Verdun and on the Somme. To the few strategic-minded planners at G.Q.G., Oberndorf was a prime target area, and one of the few of such importance within striking radius of the obsolescent bombers then at their disposal.

Heretofore, much of the French bombing force had been employed chiefly against targets of tactical significance only, and those usually not far behind the German lines. The results of these raids on ammunition dumps, supply depots, rail junctions and the like were immediate but only temporary. Moreover, the use of hard-to-replace planes and crews on targets better dealt with by long-range artillery, was as inefficient as it was costly. But to strike at the vitals of the German rifle production center would be to deal a blow, the effects of which would be long-lasting, and perhaps crippling, when the pinch of a small-arms shortage eventually made itself felt on the battlefield. Moreover, calculated the planners, the news of a successful penetration of the German homeland by a large Anglo-French force working in concert would raise the morale of the English and French populations, still suffering from sporadic German night raids.

But no one was under the illusion that Oberndorf would be an easy target to bomb. It was almost a 450-mile round trip from Luxeuil to Oberndorf; two-thirds of this distance would be flown over hotly defended enemy territory. The route would take the bombers over the nest of Fokkers based at Colmar and less than twenty minutes from the enemy fighter base at Habsheim. The raiding force would have to cross the natural barrier of the Vosges Mountains, and the even more imposing chain of the Black Forest, both areas thickly planted with antiaircraft batteries and laced with machine guns. Added to the problem was the fact that fighter escort would be able to provide cover only part of the way. The 1½ Strutters of No. 3 Wing, armed as they were, stood an even chance of protecting themselves; the planes of *Groupe de Bombardement* 4 were another matter.

Happe's contribution to the raiding force would number sixteen bombers, both the familiar Farmans and the somewhat newer Bréguet-Michelin IV; neither type could cover itself from attack from the rear, both were pitifully slow. The Bréguet-Michelin, powered with a 220 h.p. Canton-Unné engine, had a service ceiling of 12,000 feet but its top speed when fully loaded never exceeded 66 m.p.h. Handicapped by extremely poor visibility forward and upward, the pilot often was forced to depend upon the observer in the front of the crew nacelle for flight directions, especially when seeking landmarks. Cursed with an unusually long takeoff roll, the Bréguet-Michelins could not operate from many French fields, which greatly restricted their usefulness. The plane was notoriously unstable, and tended to spiral quickly if the pilot took his hands from the wheel to make some adjustment in the cockpit. Forty small bombs could be slung under the wings, but these were aimed by an optical sight "so difficult to manipulate that even the most dedicated lost heart altogether." The only modern convenience aboard the Bréguet-Michelin was the bomb-releasing mechanism, designed and manufactured by the Michelin factory in Paris. The release enabled the bombs to be dropped automatically, at precise and predetermined intervals. The timing mechanism was set on the ground before takeoff; once over the target, all the bomb-aimer had to do was trip the cockpit release and look over the side as the bombs fell away one by one to walk across the target area. Although the Michelin release usually functioned as it was intended, the bombs themselves often did not.

The first explosives dropped by French aircraft were not bombs at all, but artillery shells to which fins were attached to keep the shells from tumbling erratically as they fell earthward. When the war began there was a large supply of 90mm shells on hand, but this reserve was quickly used up, primarily against troop concentrations because of the shell's excellent fragmentation qualities. The switch was then made to 155mm shells whose 6-inch diameter admitted a far larger explosive charge—but not large enough, as it developed, in relation to the inert mass of the heavy metal shell casing. The fins on these bombs were made of lightweight metal and were easily bent out of shape, thus ruining their aerodynamic qualities and causing many of them to impact on the earth sideways, in which cases they failed to explode. The 155s were often more dangerous to the French than they were to the Germans. When Captain Happe was commanding MF.29, stationed in late 1915 at Belfort, he witnessed one of the worst ground accidents in the history of the *Service Aéronautique* up to that time. Ground crews were loading up the Farmans for one of Happe's missions when one of them dropped a live 155 shell nose-down on the ground. An explosion ripped across the field, and half a dozen men disappeared in a fine red mist. There were cases of Farmans and Voisins simply vanishing in the sky when a 155 was detonated by the strike of a machine gun bullet or bursting shrapnel from antiaircraft shells. And no pilot returning home with a shell still hung in the racks dared risk landing on any but the smoothest of fields, for fear a rough touchdown would jar loose the dangling projectile and blow the plane to eternity.

The solution to these vexing problems was found in the creation of a bomb designed solely for aerial use, the *Gros-Andreau* bomb. Unique among bombs used by either side during the war, the *Gros-Andreau* depended upon a liquid mixture for explosive effect. The mixture, an aniline, was composed of 80 percent nitrogen peroxide and 20 percent gasoline. These liquids were kept separated by storage in thin metal envelopes so there was no chance of their becoming mixed before putting them into the empty bomb casing. The casing, an elongated shape made of lightweight metal, was divided in two sections, separated by a metal partition called the *opercule*. Just prior to the mission, the forward segment of the casing was filled with gasoline and sealed. Then the nitrogen peroxide was pumped into the rear half of the bomb under pressure and sealed. At the rear of the bomb projected a small metal propeller that whirled around as the bomb fell through the air, screwing down the firing pin, thus making the bomb live. When the bomb was released from the racks, a special key inside the casing revolved, operating a plunger that pierced the *opercule,* allowing the two liquids to merge while the bomb was in free fall. If the missiles were released from low altitude and struck the ground before the liquids had time to fully combine, they exploded with incendiary effect; if they were dropped *too* near the earth by mistake, they would not explode at all. Unfortunately the thin metal of the forward part of the casing gave the *Gros-Andreau* bombs little penetrating power. They were made in three sizes: 22 pounds, 55 pounds and 110 pounds; approximately 50 percent of the weight comprised the explosive charge.

French crews at first regarded these novel missiles with distrust; a bomb that gurgled was alien to anything previously heard of in the war. This distrust quickly turned to fear and hatred when the liquid bomb's fatal flaw was discovered: the rear casing frequently leaked noxious fumes that permeated the interior of the crew nacelle, causing giddiness and nausea. If breathed long enough, these azote fumes sometimes put airmen out of the war with acute intestinal and stomach disorders. Shortly after these bombs came into general use, the crew of a Voisin from VB.101 was subjected to the capricious behavior of the liquid missile during a night mission to Germany.

Shortly after takeoff, the bomb-aimer noticed "a truly atrocious odor" seeping up from underneath the nacelle where four of the small *Gros-Andreau* bombs were slung. The pungent smell worsened, and by the time the Voisin was over the target the bombardier was clutching at his abdomen and coughing violently.

He reached for the release handle, only to discover that the bombs were hopelessly stuck in the racks. Half-blinded and nearly unconscious, the bombardier cut through the bottom of the nacelle and began hauling the bombs inside. By the time the last missile was aboard, unconsciousness overtook both crewmen and the Voisin began a slow spiral earthward. The pilot recovered after the plane had lost 2000 feet of altitude and managed to turn for home. The bombardier roused himself long enough to heave the bombs over the side so they would clear the whirling propeller blades in the rear, then fell in a stupor against the coaming. The Voisin made it back to the lines, and the crew survived, but the story was soon being told at bases all along the Western Front and crews regarded the new missiles with horror. These were the bombs the men of Happe's group would be taking to Oberndorf.

When the Escadrille had been attached to Happe specifically to escort his bombers into Germany, it was assumed that the squadron would be up to strength in both pilots and planes. But the evening before the mission was scheduled Happe discovered that the American squadron had only five Nieuports for the eleven pilots available on the active duty roster. Bert Hall had flown one of the planes to a field near Nancy, from where a diversionary force would be sent across the lines in an attempt to draw German fighter opposition away from the Oberndorf raiders; this left N.124 with planes available for de Laage, Lufbery, Prince and Masson. Thaw had taken the other pilots to the aircraft depot at Bar-le-Duc in a last-minute effort to secure more planes, but they were still waiting there when the mission became airborne. Thus Happe had four Nieuports to escort the mixed force of forty bombers, and the fuel capacity of the little fighters could carry them only as far as Ettenheim, just across the Rhine. The final forty miles to the target would see the bombers on their own across the mountains of the Black Forest, where German fighter reaction was expected to be the heaviest.

At fifteen minutes before 1 P.M., Thursday, October 12, the pilots and gunners of the Oberndorf force began shuffling from their huts to the ranks of airplanes waiting for them on the field at Luxeuil. Seen from a distance, the men resembled bears lumbering across a pasture. They moved with a slow, stiff-legged gait, encumbered by layers of heavy clothing topped with sheepskin-lined coveralls reaching from ankles to throats. Their feet were encased in shaggy, knee-length fur boots; their hands were covered with heavy leather mittens drawn over pairs of white silk gloves.

The Farman crews climbed awkwardly through the maze of wires and struts and heaved themselves into the cockpits in the jutting nacelles riding high off the ground. Mechanics hastened to the rear of the planes to pull the propellers through to start the engines. Then they scurried underneath the wings to pull the chocks away from the wheels.

At exactly 1 P.M. the first Farman began rolling down the field, kicking up clouds of dust. The entire contraption creaked and groaned with the effort to become airborne. The engine strained, working with the flat, 53-foot wings to help lift a ton of airplane from the earth. The performance was repeated until, finally, all of the Farmans were in the air. The Bréguet-Michelins came next, and the hundreds of ground crewmen who stood lining the sides of the field held their breaths as the awkward machines rose and fell back to the ground with clattering shock, straining to get off the ground. But all of them made it, with bare inches to spare, and the tension went out of the watchers in a swelling cheer.

The Strutters, precisely lined up in flights of threes, facing into the wind, began rolling smoothly down the field, their rotary engines snarling in a higher key. After the spectacle of the elephantine French bombers, the Strutters seemed fairly to race across the ground to lift cleanly and surely into the air. One flight followed another until twenty-four of the new British planes were circling the field, shifting into the predetermined formation pattern laid down by Wing Commander Davies. The combined thunder of nearly 6000 horsepower that filled the air drowned out the exultation from the ground, and to this unmuffled roar was added the angry popping of the Le Rhônes as de Laage led the four Nieuports down the field in formation takeoff. They quickly climbed above the bombers still jockeying into position, then circled overhead as the milling mass of planes moved eastward.

To the French bombardier-gunners sitting in their exposed positions in the forward part of the bathtub-like nacelles, it must have been a comforting sight to peer upward and see the stately formation of British Sopwiths flying in a flawless V of Vs; never before had they flown under such splendid cover, under so many protective guns. The observers, unoccupied as they were on the first half hour of the mission, had ample opportunity to gaze downward and watch the countryside slowly unrolling beneath them—just as it had at Avord and at Aulnat, where they had spent tedious hours suspended aloft in dummy nacelles nervously trying to master the intricacies of the optical bombsight while a simulated landscape unreeled below on a moving carpet.

The red tile roofs of the tiny villages, untouched by shellfire, were plainly visible, and the observers could see clearly the white faces of the field workers who turned their eyes upward to stare in wonder at the armada sweeping across the sky. The gentle foothills east of Luxeuil, aflame here and there with fall colors, soon gave way to the looming, dark green masses of the Vosges; the gunners sat more erect now, their senses tuned to the danger that lay just ahead.

The mission had been airborne for three-quarters of an hour before the first German opposition appeared, in the form of ranging bursts from antiaircraft batteries that splotched the cold purity of the sky with ugly black puffs of smoke. A French crewman remembered "crossing the lines at a place in the Vosges that seemed extraordinarily well defended. The air was filled with evil black clouds filled with fire and my ears rang from the concussion of bursting shells. The Farmans were barely able to rise above 2000 feet. A hail of machine gun fire from the ground swept through the formation and several of them seemed to turn and head back. The ground fire had plucked them from their flight like stricken geese. We were flying through a terrifying barrage; our planes rocked to and fro as we sailed through the sea of fire and exploding steel.

"Then one of the remaining Farmans staggered in the air. It had received a whip-like blow from a 77mm shell. The plane fell rapidly, then rose again as if the pilot were guiding its erratic flight. It fell again, then righted itself before plunging to earth. We had just lost one of our most courageous bomber pilots." [1]

---

[1] Killed was *Adjudant* Henri Baron, whose fame as a night-bomber pilot was equal to Happe's. According to a contemporary, Baron "could see clearly, no matter how black the darkness." Happe had urged Baron not to fly the Oberndorf raid, in order to save himself for nocturnal work, but Baron had refused. He had survived three grueling night-time trips to Rottweil to bomb chemical stores, but Oberndorf was his first long-range daylight mission.

The formation flew on through a continuing barrage that slackened only slightly as the planes crossed the Rhine, which appeared as a silver ribbon wandering the course of the dark green earth.

The pilots of N.124 had time for only a few minutes' worth of reflection that this was the first time any of them had flown across the Rhine; five miles past its eastern bank was Ettenheim, the limit of their radius of penetration. Regretfully they banked away from the bombers underneath them and turned for home.

Only moments later the hellish shelling from the guns below stopped as suddenly as it had begun; a flight of Fokker E-IIIs dropped from the sun and made tentative passes at the uppermost layer of bombers. But the tight formation of the Sopwiths and the disciplined gunnery of the Canadians discouraged the few Germans, who prudently sheered off to await reinforcements.

Past the lush valley of the Rhine droned the bombers. They lifted slightly as if to follow the contours of the rising hills that guarded the mighty, rolling ramparts of the *Schwarzwald*, shrouded with masses of thick trees. The planes flew onward across the forested mountains for another twenty minutes before dipping downward toward the valley of the Neckar. A few miles above the target city the formation wheeled through the air in a 90-degree turn; now they would fly down the twisting course of the narrow river as it made its way south from the town. Bombardiers were already anxiously fiddling with their sights in the Farmans and Bréguets, and the pilots were kept busy making constant minor corrections in their course in order to follow the erratic twists and turns of the narrow strip of water below. Three miles north of the town the river bends sharply inward before straightening out into a broad, level plain immediately west of the Mauser works. Steep hills flank both sides of the plain, and it was across the level ground and between the hills the bombers would have to pass in order to dump their explosives on the buildings that stood beside the banks of the Neckar.

The Sopwiths were arrayed line astern in flights of seven aircraft each; the first five Strutters were single-seater bombers, with a brace of two-seater fighters covering the rear. Piloting the lead bomber was Wing Commander Davies, equipped with a periscopic sight with a wide relief ocular that enabled him to center the crosshairs on the target without having to lower his head beneath the rim of the cockpit. Davies led the way down the valley, expecting any moment to receive withering blasts of machine gun fire from the surrounding hillsides, but no enemy fire came and he was free to concentrate on lining up his sights. When the bombs left the cells inside the fuselage behind Davies' cockpit it was the signal for the other British pilots to bomb in salvo. As the tight formation of Strutters raced down the valley, they left behind in their wake thundering explosions and a rising pall of smoke.

Minutes later the Farmans and Bréguets arrived on the scene to find the target area "obscured by clouds of dense black smoke. . . . We dropped our bombs into the center of the holocaust and quickly turned back for France. We considered the factory as practically destroyed."

Lightened of their load of bombs, the planes climbed up to 6000 feet, underneath the Sopwiths, their only protection against Fokker attacks until they could reach the Rhine and the Nieuports that should be waiting for them there. They still had fifty miles of enemy territory to cross before reaching the river, and nearly twenty miles of hostile airspace to penetrate even with the meager help the Americans could give. It was a long way home.

At the controls of one of the two-seater fighters hovering over the French formation was a twenty-three-year-old Canadian pilot flying his first big sortie. Raymond Collishaw came from Nanaimo, Vancouver Island, British Columbia. Before he was twenty he had seen half the world from the decks of merchant ships. January 1916 found him flying routine coastal patrols off England, a tedious occupation he rid himself of in August by transferring to No. 3 Wing. "The Germans," Collishaw reported, "made their most effective attacks while we were on the way home and before the *Escadrille Américaine* had rejoined. It was a running fight all the way. We adopted the tactic of flying directly into the afternoon sun so the Germans would have to fly into the blinding glare in order to attack our vulnerable rears. The Germans much preferred the clumsy French aircraft, which flew under us for protection."

The delayed German fighter reaction hit the Oberndorf raiders a few miles from the target on the homeward leg. Swarms of

Fokker E-IIIs dropped from the skies, bypassing the tight ranks of Sopwiths to fall on the nearly defenseless French. A Fokker fastened itself on the tail of one of few remaining Farmans and opened fire. But Collishaw had not been dozing. He peeled off and plunged after the Fokker and shot it off the tail of the wildly maneuvering Farman. The Fokker fell away spinning and crashed in flames in the forest below. "A whole series of engagements ensued. The Farmans and Bréguets were dashing haphazardly around the sky to avoid attack, and one was hard pressed to tell friend from foe."

Collishaw's observation is apt. A French gunner recalled seeing a Strutter pouring fire into a Fokker when, "inexplicably, a Farman drifted into the path of the deadly stream of lead spouting from the nose of the British plane. The Farman started blazing and a few seconds later my own plane was flung violently upward from the explosion that ripped across the sky."

While the confused aerial struggle was moving through the air over Germany, the four Escadrille Nieuports were streaking east to join the battle. They arrived just as it seemed disaster was overtaking the entire raiding force. Bréguets and Farmans were plunging and rearing in erratic patterns, and even the welded-together British formation was beginning to feel the fury of the German assault. One, then another Strutter fell crazily through the clouds; the first in flames, the second spinning earthward with a dead hand on the controls.

Then a Fokker sliced down like a meteor to tear itself to pieces on the ground.[2] The air was crosshatched with tendrils of blue-white smoke and the atmosphere trembled with the sound of roaring engines and the frantic chugging of scores of machine guns.

De Laage was the first to plunge into the mêlée. Targets were everywhere. He picked a Fokker sitting on the tail of a Bréguet and opened fire. The Fokker staggered and fell earthward. Then de Laage was swallowed up in the fighting.

Fokkers weren't the only planes the Germans sent up in their

[2] Lieutenant Collishaw's second kill. He ran his score to sixty by the end of the war, finishing with the rank of Lieutenant Colonel. The Canadian went on to fight in Russia in 1919 and served with distinction during World War II. He retired from the R.A.F. with the rank of Air Vice-Marshal and lives today in British Columbia.

desperate attempt to destroy the bomber force. Lufbery jumped one of the new-model Roland C-II two-seater "Whales," a type generally used for reconnaissance. He traded shots with the German gunner firing steadily with a swivel-mounted Parabellum gun until the gunner slumped from sight. Lufbery eased his fire forward and saw the pilot jerk forward in his seat and fall lifeless against the control column. The Roland began its final dive to earth, and Raoul Lufbery became the first American ace of the war.

Didier Masson found himself in the middle of a furious struggle between three Fokkers and a solitary Bréguet. He rolled over and down and came up underneath one of the Fokkers and started to line up in firing position. Then his engine spluttered and stopped cold. The fuel gauge registered empty, indicating a nicked tank that had allowed the precious gasoline to trickle away. The hunter now became the hunted, and Masson banked for the lines with one of the Fokkers sitting on his tail firing. A burst of Maxim fire carried away his windscreen and sent lead slamming through Masson's few instruments. Crouching helplessly in the cockpit, Masson waited for the next burst, which he probably expected to feel between his shoulder blades. But the zealous Fokker pilot overshot and his plane slid in front of Masson's Vickers gun. Masson quickly clamped down on the trigger and got off twenty rounds before the German could correct his error. The aim was good, and the enemy fighter spun away rapidly toward the ground.

By carefully nursing altitude, Masson managed to cross the German lines with 150 feet of altitude to spare. He "urged the ship on with the motion of his body, talking to it as he would to a faltering horse." The wheels of his Nieuport barely cleared the barbed-wire entanglements in front of the French first line, and Masson dead-sticked the plane to a rough landing in a cluster of shell holes straddling a communication trench. Hidden from German observation by a rise in the ground, Masson was able to scramble safely from the cockpit and roll into the security offered by the communication trench. Five minutes later, searching German shells found the Nieuport and blew it into matchwood. But at the time Masson was enjoying a drink in a nearby infantry dugout and wondering how he would get back home.

The savage dogfight overhead lasted until the scattered formation reached the German lines. The parting shots were fired by Norman Prince who knocked an E-III from the sky. The Germans, fought out and low on fuel, broke off the engagement that had run a course through sixty miles of their own airspace.

The sun was low as the remaining bombers flew on to Luxeuil. Not all of them made it. A Strutter pilot lost his bearings in the gathering darkness and landed in Switzerland, where he was interned and sat out the war.

A Farman ran out of fuel and the pilot had no choice except to crash-land in the Vosges. "The old chicken coop," said a survivor, "was entirely smashed. But the occupants, a lieutenant and a sergeant, were in luck and crawled from the tangle of wire and wood without the least hurt. The plane had crashed on top of a mountain 3000 feet high—just 50 feet from a sheer precipice."

Lufbery and Prince tailed the straggling bombers until they crossed the lines and the possibility of further German attack was remote. Then, low on fuel, Lufbery led the way down in the gloom toward a small emergency field at Corcieux, not far inside the French trench system. It was nearly dark when Lufbery spotted the tiny field, and he sat down quickly, skimming the trees lining the edge of the landing patch. Lufbery gunned the plane down the field to leave plenty of room for Prince, whose notoriously poor depth-perception had caused him to wreck more Nieuports than any other man in the squadron. Even on bright sunny days the others sweated out Prince's landings, for his inability to gauge space relationships exceeded that of Dud Hill's, who was nearly blind in one eye.

Lufbery stood near his plane and anxiously watched Prince turn into the wind for his landing approach. Only a remnant of twilight remained, leaving the ground an indistinct purple smudge. Prince came in fast and just managed to clear the trees, but he failed to see the high-tension cable stretched near treetop level. His landing gear caught up in the wire and the speeding Nieuport flipped upside down. The shock snapped Prince's seat belt, and he was flung to the earth with brutal force. The Nieuport somersaulted down the field and disintegrated.

Prince lay groaning on the ground, both legs broken. Through clenched teeth he begged Lufbery to order the men at Corcieux to set out flares "so another man won't smash himself up the way I have." An ambulance was summoned, and Prince suffered agonies on the rough ten-mile ride over wartime French secondary roads that led to the hospital at Gérardmer. Lufbery sat in the back of the bouncing ambulance, holding Prince's hand while the injured pilot sang and talked about his future in order to distract his mind from the unbearable pain.

At first the doctors gave Prince a good chance to recover, but the next day a blood clot formed on his brain and he lapsed into a coma. It was too late to operate, even had a skilled surgeon been immediately available for the demanding job. The hospital rang up Luxeuil with the news.

Less than an hour later, Happe, Thénault (who had just returned from leave) and a delegation of Escadrille pilots were standing silently around the bedside of the luckless flier. Happe, his face "working with emotion," promoted the unconscious aviator to lieutenant and then read off a citation.

For nineteen months in escadrille has distinguished himself by a bravery and devotion to duty beyond compare in the execution of numerous bombardments and pursuit work. Was grievously injured on 12 October, 1916, after having brought down an enemy plane. Already has the Médaille Militaire.

Then Happe leaned down and pinned to Prince's pajama jacket the medal of the Legion of Honor. Two days later, the founder of the *Escadrille Américaine* died, at the age of twenty-nine, without having regained consciousness.

What had happened at Oberndorf? Were the factory buildings destroyed? Had German rifle production been dealt a crippling blow? These were the questions being asked by the staff officers of *l'Aéronautique aux Armées*. In the *compte rendu* Happe submitted to G.Q.G. the day following the raid, there was but meager information—certainly not enough to satisfy the statistics-minded planners. Happe stated that "40 aircraft had departed on 12 October to bomb the Mauser factory at Oberndorf." He added, "9548 pounds of bombs were hurled at the objectives, all explosions verified to have taken place on the objectives or in their immediate neighborhood." Happe's brief account concluded with a claim of six enemy aircraft destroyed, while admitting the loss of six French and three English bombers. An enthusiastic account of the raid appearing in the Chicago *Daily News* spoke of "millions of dollars' worth of damage . . . a city block razed."

But the French were almost completely in the dark; they did not know the real extent of the damage inflicted—at considerable cost to themselves—upon the target astride the Neckar. No aerial reconnaissance was made, no photographs taken that might substantiate the French Bréguet pilot's statement, "We consider the factory as practically destroyed." The only first-hand description came, strangely enough, from a train traveler from a neutral country. On October 17, G.Q.G. received the following dispatch from the French Military Attaché at Berne:

"A Swiss lady returning from Berlin passed by Oberndorf the day following the bombardment by our aircraft. She was able to determine and describe part of the damage because the express train was unexpectedly halted at the Oberndorf station for passport examination. The Mauser factory, which measures more than two kilometers in length, was seriously hit: three bombs had fallen directly on the factory, of which half was razed.

"This same person saw outside the factory three craters caused by the projectiles.

"The immediate area was barricaded.

"No other impressions could be recorded. *Silence absolu.*"

The German communiqué, picked up in Berne and forwarded to Paris, was sharply contradictory. "Of 40 French and English aircraft, 15 struck Oberndorf and there dropped about 60 bombs. The other planes were dispersed by the attacks of our planes, and dropped their bombs haphazardly in the woods, in the meadows and in numerous small localities. Neither at Oberndorf or elsewhere was there damage inflicted upon military matériel. The damage, in general, was of little importance. The production in the factory was not disturbed. Three persons were killed and seven were injured, struck in the open by bomb bursts. Nine planes were shot down by our aviators or by our antiaircraft batteries. No German planes were lost, no German pilot was killed or wounded." Then, as if to offer convincing evidence that the communiqué was indeed factual, there were listed the names of five of the crewmen killed (omitting four too badly burned or smashed to identify) and eight prisoners, taken after the raid.[3]

Scanning the columns of the Oberndorf daily newspaper, *Schwarzwälder Bote*, turned up nothing startling. Not until the issue of October 17 did anything appear concerning the raid, and then the event was given only two inches of space. The additional information included only the facts that two P.O.W.s were among those killed—Peter Katzapoff, twenty-seven, and Jean Baptiste Dufour, thirty-six—and that twenty-six persons were injured. Then a curtain was drawn over the raid on Oberndorf; there remained only *silence absolu.*

In what was probably one of the unfairest decisions handed down by G.Q.G. during the war, Captain Happe was removed from command of *Groupe de Bombardement* 4 and sent back to the infantry. The reason: excessive losses in combat. While it is true that Happe's losses ran high (27 percent on the Oberndorf mission) it is equally true that few bomber chiefs displayed such personal courage and leadership in taking a command deep into Germany to strike where it hurt—using planes that were even in 1915 being called "death traps." G.Q.G. might well have probed into the question of why brave men were sent aloft in equipment that was greatly inferior to the enemy's, and to their Allies' as well.

Nor can the question of the escort be avoided. The aeronautical section of G.Q.G. was aware long before the raid that the *Escadrille Américaine* was woefully short of planes; during the height of the Verdun battle, as many as twelve French fighters were sent out to protect two observation planes—yet, for the biggest raid of the war, only one fighter was sent out for every four French bombers. Moreover, had the fighter escort been allowed to take off from a field immediately behind the French lines—instead of a full forty miles away, as was the case with Luxeuil—they would have been able to rendezvous with the bomber force at the lines to escort them to the target and back. The choice of equipment-poor N.124 leads to the speculation that

[3] Names of the dead were given as Guérinau, Baron, Georges, Jouan and Marchand. The captive airmen were listed: Rockey, Sterdec, Rouet, Delcroix, Buckerworth, Mattay, Newmann and Witty.

the decision was more political than military; publicity could then point to the raid as a three-nation affair in which Frenchmen, Britishers and Americans were seen working in concert against the Germans.

The Americans were spared witnessing Happe's ultimate degradation. Four days after they buried Norman Prince, they packed up and left Luxeuil for the last time.[4]

---

[4] Happe survived nearly two years of infantry warfare while commanding a battalion of Colonial Sharpshooters.

Rumpler C.-V

CHAPTER 9

WINTER OF DISCONTENT

Popular belief built us into legendary characters and credited us with being an heroic race of supermen without fear or reproach.

—EDWIN C. PARSONS

The valley of the Somme in winter is noted for the cold mists that come swirling down from the flanks of the wooded hills and for the gluey mud that abounds. A worse site for an airdrome can hardly be imagined, but one of the largest fields near the Front in late 1916 was near Cachy Wood, eight miles southeast of Amiens.

At Cachy the Escadrille joined *Groupe de Combat* 13, then made up of squadrons N.15, N.84 and N.65, under the leadership of Commandant Philippe Féquant, a onetime infantryman who had gained a reputation for aggressive-mindedness while subduing Tonkinese pirates before the war. No chairborne commander, Féquant frequently flew patrols with his squadrons. Remembered one of his pilots: "When the fighting was heaviest, his Spad with its anchor insignia could be seen far beyond the enemy lines, making its way calmly through enemy antiaircraft bursts. It was a heartening, an inspiring sight . . . he shared with his pilots their dangers as well as their successes; and he did this when, as Group Commander, his duties on the ground almost forbade taking part in activities over the lines."

Féquant's squadrons shared the field at Cachy with *Groupe de Combat* 12, the famous *Cigognes* (Storks), comprising squadrons N.3, N.26, N.73 and N.103—all under the command of Commandant Brocard, the officer who had helped Thaw, Bach and Hall transfer to aviation in 1914. The Storks contained the élite of French *chasse* pilots, headed by such paragons as René Dorme, Alfred Heurtaux, Armand Pinsard, Albert Duellin and spinsterish Georges Guynemer, a demigod of twenty-two with eighteen German planes to his credit.

Now attached to a *Groupe de Combat* for the first time since its creation six months previously, the Escadrille was no longer an independent unit. The Americans quickly discovered they had lost more than independence, they had lost many of their privileged comforts as well.

They gazed with dismay at their quarters. Instead of being shown to a cozy villa or installed in a first-class hotel, the Americans were directed to a slab-sided, tar-papered portable barrack erected in a sea of mud—glutinous stuff that sucked the shoes from the wearer's feet. Sloshing across the half-submerged duckboards, the pilots entered the barrack, which they found cold as a tomb and furnished only with a long row of cots and a small potbellied stove at the far end of the room. The pilots stood in the hut, their voices echoing hollowly off the thin, bare walls, discussing their apparent fall from grace and wondering where the mess hut was located. It turned out that no mess facilities for N.124 were available; indeed, no eating arrangements whatsoever had been made for the Americans. And the nearest village was five miles away over shell-torn, muddy paths that no man would dignify with the name of road.

Then it started to rain and the pilots listened to a steady *drip, drip, drip* of water that seeped through the roof. The wind rose, and icy drafts whipped through cracks in the walls. Someone asked for blankets, and was told none were available. Bill Thaw went off with Pavelka to see Captain Thénault, who had found a warm billet with Commandant Féquant. Pavelka reported: "The Captain just shrugged his shoulders and suggested we go find a place to eat with some of the other escadrilles." There was nothing for it but to slop through the mud to see if they could beg dinner—and breakfast and lunch—from one of the French squadrons until they could arrange to feed themselves.

"I tell you," Pavelka wrote McConnell, "it's just like the infantry, but here no one cares whether you are lodged or fed. Jim, your back would go awfully bad here in this fog and rain. Take my advice and stay in Paris."

The prospects for flying were equally depressing. Overhead, gray clouds scudded by, propelled by stiff, cold winds. And in the early mornings and during the evenings, white mists crept across the field, cutting visibility to a minimum. Bordering the field were trees, now stripped of leaves, but growing thickly and tall; if a man lost an engine on his letdown, these trees could kill him. The field itself was covered with a slick coating of mud that soon would turn, with the dropping of the mercury, to a hard, rutted surface overlaid with rime ice. Takeoffs would be hazardous, and landings in one piece would be largely a matter of luck and God's good will.

The Nieuports, when they came, would be kept in Bessanau hangars made of canvas supported by wood and steel. Although the hangars would keep rain and snow from the planes, they would do little toward providing the warmth necessary to keep the oil from congealing in the reservoirs. And it was only October; the real winter had not begun.

Thénault had reason to despair at the lack of planes, for which he had been waiting since before the Oberndorf strike, but not on the score of available pilots; by the end of October he could count thirteen men ready and able to wage combat. One of them was Frederick H. Prince, Jr., Norman's older brother. The two men were totally unlike; where Norman was bantam-like and hypertonic, Fred was ample and almost languorous; where Norman had been bellicose, Fred was affable. He almost immediately struck up a boyish friendship with Chouteau Johnson, whose mild temperament matched his own.

Robert Soubiran made it to the Escadrille after eighteen months in the Foreign Legion. A New Yorker by birth, and a mechanic and racing car driver by preference, Soubiran was pulled from the lines to help with the wheat harvest of 1915. Sitting atop a threshing machine, tinkering with its innards, was not Soubiran's idea of *la guerre à outrance*, and he returned to his regiment in time for the offensive in the Champagne later that year. This action resulted in a bloody knee wound and a long stay in the hospital.

Recalled a contemporary of Soubiran's: "There are towns and villages all along the battle area in France where the name of Robert Soubiran will be remembered long after those of most of us will be forgotten. Of French descent and speaking the language fluently, he made friends among the inhabitants of scores of villages where the Legion was *en repos*. He whittled his bread with the natural ease of an old *poilu* reservist; then sticking his open clasp-knife upright in the deal table, he would drink *pinard* from his *bidon* with audible zest. Old French housewives hearing him speak English were astonished. *Mais, c'est un français, celui-là!* High praise reserved to Soubiran alone of all his compatriots."

Offsetting the short, swarthy Soubiran was Willis Haviland, a square-shouldered, erect, barrel-chested, smiling Adonis from St. Paul, Minnesota; Haviland, everyone agreed, "was easily the handsomest man in the squadron and the Beau Brummell of the outfit." Like McConnell, Haviland had left the volunteer ambulance service to enlist in the rapidly expanding Franco-American Flying Corps. By the end of 1916, there would be more than fifty-eight names on the rolls of the Gros-Vanderbilt organization, with more and more volunteers coming directly from the ambulance service; fewer and fewer Americans were available for transfer from the thinning ranks of the Legion.

Although almost all of the transfers to the *Service Aéronautique* went smoothly—the men passing from the infantry (or ambulance corps) through flying school, to the replacement depot at Le Plessis-Belleville and thence to an operational squadron—the case of Emil Marshall is typical of just how muddled a man's affairs could get if the ponderous machinery of bureaucratic paper work slipped a gear.

Marshall, a onetime accountant for the Auditor of New York State, was sent to the Escadrille just before it left Luxeuil. He appeared wearing a clean, but patched and faded *poilu's* uniform of *horizon bleu,* upon which hung the medal of the *Croix de Guerre* with star; a muddy kit bag and a dented steel helmet were slung over his shoulder, and the dirt from the trenches was still under his fingernails. Marshall looked like a veteran, and he was. He quit his job and came to France in 1914, where both parents had been born. Marshall had a "baseball arm" and was made the leading bomb-thrower for his battalion, part of the 156th *Regiment d'Infanterie,* which spent nineteen months in and around the murderous Bois le Prêtre in the Champagne. Marshall had earned his decoration for leading a six-man patrol through a heavy bombardment to a German forward observation post where, armed with trench knives, grenades and revolvers, Marshall and his men hurled themselves upon a German sentry crouching in a hole. One man was caught up in the barbed wire on the way out and killed by machine gun fire, but the others ran stumbling through the rain of high explosive to reach their battered trench; the last few yards were made with Marshall pulling at the German with a painful grasp on the man's ear. Marshall survived the worst of the fighting in front of Verdun and finally received the coveted transfer to aviation. The slipup occurred when Marshall was sent directly to N.124, bypassing altogether the training schools. Weeks passed before Thénault could get the tangle straight and Marshall posted to Avord for primary flight training. At Avord the doctors discovered that Marshall was blind in one eye, and he was sent back to the Escadrille, this time as a mechanic. But Marshall hadn't even a rudimentary idea of the workings of an internal-combustion engine, and he was finally put to work in Thénault's office handling papers. Marshall was the only American member of N.124 carried on the roster as *personnel non-navigant,* a distinction the former bomb-thrower was far from happy with.

Fog, mist and drizzle grounded all eight squadrons more days than not, and it became bitterly cold. While the Americans had been welcome to share food and drink with the French, they were ashamed of endless panhandling. Thénault, whose personal contact with the pilots grew less as the weeks went by, gave no indication that he would make separate feeding arrangements, so the pilots took matters into their own hands. Bill Thaw and Didier Masson took the train to Paris, where they badgered Dr. Gros into giving them money from the Corps funds to buy enough cooking utensils "to feed a battalion." Thaw managed to borrow a large Ford touring sedan to haul the largesse back to Cachy, and Allan Muhr of the French Racing Club handled the wheel on the breakneck, 95-mile dash back to the Front. The pilots were overjoyed at the sight of so much new cooking hardware, and ecstatic at the provisions for the bar Thaw had purchased. The bar was set up first, in a tent near the barrack; then the kitchen was put in order under the direction of Masson, whom Thénault appointed *chef de popote*. The post suited Masson as long as the Paris provisions held out. When they were exhausted the job of mess officer became a thankless task. There are few men alive who can do anything spectacular with aging fish, issue horsemeat and stale bread. Masson, however, later secured the services of a onetime sauce cook at the Ritz named Sampson who became Masson's right-hand man in the kitchen. Sampson was a genial Parisian with a walrus moustache, a greasy apron and an inordinate fondness for kitchen sherry; when he was sober, Sampson accomplished wonders in disguising the distinct tang of horsemeat; when not, Masson only let him wallop pots.

With the eating problem solved, the pilots turned to work on their primitive barrack. To give a semblance of privacy, flimsy partitions were installed the length of the barrack so that each pilot would have what passed for personal quarters. An area at the far end of the hut was designated as the lounge, and chairs of varying degrees of repair and taste were grouped around the stove, kept glowing a cherry red with wood scrounged from the forested area surrounding the field. As is the case with campfires, the traditional cast-iron, potbellied stove provides but two zones of proximity—too near and too far. Part of the pilots' anatomy would blister while another part, only a foot away, would freeze. Each day brought lowering temperatures, and even when a carload of blankets arrived from Alice Weeks in Paris, the men slept in their oil-stained, fur-lined flying suits, buttoned to the throat. At Cachy these suits were seldom removed.

Despite the fame of the *Escadrille Américaine,* which by then had spread to wherever newspapers were published, the squadron had yet to choose a distinctive unit insignia. Emblazoned on the sides of the planes flown by the *Cigognes* were large storks, painted in white and in varying attitudes of flight; the Nieuports of the group to which the Escadrille was attached were even more fancifully decorated with plumed knights' helmets, black dragons spitting fire and Nungesser's well-known skull, coffin and candle motif. The Escadrille pilots had been contented with painting initials on the sides of their planes, but now something distinctive, something American, was called for. Thénault suggested the head of an Indian chief as N.124's trademark. Put to a vote, the idea was accepted. But nobody had a picture of an Indian chief to copy; there were plenty of pictures in *La Vie Parisienne,* but most of the good ones were pinned to the barrack walls—and none were of Indians. Finally a mechanic named Suchet located an empty ammunition container from the Savage Arms Corporation that bore on the front the likeness of a Seminole. Armed with the box top and buckets of brown, red and white paint, Suchet went to work painting Indians on the sides of the Escadrille Nieuports as they came up from the depot. Suchet had more heart than talent, and the original trademark was in no way handsome—but it was N.124's, and it was certainly American.

Word trickled down one day that Major General Sir Hugh ("Boom") Trenchard, chief of the Royal Flying Corps, was coming to visit Cachy to pass in review the entire command. This news put Captain Thénault into a mild panic. He thought of the splendid dress and equipment of the French aces on the field (why, even the humble mechanics managed to look like field marshals when on leave) and he remembered that Trenchard had a reputation for rigid military etiquette and was, as Thénault put it, "used to clean aviators turned out in well-cut uniforms and impeccable boots." He must have shuddered when he mentally passed in review his own, unique command. Since there was no specified uniform as yet for the French Air Service, the Americans could, and did, wear uniforms of their own choosing. Some pilots fancied choke-collared black uniforms with a red stripe running the length of the trousers as worn by French engineers. Others wore the horizon blue of the infantry, some with slacks and low-cut shoes, some with breeches and boots. Some of them preferred the plain khaki of the Foreign Legion with flared breeches and infantry lace boots that came to the knee. Then there were pilots who liked none of these styles and designed their own uniforms, sometimes with striking results. Headgear varied from the standard stiff-crowned, shiny-visored officer's hat to the large blue beret worn by the *Chasseurs Alpins,* a head covering that greatly resembled a monstrous limp cabbage leaf drooping over one side of the head. Neckties ranged in color from black to khaki to dark red, and were of varying material cut to no standard pattern. Doc Rockwell preferred artilleryman's breeches and bulky, knit sweaters. Thénault also admitted that he was worried about what impression the Escadrille's half-grown lion and assortment of stray mutts would have on the British air chief.

But Thénault's fears came to nothing. It was announced that General Trenchard was reluctantly forced to cancel his visit, and Thénault sighed with relief.

By October 30 the Escadrille was finally up to strength in aircraft, having received twelve factory-fresh 110 h.p. Nieuport 17s. The next day, Thénault, Thaw, Lufbery, Hill and Johnson took off in marginal weather and scared up a German two-seater, but the enemy plane dived away under sporadic fire and disappeared in the mist. Disappointed, the patrol returned to Cachy, where Thaw and Johnson started packing for a twenty-one-day leave in America. Fred Prince, ailing from the chilly, soggy Somme climate, left for America a week later.

Jim McConnell, who had been in the hospital since his crash at Verdun, came back to the Escadrille from Paris, where he had cajoled the doctor into letting him go by explaining that he was owed back pay, but under the system no pay could be vouchered until McConnell returned to active duty. McConnell pleaded poverty and a desire to return to the squadron; the doctor, although doubtful of the American's recovery, listened sympathetically to the tale of woe and released him. The big Southerner hobbled aboard the train bound for Cachy, where he was received with great warmth and some concern: the first time he tried to haul himself into the cockpit of a Nieuport, he failed to make it. It took two mechanics to heft him into the seat.

For once the squadron had more planes than pilots, and they flew patrols when weather permitted—cold, miserable outings over the Somme that gave them a grandstand view of the churned-up battlefields already showing patches of snow. The titanic struggle had nearly run down, and there were few German planes to be seen in the freezing sky. After spending two hours monotonously flying back and forth over their sector, the Americans would return to the field stiff with cold and cursing winter warfare. Pavelka jumped a solitary German observation plane on the afternoon of November 14 and managed to get off several long bursts before the enemy craft dropped from sight behind a wooded village secreted in a deep valley, but no confirmation was forthcoming.

If the Germans had little stomach for daylight missions in winter, they showed an annoying proclivity for operations after dark. On moonlit nights, usually just after the bars on the field had closed and the hundred-odd pilots had bedded down for the night, the screeching wail of air-raid sirens would pierce the silence, turning the slumbering camp into a shambles of cursing men who struggled to free themselves from sleeping bags and entangling blankets, frantically searching for boots in the pitch darkness of the barracks. In the distance the unsynchronized *raummm, raummm, raummm* of German engines filled the air. Pilots, mechanics and clerks piled out of barrack doors, slipping and sliding in the mud, to head for shelters spotted around the field. The raiders appeared over the field to loose 100- and 250-pound bombs that whistled from the sky with fearful shrieks. Explosions shook the earth and brilliant flashes of flame marked the places where the bombs fell.

The bombers came every night there was good weather, and there was nothing to stop them except a few machine gun pits manned by hardy souls who crouched firing into the sky, trying to protect themselves from whirling chunks of steel from bomb casings and from the heavy machine-gunning from the strafing

Germans above. To be helpless in the face of such attacks is particularly galling to fighter pilots, whose sole mission is to prevent just such outrages. Pavelka was determined to offer meaningful opposition to the raiders when they came again. He and his mechanic, Louis Bley, rigged a small generator, operated by a propeller, to a strut. They jury-rigged a primitive set of running lights and small bulbs to illuminate the few cockpit instruments. Pavelka made two or three practice night takeoffs and landings and was convinced he was ready "to show those bastards when they come again."

He hadn't long to wait. Shortly after the first big raid on Cachy, the Germans returned and unloaded tons of high explosive. Eight heavies struck the field, one plunging through the roof of the hangar where the Spads of N.3 were housed. A roaring fire erupted and men rushed from the safety of their underground shelters to drag the planes to safety, away from the gasoline-fed inferno. Pavelka ran not to the hangar blazing furiously, but across the field, shouting for his mechanic. Pavelka's night-flying Nieuport was wheeled from its hangar and Pavelka flung himself into the cockpit, hurriedly fastening the seat belt and shoulder yoke catches. He flicked switches while Bley swung the prop to start the engine. The Le Rhône caught, and Pavelka impatiently waited until the tachometer needle steadied, showing the engine would hold. He shouted for Bley to pull the chocks and then taxied rapidly across the field, using his rudder to steer clear of the bomb craters. By the flickering glare from the burning hangar, Pavelka took off, heading into the black sky above.

Just as his wheels left the earth the electrical system failed, plunging the cockpit into darkness. Pavelka was committed to flight, for there was no turning back onto the field where bombs were raining down. A thousand feet up and Pavelka was practically blind. The altimeter, tachometer, oil-pressure gauge and fuel-pressure gauge were invisible. He had no idea how high he was flying, nor in which direction; he could only guess at the attitude of his airplane, and the condition of his engine was relayed to him by its sound alone. Below, the flames from the burning hangar were dying out, but the flickering light indicated the general direction to Amiens. He turned toward what he believed was an easterly direction, hoping to intercept straggling

German bombers on their way home; always before, the enemy raiders had continued on to Amiens after bombarding Cachy.

He flew on, peering into the black void all around him, but he could see only the firefly-like flashes from the guns at the Front, indicating the direction of the earth. If he felt pressure on his right buttock, he applied a touch of left aileron, his senses telling him he was banking slightly to the right; if, when turning, he felt a blast of air on his cheek, he knew he was skidding, and he applied more rudder. Lacking a true horizon, he had difficulty in telling whether he was in a slight climbing or a slight diving attitude. He saw a few lights twinkling below and assumed he was over Amiens, and that the city had not been visited by the Germans that night. The moment the sound of his engine was heard by those on the ground, the comforting lights went out and Pavelka was truly lost. Making constant minor flight corrections, he knew, might well add up to a course that would take him far behind the German lines. He tried letting down close to the ground, but machine guns opened up and filled the sky with tracers. Were they French guns or German? He had no way of knowing. He climbed back into the sky, away from the guns. In desperation, he fished his cigarette lighter from a pocket of his flying suit, hoping to catch a glimpse of his compass and altimeter, but the cockpit was filled with a constant blast of cold wind and Pavelka cursed when time after time the lighter failed to work.

Pavelka's only hope was to last for the rest of the night without flying into the ground. Then he could attempt a landing in the first light. But he could not see his wristwatch and did not know what time it was, how long he would have to wait, how much fuel remained. If he managed to stay on his own side of the lines he had to trust the weather would hold until dawn; a heavy early-morning fog would obscure the earth with a white opaqueness, hiding shell holes, trees, barbed-wire entanglements and ruined buildings—any of which would smash his plane.

While Pavelka was groping in the friendless sky above, the other Escadrille pilots were helping subdue the last of the disastrous fire. When the flames in the hangar died down, the pilots and mechanics stepped into the embers to look at the damage. Many of the Storks' Spads had been burned to ashes. Guynemer stood looking at the blackened skeleton of wire and wood, the pride of his life, and he nearly wept. *Vieux Charles*—Old Charlie—was no more. Guynemer's plane was but one of sixteen lost that night.

In one corner of the ruined hangar, blackened men with singed hair and scorched clothing were struggling to lift the ruins of an airplane from what once had been a man. One of the *Cigognes* mechanics had run inside the hangar to wheel out the Spad flown by his *patron* and had been pinned underneath the half-ton of airplane when concussion from an exploding bomb had hurled it on its side. The mechanic had slowly roasted, his screams unheard. They had to pry loose from his hand a knife with which he had futilely tried to cut himself free.

Angry, saddened, exhausted, the pilots trudged back through the mud to their barracks—all except the Americans, who stood outside in the cold to listen for the sound of Pavelka's engine. They waited two hours, then gave up—he must have landed somewhere else or been shot down or was a prisoner in Germany. Whatever had befallen him, there was no way to help.

Pavelka heard the first splutterings of his Le Rhône. He had reached the end of his fuel supply and would have to come down whether he was ready or not. He began a shallow glide through the murky, predawn atmosphere. A few hundred feet from the ground the engine stopped cold; the propeller flicked around and froze into position. There was no sound except the sighing of the bracing wires as Pavelka's Nieuport slanted downward.

Through the mist broke the first red rays of dawn, and Pavelka had barely enough light to see to keep from smashing nose-first into the ground. The Nieuport flared out and bumped across a field and rolled to a stop. The air was still and cold, but Pavelka sat limply in the cockpit, soggy with perspiration. English soldiers appeared through the gloom and gathered around Pavelka's grounded bird; he had lucked out, coming to rest in the British lines at Martainville, twenty-five miles from Cachy. Thirty minutes later, a heavy ground fog rolled across the Somme, cutting off any chance Pavelka had of flying home. He spent the next four days in a château behind the lines being royally entertained by British Army officers. On the morning of the fourth day the fog lifted enough for Pavelka to take off and fly low to Cachy. The trip took him twenty minutes.

War is a favorite breeding ground for rumor, and the one that began circulating, saying an attempt would soon be made to change the name of the Escadrille, was lightly dismissed. Great was the shock, therefore, when official word reached Thénault that the *Escadrille Américaine* would henceforth be known as *l'Escadrille des Volontaires.* The chain of events leading to this decision began on November 4 with the receipt at the French Ministry of Foreign Affairs of a telegram from the French Ambassador in Washington. The 350-word message referred to Secretary of State Robert Lansing's pointed—but as yet unofficial—protestation that the continued use of the phrase *Escadrille Américaine* in French war communiqués "puts the United States in an embarrassing position with the German Government." The telegram ended with the suggestion that the name be suppressed.[1]

This suggestion was acted upon, and the decision reached Thénault and the pilots in mid-November. *Escadrille des Volontaires* . . . the new name was greeted with hoots and expletives. To the pilots it was a dull, colorless label that stripped them of their nationality. As could be expected, they continued to call themselves the *Escadrille Américaine.*

The new and thoroughly disliked name remained official for only twenty-one days. On December 2 the Minister of War took pen in hand and wrote a directive to General Joseph Joffre, Commander in Chief of the French Army:

"Following letter 7963 D of 11 November on the subject of squadron N.124, I have the honor of making known to you that, to satisfy a request emanating from the United States, the

[1] Pro-German newspapers in the United States had been waging a vituperative campaign against the Escadrille for weeks. Among the more implausible charges was one claiming that the American pilots were ruthlessly bombing German localities, threatening the lives of American citizens living there.

Escadrille des Volontaires will henceforth be known as the *Escadrille Lafayette.*

"Please inform the services concerned of this decision." [2]

This time the change was welcome, and permanent.

Ever since the heavy fighting at Verdun, the majority of the Escadrille pilots had been agitating for Thénault to get rid of Bert Hall. The indictments were many. Hall cheated at cards; his fantastic lies nearly involved the Escadrille's name with that of Mata Hari, the thirty-six-year-old suspected German agent; [3] from the practice of kiting checks given him by squadron mates, he had graduated to outright forgery; some time after Chapman's death he resorted to the stratagem of having his teeth pulled, one after another, in order to avoid flying patrols; he was strongly suspected of being a bigamist, and—finally—his efforts to capitalize on Kiffin Rockwell's death had made him an outcast. Thénault had as little use for Hall as the Americans did, but he had no grounds to expel him—particularly in view of the fact that Hall had been awarded the *Médaille Militaire* and the *Croix de Guerre.* Eventually, after the pilots in a body had several times asked him to go, Hall left. On his final day with the Escadrille, he entered the mess shack where the others were at lunch, and while they paused briefly to stare silently at the angry figure standing in the open doorway, Hall cursed and yelled out, "All right, you bastards, I'm leaving—but you'll be hearing from me yet." With that, he stormed out of the hut and out of the Escadrille.

"We were not sure," Emil Marshall said later, "whether Hall meant his last remark as a threat of vengeance or whether he meant he was going to show us all up with a brilliant war record." Whatever Hall meant, the facts are plain enough. He joined another French escadrille, N.103, and gained credit for another

---

[2] Subsequently Dr. Gros in Paris tried to claim credit for giving birth to the name Lafayette Escadrille, but the idea stemmed directly from the French Ambassador in Washington. Gros lost no time in renaming the Franco-American Flying Corps (né Committee) the Lafayette Flying Corps. Among his other qualities, Gros had an innate sense of the value of publicity.

[3] Mata Hari, born Margaretha Zelle, was convicted by the French of espionage and shot to death by a firing squad in October 1917 in an open field outside the town of St. Lazare.

kill; then he asked for permission to return to the United States in order to enlist in the U. S. Air Service. But Hall spent the rest of the war in America as a civilian, occasionally appearing on vaudeville circuits as a speaker on aerial warfare. He once was stopped by the French Consul in San Francisco for illegally wearing the medal of the Legion of Honor—at a time when he was being carried on the rolls of the French *Service Aéronautique* as a deserter. Nor was this the last the Escadrille, and indeed the world, would hear of the enigmatic Bert Hall—half-hero, half-heel.

As the winter closed down in earnest, days fit for flying grew fewer and fewer. Patrols were always scheduled, but the pilots were allowed to sleep until de Laage had torn himself from his cot to gauge the possibilities of launching Nieuports. Day after day the same scene was repeated: de Laage, rising at five, would hastily dress and go outside to stand shivering in the predawn gloom. Covering the field was the usual ghostly morning ground fog, and all around the horizon were low-hanging clouds that seemed heavy with sleet, threatening to dip right down to the ground to merge with the swirling mists. Standing next to de Laage, flapping his arms against the sides of his body, the orderly waited until the lieutenant had scanned the sky. Shaking his head, de Laage would mutter, *"Non, c'est affreux."* Horrible indeed, and thus having uttered reprieve, de Laage would trot back to his hut to finish his sleep.

"This weather," remarked Jim McConnell, "makes me feel bum for fair." It took its toll. Lufbery began to feel the insidious onset of rheumatism; Masson came down with the flu; de Laage was immobilized with the grippe, and McConnell's injured back worsened and he was forced to spend his days shivering in bed. On one of the days when flying seemed possible, Soubiran went aloft, ran into heavy weather and hurriedly turned back to land—only to ground-loop on the rutted surface of the field, cracking his collarbone. Dud Hill went up, got lost in a suddenly developing fog, and had to land at Montdidier thirty miles away; and there he stayed grounded for an entire week. With three pilots still on leave, the Escadrille was down to four effectives on

December 6. The war in the air all along the Western Front had ground to a halt.

To alleviate the acute depression that had Cachy in its grip, Thénault waited until some of the illness had abated, then commandeered a *camion*—a motor lorry—and the entire Escadrille went into Amiens for a night on the town. The streets were packed with uniformed men from every part of the British Empire and from a great many French regiments. Not far from the Front itself, Amiens was the natural magnet that attracted those who could grab a few hours or a few days away from the misery of the crumbling trenches whose bottoms were filled with ice water. The Americans did most of their carousing at Charley's or at the Hotel Savoy Bar, crowded, smoke-filled places ringing with song and raucous laughter. The available young women, whether *poules* or adventuresses, found their way to these places of impromptu assignation, and there the pilots gathered.

Captain Thénault had given a lecture on the subject of wenching when the squadron first moved up to Cachy; in fact, this fatherly talk by the thirty-year-old commanding officer was repeated whenever a new man or two joined the unit. He "pointed out the dangers of consorting with women who, according to Kipling, practice the oldest profession in the world."

Shot back one of the pilots: "Have you never read Nietzsche? He said, 'Man is created for war, and women for the pleasure of the warrior.' "

Nonplused, Thénault reiterated his warnings and countered with a Latin homily, *In medio stat virtus*. The pilots called the debate a draw, perhaps in deference to rank, but once in Amiens the question was purely academic.

It was late at night when the Escadrille pilots made their way up the cold, mist-shrouded streets that led to the square where the truck was parked. As they entered the square they came upon a figure lying face-down in a gutter. Closer examination proved the body, breathing heavily and reeking of whiskey, to be that of a Scottish soldier. He lay still as a post, his kilt damp with the cold rain that had begun to fall. To abandon the unconscious form—perhaps a survivor of Loos or other terrible battles—would result in pneumonia, or arrest by the military police. Glamorous flyers though they were, the Escadrille pilots were still "other ranks," and the slumbering Scot was hefted from the cobblestones and hauled to the truck for the ride back to the field.

The next morning brought only more foul weather. Nursing hangovers, the pilots gathered around the Scot when he began to show signs of coming to life. His reaction surprised everybody. He sat bolt upright in the cot and stared wildly at the men grouped around him—all wearing strange uniforms and speaking a brand of English never heard north of the Clyde. "Ah, mon," he wailed, "I've been taken prisoner!" First the pilots, then Thénault, tried to reason with the befuddled trooper; but the more they explained, the more he was convinced that he had—and God knew how—wandered into the German lines from Amiens.

Exasperated, Thénault's voice rose. "But you are free. Free, do you understand? You find yourself here at the *Escadrille Lafayette,* which fights in the ranks of the French!" The Scot muttered that he had never heard of any bloody Yank squadron and stubbornly refused to give his regiment's name or its location. It required the intervention of Commandant Féquant to bring the Scot out of the fog, after which he spent the rest of the day with the pilots before being motored back to his unit.

By now Whiskey was growing rapidly and, like all domesticated quadrupeds, he had a mania for chewing on whatever was handy, including limbs; McConnell's fingers were once mauled so badly he was unable even to grasp a fountain pen. On one of the really cold nights when the pilots were sitting close to the ineffectual stove playing poker, writing letters or pulling slowly at bottles of cognac, Whiskey sauntered over to Rumsey's cot and dragged a brand-new cap to the floor and began to reduce the expensive headgear to shreds. Rumsey glared at the lion, shouted at him to stop. But Whiskey kept munching, growling contentedly. Rumsey set down his bottle, by then nearly empty, and lurched over to the cot and tried to wrench his cap free. The lion growled playfully and sank his teeth deeper into the gabardine cover. Rumsey flew into a rage and grabbed up the nearest thing at hand, a heavy walking cane, and clouted the lion over the head. Whiskey dropped the cap and walked uncertainly across the floor, collapsing at the booted feet of the poker players. The pilots bent down to examine their cherished mascot and discovered the blow had blinded the animal in one eye. Rumsey's remorse, coupled with a chronically poor constitution, was so great he broke out all over with painful boils and had to be sent to the hospital. He was discharged from the service on grounds of poor health before the year was out.

The near-global fame of the Lafayette Escadrille drew to the field an increasing number of visitors. Some, like the R.F.C. pilots who dropped in frequently to share the Americans' mess, were welcomed and made to feel at home. Others, like the Philadelphia flying school operator Dr. Gros brought out one day "to rope in suckers in America . . . to use us for advertising this two-bit school in Philly" (so gauged Pavelka), were gotten rid of as quickly as possible. The third category of visitors—and these were by far in the minority—were those who had something to contribute to the welfare of the pilots. Such a man was William Astor Chanler, an aviation enthusiast and benefactor of the Lafayette Flying Corps. Conversations with pilots on leave in Paris on the subject of malfunctions of aerial machine guns had given him an idea.

Chanler arrived at Cachy one blustery afternoon in a large touring sedan and asked for help in unloading a number of carefully packed, elongated cases into the barrack. When the cases were opened, he proudly swept his arm in the direction of the presents—a dozen Browning automatic 12-gauge shotguns. Chanler eagerly explained that each pilot was to have a Browning to take aloft to use on the Germans if the Vickers guns failed at a critical moment. Not wishing to dampen Chanler's boyish enthusiasm, the pilots warmly thanked him, and Chanler returned to Paris secure in the knowledge that he was helping a little to win the war; perhaps, even, to save the lives of his countrymen.

Since it was patently impossible to employ the long-barreled, unwieldy, short-range bird guns in the cramped confines of a Nieuport, the costly weapons were put to the use the makers had intended. Soubiran, recovered from the broken collarbone, was the first to load up a Browning and disappear into the woods. He returned at a dead run, cached the Browning and jumped into bed fully dressed, there to begin a fine imitation of snoring. He later explained he had been chased out of the woods by *gendarmes* and feared they would arrest him. Although it developed that hunting was strictly prohibited, being pursued by the French constabulary added zest to the game and hardly a day went by but that Sampson would have a grouse or a hare for the squadron pot.

Christmas came and went, the cold grew worse and the winter seemed interminable. Lufbery's rheumatism was a nagging pain, and he moved about the barrack with the stiff motions of a man twice his age. On many nights he took the evil-smelling lion to bed with him for warmth. Finally, on December 27, de Laage walked outside to find enough sun to cast shadows on the ground. At the other end of the field the *Cigognes'* Spads were rolled from the hangars and the Hispano-Suiza engines began to crackle sluggishly into life. The Americans gulped down cups of scalding hot coffee, muffled themselves to the ears and walked over to their own tarmacs to start the Le Rhônes. The half-crippled Lufbery was on this early patrol.

The Nieuports crossed the lines and were greeted by the usual crash of bursting antiaircraft shells. Thénault, flying a new Spad, unthinkingly kept the throttle bent forward, and he gradually drew away from his men until he was lost in the clouds. Then the patrol broke up and Lufbery found himself flying alone. South of Chaulnes he observed a German reconnaissance plane, also alone, droning by underneath. A clean dive from altitude brought Lufbery into firing position and he pressed the trigger; the Vickers gun remained silent. Lufbery's plane shot past the startled German, who reacted instantly by whipping over and down on Lufbery's tail, opening fire. Holes appeared in Lufbery's wings as he twisted away from the fire and climbed up to clear the stoppage. Working the charging handle back and forth cleared the jam, and Lufbery dived down again and succeeded in getting off a long burst into the vitals of the German plane. The pilot was killed instantly, his plane plunging forward in a power dive straight to the ground. The fight was seen from the ground by French infantry, and Lufbery had his sixth confirmed victory. On the same day, Guynemer fought a successful combat and shot his twenty-sixth German from the sky not far from Lufbery.

The high spirits engendered by these victories were soon squelched by the onset of the worst winter weather France had endured for years. Pilots in the unheated canvas wash sheds quickly learned not to attempt to comb their hair with water, for between the time the water was doused on the head and a man could pick up a comb, his hair was frozen in attitudes of fright. Coffee served from steaming pitchers cooled in the heavy mugs long before it could be finished. Inside the barracks, breath condensed and men seemed to be spewing white clouds when they spoke. The isinglass in the windows frosted over and remained opaque. Men slept, dressed and walked about in temperatures little higher than those used to refrigerate meat. They put on as many layers of clothing as they could fit on their bodies; still, when they ventured outside the wind cut through their clothes like knives. Men breathed shallowly, with their chins pushed down into their fur collars; deep breaths in the frigid outdoors gave the sensation of swallowing glass. The sky became a perpetual gray dome, shutting the sun from sight, and nowhere was there relief from the cold.

Lufbery's rheumatism worsened until every movement was an agony. He packed part of his gear and went to the south of France to let the warm Mediterranean sun bake away the constant ache. Jim McConnell was all but paralyzed and Thénault was forced to send him back to Paris for infrared treatments for his ailing back. Doc Rockwell and Dud Hill got leaves, and packed immediately to begin the long trip back to America and three weeks away from the misery of the Somme.

A replacement came up to Cachy on a day when the clouds were almost hugging the frozen earth and a day so cold even Soubiran stayed in bed to keep warm, leaving the forbidden game to shiver unmolested in the snow. No flying was possible, yet the pilots gathered around the stove in the hut distinctly heard the unmistakable sound of a rotary engine blipping its way down toward the ground. The Escadrille pilots, having once peered outside that morning, knew there would not be—could not be—any man fool enough to fly in the forbidding muck that enveloped the valley of the Somme. This knowledge was final and indisputable—yet, some madman or drunk was up there trying to let down. Then they heard the intermittent popping as the plane was taxied down the field; the engine was cut and there remained only the sound of the wind whistling through the cracks in the walls.

Moments later the door of the hut burst open and what appeared to be an animated teddy bear walked down the length of the hut, unwinding layers of silk and wool as he approached the stove. When the unveiling was complete, the pilots could only gape at the bared face before them, the face of a child. Wide, blue innocent-looking eyes greeted them. A snub nose red with cold was planted between rosy cheeks that showed no trace of beard. Closely cropped blond hair topped a head that measured no more than 5 feet 6 inches from the floor. On closer inspection, a downy moustache appeared. If he was sixteen years old, it would be a miracle.

His name was Edmond Charles Clinton Genêt, he had just turned twenty and his home was in Ossining, New York—"You know, where Sing-Sing is located." Genêt was all eyes and all questions and all eagerness. There was the flare of an eighteenth-century *gallant* about him, somehow agreeably mixed with an unabashed Boy Scout's attitude toward the war; to Genêt, the Germans were not simply "the enemy," they were arch villains, "scoundrels of the worst sort imaginable," and worthy of the sternest punishment that decent men could mete out. In his haste to close with the hated Boche, Genêt had left the depot without orders to fly directly to Cachy; when he learned that most of the time was spent in bed trying to keep warm, or idling the hours away at cards, he was visibly let down.

Bit by bit the background of this unlikely-looking warrior seeped out, but few details came from him. He was the great-great-grandson of Citizen Genêt, who had been sent to America by the French Revolutionary Government in 1793. Citizen Genêt liked America so well he decided to stay and raise a family. Thus this distinguished heritage partially accounted for the diminutive corporal's desire to fight for the land of his fathers. The others at Cachy tended to regard Genêt as more of a mascot than a fighting addition to the muster roll, but when they learned he had taken part in the assault on the Bois Sabot, Genêt seemed to grow several inches.

The final phase of the 1915 French offensive in the Champagne began in September, with a massed assault against the heavily fortified positions of the Navarin Farm and an innocent-looking patch of woods called the Bois Sabot, or Horseshoe Wood. Lying across a wide stretch of featureless ground, the Bois Sabot appeared only as a dark green clumping of scrubby trees and masses of secondary growth. Close up, however, the position was revealed for what it was: a natural defense bastion formed of thickly interlocking trees and branches in the form of a horseshoe, with the open end facing the level ground across which any attack would have to come. The Germans had laced the wood with thirty-two machine gun nests, countless mortars, quick-firing fieldpieces and *Minnenwerfer,* which threw canisters filled with scrap metal and one hundred pounds of explosive. Thick belts of barbed wire crisscrossed the woods in depth—most of it hidden in the heavy undergrowth; and the carefully sited machine guns were protected by bunkers made of reinforced concrete. To withstand the bombardment that always signaled the beginning of any French infantry assault, the German troops defending the Bois Sabot were provided with deep dugouts and trenches covered over with elephant iron and, in some places, concrete roofs. With justification, German Army engineers believed Horseshoe Wood impregnable against frontal attack.

The First Regiment of the Foreign Legion, among whose ranks numbered *Soldat* Edmond Genêt, had been selected to carry the Bois Sabot following the bloody and futile attacks launched earlier by Algerian *tirailleurs.* While the wood was taking a pounding from the French guns, the Legionnaires in the jump-off trenches could look out across the naked ground in front of them and see "the ghastly wrecks of the Colonials who lay before the German line, the sickly pallor of their hands and faces in awful contrast with the pools of blood around them." Then, at three-thirty in the afternoon, the whistles blew and the First Regiment scrambled from cover and began the assault against one of the most perfectly prepared defensive positions on the Western Front. Incredibly they went forward in parade ground formation.

Genêt recalled that they "started the advance in solid columns of fours, each section a unit. It was wonderful, that slow advance—not a waiver, not a break. Through the storm of shell the Legion moved forward. Officers in advance with the commandant at the head . . . inspired us all to calmness and courage. Shells were bursting everywhere. One lost his personal feelings. He simply became a unit, a machine."

Shrapnel raked through the close-packed columns of Legionnaires, who broke into a trot and dashed across the barren plain to get at the Horseshoe. To the howl of bursting shells and the terrifying explosions of the mines was added the crackle of the machine guns as they began systematically sweeping the thinning ranks. The murderous fire was "so thick that falling men were turned over and over and rolled along the ground like dead leaves before a late autumn wind." Genêt and an Italian volunteer ran far ahead of their section and found themselves advancing alone into the gale of lead. The other man lost his nerve, then his reason, then his life. Genêt somehow made it back to the remnants of his section. The attack had failed utterly, and at hideous cost. Of two companies alone, totaling 500 men, only 31 survived. Genêt's bravery went unrewarded; all his officers lay dead in the Bois Sabot and there was no one left to write him up.

Although this *enfant terrible* had much to learn concerning the wisdom of flying in winter weather that grounded even mallards, it was evident there was little he needed to be taught about carrying the war to the enemy.

Shortly after Genêt arrived, one of the squadron stalwarts departed. The long period of inactivity along the Somme worked in Pavelka a sailor's restlessness that he could satisfy only by a change of scene. When the call came for volunteers to fly in Macedonia, Pavelka instantly responded. He said goodbye to the Lafayette Escadrille on January 24, 1917, and sailed for Salonika from Marseille.

Pavelka's illusion of basking in the warm Aegean sun was rudely shattered. He was assigned to N.391, *Armée d'Orient*, and when he reported for duty at a barren, windswept field he was assigned living quarters in an abandoned airplane packing crate placed on high ground so the occasional torrential rains could not flood the interior. And it was so bitterly cold Pavelka found it impossible to write letters in his usual neat, regular script. Pavelka was given an 80 h.p. two-seater Nieuport 12 and assigned a voluble Greek observer who knew his way around the port city of Salonika well enough, but was almost totally ignorant of machine guns and their application to aerial combat. Pavelka patiently taught the Greek to field-strip and reassemble the Lewis gun, and he spent long hours at the butts teaching him the rudiments of gunnery. They later fought several inconclusive battles directly over the city of Salonika, and Pavelka thought the Germans "nervy" for daring to venture so far inside Allied lines. Pavelka was then the only American pilot serving with the Army of the Orient, but he found good company in the mélange of nationalities fighting there. Pavelka struck up a friendship with an excitable French *adjudant* named Sicot, who provided one memorable touch of comic relief in what was essentially a grim, humorless war.

Sicot flew off alone one day and jumped a German observation plane, which scooted away for home. Sicot turned 180 degrees and saw, to his horror, a second plane diving at him head-on from less than a hundred yards away. Sicot quickly lined up his sights and clamped down on the trips, pouring a staccato burst of fire into the enemy plane. Hit, the other plane slipped off on one wing. When the stricken plane flashed by, Sicot's satisfaction quickly turned to shock when he made out the blue-white-red stripes of the Royal Flying Corps painted on the rudder of the disabled craft. The British plane, a B.E.-2c, landed safely in an open field, and Sicot made a hurried landing nearby. He rushed up to the cockpit to peer into the drawn face of a British major named Herring, the newly appointed Commanding Officer of 17 Squadron. Herring was clutching a bloody arm; the engine had stopped a slug and the fuel tank had been pierced. Sicot kept slapping his forehead and saying over and over, "*Oo, la la! Oo, la la!*" Herring, who was not badly wounded, managed a smile and comforted Sicot by telling him he was a damn fine shot. Then he invited the French marksman to dinner as soon as he was out of the hospital. "Sicot," wrote Pavelka, "is to receive the Distinguished Flying Cross, and the major the *Croix de Guerre*. Everyone around here thinks it an excellent farce."

On the day that Edwin Charles Parsons, twenty-four, of Holyoke, Massachusetts, reported for duty with the Lafayette Escadrille, Lieutenant de Laage took him for a walk around the field. As they moved through snow flurries that whipped around their knees, de Laage gave Parsons the introductory briefing that he gave all new pilots.

"First," de Laage said warmly, "let me welcome you to the *Escadrille Lafayette.* As you are well aware, we are somewhat unique in this war, and as a consequence we receive a great deal of publicity in journals both in France and in your own country. We are, as you can imagine, quite proud of our record thus far, and we intend to sustain the traditions already set by those who have fallen in combat.

"I only ask that you fly well, that you fight hard and that you act as a man. I demand that you obey, explicitly and without hesitation, any orders I give when I am leading combat patrols. We have a well-provisioned bar which you are free to patronize when you see fit—but I will not tolerate a man who cannot hold his liquor. Drink as much as you think yourself capable of and still be able to perform your duty. Any man who drinks to the point where he cannot function as an efficient *chasse* pilot does not belong in this, or in any other squadron. Accept your share of the responsibility for upholding the good name of the squadron, and we shall get along quite well."

The brief talk, given without pomp or bluster, impressed Parsons deeply.

"Ted" Parsons had made his way to France the year before on the *Carpathia* in the capacity of assistant veterinarian, although he knew nothing about horses. Once in France, he volunteered to drive ambulances and shortly afterward was promoted to section chief. Although not tall, he was well-built and wore a snappy blue uniform cut by a good tailor. Cursed with an intemperate cough and missing the first two joints of his little finger of his trigger hand, Parsons' medical report was marked by waivers; two and a half years of warfare had taught the French that minor disfigurements or the inability to run a steeplechase had little to do with success in aerial combat.

Shortly after his arrival Parsons got into a conversation with Didier Masson, who casually mentioned that he had flown as a pilot in Mexico before the war in Europe had broken out. "That's funny," Parsons said, "so did I."

In late 1913 Parsons had run into a skinny, dark-skinned

individual called Jeff de Villa in the Sheldon Hotel in El Paso. De Villa was from Martinique, and was a pilot of sorts representing Raoul Madero, brother of the recently murdered President of Mexico. Francisco de Villa got it into his head he needed an air arm, and Madero was going to help him get one. Parsons had bummed a sufficient number of rides at Dominguez Field in Los Angeles to qualify himself as a pilot, although what the *Fédération Aéronautique Internationale* would have thought of his capability was another matter.

Parsons and de Villa cornered Madero in his hotel room, and over several whiskies closed the deal; the aviators would buy a plane and go to Mexico and teach de Villa's young officers how to fly. Parsons would hold the rank of captain and would draw $200 a month, while de Villa would become a major earning fifty dollars a month more than Parsons.

Several weeks later the aviators were in Ciudad Juárez waiting for the plane to come across the Rio Grande on a flatcar. They waited in Juárez for almost a week, "which time we used to get swanky uniforms and good hangovers." The plane that arrived in Juárez, knocked down and crated, had once been a Curtiss biplane, but repeated crashes and jury-rigged repairs had slowly altered its configuration until even its own designer wouldn't have recognized it. A broken main spar had been patched with scrap lumber and bailing wire, and a makeshift rear seat had been installed, none too securely, and the leading edge of the lower wing cut sharply into the back of the unfortunate who sat there.

Attached to the top wing just over the rear seat was a six-cylinder engine capable at times of developing 1200 r.p.m. and fed by a ten-gallon gravity feed tank just atop the crankshaft. Neither Parsons nor de Villa cared to attempt to fly the thing down to Chihuahua, so the plane was left crated and shipped south on its flatcar.

On the first test flight, the major and the captain got the contraption up to five hundred feet for a six-minute hop—cut short when two valves stuck, sending a shower of flames from the exhaust stacks. On the next flight they were able to reach 2000 feet, and the pilots were ready for their first students. Two uneasy-looking Mexican lieutenants showed up at the field and de Villa gave the first one a two-minute briefing on the facts of flight, strapped the student in the rear seat and took off in a great cloud of red dust down the field.

Parsons watched the old Curtiss stagger into the air and weave an erratic course over the desert. Several bracing wires had snapped and de Villa thought he was going to lose his wings. When the magneto quit, de Villa dead-sticked to a bumpy landing and his student lurched out, looking very green. He walked over to his comrade and uttered one word, "*Vámonos!*" And that was the last the major from Martinique and the captain from Holyoke saw of those, or any other, students for the Mexican Air Force.

Fearing loss of their pay, Parsons and de Villa talked their way down to Headquarters of the *Division del Norte* where they were to fly reconnaissance missions. The airplane, thanks to daily patching, held together for numerous flights over contested territory, but since Parsons could never tell one side from the other he was never too sure how valuable his reports were to the Villaistas. In the fall they were ordered to Zacatecas to help with a planned march on Mexico City by de Villa and several other revolutionary generals.

In Zacatecas, Parsons found a beautiful landing field on a high plateau overlooking a valley some two thousand feet below. With eagerness he and de Villa strapped themselves into the plane and revved up the engine, which, for once, was running perfectly. The ship rolled down the grass runway at 40 m.p.h. and sailed out over the edge of the plateau. Parsons hauled back on the stick, but nothing happened except the plane began to mush sickeningly downward as though the laws governing flight did not exist. The plane, engine running full out, fell flatly to the bottom of the valley. The landing was a sensation. The wheels pushed up through the wings, almost cracking Parson's elbows, the seats came unbolted and everything came apart except the wings and the power plant.

Parsons and de Villa walked back up to the field and hitched a ride into town. The mystery of the aborted flight was solved when Parsons noticed a sign on the railway station that explained everything. The sign read: ZACATECAS, ELEV. 8523 FEET. There had been nothing wrong with the airplane; they had tried to take off a full three thousand feet higher than its absolute ceiling.

Parsons, greatly chagrined, caught the train back to Chihuahua to buy spare parts for the smashed plane. While in the city he struck up a conversation with a German he knew who ran the small cigar store in the Palace Hotel. The German asked Parsons up to his room in the hotel, poured him a drink and told him to get out of the country. "Listen, Ted, my advice to you is not to go back to wherever your plane is, but to leave Mexico for good. Within a few months de Villa is going to get in a brawl with your country and you will have to fight Americans. You'll be in a hell of a fix."

It dawned on Parsons that his friend, a onetime Uhlan, was a German agent. He shipped the spare parts to de Villa and included a warning. Then Parsons packed his bags, put on civilian clothes and went back to El Paso. He learned later that de Villa had managed to get out of Mexico, but he never saw his German friend again.

Parsons' debut in the air war over the Western Front nearly provided the setting for his finale. Like all new pilots just assigned to an operational squadron, Parsons' attitude was compounded of brashness and fear—fear that he might not acquit himself nobly in the face of enemy guns. It is this fear that has driven countless inexperienced soldiers to expose themselves to dangers that older and wiser hands would avoid.

On a day when the weather was passable enough to allow flying, Captain Thénault gave permission to Parsons, Genêt and a new pilot named Hoskier to make a practice patrol on their own side of the lines; they could stay aloft as long as the weather and the fuel held out, but under no circumstances were they to approach the German lines. Thénault's manner reminded the three neophytes of a mother cautioning her children against straying from their own backyard and into that of the tough kids' next door. Filled with bravado, the pilots roared from the field at Cachy and headed north.

For an hour the three Nieuports flew back and forth behind their own lines and saw nothing whatsoever of interest, although the knowledge that they were actually flying at the Front—or nearly so—gripped them all. Over there, not three minutes away, was German territory, the lair of the hated Boche. It was too much to bear; the Americans swung the noses of their planes toward no man's land and soon found themselves in German territory. Now what? First of all, the formation drifted apart and the planes disappeared in the scattered clouds. Genêt and Hoskier sensibly turned around and flew back to Cachy. Parsons bored on toward Germany.

Looking over the side of the cockpit, he thrilled at the sight of five German two-seaters holding a steady formation 2000 feet below. Parsons tried to remember what his instructors back at Pau had told him. *Altitude?* He had an obvious advantage. *The sun?* He banked around until it was at his back. Everything else he had learned during the long months of training was forgotten, along with his commanding officer's recent orders. Lacking top cover, alone in enemy territory, facing suicidal odds, Parsons pushed the stick forward and dived to the attack.

He began firing while still five hundred yards away, and the German formation scattered like flushed quail to deploy in a combat circle. The German gunners opened up and proceeded to shoot Parsons' plane full of holes. Bullets zipped past his head, and he felt the dull thuds as slugs ripped through fabric to bury themselves in laminated wood. Parsons was firing into empty space, his hand clamped in a paralyzed grip on the trigger handle. The engine was roaring full out, the bracing wires were screaming like banshees and the Nieuport began vibrating so viciously Parsons feared it would shake itself to pieces. He flashed down past the tail of one of the deadly two-seaters, painted a garish green and yellow, and had a fleeting glimpse of "the observer's gun muzzles with red flames curling from their black mouths; behind them, the observer's grim white face and fur-clad body." Parsons now had only one thought: to get away from those spitting guns and back home to the safety of the field. He banked sharply to the south and out of range. Looking back, he saw the five two-seaters smoothly close up their formation and fly on unconcernedly.

Parsons leveled out and headed for Cachy. Just as his knees stopped quivering from side to side and he believed he would live to eat lunch, dark shadows passed over his eyes in quick succession. He jerked his head upward to see "huge black crosses, outlined in white, whirling propellers and dirty gray, oil-streaked bellies." Fear flooded over him in waves. He hunched himself down in the cockpit, hoping to make himself a smaller target. Despite the intense cold, sweat broke out on his forehead. He sat helpless, waiting for the enemy fire, but none came. Looking back over his shoulder, he saw why.

The Germans—they were three two-seaters—were pulling away, diving for home. Behind them, weaving in and out, firing short bursts, was a Nieuport. The plane flashed across Parsons' line of flight and he saw the Indian head insignia, but he had no idea who his rescuer might be. He watched, fascinated, as the Nieuport sliced down on the rearmost two-seater and poured fire into its fuselage. The two-seater fell away and dived out of control. Parsons flew on back to Cachy.

When his plane rolled to a stop, he sat in the cockpit for a few moments, then pushed up his goggles and wiped the sweat from his brow. Unstrapping himself, he climbed out and stepped down to the ground—promptly grabbing a strut to keep his legs from collapsing. His mechanic rushed up, thinking Parsons had been shot. The sound of a Le Rhône blipping like a Nieuport coming in for a landing caused both men to look up. The plane glided in and touched down smooth as glass. Parsons watched the pilot cut his switches and climb from the cockpit.

"I could stand by this time," said Parsons, "so I walked over to thank the man who had saved my life. As I approached, he raised his goggles and unstrapped his helmet. It was Lufbery, just back from leave. He had arrived at the field without warning, and when he had learned there was a patrol of newcomers out he had taken off almost immediately.

"Before I could blubber out my thanks, he proceeded to chew me out in that funny accent of his. He raked me over the coals for several minutes and called me six kinds of a fool. Then he said that I showed good spirit and that we should have a drink. We did, toasting my own blind luck and Lufbery's seventh Hun, which was soon confirmed."

Morane-Saulnier L.A. "Bullet" Scout

CHAPTER 10

ATTRITION

L'heure est venue! Confiance! Courage! Vive la France!
—GENERAL ROBERT NIVELLE

Living conditions at Cachy were considered unbearably primitive, especially by the Americans, whose love for warmth and adequate plumbing had not been noticeably dulled by a day-in, day-out contact with the French over the long months that lay behind. The news that the *Groupe* was leaving Cachy's ramshackle dwellings and the inhospitable climate of the Somme was loudly hurrahed. Eagerly searching maps, the pilots were further encouraged by the fact that the new destination, a place called Ravenel, near St. Just-en-Chaussée, was twenty-five miles closer to the Arc de Triomphe; in fact the outer limits of Paris could be reached in less than an hour south down the main road that led from St. Just to the Porte de la Chapelle. On the afternoon of January 26 the Nieuports and Spads climbed out over Cachy

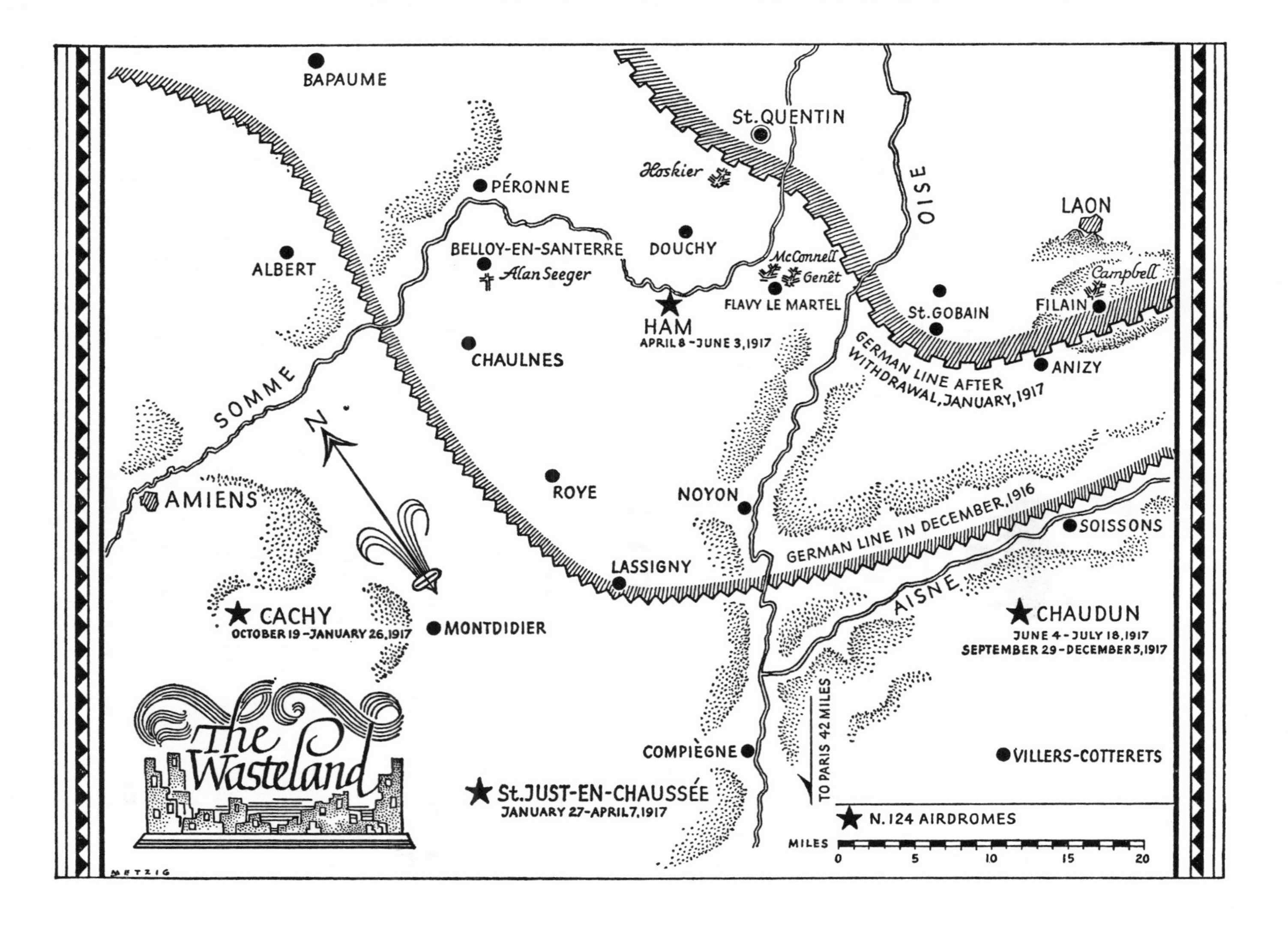
The Wasteland
BAPAUME
St. QUENTIN
Hoskier
PÉRONNE
OISE
LAON
BELLOY-EN-SANTERRE
Alan Seeger
DOUCHY
McConnell
Genêt
Campbell
ALBERT
HAM
APRIL 8 - JUNE 3, 1917
FLAVY LE MARTEL
St. GOBAIN
FILAIN
ANIZY
CHAULNES
GERMAN LINE AFTER WITHDRAWAL, JANUARY, 1917
SOMME
N
ROYE
NOYON
AMIENS
GERMAN LINE IN DECEMBER, 1916
SOISSONS
LASSIGNY
AISNE
CACHY
OCTOBER 19 - JANUARY 26, 1917
MONTDIDIER
CHAUDUN
JUNE 4 - JULY 18, 1917
SEPTEMBER 29 - DECEMBER 5, 1917
TO PARIS 42 MILES
COMPIÈGNE
VILLERS-COTTERETS
St. JUST-EN-CHAUSSÉE
JANUARY 27 - APRIL 7, 1917
N. 124 AIRDROMES
MILES
0
5
10
15
20
METZIG

Wood, the trees white with frost, and flew south to the new billet.

Disillusion was theirs. Where Cachy had offered barracks with perforated walls and leaking roofs, Ravenel offered no barracks at all. Pacing jerkily across the snow-swept field with a cold wind moaning around their ears, the pilots searched in vain for the familiar sheds with the friendly-looking stovepipes poking through the roofs; but the field at Ravenel was new and only three-fourths completed. Underground shelters had been built first, hangars next; last in order of priority were quarters for the pilots. They moved under the earth like badgers, sleeping on blankets smoothed out on the cold dirt floors of the bomb shelters. Wood fires were built—large ones at first—but the pilots were driven outside, their eyes streaming tears, by the suffocating smoke that boiled up in the nearly airless *abris*. For a week the pilots cursed and froze; then army carpenters, lashed on by the acid tongues of their sergeants, managed to erect a block of wood and tar-paper living huts. Genêt, whose enthusiasm could not be dampened, borrowed buckets of paint and brushes and proceeded to paint heroic murals that covered every square inch of the pasteboard that had been nailed up on the walls of the Escadrille barrack to keep out the wind. The wall nearest the stove that provided a semblance of heat in the "drawing room" area was splashed with the Indian head insignia done in garish colors; the others blazed with imaginative scenes of epic battles in which Fokkers, Alabatros and Hanoveranners were being blasted from the sky. The murals were good—too good—and eventually became a source of depression instead of the inspiration "the poor little dreamer" had intended.

Dud Hill came back from leave bringing a small crate carefully packed with quarter-inch-thick phonograph records. The hand-cranked gramophone was kept going late into the night scratching out *Poor Butterfly, Pretty Baby, Allah's Holiday.* Ukulele renditions were much in vogue in America, but the French found them "bizarre, barbaric." Music was a diversion for Lufbery, who would sit near the horn with a glass of cognac in his hand, allowing the jangling strains of Oriental recordings he bought in Paris to stir the coals of his memory. On the rare occasions when he spoke about himself he drew a rapt audience, absorbed in Lufbery's soft-spoken, fragmented recounting of the odyssey that had led him, finally, to war.

Raoul Lufbery could trace his American heritage back for several generations. His ancestors had settled in New York at the close of the Revolutionary War, the descendants remaining there until Lufbery's father emigrated to France shortly before the future fighter pilot was born. When his mother died, Lufbery was only a year old; his father placed him with a foster family in the Auvergne mountains. When he was five, his father remarried and returned to America, settling in Wallingford, Connecticut. Raoul was left in France.

The wanderlust infected Lufbery when he was nineteen. He quit a factory job at Clermont-Ferrand and set out to see the world. Three years later, having worked at odd jobs from Marseille to Cairo, Lufbery signed up as an ordinary seaman on a freighter out of Hamburg. He saved his pay and sailed to America to see his widowed father; his ship docked only hours after his father's had left for Europe, and they never saw each other again. Lufbery's trail followed an erratic course from New Orleans to San Francisco to the Philippines, thence into China, Japan and India. It was in Calcutta that he met Marc Pourpe, a man whose destiny was to become irrevocably linked with his own.

Pourpe was a young French pilot who earned his living by giving demonstration flights in a Blériot that he had once flown across the English Channel. Pourpe had lived for thirteen years in Suez and was as widely traveled as Lufbery. He had flown his Blériot in India, Annam, Indochina, Tonkin and Cambodia. European *colons* said of him: "His presence of a few months did more for France's influence than fifteen years of colonization."

Lufbery signed on as Pourpe's mechanic and the pair went first to China, then to Egypt, where Pourpe discussed the uses of aerial reconnaissance with Lord Kitchener. Together they worked out an itinerary covering the 2700 miles between Cairo and Khartoum. Lufbery followed or preceded Pourpe every step of the way. He sailed down the Nile on steamers and cargo rafts, plodded across the burning desert sand on swaying camels and endured unmerciful poundings aboard bump-gaited donkeys. And he walked many miles overland carrying a brutally heavy canvas bag filled with tools and canned rations. When the grueling trip was finished, so was the Blériot, and the two adventurers sailed for France to shop for another airplane.

They arrived to find Europe engulfed in war. Pourpe volunteered his services as a pilot, and his fame at home was such that he managed to have Lufbery assigned as his mechanic. With the devoted Lufbery in trail, Pourpe joined a reconnaissance squadron in September 1914. Within eight weeks Pourpe had logged seventy-eight hours behind the German lines, had been wounded and had twice brought back planes riddled with shrapnel. Despite his prewar fame and the dogged bravery he had shown, Pourpe remained a private. On December 1, he wrote to a friend in Paris admitting that he "liked making war, but these injustices really make me suffer." The letter was never mailed. The next day Pourpe took off in foul weather. Ice formed on the wings of his plane as he climbed up through the clouds in the bitter cold, and he crashed to his death.

By the summer of 1915 Lufbery had gained his wish of piloting his own plane across enemy lines, but after six months of routine observation work with VB.106 he was dissatisfied with the lumbering Voisins and gained admittance to the fighter school, then located at Le Plessis-Belleville. But at the controls of the sensitive little pursuit craft Lufbery proved ham-handed and awkward; he flew Baby Nieuports as though he were manhandling trucks across the sky. His instructors hinted that he was on the brink of washing out. The determination that had enabled him to trek across the Egyptian desert carried him through; he learned to relax at the controls, to caress the stick, not maul it, and on May 22, 1916, he was graduated. Nine months and one day later, Raoul Lufbery—factory hand, chocolate-maker, seaman, waiter, ticket-taker, wanderer, mechanic—stood on the field at Ravenel and grimaced in embarrassment as Commandant Féquant kissed him on both cheeks after pinning on his rough soldier's tunic the red silk ribbon and white enameled cross of the Legion of Honor.

In his capacity as caretaker of squadron morale, Bill Thaw had no peer. Observing that Whiskey's milky white, opaque blinded eye was having a depressing effect, he took up a collection to buy the mascot a custom-made glass eye to replace the original. In

Paris he began making the rounds of the oculists along the Champs-Élysées. Reception in the waiting rooms varied. The more urbane Frenchmen gazed noncommittally at the handsomely uniformed officer holding a leash to which was attached a nearly grown lion, lying beside Thaw's boots; others panicked and bolted through the door. The oculists reacted similarly; many were indignant, some sympathetic, but none would risk a hand to measure the lion for an eye. Thaw gave up and went back to the airdrome. He brought with him, however, two remarkable gifts. One was a handsomely made roulette table for the pilots' recreation, the other was a three-month-old female lion cub purchased at the Paris Zoo for a consolation prize. A few minutes after the rotund cub was placed on the floor to lap at a bowl of hot milk, she was christened; the name, *Soda,* was probably inevitable.

March of 1917 was the coldest on record. The mercury plunged to zero and stayed there. Cold alone, however, did not cancel scheduled patrols. The working day for a pilot began at 5:30 A.M. with a gentle, relentless shaking of one shoulder and the whispered voice of the faceless orderly hissing the dreaded words, *"C'est l'heure, monsieur. Il fait beau temps."* The pilots came awake like bears emerging from hibernation; pushing the mound of blankets and overcoats from them, cursing softly or groaning, they forestalled the moment of swinging their legs over the side of the cot and placing their feet on the bare, cold flooring. Reluctantly they reached for fur-lined boots and made the trip through the slumbering hut out to where the stars glittered in the cold, dark sky. Around the hangars fires blazed, heating the cut-down drums filled with castor oil; unless the oil was preheated it congealed in the reservoirs, making it impossible to start the engines.

In the mess tent they could hardly feel the coffee scalding their lips. Aloft, the pilots sat like frozen statues in the cockpits. They flew with one hand on the stick while beating the other on the top of a leg to restore circulation. When the stick hand froze it was pried loose finger by finger and was pounded on the other leg. This procedure was repeated at three-minute intervals for the duration of the patrol. But in the open, wind-lashed cockpits there was nothing that could be done to protect the feet and exposed portions of the face from frostbite. Ted Parsons froze a toe and couldn't walk for a week, and Genêt was put out of action when cold attacked his nose and one side of his face; the flesh swelled up grotesquely, turned white and the skin sloughed off.

Sudden snowstorms would blow up, blinding the pilots, scattering planes across the sky. A five-man patrol left Ravenel before noon one day, and only one pilot made it back to the field. Thénault dived through an opening in the clouds, with Soubiran following close behind. But when Soubiran came out of the dive, Thénault's plane had vanished.

"I suppose the captain was lost," Soubiran explained, "and Heaven knows I couldn't have helped him find the way. I found myself low over Cachy, our old hunting grounds. I set out for home and passed Montdidier all right, but the bad weather was forcing me right down to the ground. Over the end of our home wood I swung right and saw a black wall of cloud almost close enough to touch. I dove down to 300 feet, but the storm was right down on the ground and landing was out of the question. There remained but one thing—to climb.

"The storm was all around me and the snowflakes were dashing by and into my face. My goggles began to freeze over. I was shut into my machine as by a gray curtain. I could not tell at which angle I flew. All I could do was put my controls in center and watch the altimeter go up. Then I threw up my elbow to look at my compass; it was revolving, I was turning! I sat and endured something of hell and prayed very earnestly.

"For almost ten minutes I flew in the gray light you would find in a broken tomb. At 8000 feet I saw the blessed sun and the blue sky. I dropped down through a hole and onto the field at Mesnil-St. Georges, where I waited for better weather to come on home. I conceived a sort of affection for my ship; we had pulled it off together."

Parsons, having lost the rest of the patrol in the billowing muck, turned to his compass for guidance, only to discover that the liquid in which it floated was frozen solid, cracking the glass plate. He flew for an hour absolutely blind, never sure whether he was right side up or in which direction he was headed. Just at the point when his fuel was running out, he caught sight of a hole in the clouds and dived through, landing safely, but not knowing where. "I could have been twenty miles inside Germany, for all I knew. Figures walked toward me out of the mist, and one of the greatest thrills of the war was when a voice over my left shoulder broke the silence with a Cockney accent. I had landed behind the British lines south of Arras, fifty miles from home."

Genêt, who got up to 12,000 feet before breaking into the clear, got a bearing home, but the storm soon erased from view his landmarks and he knew only that he was flying south, and therefore away from the German lines. He kept on until he ran out of fuel, then managed to land in heavy mist some miles below Paris. Refueled, he waited until the mist lifted, then took off for home. Twenty minutes later, fog rolled up from the ground and he was lost again. He landed this time on an R.F.C. field east of Ravenel. He eventually made it back, but only after covering 270 unnecessary miles.

Captain Thénault fared best of all. After diving through the hole in the cloud, he roamed around in the lowering storm until he spotted a large park walled in with stone, which could only mean one thing, a château. Thénault set down in the park, stepped from the cockpit to be greeted by the landowner, and spent three days enjoying the hospitality before the weather cleared and he could return to Ravenel.

Rumors of the big spring "push" were all over France that March, rumors given substance by the increasingly heavy traffic rumbling up from the interior toward the Front. Jim McConnell, still ailing and partially crippled, packed his duffle and returned to the Escadrille. Four new pilots reported to Thénault shortly afterward: Stephen Bigelow, Walter Lovell, Edward F. Hinkle and Harold Buckley Willis.

Bigelow was known as "a 23-year-old, pleasure-loving near-graduate Boston playboy of several colleges." Bigelow quickly made himself popular on the first rainy day when he displaced Thénault at the keyboard of the rented piano, where he demonstrated a near-virtuoso talent.

Easy-going Walter Lovell, thirty-three, was a Harvard graduate and the most overtrained man in the Escadrille. He learned to fly on Blériots at Buc at a time when the graduation rate was maddeningly low and spent ten long months repeating courses usually finished in three. This excess air time paid dividends in piloting skill, and when losses in the Escadrille began to mount, Lovell was speedily made flight leader.

The younger pilots believed that thirty-three was relatively old to begin the exacting task of learning to survive as a fighter pilot; thus when Edward F. Hinkle reported for duty, the others thought there must have been some mistake: Hinkle was past his forty-second birthday, more than twice Genêt's age. This ancient had graduated from Yale and had studied design at the Beaux Arts in Paris. Despite a rugged physique, Hinkle had been forced to pull wires to gain admittance to flying school, where he performed creditably for a man that old. Inevitably he was called Grandpa by the others.

The biggest of the replacements was Harold Buckley Willis, who stood 6 feet 2 inches in his stockinged feet. Willis, another Harvard alumnus, was practicing architecture in his native city of Boston in 1915, when he quit to join an ambulance unit in France.[1] On one of Willis' first patrols he demonstrated that his passion for art could not be cooled by the demands of war.

Just before dawn, March 17, the telephone in Thénault's office began ringing. Thénault stumbled from sleep and picked up the receiver. The voice at the other end was hysterical with excitement—Zeppelins were at that moment headed for Paris, there to unleash terror on the city. Thénault slammed down the receiver and ordered up a patrol. Pilots were roused from slumber to struggle into their heavy flight clothing. They ran outside for the hangars. Parsons and Willis were the last two pilots to take off, and they headed for Compiègne, where the airship was supposed to pass before going on to Paris.

"None of us," said Parsons, "had had an opportunity to take a crack at a Zep before and we were keyed up. Willis and I arrived over Compiègne at the same time ready to do battle, but we saw that we were too late, the French antiaircraft had beaten us to it. The big gas bag lay on the ground a smoking tangle of twisted metalwork, surrounded by hundreds of curious *poilus*. Fasci-

[1] **One of Willis' passengers had been Kiffin Rockwell, wounded in the battle of Artois.**

nated, I circled around and around, gazing over the side of the cockpit at the wreckage. It got too damned cold to stay up, so I looked around for Willis thinking we could fly home together. He was nowhere to be seen, so I went on back to Ravenel to thaw out.

"An hour passed, and still no Willis. We were getting worried about the big lug. Had he run afoul of a German patrol? Had he flown across the lines and gotten lost? Was he somewhere up there fighting for his life? We didn't know. When the second hour approached, we sighed and gave him up. Too bad, we thought, he seemed such a hell of a fine man. Then the unmistakable sound of a rotary engine brought us all running back outside. There was Willis' Nieuport coming in for a landing. We rushed out to see if he had been shot up, but his plane was untouched. We asked him where the hell he had been. He replied casually in deep, cultured accents that having seen there was no need for his services to combat Zeppelins, he took what he called 'the splendid opportunity' to fly to Chartres—nearly a hundred miles to the south—to get an aerial view of the cathedral there. He walked across the field to the barrack to warm up, still expounding on the glories of Gothic architecture." [2]

Jim McConnell refused to stay grounded, despite the pleadings of Thénault and the pilots. He could walk little better than before his stay in the hospital, and the aching stiffness had reached to his neck, rendering him capable of turning his head barely a few degrees to either side; this was potentially the most dangerous result of his crash months before. Unable to swivel his head, to peer straight up, to see behind his shoulders, McConnell might as well have been wearing horse blinders. He nonetheless insisted on flying his patrols.

The weather was far from promising on the morning of March 19, but by ten the ceiling had lifted to permissible heights; dirty

[2] The Zeppelin futilely sought after by the Escadrille patrol had not been headed for Paris. The Zeppelin, L-39, was one of five sent out to bomb London and turned back after encountering 40 m.p.h. gales. L-39 was, in fact, drifting helplessly over France with dead engines when shot down by anti-aircraft fire. French ground controllers, of course, had no way of knowing this when the patrol was ordered up.

gray clouds driven along by sharp winds scudded across the field, but these were high enough. Parsons, Genêt and McConnell bundled up and started for their planes, chatting and wisecracking as they walked across the field. Parsons and Genêt climbed nimbly into the cockpits, but McConnell could not make it. His anxious mechanics moved in and helped him ease his bulk painfully into the bucket seat. The engines were revved up, pilots carefully watching the tachometers. With a wave of the hand, each pilot signaled for the chocks to be pulled and the three Nieuports bumped across the field and rose into the air. Moments later, Parsons' oil line clogged and the cylinders seized. He put his nose down and glided to a forced landing a mile and a half away. He climbed out of the cockpit and watched McConnell and Genêt disappear into the clouds.

The two Americans crossed the lines and veered to the northeast of Ham, headed for St. Quentin. Over Douchy, in scattered clouds, McConnell discovered a pair of German observation craft flying toward France, some distance above. He started climbing, with Genêt following closely behind. A few minutes later McConnell's plane disappeared in a cloud. Genêt kept climbing until he reached 7000 feet, where he began stalking one of the two-seaters that loomed up out of the mist. The two planes began circling, with Genêt on the inside. The German gunner opened up first and a center-section strut exploded in Genêt's face. Then an aileron control coupling was struck, part of the slug ricocheting into Genêt's face, gouging out flesh. Bullets hit the upper wing and peppered the fuselage.

Genêt banked away from his opponents and lost them in the clouds. Stunned, the wound in his face burning like fire, he flew the plane with one hand while he tried to staunch the flow of blood with a silk scarf. He flew on down looking for McConnell. The sky was empty of planes. Genêt flew around for a quarter of an hour, but all he could see were burning villages below and clouds above. Bursting shrapnel fired from the ground reached for his riddled plane, and with the wing dangerously near to snapping off, Genêt gave up the search and flew home through a haze of blood and tears.

It was three days before the Escadrille learned the fate of the missing pilot. "We were sitting around the big table in the barrack playing roulette," recalled Parsons, "with the set Thaw had brought back from Paris, when word came about Jim. Bill was playing banker that afternoon, and the only sounds in the hut were the clicking of the little ball and Bill's voice droning *Faites vos jeux . . . vingt-trois, rouge . . . faites vos jeux.* Then the door to the hut suddenly burst open and we all looked up, startled, and saw de Laage standing in the doorway. He stood there, silent, with a godawful expression of unbearable sorrow and pain on his face. Finally he said, 'They have found him. Jim is dead . . . one of the best—' Unable to finish, he turned from the door and walked back outside. The little ball clicked into place and the wheel slowly stopped revolving. As one man, we scraped our chairs back and went to our separate rooms, where we stayed for the rest of the afternoon."

McConnell's body, sprawled beside the twisted junk that had been his airplane, was found by French troops. He had been hit by several bullets, any one of which could have killed him. The Germans had stripped the corpse of identity papers, wristwatch, rings, money and clothes—including his shoes. The plane had impacted going full throttle, and identification was possible only from the number, 2055, painted on the rudder. McConnell was buried where he fell, near Flavy-le-Martel, six miles east of Ham, just behind the St. Quentin Canal.

McConnell's last letter, found among his effects, willed Ted Parsons his sleeping bag and concluded:

"My burial is of no import. Make it as easy as possible on yourselves. I have no religion and do not care for any service. If the omission would embarrass you, I presume I could stand the performance.

"Good luck to the rest of you. God damn Germany and Vive la France."

McConnell's death crushed Genêt's spirit. He shunned all offers of sympathy, rejected the idea that McConnell's fall was anybody's fault but his own. He refused to turn himself into the hospital to have his face wounds treated, and his features grew puffy and his complexion turned sallow. He became morose and edgy, and spent his free time alone, brooding. To "Dear Little Mother" in Ossining, Genêt wrote in a neat tiny hand: "My blood boils and thirsts after those accursed Huns. They're brutes and fiends and daily they grow worse. I'll get a Boche yet, or more than one, to avenge poor Mac. I've already been told I was reckless in the air over the lines, but after this I vow I'll be more reckless than ever, come what may . . ."

Throughout the month of March 1917 the question *When?* ran through the minds of the Escadrille pilots like the title of a familiar and disturbing refrain. There was no longer any doubt that America was finally coming into the war; and it was manifest that the much-heralded—too much, it seemed—French spring offensive was nearing the end of its gestation period. And on their destinies both eventualities would have profound consequences: one, delayed; the other, immediate. The two totally unrelated events occurred within ten days of each other.

It was nearly eight o'clock in the evening of April 6 when word was flashed to Group Headquarters at Ravenel that President Wilson had signed the declaration of war against Germany. Men flooded from the warmth of the barracks and began dancing and shouting in the open air, their faces bathed in red, blue and yellow from the Verey lights drifting down from the sky. The lingering cold drove them back indoors, where the celebration—and the speculation—went on into the night. The pilots assumed and accepted as a certainty that within a few days at most their government would be calling for them to help forge America's air arm. They waited nearly a year.

In the avalanche of copy that poured from the presses immediately after Wilson's proclamation, the Lafayette Escadrille was not overlooked. American journalism rose to the occasion to provide fresh examples of ludicrousness. The following "eyewitness account" became a squadron classic:

> "Uncle Sam is with us, boys! Come on! Let's get those fellows!" These were the stirring words of Captain Georges Thénault, the valiant leader of the *Escadrille Lafayette*, upon the morning news was received that the United States had declared war upon the rulers of Potsdam. For the first time in history, the Stars and Stripes of Old Glory were flung to the breeze over the camp, in France, of American fighting men. Inspired by the sight, and spurred into instant action by the ringing call of their French

> captain, this little band of aviators from the U. S. A. sprang into their trim little biplanes. There was a deafening roar of motors, and soon the last airman had disappeared in the smoky haze which hung over the distant battle-lines . . .
>
> Far back of the German lines, they encountered a formidable battle-squadron of the enemy. Heedless of risk, they swooped down on their foe. One of our boys was attacked by four Germans at the same time. One he sent hurtling to the ground 15,000 feet below. He caused a second to retire disabled.
>
> Another American accounted for another in a running fight that lasted for more than a quarter of an hour.
>
> A third man, his biplane riddled with bullets, succeeded by a clever ruse in decoying two pursuers, bent on his destruction, to the vicinity of a cloud where several of his comrades were lying in wait for further victims. A moment later, both Germans were seen to fall earthwards spinning like leaves in that last terrible dive of death.
>
> These boys are Yankee aviators. They form the vanguard of America's aerial forces. We need thousands of others just like them.

The day following America's entry into the war was moving day for *Groupe de Combat* 13, and no epic struggles were waged by the pilots of the Lafayette Escadrille. However, an American flag *was* carried across the lines, a small one given to Ted Parsons by his mechanic, Félix Henriot. The handkerchief-sized banner was tied to a cabane strut and Parsons flew it inside German territory—the first Stars and Stripes to make the trip—and brought it back tattered and raveled from the wind.

A story in the New York *Tribune* capriciously transferred Thaw to piloting two-seaters, dressed him "in the khaki uniform of the American air service," and "with the Stars and Stripes fluttering side-by-side with the Tricolor, underneath his French battle plane," had Thaw taking off "twenty minutes before the charge of the infantry." The story related how Thaw encountered a Fokker over the lines, but by "mounting in swift spirals," managed to overtake the enemy and send him down in flames. Twenty-five miles behind the German lines, Thaw's engine quit and he landed in a plowed field just outside a small town. Villagers rushed out and began pelting Thaw with questions. "I am an American aviator serving with the French," he replied. "Didn't you know America has declared war on Germany? Here is my

American flag." This was news to the villagers, and "many men and women sought to embrace him, others gave him flowers." Within ten minutes, Thaw's observer had fixed the engine, and "as the last screw was tightened into place," a villager rushed up with the alarming information that a large German patrol was approaching. "*Sauve qui peut!*" he shouted. "*Les boches y sont!*" Taking him at his word, Thaw gathered up his flag and took off for home.

For weeks the new Commander in Chief of the French armies, General Robert Nivelle, fifty-eight, had been boasting to politicians and *poilus* alike that his grand spring offensive would end the war. An aura of invincibility hung over Nivelle's head since the spectacular reconquest of Fort Douaumont the previous autumn, and Nivelle's suave assurances fell on eager ears. These same optimistic utterances fell also on alert enemy ears; on March 14 the Germans began to withdraw silently to the iron-and-concrete Hindenburg Line. The withdrawal shortened the German front by nearly twenty-five miles, thus freeing thirteen divisions, which were added in a defensive posture in the area where the offensive was expected. The Germans brought up more guns, prepared deeper dugouts, sited new machine gun nests, spun fresh barbed-wire webbing, and sat down to await the coming of Nivelle.

For the approaching offensive, *Groupe de Combat* 13 was attached to the French Fifth and Tenth armies, and the Lafayette Escadrille was assigned a new role: aerial reconnaissance. From Ravenel, the combat group—now numbering five squadrons with the addition of N.88—moved thirty-two miles northeast to an abandoned German airdrome at Eppeville, just on the outskirts of Ham. Again they moved into a wasteland. The departing Germans had scorched every square yard of ground they had given up; fruit trees had been wantonly cut down or ringed, wells poisoned—sometimes by dropping a cadaver to the bottom—buildings razed, roads torn up, villages put to the torch. A pall of smoke hung low to the ground and the smell of putrefaction was everywhere.

Area familiarization flights were scheduled for the morning of April 8, but a series of misfortunes struck a third of N.124's aircraft from the operational list before the morning was well under way. "Grandpa" Hinkle completed a circuit of the field and landed heavily on the right wheel, which sheared off. The lurching Nieuport dragged along the ground on the axle and right wing tip, and when it skidded to a stop the lower wing was in splinters. The plane was dragged away. Willis had his armorer load up the Vickers gun for a firing test. He ran the engine up to combat r.p.m. and squeezed the trigger. The plane rattled and vibrated and Willis shook with recoil as the propeller disappeared in flying splinters. When Willis stopped the engine, the armorer commented, somewhat unnecessarily, "*Monsieur,* the synchronizer does not work." Walter Lovell got into his plane and started the engine. It roared briefly, then stopped with a sickening clatter as it seized. The plane was towed away for a new power plant. Genêt was rolling down the field preparatory to takeoff when a piston rod sheared off, grinding up a cylinder. His plane too was towed off, making the way clear for a new pilot named Kenneth "Siwash" Marr, a mature, solid, tough former Alaskan sourdough.

Marr got off all right and circuited the field without difficulty. Coming in, however, his wheels caught up in some twisted railroad tracks at the end of the field. The Nieuport somersaulted, skidded upside down and came to rest with a crash on the opposite side of the railroad embankment. Marr was pulled from the wreckage with only bruises, but the plane was written off the books. Thénault, watching his supply of aircraft dwindle, called off flying for the morning.

After lunch, de Laage decided to try to break the jinx. He got off the field in a tearing climb and zoomed upward, heading for the balloon line. He reached the tethered, swaying bags in time to witness an uneven struggle between a solitary Nieuport and four German fighters; the Nieuport pilot was doing what he could against odds to keep a balloon from being flamed, but was being driven lower to the ground with each maneuver. De Laage, with the advantage of altitude and surprise on his side, plunged down on top of the Germans and shot two of them from the sky. The double kills were confirmed, and de Laage was later named *Chevalier* in the Legion of Honor.

By early 1917, Army and Army Group commanders were utilizing their fighter aircraft strength for three primary roles:

Defensive, which placed the fighters on their own side of the lines in order to intercept enemy observation planes and thus preserve secrecy of movement and intention; Offensive, in which squadron and even group sweeps were carried out inside enemy territory to seek and destroy whatever hostile aircraft were found, and Contact, that saw the fighters roaring at suicidally low altitudes to discover new German positions and troops-on-the-move—tactical targets the high-flying, slow-moving observation planes sometimes took overlong to ferret out. Subject to merciless machine-gunning and rifle fire from the ground, having no room for maneuver or escape and thus easy prey to enemy fighters overhead, pilots universally hated this low work more than any other. It was this kind of job that was assigned to the Escadrille during the week preceding the Big Push. Thaw made of it a specialty.[3]

First sortie was always at dawn, with the sun rising at his right shoulder to burst into a brassy glare in the eyes of German gunners crouched in their holes. Once clear of the field, Thaw's wheels were seldom higher than a hundred feet from the ground, rising and falling to hug the contours of the earth flashing past his wings. Through the blur of the propeller he kept his eyes focused 200 yards ahead, which allowed four seconds to identify and locate a target on squared map (kept strapped to his leg) before passing it directly overhead. From dawn to dusk Thaw raced over crumpled villages, the scattered rubble of farms, shattered woods, drained and sandbagged canals, smashed churches and new trenches hacked from the torn earth; he flew so low he made out the startled features of the white, upturned faces underneath the coal-scuttle helmets. He looked into the black muzzles winking and spitting red flame, felt the lead smacking into his speeding plane. He sought out hidden machine gun nests, troop concentrations, pillboxes, secreted artillery—anything that might stand in the way of the advance. When feasible, he saved valuable time by landing bare yards away from brigade or even battalion headquarters to deliver his marked-up map so that the targets could be dealt with immediately by artillery. Often, he had

[3] Rifle fire was not to be lightly dismissed. To cite perhaps the most ironic example, on July 26, 1918, Major Edward Mannock, the R.A.F.'s virtuoso ace with seventy-three confirmed victories, was shot down and killed by a random shot fired by a German infantryman.

the satisfaction of listening to a barrage being called down on a target he had flown over less than a quarter of an hour before. Thaw returned from these dirty, unglamorous missions red-eyed with fatigue, but his hands never shook to betray a case of nerves stretched to the breaking point. Legend had it he was born without any.

Lufbery always volunteered to be among those flying top-cover for Thaw, but once the low-level work was done for the day, he went hunting alone. On April 8, he jumped a two-seater across the lines and forced it to land intact in a cratered field. Five days later he pounced on two more, and after a stiff fight shot one of them spinning through the clouds. A French forward observation post confirmed that the German had smashed heavily into the ground, and that made eight for Lufbery.

To the east, where the main blow of the Nivelle offensive was due to fall, the muttering of the guns rose to drumfire pitch. Standing on the field at the first hint of dawn on April 16, clusters of pilots and mechanics of Combat Group 13 watched the distant horizon redden with the flashes of artillery fire as a tornado of shelling fell along the Chemin-des-Dames. Genêt and Lovell were the first up that morning, but returned after an uneventful flight. Lovell commented on Genêt's sunken eyes and wax-like complexion and suggested that he turn in for the rest of the day. Genêt snapped out a no, and brooded around the field, listening to the bombardment. That afternoon, with the offensive well under way and the squadron back to offensive work, two-man patrols were kept shuttling back and forth from Ham to the region of St. Quentin. At 2:30 P.M. Willis Haviland got ready for a flight with Lufbery, but was told by his mechanic that his engine needed adjustment. Haviland asked Genêt if he could borrow his plane for the patrol, but Genêt refused and got in the cockpit himself to fly with Lufbery.

The ceiling dropped and the two Americans were forced below 5000 feet as they approached German antiaircraft concentration in the woods near St. Quentin. This battery was the terror of every man who flew over it; the gunners were crack shots who used not only 77mm shrapnel, but 105mm high-explosive shells whose concussion alone could destroy an airplane.

Lufbery and Genêt were embroiled in a sea of fire-centered clouds of black smoke; ringing detonations slammed against their eardrums and their fragile planes were tossed in the sky like corks. Lufbery shot a glance over his shoulder in time to see Genêt's Nieuport bracketed by three bursting shells. Immediately Genêt banked away and headed for home. Lufbery banked around to follow, but after seeing that Genêt maintained a straight and level course for three or four minutes, turned back again to finish the patrol alone.

What happened next was observed by French *poilus*. They watched Genêt's plane snap into a vicious spin from about 4000 feet with the engine still running full out. One wing snapped off, and the fuselage hurtled earthward with the sound of an express train. It tore into a hard-packed road doing 200 m.p.h., burying the engine five feet into the ground. Genêt lay crumpled on the ground, looking like a bag of bloody laundry. Had he been mortally wounded by shrapnel? Had he—as many believed—fainted in the air? Nobody ever knew. In any event, he was the first American citizen killed at the Front after the United States' declaration of war. Could he have known, this distinction undoubtedly would have gone far to erase the secret shame he carried with him to his death.[4]

The funeral was held at Ham on a dismal day that threatened rain. As Thénault closed the prayer book over the plain pine box the heavy clouds parted and a brilliant shaft of sunlight burst from the sky and fell across the bier. An instant later the dark curtain closed. The phenomenon was termed by Thénault "a benediction from heaven."

Hoskier, who had joined the Escadrille in December, fell heir to Genêt's only legacy—a misshapen runt named Archie, offspring

---

[4] At the time of his death Genêt was listed as a deserter from the U. S. Navy. A seaman aboard the U.S.S. *Georgia* in August 1914, he sought to buy his way out, but failed. On leave in Washington, he obtained a passport on a spurious pretext and sailed for France. His name was cleared after the war by the Secretary of the Navy, Josephus Daniels, who wrote Genêt's mother praising her son: "I myself am honored in having the privilege of declaring that the record of Edmond Clinton Genêt, ordinary seaman, United States Navy, shall be considered in every respect an honorable one."

of de Laage's mongrel bitch, Miss. The mutt wheezed with distemper and limped cruelly from having been hit by a motorcycle, but the balding (he was only twenty-three) Hoskier fixed up a box in the squadron's hangar for Archie, and shyly laughed off the suggestion that the dead man's dog would bring bad luck.

For some time Hoskier had been eyeing the squadron gunnery trainer, a Morane Parasol; he mentioned to Willis that he "could really do some fighting" in the Parasol, if he had the chance. Four months had dragged past since he began his career as a combat pilot, but a victory had eluded him. He somehow reasoned that the Parasol might bring him luck. More experienced pilots pointed out that although the plane had been admirably suited for the reconnaissance role it had performed in 1915 and in 1916, it was no match for the Albatros D-III fighters the Germans were then using.

These sleek, shark-like single-seaters were powered with 160 h.p. Mercedes in-line water-cooled engines that drove them to 110 m.p.h., and they had an initial rate of climb of a thousand feet per minute. Armed with twin Maxim guns—and when flown by good pilots—they were formidable opponents indeed.

Verdicts on the 70 m.p.h. Parasol's handling characteristics ranged from "sweetest flying ship at the Front," to "tricky, treacherous beast you have to fly every minute—*or else.*" Hoskier determined to find out for himself, knowing that the Parasol was soon going to be returned to the depot. He approached Thénault and pleaded for permission to fly it on one offensive patrol. He would take with him, he said, de Laage's orderly, Jean Dressy, a qualified aerial gunner. Thénault gave in and told Hoskier he could accompany one of the regular patrols.

Hoskier's chance came a week after Genêt's death. On the morning of April 23, he and Dressy climbed into the high-winged monoplane and took off to follow Thaw, Haviland and Willis over enemy territory. Hoskier trailed the others all the way past the line and to St. Quentin; the Parasol's poor performance barely enabled him to stay within a half mile of the faster Nieuports. Over St. Quentin they were forced to fly through nether fringes of cumulus; goggles and windscreens misted over, and in the ghostly translucence the planes appeared as indistinct gray shapes bobbing up and down, skidding this way and that, in a white sea. Suddenly darker shapes flashed through the mist, noses winking flame. A lurking gaggle of Albatros had jumped them from high up. The fighting was confused, sporadic. The Americans climbed into the clouds, where in the dark wetness they lost the Germans—and each other. Three Nieuports came out on top of the cloud cover, miles apart; but the Parasol had vanished.

Somewhere in the murky half-light, Hoskier had fastened the Parasol on the tail of a diving Albatros; together they plunged through the mist, Dressy working the Lewis gun. When they streaked beneath the cumulus and into the clear, ground observers saw two or three other Germans riding the tail of the Parasol, which was caught up in a web of tracers. The broad, fragile-looking wing of the French plane tore loose from its moorings to flutter lazily into the sky, but the fuselage plunged earthward like a comet for several thousand feet before disintegrating in a spray of splintered wood, jagged metal and shredded fabric. Flames licked at the bits and pieces, but there wasn't enough left of the airplane to make a good bonfire.

Retribution came quickly. The following day Lufbery increased his score to nine confirmed, by blowing a German plane out of the sky. Two days later the Escadrille victory tally rose to twenty-four when the offensive patrol collided head-on with a German counterpart over no man's land. The battle was fought in broken clouds and the close-knit formations were split into packets of two and three fighters wildly climbing, diving and zooming through the scattered clouds, emerging into open pools of blue sky, there to snap out frenzied bursts of fire. The battle was "like a frontier affair in the Wild West, with clouds instead of rocks for cover, and machine guns instead of Winchesters for weapons." Chouteau Johnson bushwhacked an Albatros he caught breaking into the clear, blasted it at close range for his first and last kill of the war. Haviland, the "Beau Brummell," also got his first by waylaying another Albatros, which he sent flopping to earth. The fight ended as abruptly as it had begun. The Germans had been routed and the Escadrille patrol returned intact, flushed with success.

Two days later Thaw took Haviland for a late-afternoon flight over the happy hunting grounds of St. Quentin, where they flushed a two-seater headed for home. The Americans hurtled down and Thaw's first long, hammering burst slammed into the surprised occupants of the reconnaissance plane, which fell off and slipped and skidded through the air to crash just southeast of the ruined town. French artillery observers clocked its fall at six-thirty.

But despite unprecedented help from the air, the Nivelle offensive, upon which so much of the hope of France depended, had failed disastrously. On the eve of the battle, Nivelle told his troops, by then keyed to fever pitch, "The hour has come!" For a depressingly large number of them, it was all too true. At Zero Hour, nearly a quarter of a million men wearing the horizon blue of the French infantry rose cheering from their trenches to advance over the barren ground evacuated by the enemy. The massed waves of *poilus* began the assault at a fast walk that soon changed to a quick, jogging gait so as not to fall too far behind the rolling barrage that swept ahead of them. For a few delirious moments it seemed that all opposition had been beaten down, that the advance would go as they had been told. Then suddenly their cheers were drowned in a hail of high explosive shells that engulfed them, in a terrible scything fire from thousands of machine guns firing from shell-proof bunkers. Entire companies melted away before the withering blast of fire that swept down from the long crest of the Chemin-des-Dames. German gunners methodically traversed the heated barrels of the heavy Maxim guns back and forth across the swaying lines of French infantry until the slopes were carpeted with writhing figures. Those who reached the barbed wire were shot while they struggled to cut their way through. Here and there the fury of the French assault reached the limited objectives set for companies, platoons, but the great blue tide lapping at the crest swiftly receded and faded away. By the end of the first day, on a front of barely thirty miles, French casualties reached the shocking total of 125,000 men killed, wounded and missing. Most historians agree that on this first day the French Army was broken; but Nivelle kept the futile attempt to dislodge the Germans going, and the offensive—crippled and half-hearted—butted its way into May.

Although the main fury of the ground battle was being spent east of the patrol sector assigned to Combat Group 13, the

Germans had plenty of air power west of the Chemin-des-Dames to oppose fighter penetrations of its air space on the western end of the Hindenburg Line. Following the lacing handed them by the Escadrille in late April, the German squadrons opposite stiffened and the Americans found it difficult to fight their way home in one piece.

Parsons—now a veteran of four months—and Lovell jumped a two-seater near Moy, but instead of falling easy victim, the Germans battled the two Americans all the way down to the ground, where fire became so hot the Escadrille pilots were forced up to safer altitudes. At 12,000 feet Parsons' plane was knocked sideways through the sky by a bursting shell fired by a German battery at La Fère. Parsons' stomach rose up within him when he heard the splitting, cracking noise as an interplane strut wrenched itself loose from the wings and shot away into the slip-stream. He gingerly nursed the plane back to Ham.

The following day Doc Rockwell got separated from the formation and was bounced by an Albatros that chased him from 15,000 down to 6000 feet, firing short, murderously accurate bursts all the while. Rockwell kept kicking his rudder bar to throw off the German's aim, but felt his plane shudder as slugs repeatedly struck the fuselage. Rockwell put his nose down and dived away from the German—normally a fatal maneuver—but by then the Albatros pilot had exhausted his ammunition. When Rockwell climbed out of his Nieuport the first thing he did was to count the bullet holes in his plane; there were twenty-seven of them on either side of the cockpit, and Rockwell never understood how he had not been killed.

The offensive died, leaving a shambles of the French Army and ruining its creator. Robert Nivelle was fired, replaced by the more cost-conscious Pétain. Mutinies broke out in no fewer than fifty-four French line divisions, and when the courts-martial were at an end at least fifty-five men were shot. The Hindenburg Line remained unshaken, the Germans still looked down on the Aisne Valley from the seemingly impregnable barrier of the Chemin-des-Dames. The sixty days of labor on that part of the Front were at an end for Combat Group 13; the Lafayette Escadrille had sustained casualties, but its pilots had dealt harder losses to the enemy. They were professionals, now, growing in competency as well as in numbers. Ground leadership was still—and always would be—the weak link, but this deficiency was to a great extent being made up for by high morale and steadily increasing individual combat experience of those who survived. Bill Thaw, who had virtually replaced Thénault as Air Commander, was slowly welding the pilots into a coordinated fighting unit.

Never discussed, but always remembered, was McConnell's solidness, his booming laugh, the fact that he would have been married (to a girl he met in Paris) in the spring; Genêt's quizzical, chipmunk expression, his almost child-like outrage at his country's aloofness during the dark and uncertain winter. ("I can't see," he said uncomprehendingly, "how any genuine, self-respecting American can feel justified in holding his head up any more. Don't they know anything about the invasion of Belgium, the submarine warfare against their own countrymen and all the other ruthless deeds which all neutral countries, headed by the United States, long ago should have risen up and suppressed and which, because of the Administration's 'Peace at any Price' attitude, have been left to increase. Damn the Boches! I hope and pray I can live long enough to make them realize there's one American who refuses to remain neutral in the face of their confounded audacities.")

They remembered Hoskier's gentle, young-old face, the way he quietly sought advice on how best to gain the advantage over an opponent in the air, and how his father—then head of the Norton-Harjes Ambulance Corps in Paris—had stood in the makeshift morgue at Ham where his son lay in the wooden box that, without warning, began to leak blood on the concrete floor. The sounds were terrifyingly loud, like the steady *drip-drip-drip* from a stalactite in the unlighted hollowness of a cavern—but the older man had only turned away to walk through the door into the spring sunshine.

These men had died in the expected manner—in combat against an armed enemy—and their loss, though keenly felt, was accepted along with every other unpleasantness of war. But what happened next at Ham, and only a week before they were to leave, stunned them all in its senseless tragedy.

The field at Ham dictated a quick-climbing takeoff with a sharp bank to the left as the airplane rose into the air; the tiny village of Eppeville was adjacent to one end of the airdrome, and engine failure on takeoff could drop the airplane in the town square. The problem was worsened by the spring thaw and occasional rains that coated the field with a muddy gruel, forcing the pilot to slam the rudder back and forth in an effort to keep the takeoff roll in something approaching a straight line. Although takeoffs were sometimes ludicrous in appearance, they were nonetheless dangerous in execution; no time in an airplane is as critical as when it is struggling to become airborne, straining for the critical speed necessary to give the pilot control over its flight attitude. Every takeoff is an adventure, but at Ham they were calculated risks as well.

Few pilots can resist the temptation to sit at the controls of an aircraft different from the one they habitually fly, and if given the opportunity almost none can stifle the urge to take it into the air. And so when one of the rarely seen Morane Monococque single-seat fighters appeared at Ham, it aroused great curiosity. The bullet-shaped fuselage with the oversized spinner, the single broad, flat wing braced from underneath, the small triangular rudder and the open cockpit offering unexcelled upward and peripheral visibility—all promised the same exciting flight characteristics built into racing planes, which the Morane greatly resembled. Landing speed was high, the stall point unpredictable and the longitudinal stability poor, but the sight of the rakish-looking mid-winged Morane—so different from the familiar Nieuports and the newer Spads—aroused in Lieutenant de Laage an irresistible urge to master its eccentricities. A superb pilot, buoyantly confident, de Laage flew with the same nonchalant skill that had earned him unstinted praise for horsemanship in the 14th Dragoons. When he stepped jauntily into the cockpit of the Morane on the afternoon of May 23, he doubtless believed he would have as little trouble taming the 110 h.p. fighter as he would have had in settling a two-year-old gelding.

A crowd gathered to watch, for de Laage was famous for hair-raising takeoffs. He strapped his helmet tightly under his chin, lowered his goggles and expertly flicked switches while the propeller was pulled through. The Le Rhône started with a puff of blue smoke shooting from the cowling, then settled down to its clattering roar. De Laage ran it up to full r.p.m. and waved for the chocks to be pulled. The mechanics ducked out of the way as the Morane gathered speed and rolled down the field spraying carbonized castor oil and gouts of mud in its wake. To watchers on the ground, it seemed that de Laage had barely got the tail up when he hauled back on the stick and zoomed upward in a dangerously steep turn.

Then, at 150 feet the roar of the engine stopped abruptly. The Morane fell off on one wing and tumbled into the ground with a sickening crash. An ambulance began to roll down the field in the trail of pilots and mechanics who ran slipping and sliding toward the wreckage. De Laage had been crushed in the fall. He was already dead when they pulled him from the cockpit and laid him gently on the ground.

The man who had so often wept openly and unashamedly at the death of others, was in turn wept over by those who asked: How can we ever replace him?

Spad S-7

CHAPTER 11

REPLACEMENTS

Of all the vexing problems facing Georges Thénault, none was as easily solved as filling the vacancies in the Escadrille created by the painful operational losses, or of bringing the squadron up to the strength required by the continued expansion of the *escadrilles de chasse*. From an early 1916 low of seven, the complement of fighter squadrons in the *Service Aéronautique* by the spring of 1917 ran as high as twenty pilots. Although the French were beginning to feel the pinch of a shortage of qualified raw material, the pool of pilots available for N.124 was, for all practical purposes, inexhaustible. Following the declaration of war by the United States, enlistments in the Lafayette Flying Corps rose sharply: in the three-month period beginning April 6, ninety-four additional Americans either had begun flight training, or were breveted pilots. In the majority of cases, replacements for the Lafayette Escadrille were handpicked. Before his death, de Laage accompanied Bill Thaw on frequent scouting trips to the advanced schools, where they earmarked promising students for assignment to the Escadrille as vacancies occurred. In a few instances the choices later proved embarrassing, but in the main this personal attention paid handsome dividends.

The last of the Foreign Legion infantrymen sent to the Escadrille was a short, cheerful former banana-plantation manager named William E. Dugan, Jr., whose home originally was in Rochester, New York. Dugan's trail, like so many before him, led from the well-paying security of a civilian job to the monotonous horror of the trenches, and from there to the hospital, out of the infantry and into aviation. Dugan's foot-slogging days came to an end in Caillette Wood in front of Verdun, where shell fragments lacing his arms and back earned him a long stay in one of the wretched, overcrowded French military hospitals. Standing only 5 feet 6 inches tall—an inch shorter than Lufbery—Dugan was, along with Genêt, the smallest man in the squadron.

Henry Sweet Jones, a Lehigh University undergraduate from Hartford, Pennsylvania, was, like Ted Parsons, a former ambulance driver. When the supply of red wine temporarily gave out one evening, Jones shocked his mates by mixing, and drinking, a cocktail made of bay rum, olive oil and vinegar.

The problem of keeping the living huts adequately lighted, generators in the workshops humming and magnetos properly wired was no longer left entirely in the hands of the French mechanics once Charles H. Dolan II was put on the rolls. Dolan, Boston-born, had learned to solve the thorniest of electrical mysteries at the Massachusetts Institute of Technology and was a practicing engineer with the Paris branch of the Sperry Gyroscope Company in 1915, when he resigned and directed his steps to Dr. Gros's office at 23 Avenue du Bois de Boulogne.

There was intellectually inclined Ray C. Bridgman, from Lake Forest, Illinois, a slender, wavy-haired youth who impressed the others with his devotion after hours to the works of nineteenth-century authors and his outspoken and detailed analysis of why the world would be safe again only with a demilitarized Germany. At the opposite end of the pole stood big, tough Douglas MacMonagle from San Francisco, who established a reputation as a warm friend and a relentless enemy; fight was written all over MacMonagle, and his caustic tongue and capacity for hard liquor steered him inevitably in that direction. Few of the "rear-echelon goldbricks" he loved to taunt while in Paris bars, however, cared to test his mettle.

John Armstrong Drexel, everyone agreed, was the most unintentionally humorous pilot they had ever known. Drexel was one of the wealthiest men in Philadelphia, and although a Pennsylvanian by birth, he was an Englishman by preference. He had lived for many years in the British Isles and spoke with a carefully cultivated Oxford accent. Drexel, who had learned to fly in 1909 and who once held the world's altitude record for Blériots, was a good pilot; but those who knew him in school remembered him mostly for his air of detachment and almost unbelievable absent-mindedness. He dressed himself for flight with all the meticulous, time-consuming care of a bride before the wedding, only to have somebody call, "Hey, Drexel, you forgot your helmet." Grieved, he would return for the headgear, carefully strap it into place, and once again head for the waiting airplane. Then, "Oh, Drexel-l-l, how about your gloves?" It became a game, and once they let him get all the way out to the airplane and into the cockpit before reminding him that he had left behind the barograph for the altitude test.

At the Escadrille, he provoked stifled mirth the first night as the other pilots watched him getting ready for bed—a process that for most of them meant shucking boots and outerwear and crawling under the blankets in their long johns. Drexel, however, slipped over his head a long flannel nightgown that hung to his ankles. He then adjusted a tasseled night-cap on his head. Fascinated, the other men watched him carefully tie up the ends of his flowing black moustache with a silk string, knotting it behind his head tightly so as to keep the moustache firmly in place while he slept. Once Drexel had tucked himself snugly in, he fell into a serene and deep sleep, undisturbed by the noise around him. Drexel proved to be a snob about money and family background—qualities of little value on the Western Front—and when he left the Escadrille a month later to accept a major's commission and a liaison job with the U. S. Air Service, nobody was distressed to see him go.

The origin of the saying, "There's one in every outfit," is vague, but the foundations of this military truism undoubtedly reach back through centuries of martial tradition. The referral is to the one man in twenty—or forty, or sixty—who can't get anything right, who bungles every assigned task, misinterprets orders, forgets instructions, doesn't know his left foot from his right and, in general, proves to be a liability to his unit, a nuisance to his fellows and an embarrassment to his commanding officer; he is the Eight Ball, the Black Sheep, the Untouchable.

The misfit of N.124, the Lafayette Escadrille, was Thomas M. Hewitt, Jr., of Westchester, New York. At Pau, he had dazzled his instructors with the facility he demonstrated in putting Nieuports through the demanding acrobatic curriculum; at Cazeaux, his marksmanship drew approving nods; and when interviewed by de Laage and Thaw, Hewitt seemed cocky, aggressive and impatient to unleash his skills on the Germans. When he arrived at the Escadrille, the older hands guessed, correctly, that Hewitt came from a well-to-do home, for he wore an expensive, black wool uniform cut by a good tailor. But as the days passed, the handsome uniform betrayed the wearer as having been hopelessly coddled: bits of fried egg, carelessly spilled on the front of the tunic, dried to a shiny yellow crust and stayed there; the creases vanished from the slacks and were not replaced; the high-topped leather shoes lost their luster and became dull and scuffed. It seemed to the others that Hewitt was somehow waiting for his mother to come and put things straight.

Hewitt's first exposure to the enemy was a revelation. It was the Escadrille custom to guide new men over the crack German battery near St. Quentin to gauge their reaction to the terrifying *crack-whoompf!* of bursting shells; the initial exposure to shelling was always momentarily unnerving, but determined men conquered their fear and maintained the integrity of the formation. The day Hewitt was flown over the battery the Germans put up an unusually vicious barrage; the metallic thunder that shook the skies sounded like the crack of doom in Hewitt's ears, and he turned for home. Hewitt found life with a Frontline squadron filled with dangers he had not foreseen when he was flying in the untroubled air over the Pyrénées. He watched the planes returning from patrol in twos and threes, not all together as when they had left. He observed the mechanics huddled around the planes counting the bullet holes, examining loose flying wires and fingering splintered struts. He noticed how when the pilots climbed stiffly from their cockpits, they looked tired and aged, their faces black and grimy from burnt castor oil and gun powder, showing white only where the goggles and helmet covered their eyes and cheeks. He wondered how a man could laugh when he poked a finger through a hole in his flying suit. Then, when Genêt and Hoskier were killed in quick succession, Hewitt realized that death might be only a few minutes away once he got near the lines.

The sight of de Laage's crushed body being taken from the wreckage of the Morane further unnerved him, heightening the realization that his life, like every pilot's, could be snuffed out by the failure of a short section of copper tubing, a turnbuckle or a petcock. Hewitt's fear of death under enemy guns now spread into a fear of sudden extinction because of the vagaries of aircraft, and this fear robbed him of his last asset, the ability to fly well.

Nieuports were being phased out of service, replaced by Spads. Built by the *Société pour Aviation et ses Derivées*, from whose initials it received its name, the Spad VII looked nothing at all like a Nieuport; Spads gave the visual impression of brute strength, not beauty. The broad, square-tipped wings spanning just over twenty-six feet were solidly wedded to each other by a double set of interplane struts and numerous heavy bracing wires. Anchoring the center section of the top wing to the thick circular fuselage were short, sturdy cabane struts. The entire rigging inspired confidence. The tail surfaces were large in area, and the ample rudder was preceded by a long, straight vertical stabilizer, a feature lacking altogether on Nieuports.

The trailing edges of the wings, rudder and elevator were fashioned of heavy piano wire, and when the fabric was stretched tight on these surfaces and doped, the shrinkage resulted in characteristic scalloped edges. The landing gear was set well forward, which made crosswind touchdowns less hazardous, and was solidly built to withstand the roughest of landings. Centered on the fuselage directly in front of the pilot was a single Vickers gun, belt-fed with 500 rounds of .303 caliber ammunition. Missing was the familiar nine-cylinder rotary engine; in its place was a V-type Hispano-Suiza water-cooled engine that delivered

150 h.p., later increased to 180. Spads would do 120 m.p.h. level, and pilots had no fear of diving them to the limit. They were more powerful, faster and stronger than any airplane yet flown by Allied pilots. But because they were heavy, grossing out at nearly 1600 pounds, and because the very thin airfoil section provided only nominal lift, the gliding ratio was poor and Spads had to be flown almost into the ground for landing; they did not hover or float like Nieuports, nor were they as maneuverable. However, the Escadrille pilots gladly traded handling ease for the added strength and the added speed.

Spads were coming up to the squadrons slowly, and once arrived were jealously looked after. By June 3, when the Escadrille moved from Ravenel to Chaudun, below Soissons, Hewitt had been allotted one of the coveted new fighters. Before the departure of Combat Group 13 for Chaudun, the pilots were warned of a deep irrigation ditch that ran the width of the new field. Although the ditch was marked with red flags and was clearly visible from the air, squadron commanders gathered their pilots together for a verbal reiteration of the danger of exceeding the normal landing roll when setting down on the new terrain.

One by one the squadrons departed, leaving the Lafayette Escadrille to fly in last. Finally all seventy-five Nieuports and Spads were safely down at Chaudun except one. Hewitt was the last man in the Group to make his circuit of the field. Twice he flew across the landing ground, marking the position of the irrigation ditch. Thénault and the rest of the N.124 pilots stood on the edge of the field watching as Hewitt made his approach. He let down uncertainly, as if afraid to get close to the earth. Just over the center of the field, he finally committed himself and came down with a jarring lurch, bounced once in the air, then settled heavily on the ground, rolling fast for the end of the field. "The ditch! The ditch!" the watching pilots screamed, but Hewitt's Spad rolled straight for the red flags flapping in the wind. His wheels caught in the lip of the trench and the plane whipped over on its back with a dismal crunching sound. The new Spad was a write-off, but Hewitt emerged unhurt, if pale.

Thénault flew into a rage, the first demonstration of lost temper ever witnessed by the others. His face livid, he cursed out Hewitt in two languages, hardly bothering to separate one from the other. Then he ordered Hewitt to drive back to Ravenel and ferry back Soubiran's Spad—Soubiran then being on leave in Paris. Thénault later explained that the jolting, two-hour trip by car over muddy, shell-torn roads would be punishment enough for Hewitt—but he was to regret his quaint notion of discipline. The next morning, Thénault and a horde of watchers gathered on the field when they heard the sound of the Hispano-Suiza engine roaring across the field. Again, Hewitt skimmed over the field, his eyes probably riveted on that menacing ditch. He zoomed up and banked into the wind and let down for his second landing attempt on the greensward of Chaudun. His approach was lower, and he touched down well within the permissible limits, but he forgot to cut the throttle. The result was inevitable: the Spad landed fast and bounced inexorably toward the fatal trench. The others watched in disbelief as the new Spad once again demonstrated the hypnotic attraction the ditch seemed now to hold for Hewitt, who could only sit frozen at the controls until the willful airplane piled up not ten feet from where he had crashed the day before. Shaken, Hewitt crawled from the fresh wreckage to face Thénault's wrath. Within less than eighteen hours he had set the French Government back the equivalent of $20,485.22. Grounded on the spot by Thénault, Hewitt retreated to the bar, where he drank alone; after two months with the squadron, he had no friends, only the bitter nickname "Horrible."

The new field at Chaudun was the largest yet laid out for the use of *groupes de combat,* but it was not large enough to contain Sergeant Andrew Courtney Campbell, Jr. Campbell, a dapper playboy from Chicago who sported a walking stick and wore the bellows-pocketed, long-skirted British officer's tunic with Sam Browne belt. He looked upon the war primarily as a stage where he could roam at will, demonstrating his love for low-altitude acrobatics and his utter disregard for lives and property. Known as a "jester in the Shakespearean sense" on the ground, Campbell carried his mania for collegiate pranks into the air. He handled his Nieuport in formation the way he had driven his Stutz Bearcat in heavy traffic along Lake Shore Drive—dodging, weaving, roaring full out and stopping just short of collision. He delighted in seeing how close he could come to others before their nerve gave way and they were forced to jink up or down, slew left or right, to keep Campbell's hovering undercarriage out of their cockpits. The other pilots pleaded, cajoled, then threatened Campbell; Thénault sternly lectured him, forbidding him to endanger lives and property belonging to France, but Campbell flew merrily on to a near-disaster that became known as the Miracle of Chaudun.

While aloft one morning waiting for the others to form up for patrol, Campbell began a series of violent acrobatics. He dived low at the hangars, zooming up steeply to half-roll off the top. He repeated the maneuver several times, gaining altitude with each roll-out. When he was about 4000 high on the third or fourth pass, he dived and pulled up sharply in a screaming climb. Just as he entered the top of the loop the lower left wing snapped off with a crack that was heard on the field below and fluttered away in the slipstream. The narrow-chord wing had sheared off at the root, leaving the outer V-strut and bracing wires still attached to the upper plane. Watchers on the ground prepared for the inevitable spin and violent crash; the ambulance was started up and men hopped on the running board.

But Campbell got the nose down and began a precarious glide that carried his crippled airplane six miles away from the field. He sat down with a feather-touch landing in the center of a beet patch and climbed from the cockpit to light a cigarette. After posing for photographs in front of the amputated Nieuport, Campbell returned to the field. He spent an hour in the bar describing his masterful handling of the situation, then borrowed somebody else's airplane to go on patrol. If Campbell's own close call could not sober him, neither could the violent deaths of others who imitated him.

The brooding Herman Chatkoff—former car-washer from Brooklyn and "Salvation Army Veteran" who had joined the Foreign Legion in 1914—had made his way to the Lafayette Flying Corps and in the summer of 1917 his squadron, C.11, was based near Chaudun, where it had been engaged in artillery missions during the abortive Chemin-des-Dames offensive. Chatkoff, a longtime admirer of pursuit pilots, was a visitor to

Chaudun, where he was frequently invited to stay for lunch. He flew in just before noon on June 15, bringing with him a passenger, a young ambulance driver named Benjamin Woodworth. The lunch was punctuated with good-natured insults directed toward "truck drivers," pilots who flew the cumbersome observation and bombing planes. The ragging continued until Chatkoff and Woodworth were ready to leave.

Chatkoff revved up the two engines on the Caudron and began his roll down the field in front of the yelling, jeering crowd of fighter pilots. He pulled back hard on the control column and the heavy, awkward-looking airplane lunged into the air. Chatkoff then began a series of steep banks and climbing turns at 200 feet; few of the Escadrille pilots could bear to watch. The inevitable happened: the Caudron, pushed beyond the limits of its aerodynamic ability to sustain flight, lost airspeed and stalled out. It crashed heavily at the end of the field, but did not burn. Woodworth had been cut in two, his skull crushed and the lower part of his body scraped clean of flesh, revealing the naked whiteness of exposed bone. Chatkoff was pulled from the crumpled wreckage alive, but brutally mangled; his skull was fractured in three places, both legs were broken at the hip and a jagged splinter of bone had pushed through his intestines. When they lifted him to a stretcher, he managed a ghastly smile, then fainted.[1]

The grisly accident had a sobering effect on most of those who witnessed Chatkoff's fall. "It cured forever," said Parsons, "my desire to indulge in low-level acrobatics." To Lufbery, the death of Woodworth was "as much plain murder as anyone could see. Chatkoff had no right to risk another man's life just to show off." And Campbell? He spent the next patrol hovering behind Ted Parsons' Spad, moving his whirling propeller back and forth about six feet from Parsons' tail. "I spent more time trying to stay

---

[1] Chatkoff, who had changed his name to Lincoln from the Germanic Herman, spent the rest of the war in a French hospital. Returned to the United States after the Armistice, he was confined to a mental institution. Due to a controversy between the French and American governments as to his status, Chatkoff remained virtually a man without a country for thirteen years. But on February 6, 1931, President Hoover signed a bill put through Congress after a seven-year legal struggle that awarded Chatkoff a pension of $100 a month and perpetual care in a Veterans' Hospital.

out of the damn fool's way," said Parsons, "than I did looking for Huns. I shook my fist at him and cursed back into the prop wash, but he only grinned and waved and threw kisses; it was maddening."

James Norman Hall joined the Escadrille at a time of triumph and tragedy.

On June 12—four days before Hall's arrival—Lufbery had rolled out of bed before anyone else and climbed into his Spad for a predawn solo patrol. He got the sturdy fighter to 16,000 feet, climbing easily; up there, the sky was pale blue, edged with pink tracings from the rising sun. As he crossed the lines, Lufbery made out the shapes of seven German planes moving slowly across the earth that was still half-shrouded in darkness. Lufbery kept his position, carefully counting the enemy; two of the planes were observation machines up to regulate an artillery shoot on a supply route over which moved food and ammunition to the French first line. The two-seaters were protected by a top cover of five Albatros fighters weaving slowly back and forth a thousand feet overhead. Here was the classic mid-1916 situation that would have seen Kiffin Rockwell or Victor Chapman impulsively attacking; but Lufbery had long ago learned his lesson and he maintained his distance, waiting for one of the Germans to make a wrong move. One did. A two-seater drifted from underneath the shelter of the Albatros and moved crabwise across the sky. Lufbery waited until the two-seater was off by itself a good hundred yards from the others, then he put the nose of his Spad down and dived all out with the throttle open for the one firing pass he would have time to make before the Albatros pilots got wise and came to the aid of the drifting observation plane. Lufbery howled down until the gray hulk of the German straggler filled his ring sight. Lufbery's single Vickers gun rattled off a scorching twenty-five rounds, and he had a fleeting glimpse of the German pilot thrown forward against the cockpit rim as the weight of the lead caught him in the back. The two-seater plunged straight down and came apart in the air, the wings crumpling backward, ripping loose and sailing through space. The fuselage plummeted to earth between the lines, and some time later the wings and loose struts drifted down and fell inside a French trench.

It was an easy confirmation, his tenth, and the Commanding General of the French Sixth Army was so pleased he invited Lufbery to share luncheon with him at his Headquarters, where he presented the new double-ace with a citation:

> VIe *Armée Etat-Major*
>
> LUFBERY, RAOUL, *Adjudant Pilote à l'Escadrille* N.124 (*Aéronautique*). *Pilote de chasse merveilleux. Est, pour son escadrille, un example vivant d'audace, de sang froid, et de dévouement.*
>
> *A abbatu le* 12 *juin,* 1917, *son* 10è *avion ennemi.*
>
> (*Signé*) MAISTRE

On the heels of Lufbery's success came Chatkoff's horrible crash, and the following day Hall was enrolled on N.124's duty roster as one of the available pilots. But at thirty Hall was no stranger to reality and was already well acquainted with the toll exacted by war.

Hall, a slender, shy, soft-spoken romantic from Colfax, Iowa, had been graduated from Grinnell University in 1908. For several years he worked as an investigator for the Massachusetts Society for the Prevention of Cruelty to Children, a poorly paying job that led him to the slums of Boston. The parents of the children whose welfare he was investigating tempted him with liquor and sex, and his polite refusals, coupled with a dogged determination to get at the facts, often triggered primitive emotions: once he barely escaped with his life after being chased around and around a kitchen table by a drunken giantess armed with a butcher knife.

Hall left the States in the summer of 1914, intending to settle in Europe and earn his living as a writer. "It was a happy, hopeful woodshed poet," he remembered later, "who early in June arrived in London, a suitcase in one hand and a portable typewriter in the other." But the early Hall remained unpublished. The war caught up with him in the Welsh village of Beddgelert, a way station on a literary pilgrimage he was taking by bicycle. After an agony of indecision, he took the King's shilling and became Private J. N. Hall, No. 690, 9th Battalion, Royal Fusiliers.

In France, Hall fought as a machine gunner through the bloody battles of Loos and Hulluch, surviving where many thousands did not. His luck was phenomenal. During a protracted lull in the Flanders fighting, Hall was sitting in a ruined dugout brewing tea. A trooper named McHard was manning the Vickers gun in the fire trench. McHard beckoned to Hall, asking if he would mind the gun for a moment while he searched through the dugout for a missing canteen. Hall agreed, and moments later the earth was convulsed with a sudden barrage from German guns. In the midst of the furious shelling, Hall saw from his crouched position by the gun the dugout take a direct hit. When the fury had spent itself, Hall scrambled down the ruined trench and began digging. Seven of his friends had taken refuge there—men he had been chatting with only minutes before. Three had been killed outright, three more died a short time later, and the seventh was taken to the rear where his leg was amputated. McHard's skull had been split cleanly down the middle.

Hall served a year and ninety-nine days with the Fusiliers before applying for home leave; he was given instead an honorable discharge. He spent only five months in America, then sailed to France and enlisted in the Lafayette Flying Corps. His first tour of duty with N.124 lasted only ten days.

On his first patrol, he got lost. Absorbed in the panorama unreeling beneath the wings of his Spad, Hall suddenly awoke to the fact that he was 12,000 feet above the earth, surrounded by masses of clouds, his companions vanished from sight. While searching for the rest of the patrol through the canyons of heaped-up cumulus, his attention was drawn downward by the bursting of white antiaircraft shells; flying serenely through the French barrage a large German two-seater photographic plane was making its way deeper into Hall's territory, utterly unaware of the Spad flying only a thousand feet above. Hall, seeing his chance for an easy first kill, throttled back and glided down until he was in perfect firing position. He could see the observer bent over his camera in the rear cockpit, his gun pointing idly at the sky. Hall slipped his gloved finger through the trigger guard . . . and couldn't fire. He flew so close to the startled Germans he nearly rammed them. The observer grabbed for his gun; the pilot wheeled his plane around and plunged into a cloud and was lost to Hall forever. Stupefied, Hall flew home. He could never explain, even to himself, his inability to close his hand the final quarter of an inch that would have sent lead streaming from his Vickers gun into the German plane. He kept the secret from the others and—in view of the greater failure—accepted Thénault's dressing-down for having strayed from the patrol with what amounted to gratitude.

On June 26, Jim Hall flew his third patrol—a command performance by six of the Escadrille pilots for a group of visiting American officers recently arrived in France. The honor fell to Thaw, Lufbery, Parsons, Dugan, Bridgman and Hall. Thaw, as patrol leader, gave the others explicit instructions: they were to rendezvous at 9000 feet over a reservoir near Soissons, then fly in formation to the lines, nine miles distant. Thaw emphasized to Hall, the greenest of the lot, that should he get lost again he must not attempt to find the others, but should turn back for the balloon lines and wait for their return; he was certain that the visiting Americans, having seen six Spads leave the field together, would expect to see them return together.

Five of the planes left the field at Chaudun just before sundown, but Hall was piloting a plane with a rebuilt engine that proved difficult to start. With some dismay, Hall watched the five Spads disappear from sight while he sat immobliized on the ground waiting for his mechanic to clear a fuel-line stoppage. When Hall's engine finally burst into life, he was a full ten minutes late, and he rushed from the ground to attempt to reach the rendezvous area in time. He arrived over the reservoir, but his heart sank when he found no sign of the patrol. He circled uncertainly, then started climbing for the assigned patrol altitude of 15,000 feet. The rebuilt engine acted sluggish and balky and was beginning to overheat. He could climb no higher than 12,000 feet. Instead of heading back for his own balloon lines, Hall swung toward Germany, determined not to be left out of the showcase patrol. Watching the rising cylinder-head temperature gauge and frantically scanning the reddening sky, Hall flew on. Then, in the gathering darkness, he made out the shapes of single-seater fighters ahead of him. One of the planes was above the others, indulging in a series of well-executed barrel rolls, which Hall recognized as the characteristic exuberance often displayed by Bridgman. With a sigh of relief, Hall nosed his Spad toward the planes a thousand yards away.

One of the fighters dropped down to Hall's altitude and "suddenly loomed up in front of me like an express train, as you have seen them approach from the depths of a motion picture screen, only ten times faster, and he was firing as he came." Tracers flashed through Hall's Spad, and he realized too late that he had flown into the middle of a six-plane Albatros formation.

It was over within sixty seconds. Hall had started to bank for home when he was slammed forward by the impact of a Maxim slug that struck him behind his left shoulder blade, emerging under his arm; a second bullet parted his goggles where they were joined over his nose; a third slammed through the wicker seat, grazing a testicle. Dazed, Hall reached up to cut the switches, but his left arm failed to respond to the command issued by his fast-numbing brain. Believing the arm had been blown over the side of the cockpit, he looked down to find it still attached to his body, but it hung lifeless and insensitive to feeling. Then he blacked out.

He came to, dimly realizing that the Spad was hurtling earthward with the Germans still on his tail, firing. A bullet grazed his right leg, but Hall didn't feel it. The Spad fell off in a half-spin, and the Germans pulled away. Through the curtain of fog that had descended on his brain, Hall asked himself, *Am I on fire?* The thought jerked him into full consciousness. He pulled back on the stick and held it between his knees, reaching up with his serviceable right hand to cut the ignition and fuel switches. This done, he fell back again, overcome with listlessness. Air left his lungs in great heaving gasps, and he could barely catch his breath. With the propeller stopped, the Spad began falling out of control again. Through the haze, terror penetrated, and Hall screamed aloud, "I'm going to be killed! This is my last sortie!" With one final, almost superhuman effort of will, he roused himself long enough to haul back on the stick to level out 500 feet above an endless expanse of shell holes, trenches and snarled strands of barbed wire. Just before he lapsed into unconsciousness, he groggily wondered if he was coming to earth in French or German territory.

Hall's Spad plunged directly into a French first-line trench in the Ravin d'Oisel, one of the shallow ravines leading down from the Chemin-des-Dames. The wings were ripped off by the raised edges of the deep excavation, absorbing the greater force of the impact. Hall's unconscious form was pulled from the fuselage, which had plunged to the bottom of the trench. He was carried, under heavy bombardment, to a dressing station, and from there to a field hospital. By eight that evening he was lying between clean white sheets in a section reserved for officers. ("It's a pity," he remarked later, "that the French can't treat Americans as though they belonged over here.")

Two weeks later, news reached the Escadrille that Corporal Hall was to be awarded the *Médaille Militaire* and the *Croix de Guerre*, with palm. Reasoning that Hall was done for, a delegation of pilots piled into a car and roared over to the hospital to pay their last respects. They entered the ward with caps in their hands, expecting to find Hall breathing his last; instead, they saw him sitting propped against the pillows, happily absorbed in *The Oxford Book of English Verse*.

When James Ralph Doolittle (no relation to General James H. Doolittle of two decades hence) of New York City checked in at Chaudun, he looked as if he had lately emerged second-best in a saber duel; raised welts of pink scar tissue marred an otherwise handsome equine face, and his head was crisscrossed with white furrows where the hair refused to grow. Marking time at Le Plessis-Belleville while waiting for assignment, Doolittle had piled up a Nieuport in landing, and his injuries required two months in the hospital to heal.

The urge to create a home-like atmosphere in even the meanest, most antiseptic of surroundings is instinctive with nearly every soldier; the framed photograph, the bit of curtain, the private shelf, all help to take the edge from the curse of loneliness and the loss of identity that go with military life. Thus nobody was surprised when newcomer David McKelvey Peterson, of Honesdale, Pennsylvania, went quietly to work sprucing up his living area in the Escadrille's wooden hut at Chaudun.

The tall, phlegmatic Peterson efficiently erected a staggered series of shelves, where he neatly arranged his possessions. He carefully constructed two small wooden tables that he varnished with painstaking care, then fashioned a small reading lamp with a cone-like shade so he could read at night without disturbing the others. He filled in knotholes in the floor and conscientiously sealed up cracks in the walls. Peterson's meticulously contrived renovations required the better part of two weeks, and when he had finished, his section of the hut fairly glowed with inviting warmth.

When, a few days later, the order came to pack up and move, the emotionless Peterson began to disassemble his handiwork as quietly and carefully as he had put it together. Pilots passing his end of the hut heard him whistling as he went about it. They noticed that Peterson could not carry a tune.

Albatros DVa

CHAPTER 12

WESTWARD TO THE SEA

No ground along the Western Front offered less promise of a breakthrough than did that part of the Flemish plain stretching wetly from below Ypres to the windswept beaches along the Belgian coast above Nieuport. In this region, with its essentially maritime climate, the war assumed an altogether different character. The marshy ground, almost at sea level, is further sodden by constant rain and heavy mist, forming a spongy mass in which it was virtually impossible to dig trenches or underground shelters; a spade shoved into the yielding earth slid immediately into the water, only inches below the ground. Shell holes—elsewhere a source of refuge—became death traps. Soldiers weighted with equipment who sought shelter in one of these holes during a bombardment found themselves in danger of drowning. One British regimental commander complained: "The ground on which we are fighting is awful. Underneath the thin crust is bottomless mud. Men standing in trenches only four or five feet deep are almost unable to get out, and gradually sink until it takes four or five men to extricate them."

Across this ground, on a nearly twenty-mile front, Field Marshal Sir Douglas Haig prepared to launch an offensive that became known as Third Ypres. At its most optimistic, Haig's plan envisioned a breakthrough along the coast that would "root out the hornets' nests of Zeebrugge and Ostend" (from where German U-boats sallied to exact such heavy toll) and in doing so the offensive would push the German flank inland, from where further flank attacks could be launched. At its most pessimistic, Haig's scheme would, over a series of carefully staged attacks, clear the Germans from before the ruined city of Ypres itself, relieving that beleaguered town once and for all.

Some five hundred British and two hundred French aircraft were scheduled to take part in the offensive. The weight of the infantry would be preponderantly British; but to share the cost of possible victory was the French First Army, to which was attached Féquant's *Groupe de Combat* 13 operating from the field at St. Pol-sur-Mer, on the western side of Dunkerque Harbor.

The migration began on the morning of July 18 in threatening weather. It was 122 miles to St. Pol, and most of the route proved to be enveloped in rain and fog. The formations began battling through sudden squalls that drenched the pilots; when they broke into occasional clear patches the sun failed to warm them and their heavy, wet flying suits clung to them coldly and uncomfortably. Goggles fogged over and were pushed up, exposing eyes to the punishing blast of air flung backward by the propeller. Constant changes in altitude were forced on them as they tried to avoid plunging into suddenly looming banks of fog. Tight formations broke up into elements of two or three aircraft, boring blindly through the overcast. With most ground references obscured, maps were useless; the pilots flew a compass course of 270 degrees and hoped for the best.

The inexperienced Ralph Doolittle got hopelessly lost. After plowing through a fog layer he emerged to find himself separated from the Spads that had been flanking him. He entered the damp confines of a cloud and was alone in the world except for the roar of his engine. He flew on until he could stand the uncertainty no longer, then put his plane into a shallow dive to seek the friendly earth below. He came out of the cloud and into the sunshine 500 feet above an airdrome. He saw the canvas hangars and the planes lined up on the sun-drenched field; it was not a field he knew, but it was a haven nevertheless. He began letting down to land and ask directions.

He dropped lower and got his nose into the wind, but was startled when tracers began flashing upward at him from the ground. He was now close enough to notice that the planes on the field were marked with large black-and-white crosses. He hauled back on the stick and gave it full throttle. The clouds above were no longer his enemy, but his salvation. He climbed until the protective moisture enveloped him completely, but once again he became unnerved at the helpless feeling of flying blind over unknown territory. He angled downward, and found himself only a short distance from a British observation balloon floating a thousand feet above the ground. Doolittle relaxed, but only momentarily; the balloon was sinking rapidly. Then Doolittle took in the combat that was raging above his head. Two German fighters were firing at the balloon, which was being winched down, and were in turn being harried by a lone British Nieuport. Doolittle climbed up to aid the Britisher.

The Germans quickly dropped their attacks on the balloon to devote their full attention to the intruders. One slewed around and fastened his guns on Doolittle's tail and opened fire. A hammerblow struck the American in the calf of his leg, jerking his foot painfully from the rudder bar. The Spad plunged down out of control, with the German still in pursuit. A second burst of lead spattered against the engine, and Doolittle, giddy with pain, slipped earthward with the wind sighing through the bracing wires. He began to straighten out too late to avoid landing crosswise in a plowed field. His wheels struck a furrow, flipping the Spad over on its back. Doolittle's head was thrown forward violently, cracking against the cockpit rim, and the recently healed scars opened anew, drenching him with blood. British soldiers rushed over to the wreckage, unstrapped the big half-conscious American and lowered him to the ground, where his wounds were staunched with compresses. A few minutes later, Ralph Doolittle was on his way to the hospital and out of the war. He never did learn what happened to the Nieuport and the balloon.

Parsons and Willis had safely completed over half the journey through heavy weather and were nearing Arras, which was partly in the clear. Willis, who had rigged a small stereoscopic camera to his plane, circled for a shot of the earth below. Parsons dropped behind Willis to follow. A cloud loomed up ahead, and Parsons saw Willis bank violently to the right. Instinctively he jammed his own foot on the rudder bar and tore around after Willis. He shot past the gray hulk of a British balloon that lay hidden in the cloud, the basket dangling below in the clear. Photography abandoned, they flew straight on to St. Pol. The trip had taken them one hour and fifteen minutes.

The role of the Escadrille during the Ypres offensive would be purely aggressive. The mission of the Group was "to attack and, if possible, to paralyze enemy aviation on its own terrain." This was interpreted by the Americans to mean their work would consist of offensive patrols only, to seek and destroy German aircraft behind their own lines. But they were only partially correct. Headquarters of the *Service Aéronautique* planned to inaugurate a tactical bombing program against German airdromes, utilizing Spads adapted to carry four 22-pound Gros-Andreau bombs. It was admittedly an experiment, but why Headquarters believed that pinprick raids carried out by single-seat fighters—which were not fitted with even the crudest of bombsights—would prove to be as destructive as missions undertaken by waves of bombers designed for the job was a mystery to Spad pilots, who looked upon the assignment with loathing.

Ask anything of a pilot, but do not ask him to carry aloft a single ounce not necessary to his well-being or to the success of his flight. More fuel, extra ammunition, added instruments—these he will welcome, gladly accepting the penalty imposed by their weight upon the flight characteristics of his airplane. But in the case of disfiguring the underside of a Spad with four drag-producing bulbous objects whose weight totaled half that of the pilot, the penalty could have been steep—especially when operating from St. Pol-sur-Mer, where every flight was an adventure in uncertainty. The sharp prevailing winds were westerly, dictating takeoffs directly over the ocean. A large concrete seawall loomed up at the edge of the field, which was shorter than most. Engine failure could mean either crunching into the wall or plunging into the sea; the load of touchy liquid bombs added greatly to the possibility of sudden death in either case.

Captain Thénault picked Rockwell and Parsons as the Escadrille's contribution to the bomber force mustered by Group, and they watched glumly as the armorers went to work installing racks and release handles to their Spads. Parsons' reaction was one of "sorrowful anticipation and deep distress of mind . . . it seemed like suicide to us, and our opinion of the Einstein of the nonflying personnel who had conceived the idea was anything but flattering to him and his ancestors." Resigned to carrying the toxic cargo, Rockwell and Parsons demanded instructions on how they were to get the bombs on target; none had been supplied with the missiles. The Group Armament Officer, a mathematician in civilian life, came up with the following: "Fly to 3000 feet, maintain a straight course until the target disappears beneath the lower wing. Then dive at a 45 degree angle for 1500 feet, level out, count to ten and immediately release your bombs." In lieu of anything more concrete, this piece of whimsy was accepted by the Escadrille pilots as a means to further paralyze German aviation. The practice target, a red-painted barrel, was moored a few hundred yards out in the ocean, and Parsons was the first to test the mathematician's theory. He got off the ground, missing the top of the seawall by inches, climbed to altitude and executed the prescribed maneuvers. Parsons returned immediately and reported to Thénault that his bombs had struck nothing but the ocean. Pondering the possibilities of getting jumped by enemy fighters while weighted with bombs, considering what they would do if the bombs began to leak the deadly fumes while en route to the target, weighing the chances of the bombs getting stuck in the racks and having to land with them clustered under their feet, Parsons and Rockwell made out informal wills and awaited the coming of the offensive.

The drive began at four on the morning of July 31, 1917, in a torrential rain, turning the ground into a quagmire in which the heavily loaded infantrymen bogged almost to the knees as they moved through the mud to get at the Germans firing at them from the shattered woods, ruined farm buildings and parapeted crests. At St. Pol the pilots sat fully dressed, waiting, listening to the rain drumming on the canvas tent tops, smoking cigarettes and drinking coffee from thick mugs. Mechanics huddled in the doorways of the hangars where the Spads were kept, watching the rain sweep horizontally across the sodden field, driven along by stiff winds blowing in from the North Sea. As the morning wore on, the wind abated, but the rain settled into a steady downpour that gave every indication of lasting throughout the day. The pilots took off their heavy flight suits and moved to the bar, where they sat listening to the ceaseless rumble of the guns. There was no flying that day, or on the three days following; the heavy rains grounded both sides.

By the time the skies cleared, Headquarters had unexpectedly reversed its decision to bomb German airfields. The state of the ground was such that no real push could be made along the coast toward Ostend and Zeebrugge, but substantial gains were being made in front of Ypres, where the fighting degenerated into a muddy foot-slogger's war that aviation could neither hinder nor help. The racks were taken off the Spads, the bombs returned to the depot and the Escadrille resumed high-altitude patrolling.

They almost immediately ran afoul of the Richthofen Circus—so called because of the wild color schemes of its aircraft and its peripatetic nature—based across the lines near Courtrai. *Jagdgeschwader* 1, to give it its proper name, was run by a humorless Prussian named Manfred von Richthofen, who had been one of Oswald Boelcke's star pupils. He had learned his lessons well; he began his victory string only two days before the Escadrille had formed up at Luxeuil in April 1916, and within fifteen months his confirmed kills stood at fifty-seven—more than twice that of the combined total of N.124. The four squadrons under his command were staffed with picked men flying garishly-painted improved Albatros D-Va fighters that were nearly as fast as Spads. As the Battle of Third Ypres opened, the Richthofen Circus took to the air without its ringmaster, who was forced to stay on the ground recovering from his first wound; on July 6 a British observer named A. E. Woodbridge, manning a Lewis gun in a two-seater F.E.2d, creased von Richthofen's skull with a slug fired at an estimated range of 300 yards, and the German lurched from the fight to land in the Flanders mud. Although von Richthofen was back with *Jagdgeschwader* 1 three weeks later, he was in no condition to resume aerial combat. However, this twenty-five-year-old virtuoso of German fighter pilots was not the whole show; some of the Circus pilots had scores as high as thirty-four, and the multihued Albatros of JG.1 were always approached with the respect one professional reserves for another.

On the afternoon of August 5, four pilots of the Lafayette Escadrille made the squadron's first acquaintance with the capabilities of von Richthofen's men. Lufbery, Parsons and Lovell formed an escort for Willis and his Spad on a deep-penetration photographic mission of German rear areas. The bulk of French aerial photographic work was carried out by two-seater reconnaissance aircraft mounting monster cameras taking 7 x 9½-inch plates through 520mm lenses, but during the spring and summer of 1917 increasing use was made of Spads equipped with more compact cameras taking stereoscopic pairs of 5 x 7-inch negatives through 240mm lenses with speeds ranging from f/4.5 to f/6.3. Photography was accomplished by the pilot with the aid of a stopwatch and a graph; the graph indicated the speed, height, base of coverage for each exposure and exposure interval. To give one example: at a speed of 120 m.p.h. from a height of 10,000 feet, each exposure included a base length of 800 yards of terrain, and with a given load of thirty-six plates, the pilot could cover stereoscopically slightly more than seventeen miles of terrain features, clicking off exposures at precise 15-second intervals. When the negatives were printed in stereo pairs and examined under matched pairs of magnifying glasses, such details as machine gun emplacements, camouflaged artillery batteries, ammunition dumps and even individual observation posts leaped up with startling clarity. The work—especially stereo missions—required flying finesse, for the maximum benefit could be achieved only by maintaining constant speed and elevation and—even more important—keeping the axis of the lens as nearly perpendicular to the ground as possible during the long, rigidly determined flight path while the exposures were in train.

The Escadrille photographic sortie left St. Pol at 4 P.M. The four Spads flew out across the ocean, gleaming in the sunlight, then turned sharply in to cross the narrow white strip of sandy coastline and began the depressing trip across the muddy brown swamp that stretched eastward as far as the eye could see. Willis was leading, with Lufbery and Lovell flying the flanks; Parsons held station above and to the rear. With the first beautiful flying weather in over a week, the sky over the lines was fairly crawling with British and French planes, but of the enemy there was no sign.

Fifteen miles inside the German lines, with the photography completed, Willis waggled his wings and pointed downward with his gloved hand. Parsons recalled: "Below us we caught sight of six Boche planes performing all sorts of fantastic evolutions . . . we had the advantage of height and decided to attack. Each of us picked a German and dived. We opened fire, only to have the Germans disappear from in front of our guns. They dropped in baffling twists, whirling about with devilish skill, bringing into play all the tricks of aerial acrobatics we had ever heard of—not even the great Lufbery could get inside their guard.

"We kept after them for thirty-five minutes—an eternity in combat—but got nowhere. We should have known better than to stay so long that far inside German territory, but we kept at it minute after minute, hoping one of us would score."

Hotly engaged, the Americans did not see a second layer of Albatros dropping down from above until it was almost too late. The first warning came when Parsons' Spad was jumped and he heard "the depressing sound of bullets whining and crackling over my head." To warn the others, who were battling at lesser altitudes, Parsons shoved the stick forward and streaked through the milling planes beneath him, flashing past Willis like a meteor, with the German still on his tail. With the arrival of the new enemy, the Americans quickly broke off the fight and scattered for home. Willis, who was already in a dive, steepened it when he saw a thick fog bank 1500 feet below. But he and Lufbery and Lovell managed to become swallowed up in its clammy embrace before the Germans had a chance to nail them. They found the earth clouded over when they reached the lines, so they flew out to sea and dropped down near the waves to fly along the coast until the familiar sight of the Dunkerque lighthouse signaled that they were home. They landed safely in the mist and awaited the arrival of Parsons.

The one great advantage of a Spad was its ability to outdive anything else in the air and recover without losing its wings—a quality lacking in the structurally weaker Albatros. With the Albatros on his tail firing steadily, Parsons pushed his one advantage to the limit. He held the stick forward with both hands and watched the altimeter rapidly unwind as the engine screamed in protest. He held the dive for 6000 feet and risked a glance over his shoulder; the Albatros was still following, but was at least 300 yards behind—too far for accurate marksmanship. Parsons hauled back on the stick and came out of the dive with the Spad quivering and vibrating, the wires howling like banshees. The plane eased up from the bottom of the curve and Parsons leveled out with full throttle. The German pilot tried to follow, but came out at least 500 feet below Parsons. Still game, he climbed back up and continued the chase.

Parsons flew home through a heavy antiaircraft barrage and was surprised to see the Albatros plowing through the explosions, determined to renew the battle. Parsons reached the British lines, then decided to go back and fight. "We jockeyed for several minutes, neither of us gaining the advantage. It was getting late, and both of us were running short of fuel and ammo. On the next circle, I waved at Fritz—somewhat derisively—and nearly fell out of the cockpit when he waved back. It was my first and last experience of exchanging personal courtesies in the air with the enemy." Parsons landed at St. Pol with two minutes of fuel remaining in his reserve tank, and learned he had been reported missing in combat.

The Circus pilots had demonstrated flying ability and courage well above the ordinary; their marksmanship left the Americans unimpressed. All four Spads were carefully gone over, but only one small hole was found in Lovell's elevator.

The Escadrille spent another week at St. Pol before the Group was recalled, but the time passed without incident. Off hours the pilots waded through strands of rusting barbed wire to swim in the gentle surf, or rode into nearby St. Omer, where the streets were jammed with troops, the stores garrisoned with avaricious merchants and the nights filled with importuning females. Near the field, Bill Thaw came across a derelict Nieuport fuselage and devoted several afternoons to calking the seams, shellacking the linen bottom and sides and fitting a thwart where the seat had been. He called the result a boat, and much to everybody's surprise, it floated. The kayak-looking craft was launched every fair afternoon with *pinard* and bottles of stout English beer.

They were marking time, waiting for word to come that would decide their fate as individuals and as a squadron once America became a *de facto* combatant. Already there were signs. The formerly indifferent War Department was now begging the French to release any willing Lafayette Flying Corps pilots to come home to instruct American cadets. In the memorandum Thénault received from G.Q.G., it was pointed out that applicants for Stateside instructors must not be commissioned officers (almost no American was) and must hold the *Croix de Guerre* (few Americans were without). Masson, Johnson and Bigelow—with thirty-five months of service between them—immediately applied for transfer.

As it turned out, Bigelow's health failed him before his application was processed, Johnson waited almost a year before he received orders for Stateside duty, and Masson didn't reach home until the war was over. Their hopes were thwarted by the chaotic affairs of an unprepared nation frantically muddling forward to fight a war it had never dreamed of entering.

Nieuport 28C-1

CHAPTER 13

GREAT EXPECTATIONS

The General Staff is now trying to run the Air Service with just as much knowledge of it as a hog knows about skating.
—BRIG. GEN. WILLIAM MITCHELL

In writing about United States preparedness for aerial warfare as late as 1917, General John J. Pershing commented: "The situation . . . was such that every American ought to feel mortified to hear it mentioned. Out of 65 officers and about 1000 men in the Air Service Section of the Signal Corps, there were 35 officers who could fly. With the exception of five or six officers, none of them could have met the requirement of modern battle conditions."

And in France the visionary renegade Lieutenant Colonel "Billy" Mitchell observed, "Our air force consists of one Nieuport which I used myself, and that is all."

The American trait of brash optimism was never more evident

than during the first few months following the entry of America into the war. Congress rashly promised "to darken the skies over Germany" with American-built aircraft powered by American-designed engines and manned by American-trained pilots. To this end, on July 24, $640 million was voted for military aeronautics. The appropriation included funds for the construction of 22,625 aircraft (four times the number then in service with the French, British and Italian air services) and 44,000 engines. The sum was the largest ever voted for a single purpose in the nation's history, and was intended to assure the elevation of America to the world's leading air power.[1]

Even with unlimited funds and an awesome industrial potential, a nation that had been aeronautically asleep for more than a decade could not be turned overnight into a country capable of mass-producing machines for warfare in the new dimension. Denied access to research and development data by the French and British governments for nearly three years, America began its aviation program virtually from scratch. As a consequence, the first American-built aircraft—a British-designed D.H.-4—didn't reach France until thirteen months after the United States entered the war, and when the Armistice was signed, a tally of U. S.-constructed combat planes on the Western Front revealed the dismal figure of 196—hardly enough to darken the skies over a cow pasture, much less a nation.

When it became evident, during the summer of 1917, that America was planning to create a truly formidable air arm, the executive committee of the Lafayette Flying Corps decided that it would serve the best interests of the nation if all American pilots then serving in French squadrons were formally asked to make application for transfer to the U. S. Air Service. Dr. Gros somehow managed to obtain a direct commission as a major—not in the Medical Corps, but in the Air Service—and, outfitted in a choke-collared tunic and black boots, paid a call on the pilots of the Lafayette Escadrille, to whom he was jokingly known as "our Secretary of War." Gros explained that he had already had talks

[1] In 1914 the United States ranked fourteenth among nations in air strength and appropriations for its development—below near-medieval Russia and feudal Japan. In 1917, as in 1941 and 1951, America's preparations for a major war were undertaken only after its outbreak.

with the French authorities, who had agreed to release the Americans in order that they could accept commissions in their own army. Pressed for details, Gros replied that he really hadn't received any firm commitments from the U. S. Air Service, but that he nevertheless believed they should offer their services to their own government. Then he made the mistake of asking that the pilots remove the French cocardes from their planes and substitute American ones, which had white centers instead of blue.

"At this," reported Willis, "the row was on. When the dust settled, the Captain discovered that the entire Escadrille intended to fly under French colors as long as we are a French outfit—that we do not intend to lose our identity—that American officers now in training in France are not going to take charge of us until they prove worthy of the responsibility, and lastly that the Escadrille remains French until the question of machines, mechanics and grades as officers under American colors are satisfactory . . . they are not going to hang anything on us."

Gros was unprepared for this vehement opposition; he was never able to appreciate the strong emotional bonds the Escadrille pilots had formed with the French nation—bonds literally cemented in blood—and could not imagine why the Americans were not eager to muster under U. S. command. When Gros began sounding out the feelings of the Americans serving in various French escadrilles he found the same hesitancy and doubt; nobody was willing to commit themselves until Gros could provide a definite offer from the War Department.

Late in August, Gros sent each of the American pilots a form letter that began, "Dear Sir," and continued, "I hear that a certain number of you do not wish to be transferred to the U. S. Air Service. I believe you will be given your choice, but in your decision remember that positively no further allowances will be paid from the Lafayette Flying Corps funds. . . . As I am anxious to know immediately your intentions in this matter, will you let me know without delay what you intend doing? If you pass the U. S. Air Service physical and mental tests, you will probably be proposed for a commission, sub or full lieutenancy."

This letter, containing as it did no firm offer of rank, drew no replies. Few of the Escadrille pilots believed they could pass the reputedly stiff U. S. physicals, and they did not like to be told they would "probably" be commissioned—particularly skeptical were Thaw and Lufbery, who were already *sous-lieutenants*. And the fact that their Corps allowances would be cut off—which amounted to two-thirds of their total pay—seemed to be a lever to force them into transferring. Gros's letter caused uneasiness and endless debate. Word of the pilots' outspoken criticism of the way in which their affairs were being handled reached the ears of Commandant Féquant, whose own sharply contradictory reactions were, to say the least, baffling.

First, on August 3, 1917, he had written a four-page memorandum addressed to G.Q.G. in which he pointed to "the splendid spirit of the *Escadrille Lafayette* and its devotion to duty that has been a matter of pride to all Americans and has helped to bring their country to our aid in the war. The spirit of sacrifice of these men, who came as volunteers to fight for us, is revealed in the last words of those who have been killed. All of them said they would gladly give their lives in the service of France. Their example has raised morale even of the pilots in the French squadrons who have fought at their side. In order, then, to reward in some measure, the *Escadrille Lafayette* for the valor of its pilots and for its success as a squadron, I ask that it be cited in the order of the army."

Twelve days later the Escadrille was presented with a handsome, hand-decorated scroll signed by Marshal Pétain that extolled the squadron for its "exalted morale," and concluded with the following accolade: "It has excited the profound admiration of the officers who have it under their command, and of the French squadrons which, fighting by its side, have striven to vie with it in valor."

Féquant's second memorandum on the subject of the Escadrille followed on September 5—only three weeks after the squadron was cited—and began: "For some time, now, I have been aware of a certain uneasiness pervading the *Escadrille Lafayette*." He went on to say that "the majority of the pilots seem to be disinterested in maintaining the high reputation of their unit . . . only the best among them continue to be motivated by the most notable sentiments of duty." Féquant blamed the "low morale" on the pilots' uncertainty about their future in the U. S.

Air Service or in the *Service Aéronautique* in the case of those who planned to remain. He said he feared this negative attitude would damage the reputation for valor the Escadrille had established. Féquant strongly urged that the Lafayette Escadrille ("whose soul has fled") be "cleanly and quickly" wiped from existence, its pilots scattered throughout other French squadrons, their places at N.124 filled by other French pilots.

This astonishing request, which came on the heels of hard fighting that saw two more German planes go down under the guns of Lufbery and Parsons, was immediately turned down. Féquant's views on the state of morale seemed extreme, and the sudden erasure of the famous squadron would have been impossible to explain away. There was no legitimate excuse for Féquant's drastic suggestion—one which he never made again. The best explanation is that he mistakenly equated soldierly griping for moral disintegration.

The next letter from Major Gros offered greater encouragement to the Escadrille pilots, who were informed that applicants who failed the U. S. Army physical would be "passed judgment on in the broadest sense, taking into account your record at the Front and your ability as fliers." He then assured them that those accepted would "get at least a 1st lieutenancy, some may get a captain's commission. My advice," he concluded, "is to trust us and you will not regret it." Put to a vote, the Escadrille pilots agreed to request transfer in a body to the U.S.A.S.

A four-man team of examiners, including the ubiquitous Major Gros, appeared at the Escadrille early in October and spent the better part of a day probing into the health of the pilots. "The physicals," said Parsons, "included a long series of rather ridiculous demonstrations—which weren't helped by frequent visits to the bar to bolster our courage." The pilots were blindfolded and made to hop on one foot, then the other, in a straight line; they were spun around in a revolving chair until they were giddy, then told to keep their wavering eyeballs focused on a pencil point swinging back and forth a few inches from their nose; water, heated to 70° F, was poured into each ear to induce nystagmus—oscillation of the eyeball; nonsense rhymes were whispered from twenty feet away and had to be repeated verbatim; blood samples were drawn, urinalysis was done and stethoscopes applied.

When the ordeal was over and the results analyzed, hardly a single Lafayette Escadrille pilot was judged physically capable of piloting an airplane. Lufbery, Marr and Doc Rockwell were overage at thirty-two, as was Soubiran at thirty-one. Jones had flat feet. Hill's vision in his right eye was limited to finger perception. Thaw's left eye was partially atrophied, testing at 20/80, his hearing was defective, one knee was not fully articulated, and his wounded elbow was permanently crooked. Dolan proved to be myopic. Lovell, an ancient thirty-three, was surprised to learn that he was color-blind and suffered from poor hearing. The doctors packed up their testing apparatus and the dossiers on the unpromising material at N.124 and moved on, wondering what the staff officers of the A.E.F. would think.

When Pershing arrived in France in the summer of 1917, he set up his headquarters at Chaumont, from where the American war effort would receive its field direction. He chose Brigadier General William Kenly as his Chief of Air Service. Kenly was not an aviator, but he plunged into the job with the determination to create an air arm superior to any on the Western Front. Equally dedicated was his G-4 (Staff Supply Officer) Colonel Raynal C. Bolling, who, along with Mitchell, was drawing up recommendations for the type of equipment to be produced in America in order to speed up the aerial offensive against Germany. One of Kenly's first tasks was the processing of the reports on American aviators who had applied for transfer from the *Service Aéronautique* to the U.S.A.S. Kenly, a realist, was not troubled by the adverse physical records and quickly persuaded Pershing to recommend unconditional waivers. No doubt both Kenly and Pershing were strongly influenced by the written summation of the pilots' characters and motivation. The examining team reported:

"The Board was much impressed by the class of men examined, the fine reports of their work given by their commanding officers, and their great desire to serve under their own colors. The material is valuable as a nucleus of aviators, experienced at the Front, around whom can be grouped the less experienced pilots recently trained or undergoing training here. It is capital with which to build and should be preserved. . . . It is the opinion of the Board and of the French officers commanding these Americans that their position should be settled as soon as possible; that they should be allowed to remain at the Front until required by the A.E.F., and that as soon as they are required they should immediately undertake the new duties assigned to them."

Plans for incorporating the Escadrille into the U.S.A.S., for grouping the hundred-odd American pilots scattered across France into U. S. squadrons, were going rapidly forward when the blow fell. President Wilson stunned those at Chaumont by the sudden removal of Kenly, replacing him with Brigadier General Benjamin Foulois who was neither an active pilot nor had ever been in France to study conditions there.

Mitchell remarked that Foulois brought with him "a shipload of aviation officers, almost none of whom had ever seen an airplane —a more incompetent lot of air warriors had never arrived in the zone of active military operation. As rapidly as possible, the competent men who had learned their duties in the face of the enemy were displaced and their positions filled by these carpetbaggers. Colonel Bolling was relieved of his command, and the contracts he had made with the French for aeronautical material were cancelled. "This was serious," Mitchell pointed out, "as it occasioned another long delay in getting suitable planes."

Major William W. Hoffman, one of the four members of the examining board, recently recalled: "I had never seen Pershing so angry. He fully approved of everything Kenly had been doing and had the utmost confidence in his staff. Kenly was fired without foreknowledge on Pershing's part . . . Foulois was shoved down his throat. 'If they send me any more like Foulois and that bunch, I'll resign!' Pershing said, and he meant it. Foulois probably meant well, but neither he nor his staff had a tenth of the knowledge that Kenly and Bolling did.

"Bolling, one of the finest men I have ever known, was shaken to the core by the turn of events and wanted to flee the poisonous atmosphere prevailing in Paris and at Chaumont. He perfected his flying and later managed to get permission to go out with a British squadron at the Front."

To reach the R.A.F. airdrome where Bolling hoped to begin a new life as an operational fighter pilot, he secured the loan of a staff car and a nineteen-year-old A.E.F. driver. Once past the Zone of Interior, they began making their way over unmarked shell-torn roads that led up to the Front, which was then in a state of flux. They got lost, and the driver unknowingly drove past the British lines and into no man's land. Proceeding at a crawl, the car topped a rise and then the driver slammed on the brakes. Twenty yards ahead, coming at them in double-time, was a platoon of heavily armed German infantry.

The driver opened the door and bolted out one side of the car, while Bolling leaped from the back seat and flung himself into a shell hole. The driver, seeing they were hopelessly snared, threw up his hands and was captured. The Germans yelled out for Bolling to surrender. Instead, he jumped upright and opened fire with a .45 Colt automatic. The driver watched helplessly as the waiting Germans riddled Bolling with rifle slugs, knocking him backward in the shell crater.

Mitchell was kept on as Air Commander, Zone of the Advance. Foulois moved his staff from Paris to Chaumont, whereupon Mitchell shifted his headquarters to Neufchâteau. "My new office," he wryly commented, "was at 10 rue de la Comédie—which was a good name considering the state of our air organization at the Front."

Foulois' accession to power frustrated the Escadrille's hopes of quick transfer. Kenly's meticulously worked out plans were shelved, and the new staff began a wasteful re-examination of the character reports of every American pilot in the *Service Aéronautique*. It seemed to the disgusted Escadrille pilots that they were no nearer to wearing American uniforms than they had been seven months before when Congress declared war.

This turmoil within the squadron began during a frantically busy period—the most hectic in the Escadrille's eighteen-month history.

Gotha G-V

CHAPTER 14

COMBAT

When all is said, L. L., ours is a beastly business, isn't it?
—JAMES NORMAN HALL

In the predawn darkness of August 13, 1917, the deadly passage of thousands of heavy shells rent the air with awful shrieks and once again the hills in front of Verdun erupted in a cataclysm of smoke and flame. But this time the guns were French, 2500 of them, and the hurricane of destruction was falling on German heads. Along the fifteen-mile stretch from Avoucourt on the left to the Bois des Caurières on the right, nearly 100,000 French assault troops crouched in shallow trenches or rested in battered dugouts, listening to the awesome thrumming as shells ripped across the sky. They waited expectantly for the days to pass and the lifting of the bombardment; then they would surge forward across the tortured hills and hurl the Germans back, away from Verdun. This was to be a Pétain offensive, leaning heavily on the weight of artillery, sparing of men, designed to shove the enemy

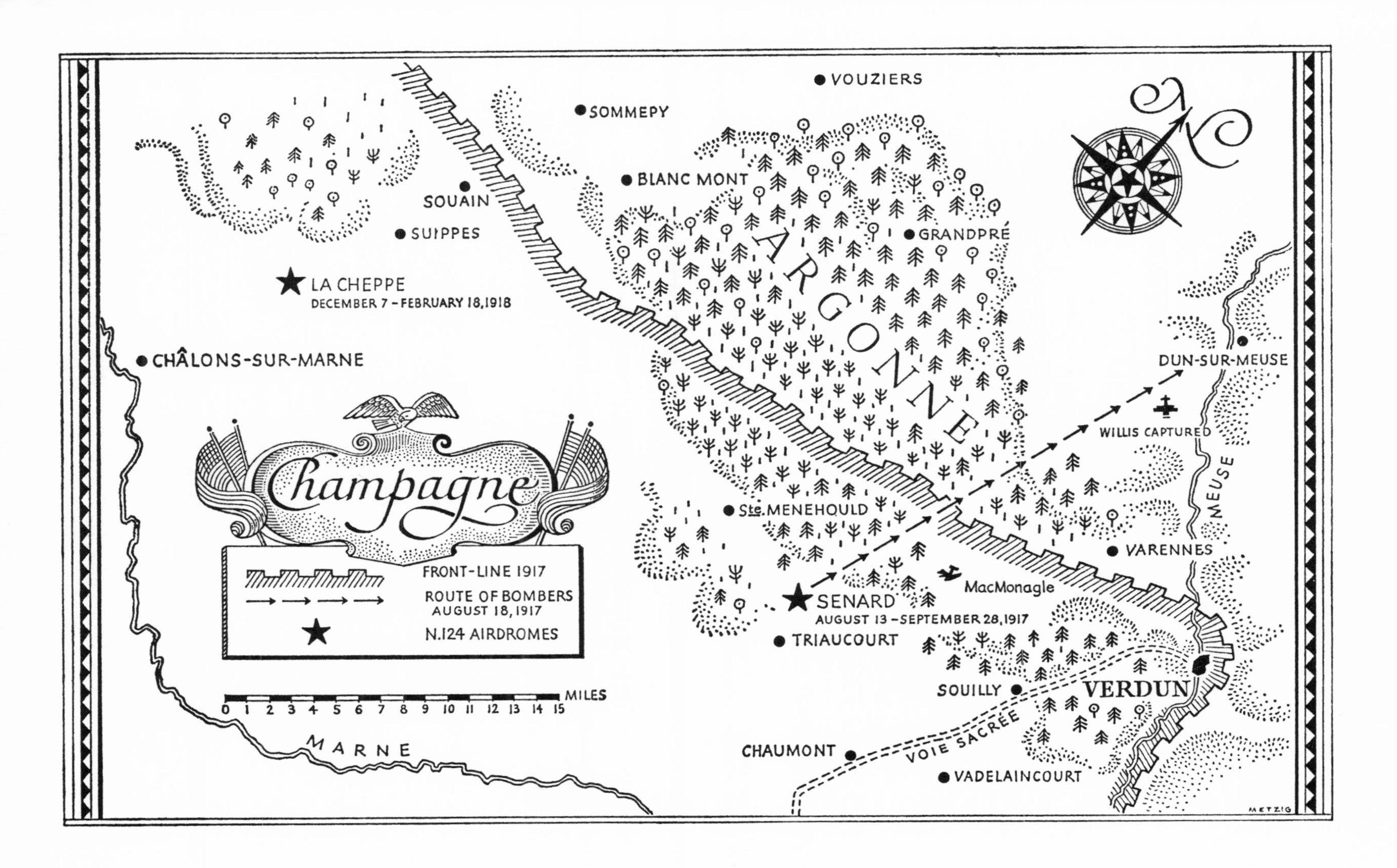

VOUZIERS
SOMMEPY
BLANC MONT
SOUAIN
SUIPPES
GRANDPRÉ
ARGONNE
LA CHEPPE
DECEMBER 7 - FEBRUARY 18, 1918
CHÂLONS-SUR-MARNE
DUN-SUR-MEUSE
WILLIS CAPTURED
MEUSE
Champagne
FRONT-LINE 1917
ROUTE OF BOMBERS
AUGUST 18, 1917
N.124 AIRDROMES
Ste. MENEHOULD
VARENNES
MacMonagle
SENARD
AUGUST 13 - SEPTEMBER 28, 1917
TRIAUCOURT
SOUILLY
VERDUN
0 1 2 3 4 5 6 7 8 9 10 11 12 13 14 15 MILES
MARNE
CHAUMONT
VOIE SACRÉE
VADELAINCOURT
METZIG

back to his start-line of February 21, 1916. This done, reasoned G.Q.G., the bitter tea of Nivelle's bloody fiasco along the Chemin-des-Dames might be better digested—and no better place for a grand tactical victory than at Verdun, the very symbol of the nation's will to endure.

The Spads of *Groupe de Combat* 13 flew into Senard from St. Pol on the afternoon of the first day of the bombardment. From the field at Senard, in the foothills of the Argonne and only twenty miles below Verdun, the ceaseless drumming of the cannonading beat the air with awesome intensity. Dinner that evening was accompanied by the clamor of the guns, the pilots went to sleep with the drumfire ringing in their ears, and when they got up the next morning to dress for patrol they noted that the fury was not abating. It was to be a nonstop bombardment, lasting until the bugles shrilled for the assault to begin.

That morning, August 14, Thénault led Parsons and Willis over the right bank of the Meuse, where they were jumped by four aggressive German pilots flying Albatros fighters with orange fuselages. They fought the Escadrille pilots to a standstill. That afternoon Lufbery took Parsons and Lovell over the smoking battlefield, and they tackled five two-seaters which immediately tightened up in a defensive formation that resisted effectively every firing pass the Americans made. Every time Lufbery pulled up underneath and directly astern—the two-seater's blind spot—he came under fire from one or more of the other gunners and had to break off his attack. The Americans returned scoreless to Senard, where Lufbery counted a dozen holes in the wings of his Spad. "Then we realized," said Parsons, "that we were to have no easy time of it at Senard, and we began to look back upon our pleasant stay at St. Pol with no little misgiving."

Air strikes on enemy resources as a prelude to large-scale ground offensives were finding increasing favor with the French. Seventeen miles north of Verdun lay Dun-sur-Meuse, the vital rail center feeding a constant stream of men and munitions to the dug-in German Army, which was beginning to suffer heavy losses from the murderous bombardment. And nearby, at Bantheville, French photographic planes had uncovered a vast, heavily camouflaged ammunition dump where thousands of shells were stacked. A strike on the strategic targets—disrupting rail traffic, robbing the German guns—would pay tactical dividends when the four French army corps rolled forward on August 20. Accordingly G.Q.G. ordered Dun bombed forty-eight hours before the ground assault was to begin.

The strike force consisted of thirty-one Sopwith 1½ Strutters belonging to *Groupe de Bombardement* 1, whose commander called on Captain Thénault and asked for fighter escort for this mission, which he said he expected to be hotly opposed. Thénault agreed, and assigned six Spads to the raiding force. The bomber chief had fixed ideas about how a fighter escort should be utilized; he explained that he wanted the escort split into two elements of three planes each, each element to take up station on either flank of the bomber formation, and at the same altitude. Moreover, he wanted the Spads to stick with the bombers and not attack enemy fighters unless they were making firing passes directly on the flanks. It was argued that effective fighter protection could only be carried out if the escort was given flexibility, was kept together and was stacked *above* the bombers. But the Sopwith chief remained adamant, and since he would be the air commander that day, there was no appeal.

The Escadrille Spads left Senard at ten on the morning of the eighteenth and arrived in formation at the rendezvous point in space, 14,000 feet above the sprawling green Argonne Forest. They circled lazily, waiting for the heavily loaded Strutters. When the massed Sopwiths thundered by below, the Escadrille fighters split into two tiny groups and obediently dropped down and took up station beside the bombers. Even throttled back, the Spads were much faster than the Sopwiths, and the Americans were forced to fly continual lazy S-patterns in order not to outstrip the others.

Ten minutes before the formation reached the target, Albatros interceptors began dropping out of the sun in twos and threes. Hank Jones, who was flying on the starboard wing of the formation, watched as a trio of Germans "filtered right straight through the whole formation," firing as they went. It quickly became apparent that the French Sopwith chief's rigid idea was hopelessly wrong. Forbidden to engage, the Americans watched in frustration as the Germans flashed in and out of the formation, trading shots with the French gunners. But they stayed beside the bombers, still S-turning as though on a practice flight.

More Albatros joined the attack on the Sopwiths, and some of them bored in on the flanks. Parsons, intent on keeping his distance from the Sopwiths flying to his left, did not see the Albatros diving on him from his right rear. The first inkling he had that he was being attacked came when tracers began flashing between his wings. A hundred yards behind, Willis swung into position and hurriedly opened fire on the German, who banked sharply away, taking his guns from Parsons' back. Seconds later, tracers began flying around Willis' head, and he pulled up steeply into an Immelmann turn to shake loose a second Albatros. The two paired off and began a close-in duel, which was soon joined by two more Albatros.

"It would not have been so bad," observed Willis, "had my engine not been hit at the first volley. It worked only intermittently, causing loss of height. We had a wild fight almost to the ground, sometimes missing collision by inches. I was badly raked by cross fire and heard the music of bullets striking engine and control cables. Toward the end, my windshield was shattered, and my goggles were broken by a ball—which slightly stunned me. I had an awful feeling of despair at the thought of the inevitable landing in Germany. As I neared the ground, I had an instant's desire to dive into it.

"I saw a wood in front of me, jumped over it and landed instinctively on the crest of a hill. One of the Germans flew over me, waved his hand, turned and landed nearby—followed by his two comrades.

"They all saluted very properly as they came up—young chaps, perfectly correct. My machine was a wreck: thirty bullets in the engine, radiator and fuselage; exactly half of the cables cut, tires punctured, wings riddled. It was a beautiful machine and had always served me well. I thought it was all too bad . . ."

Less than an hour later Willis was sitting at a mess table having breakfast with the men who had been doing their best to kill him only a short time before. When the last cup of coffee had been drunk, Willis got into a German staff car and was driven away to the prison-fortress at Montmédy. When the door clanged shut behind him, Willis regretted he had left the ground that morning wearing only pajamas under his flying suit; he carried no identification, no cigarettes and no money. Alone in his cell, a prisoner in Germany, Willis sat down on his cot "and cried like a baby."

Parsons had seen Willis take the Albatros off his tail and go climbing upward, but another enemy fighter jumped him and he lost sight of Willis as he fought off the second attack within as many minutes. The Sopwith formation, under the press of repeated assaults, began to widen and drift, but the Frenchmen bored on and unloaded their bombs from 12,000 feet; then they wheeled in a huge circle and began fighting their way back home.

More Albatros came down—how many, no one was able to estimate—and the battle turned into a mêlée. A Sopwith drifted away from the formation, a small jet of flame licking from the fuselage—a bright orange spot that quickly grew into a sheet of fire that engulfed the pilot's and gunner's cockpit. The doomed plane nosed down out of control, trailing a ragged column of black smoke.

Through the swarming mass of planes, Walter Lovell picked out a straggling Sopwith boxed in by six German fighters. Lovell hurled his Spad at them and shot one of the Albatros down in flames; the ferocity of his attack scattered the others, and the 1½ Strutter limped safely away.

Steve Bigelow suddenly saw an Albatros hurtling at his Spad head-on, guns winking fire. Before he could react, a burst of lead tore away his windscreen and a split second later the German had disappeared. Fragments laid Bigelow's cheek open nearly to the bone, and he steered erratically away from the fight, trying to sop up the blood with his scarf.

The German fighters pressed their attacks all the way to the French lines, and before the bombers could reach the sanctuary of their own territory a second bomber slipped drunkenly from the formation and fell through the sky to crash in the Argonne. Then the hammering of the guns fell silent; the battle was over, and there remained the descent through friendly skies to the field at Senard.

The field was long and narrow, with all the hangars ranged along one side. Jammed as it was with aircraft belonging to two groups, the ground traffic at Senard was strictly regulated; an inflexible rule required landing bombers and fighters to taxi to the far end of the field, turning to taxi back to their own hangar area—U-turns anywhere on the airdrome were prohibited.

Courtney Campbell, the Escadrille's practical joker, was one of the first to land at Senard. He touched down at the near end of the field, cut back on the throttle and began rolling down the grass. In his ears beat the clattering roar of Clerget rotary engines belonging to the Sopwiths, many of them returning badly shot-up. As Campbell neared the Escadrille hangar, he shoved the throttle forward and kicked sharply on the rudder bar, intending to turn directly into the hangar, thus saving himself the long trip to the opposite end of the field and back again. The next few seconds were a nightmare.

A bomber following closely behind Campbell in the landing pattern settled almost on top of the Spad turning in the center of the field. The French pilot frantically hauled back on the stick and the Strutter lurched upward, but not before its propeller had ripped into Campbell's top wing, gashing it to splinters almost down its length. Terrified, Campbell ducked and grabbed the cockpit rim and held on as his Spad was flung on its side and rolled over in a grating, ripping crash of sound. The 1½ Strutter bounced heavily to earth and slewed down the field. Scores of hands helped untangle Campbell from the wreckage, which was jerked and hauled out of the landing path. Campbell, shaken but unhurt, lit a cigarette and nonchalantly strolled off to the bar, oblivious of the uproar his flagrant violation of orders had created.

To the outraged bomber crews, it was a foregone conclusion that Campbell would be summarily kicked out of the *Service Aéronautique*—they had seen French pilots sent back to the infantry as a result of far less serious infractions. But if they expected Draconian measures from Captain Thénault, they were disappointed: Campbell was in no way punished.

This incredible lapse in military procedure was due to Thénault's peculiar status as commanding officer. When he had accepted command of N.124 under the Ministry of War's dictate that the Americans were not to be handled with standard French Army discipline, he placed himself in an almost impossible position. Effective command of any body of men—especially in wartime—rests upon absolute authority and the discretionary power of discipline, and these Thénault did not have. This frustrating handicap, a purely political consideration running counter to common-sense military considerations, whittled down Thénault's authority until he was exercising only routine leadership. But at no time did he seek to relinquish his responsibility. Georges Thénault was a professional soldier infused with the traditions of St. Cyr; to quit his post, no matter how cross-grained to his nature or disagreeable it was, would have been unthinkable.

After seven days of around-the-clock bombardment, Pétain launched his offensive. It began on the morning of August 20, a hot cloudless day, and the dry ground offered sure footing for the infantrymen who swept forward behind a rolling barrage. That day the pilots of *Groupe* 13 were up before dawn, some of them preparing for takeoff while the stars were fading in the lightening sky. The Spads ranged deep inside the German lines to beat back flights of enemy observation planes, summoned by the desperate artillery, and they roared low over the yellow-brown smoking battlefield, strafing tiny figures in field-gray. They saw the white signal rockets arcing up from the French line of advance, rockets that told them the offensive was rapidly gaining ground. These rockets, indicating to friendly artillery the position of leading elements of the advance wave, began appearing over terrain the Germans had tenaciously held for long, bloody months . . . Hill 304, Samogneux, Regneville and bitterly contested Mort Homme all fell to the exultant *poilus*.

On the sixth day the offensive slammed to a victorious halt. Both banks of the Meuse were cleared and the Germans were flung back four miles in the center, ousted from thirty square miles of territory. Just as Pétain ordered his men to stop moving forward and consolidate the gains, the skies opened and torrents of rain fell for eight straight days. On September 3 the clouds melted away and the sun blazed down.

"The Boche came out in full force," wrote Lovell. "At different points of our sector Hun observation machines kept crossing our lines at very high altitudes, and we were on the jump all day driving them back. Lufbery and I were out on the same patrol and no sooner had we reached the lines than we found two big fat Hun bi-place machines waiting for us. They were using incendiary bullets, and for a while it looked like a Fourth of July celebration. The Boche finally beat it off. In this mix-up, Lufbery received three bullets in his machine—an incendiary was still smoking in his landing gear when we got back.

"Shortly afterwards, we discovered a solitary Hun bi-place trying to sneak into our lines. We pounced on him and gave him a warm reception until four of his comrades came to his rescue. One machine I attacked was apparently badly hit. He went volplaning back into his own lines. If this good weather keeps up, I see some very active times ahead."

Lufbery was aloft at dawn the following morning and jumped a two-seater that was alone over the battlefield. He had his hands full, for the Germans were giving as good as they were taking; the observer put several holes in Lufbery's Spad, and when he tried to take them from the front, the pilot took a crack at him with his synchronized Maxim. The battle lasted for several minutes, Lufbery firing short bursts almost constantly. On his last pass from the rear, he observed that the German gunner had dropped from sight and was no longer firing. He came up underneath the looming two-seater and clamped down on the trigger grip. But his Vickers gun remained silent; he had no ammunition left. The German plane got away.

When, on the same morning, Parsons, Doc Rockwell and Dud Hill were getting ready to take off to patrol the left bank, the others noticed Parsons was wiring something to an inboard strut. The object was a life-sized, stuffed black velvet cat—a gift from a beauteous Parisienne named Renée de Ranville, with whom Parsons had spent many pleasant hours while on leave in the city. The spitting cat, with flowing silk whiskers, was a talisman Parsons hoped would break his streak of bad luck in not getting confirmations for what he knew were sure kills.

They were at 15,000 feet over the Meuse when Rockwell and Hill began jumping their planes up and down, the signal for engine trouble. Parsons watched the others turn for home and decided to finish the patrol on his own side of the lines.

He recalled: "It was a clear, beautiful day and my engine was running like a fine Swiss watch. Suddenly, a flock of Germans appeared, headed for our lines. I counted ten Albatros, but instead of crossing the lines they turned and began flying back and forth behind their own trenches. I watched them closely, paralleling their movements. I wasn't afraid of their numbers, because I had superior altitude and knew I could outrun them if I had to. Twice, we flew from the Meuse to the Argonne and back, neither of us making an offensive move.

"At the end of the beat, the Hun leader would whirl and the nine planes behind him instantly wheeled around behind him with the precision of wild geese. During this time, French observation machines were at work several thousand feet below —I particularly noticed a twin-engined Letord.

"Two of the Albatros detached themselves from the rest and went down for the Letord; I wasn't worried about the Frenchmen, for the Letord carried three crewmen and had machine guns firing fore and aft and could take care of itself. I reasoned that I might take a chance and dive on one of the Albatros and get him while he was going down. I put my nose down and started after the one nearest to me. Then I got the shock of my life. Shooting into my line of flight was a German two-seater; I had a quick glimpse of camouflaged wings and a dirty, oil-stained belly. *Where had he come from?* Collision seemed certain, and my heart skipped a beat.

"Then my instincts took over from my partially paralyzed brain. I wrenched the Spad violently around in a brutal right bank. The plane was new, and the wings held, but I fell off in a vicious spin. Putting the controls in neutral, I eased back on the stick and leveled out. There, not more than a hundred feet ahead, flew the big two-seater in perfect position to be attacked. I was so close I could see the observer's face—the first time I had ever seen the countenance of the enemy. I thought he was smiling, although in the circumstances I could not imagine why. I squeezed the trigger.

"The Vickers rattled off only ten rounds, but I saw the observer fling up his arms; the same shot that got him probably got the pilot as well, for the plane fell off on one wing and headed down. It swung back and forth like a falling leaf, then pitched forward on its nose and dropped like a plummet.

"I followed them down to make sure I had got them. Suddenly the top wing ripped loose, and I knew they were going to crash. I had been robbed too many times of confirmations, and was determined to make this one official. I checked my watch, then pulled the map case out from its hiding place underneath the front of the cockpit rim; the case, a flat, oblong box with a map inside that moved on rollers, was loose on its moorings, but I reached the map and scribbled down the time, 9:22 A.M., and the place the two-seater fell, near Neuvilly on the edge of the Argonne. I slid the map case back into place and turned for home.

"I lined up with the field, heading into the wind, then cut back the throttle as I eased the stick forward. When I pulled the stick back to level out, it wouldn't budge. I grabbed it with both hands and frantically heaved, but the stick was frozen solid. I was pointed at the ground in a shallow dive, and I watched in horror as the field rushed up to slam me in the face. Seized with a wild kind of panic, I sat momentarily paralyzed, then jammed my hand down to the base of the control column, where I found the map case wedged between the stick and the seat; the case had slipped unnoticed from its hiding place, its fastenings having worked loose in flight. I flipped the case aside and jerked back on the stick barely in time; the Spad lifted and then slammed down on the grass in the roughest landing I had made since my Blériot days—but I was alive."

Parsons' kill was confirmed the following morning. He gave credit for his first confirmation and for his narrow escape from death to the stuffed velvet cat, and he never again left the ground without the talisman riding the starboard wing.

When de Laage had been killed in May, a French pilot named Antoine Arnoux de Maison Rouge had been sent up as the Escadrille's new executive officer. Slight, pale, high-strung and reserved, Lieutenant Arnoux was the opposite of de Laage in every way. Coming as he did from a regular French operational squadron, N.67, he was aghast at the Americans' freewheeling attitude toward authority, and he held himself aloof from the mess-hall garrulity. To Arnoux, Americans were "savages." Even his most outspoken detractors admitted that he was in a difficult position; any officer stepping into de Laage's shoes would have found it rough going—just how rough was revealed during a patrol on September 19.

That day, hot and brilliantly blue, Arnoux led Bridgman, Peterson, Marr and the irrepressible Campbell across the lines on the right bank of the Meuse, where they jumped a six-plane enemy formation. Peterson was the first to engage. He got on the tail of one Albatros and the German pilot made the mistake of trying to dive away from the faster Spad. Peterson stayed glued to his tail, lacing the German plane with fire all the way down to 500 feet. The Albatros, which had been slipping and skidding across the sky, suddenly nosed steeply downward and plunged into the ground. It was Peterson's first kill. The others fought to no decision, and Arnoux led them home.

As they neared the field, Campbell pulled his Spad up until it was hovering just over Arnoux's head. The Frenchman waved Campbell away, but the Spad remained menacingly overhead. By looking over the side, Campbell could see the white, upturned face of his executive officer, his patrol leader, and the look of astonishment and outrage he saw there only made him more playful. He began bouncing up and down, each time dropping his slowly revolving wheels closer to Arnoux's top wing. The French officer was still vainly trying to wave the madman off when Campbell miscalculated and both wheels crunched into the other Spad's top wing and locked there. By now they were over the field and the hutments emptied of men, who stood gaping upward at the piggyback fighters struggling to free themselves. They made two circuits of the field, then Campbell, at a loss, put on full throttle and heaved back on the stick. The wheels ripped loose with a splintering sound that must have made Arnoux sick with fear.

He immediately throttled back and put his nose down as gently as he could, fearing that at any moment the weakened upper wing would tear loose, leaving him at the mercy of gravity. But the wing held, and he managed to get down safely. His nerves were as tattered as the wing, and he was never quite the same afterward. All along, he had believed the Americans were uncivilized; now, Campbell's harebrained performance convinced him they were lunatics as well.

Campbell, who had successfully evaded punishment following the near-disaster on the field after the raid on Dun-sur-Meuse, assumed he could get away with anything. In this he was correct: no action was taken against him. Parsons remembered that Campbell "demanded approbation for the clever way he had handled the whole affair."

The weather continued fair, and Lufbery took full advantage of the clear skies to fly one or two solo patrols a day in addition to the flight missions that came on the operations schedule. On the morning of September 22, he was out by himself at dawn, and while cruising high over the left bank of the Meuse intercepted a pair of German reconnaissance machines. He sent one spinning to earth for his twelfth confirmed kill; the other he drove back inside its own lines. Lufbery returned to the field in time to wish MacMonagle and Dolan a good time on their forty-eight-hour leave in Paris.

MacMonagle's first hours were spent with his mother, who had been in the capital for some time working as a volunteer nurse. Afterward, he and Dolan began making the rounds. They went from Harry's to the Chatham and from there MacMonagle lost track of both place and time. The next morning he again called on his mother, and again followed the pattern set the afternoon and evening before. That night on the train back to Senard, Dolan urged MacMonagle to try to get some sleep—a suggestion that the rugged MacMonagle vetoed as foolish. At several stops along the line, he got off the train and bought bottles of champagne, which he shared with the other fliers and infantrymen returning to the Front. Dolan, who knew there was a hard day ahead, stayed sober.

The train pulled into the station two hours before dawn, and it wasn't until after 3 A.M. that the two Escadrille pilots managed a ride on a truck into Senard. MacMonagle, who had lapsed into a doze on the final hour of the journey, came to life again as soon as he and Dolan were back at the field, still wrapped in darkness and in slumber. It occurred to MacMonagle that it would be a good idea to pay a call on the Captain. Dolan did his best to persuade MacMonagle that this was a notion best left alone at that hour of the morning, but MacMonagle shook off Dolan's restraining arm and bore down on Thénault's sleeping quarters. He flung open the door, walked across the floor and raised up one end of the cot where his commanding officer lay sleeping. He dropped the cot to the floor with a bang, ripped the covers from Thénault's reclining figure and shouted, "Come on, you old sonofabitch, get up!"

Thénault boiled out of bed in a blind rage, and shouted that he would teach the sergeant a lesson. He ordered MacMonagle to join the early patrol, due off the ground in little more than an hour. MacMonagle, far from subdued, only laughed defiantly and stalked from the hut.

By the time the patrol was due to leave, Dolan had managed to get almost a pot of black coffee inside MacMonagle. The pilots got into their cockpits and strapped themselves in. One after another, the Hispano-Suiza engines roared into life—except Parsons' and Hill's, which stubbornly refused. Lufbery waited patiently, his own engine ticking over smoothly, but after five futile minutes he raised his hand and gunned his Spad down the field, closely followed by Dolan, Rockwell and MacMonagle, who seemed to have command of his airplane.

As they climbed upward over the dark green swath of the Argonne, Dolan repeatedly looked back over his shoulder to keep track of MacMonagle, whose Spad began to wander to all points of the compass; first MacMonagle would sweep far to the east, then slide down underneath the others, then zoom sharply up off to the west. At various times he was above, below, behind and in front of the three Spads flying a tight V at 15,000 feet. Then, off to the east, against the rays of the sun that was lifting from the horizon, Lufbery made out eight Albatros fighters flying about 1500 feet above. He signaled to the others, and began a 360-degree climbing turn that would bring them behind and above the Germans, with the sun at their backs. Rockwell and Dolan pointed the noses of their Spads upward and followed hard on Lufbery's tail. When they noticed that MacMonagle wasn't with them, but was headed directly for the enemy fighters, they reversed course and turned to head him off. At the same time,

Parsons and Hill—who had left the ground twenty minutes late—were climbing up from far below to join the fight.

But none of them made it in time to help MacMonagle. They saw him plunge into the middle of the Albatros formation, and almost immediately fall away in a power dive that ended three miles below in the woods near Triaucourt. He probably never knew what hit him; when his body was pulled from the wreckage they found a single bullet hole in one temple, the slug passing through the other side of his head. Apparently satisfied with this murderously quick, absurdly easy victory, the Germans dived for home before the Spads could engage.

As soon as the patrol landed and reported the tragedy, Dolan drove off in a truck to recover MacMonagle's body, which lay inside the French lines. He brought it back wrapped in a tarpaulin, and the next day MacMonagle was buried at the military cemetery at Triaucourt, the firing squad furnished by engineers from the 1st American Infantry Division, then in training behind Verdun.

As a rule, pilots were kept off the duty roster for an eight-hour period following their return from leave; but there was not then, nor is there now, any question but that Thénault had the constituted authority to act as he did.

Whether or not MacMonagle would have been killed had he not gone up immediately after coming off leave is a moot question. James Norman Hall, who had known him since their training days together, pointed out that "Mac was a man to take chances, even very long ones. Furthermore, I know how keen he was on getting his first victory." Lufbery added that he wasn't positive MacMonagle had even seen the Germans, who were flying directly in the sun, before it was too late.

Essentially, the blame must fall on the system created by political expediency that allowed discipline to be flung to the winds, thus cultivating a climate that encouraged sergeants to believe they could flaunt their commanding officer with impunity, almost like upperclassmen hazing a freshman.

Since August the Germans had been waging a night-bombing campaign against the French aviation fields in the immediate vicinity of Verdun. They used twin-engined Gothas—black, narrow-winged monsters spanning 77 feet carrying three crewmen and more than a half ton of bombs. One of the most destructive nocturnal raids fell upon the mammoth field hospital at Vadelaincourt, and was witnessed by an American pilot whose squadron was based 800 yards south of the hospital. One Gotha had unloaded on the field, escaping safely through a hail of fire poured upward from the field, when a second bomber was seen approaching the packed sheds of wounded.

"We turned as one man," recounted the pilot, "to be greeted by the crash of the first bombs. It exploded fair in the center of the largest hospital building. A quick flash of flames showed the entire group of buildings with the huge red crosses on their roofs and, plain as day, we saw the great bird of ill omen circling above. Five times he turned, dove, dropped two bombs from less than 300 feet high, and disappeared into the night. The sixth time we saw the two gunners lean far out of their cockpits, while they poured streams of machine-gun bullets into the burning hospital buildings. . . . All night long the Huns came, and in the morning we learned that every hospital behind the sector in which we had attacked had been bombed and set afire.

"At Vadelaincourt, seventy Frenchmen, recent *amputés*, had been burned alive because they could not be quickly moved. Two heroic nurses, who had refused to leave their charges, died at their posts, and a score of wounded German prisoners were killed by their own steel."

Senard was spared visits by the Gotha intruders until the night of September 25, when a lone bomber—apparently probing the field's defenses—swept low over the field and loosed several bombs, which exploded with fearful detonations in the middle of the landing area without causing any damage. Encouraged by the apparent lack of ground defenses, and emboldened by the absence of night interceptors, the German raiders came in force two nights later.

The growling whine of the sirens dragged the sleeping pilots from their beds and sent them running to the slit trenches outside. The inky-black skies toward the north were crisscrossed with the probing beams of searchlights and sheeted with the bursts of antiaircraft shells reaching for the bombers. Scorning shelter, Thaw and Lufbery crouched behind the post-mounted

Lewis guns and squinted up at the blackness above, seeking the telltale blue streaks of exhaust. The first Gothas came in low with their engines throttled down and began unleashing salvos of 220-pound bombs. The earth heaved and shook as the missiles exploded in blinding flashes of flame. Tracers from the muzzles of the Lewis guns arced upward in irregular white streaks toward the low-flying monsters, which were almost invisible against the protective covering of night. Above the din of exploding bombs and the crackling of machine guns, Dud Hill's voice rose, nasal and unnaturally high, "Ain't you glad you joined the army, boy!" Hill's cliché was greeted with nervous laughter, and he repeated it after each thunderous explosion, sounding like a cracked phonograph record.

A hangar was struck and immediately was engulfed in flames. Men scrambled from the trenches to try to drag the Spads to the relative safety of the open field, but were driven back by the gasoline-fed inferno. The Gothas came in waves spaced fifteen minutes apart, and they kept up the attack for four hours. When the last bomber had gone, the men rose wearily from their holes and counted the damage; the raid had cost the Group twenty Spads, burned to ashes.

The Group moved back to Chaudun two days later, where it received replacement Spads for the job of clearing the skies of German reconnaissance aircraft preparatory to a limited objective drive on the eastern flanks of the Chemin-des-Dames. Two and a half months had passed since the Escadrille was last at Chaudun; little had changed, except summer's greenery had turned to muted browns, and cold autumn winds laced with rain whipped across the field—reminders that another winter was not far away.

October 1 was clear and cold. The early morning patrol got off and returned without incident, and at eleven Hank Jones got ready to lead the mid-morning patrol to the east of Soissons and over the valley of the Aisne. Jones, Dolan and Campbell were successful in running up their engines to full r.p.m., but Bridgman's Hisso popped erratically, backfired and then lapsed sluggishly into silence. Bridgman swore as his mechanic worked up a sweat trying to coax the power plant into life. After several minutes they were forced to give it up, and Bridgman sat on the ground and watched the others roar away from the field without him.

The three Spads flew northeast, climbing slowly under a suddenly lowering sky. At 2500 feet the even staccato of the trio of Hispano-Suizas was broken, and Jones looked across at Dolan, who gave the rough-engine signal and turned for home. Campbell closed up on Jones and they continued climbing toward the lines. When they reached 8500 feet, Jones discovered four Hanoveranner two-seater observation planes turning in large circles below them, apparently directing an artillery shoot. Jones glanced over his shoulder to make sure Campbell was still with him, then put his nose down and dived at the Germans.

He shot past the wheeling planes, then pulled up underneath the tail of one of the enemy biplanes, prepared to open up on the blind spot. But a storm of lead came pouring from the belly of the German plane—the observer was firing through a hole cut in the floor. The stick was suddenly wrenched from Jones's grasp as a burst of lead severed four control cables, the bullets passing within inches of Jones's foot where the cables ran outward to the ailerons. The Spad fell off, and Jones grabbed the stick to regain control. But the engine, apparently struck as well, began to vibrate badly and Jones quickly throttled back and started a shallow dive for home, casting fearful glances at the upper wing, where small shreds of fabric were snapping in the wind. If Campbell's Spad was anywhere in the sky, Jones did not see it.

Jones made it back to Chaudun and landed. He got out of the cockpit and started counting the holes in his plane—there were thirty-four places where the 7.92mm slugs had penetrated his wings and fuselage. Of Campbell, Jones could tell the others nothing. Thénault got on the telephone and called observation posts all along the sector. He turned up only one clue: an unidentified French plane was seen going down inside the German lines north of Soissons; no further details were known.

Days turned into weeks, and there was no word from the missing airman. He was carried on the rolls as *missing, presumed dead* until November, when the presumption was proved correct;

a message dropped over the lines by a German airman reported Campbell killed in combat, and a sketch map was included that indicated his final resting place.

James Norman Hall returned to the Escadrille two days after Campbell's death. He made it back following a two-month stay in the hospital and a losing battle with the rear echelon. After waiting futilely for orders at the depot at Le Plessis-Belleville, Hall decided to return to the squadron without them. He ran into Ken Marr, who was returning to Chaudun following a forty-eight-hour leave, and together they reported at Headquarters of G.C.13. Féquant promptly ordered Hall back to the depot. At Plessis, Hall was met by a French captain "with Teddy Roosevelt teeth and a sentence of 21 days' prison for being absent without leave." The captain assumed that Hall had been in Paris having a good time. "I was red-hot about this," said Hall, "and wanted to tell the captain that insofar as I was concerned, France could save herself as best she might—I was through with this eager-volunteer business. But he didn't give me a chance."

Hall was posted to N.112 instead of going to jail, although pilots returning to duty after a combat wound were almost always sent to their original unit. The new squadron was part of *Groupe de Combat* 15, then operating near Verdun. There was one other American in N.112, Sergeant Leland L. Rounds, a doctor's son from New York who had distinguished himself by shooting down an Albatros on his maiden flight across the lines.

Hall immediately sent a request to Thénault for transfer back to the Escadrille, but before any action could be taken, N.112 was sent on temporary duty to Belfort to keep German aircraft on their own side of the lines while Italy's King Victor Emmanuel was visiting that part of the Front. After a week of monotonous patrolling within sight of the glittering Alps, the squadron was ordered back to Verdun.

Over the Vosges while en route home, Hall's engine began to splutter when the main fuel pump went out. He manipulated the auxiliary hand pump, until it too gave way. He then switched on the small nurse tank fed by gravity from the center section of the upper wing. With about ten minutes' flying time available, he began searching the uneven terrain below for a likely field. He picked what he believed to be a pasture atop a small mountain and came down to land. Too late, he discovered the field was a natural obstacle course. Sweeping in low over the earth he narrowly avoided colliding with a herd of cows grazing atop the hill. His wheels touched down and he went barreling through a wire fence and started a wild, rolling ride down the reverse slope. He hurtled between two apple trees, losing his wings in the process, then bumped madly on over small brush, over rocks, past trees and finally came to a shattering halt against a stone wall. He was thrown forward against the coaming and bloodied his nose.

A few minutes later the mayor of the small village near where Hall had crashed came panting up and asked if he could be of service. Chagrined, Hall borrowed money from the official to get him to Verdun.

Hall spent the month of September with N.112, and then Thénault succeeded in getting him back to the Lafayette Escadrille. When he returned after nearly four months' absence he found the weather "cold and miserable, numbing my hands so that I can hardly hold a pen."

Hall's arrival coincided with the departure of Lieutenant Arnoux, whose replacement proved an immediate success. Lieutenant Louis Verdier-Fauvety, a once-wounded cavalry officer, and once-victorious aerial fighter with the Legion of Honor on his tunic, was known in Combat Group 13 as a man with incredible luck. Following the raid on Dun-sur-Meuse in August, Verdier-Fauvety had collided with another Spad at 12,000 feet; locked in mortal embrace, the two planes began a dizzy spin earthward, each pilot waiting helplessly for the death that would claim them when they reached the ground more than two miles below. But incredibly the Spads fell into the tops of large trees, and neither man was badly injured. "Verdier," reported Hall, "is so cheery and self-possessed it makes us ashamed to mope in his presence—we do a little too much of this sometimes. Nerves have a way of getting jangled, and then too we have lost three men recently, which has made us all feel rather gloomy. The change since Lieutenant Verdier's arrival has been remarkable . . . simply because of his healthy, wholesome outlook on life. Already the older men speak of him as a second de Laage."

Following a spell of bad weather, the morning of October 16 dawned cold but clear, and Lufbery was off alone before breakfast over the lines. He stalked a two-seater at 17,000 feet, and after a spirited fight in the freezing heights sent it falling drunkenly through space. But before the hapless plane started its final dive, the doomed observer put a burst into Lufbery's Spad. The engine sputtered, then stopped. Lufbery glided safely inside his own territory and landed at a strange field. There, mechanics discovered that a slug had penetrated the radiator and lodged in the carburetor. An inch either way, they figured, and Lufbery would have caught the slug in his stomach; and had the bullet been incendiary, he would have fallen three miles wrapped in flames. When his engine was repaired, Lufbery flew back to Chaudun where his thirteenth victory confirmation had already been telephoned through.

October 24, the second day of the offensive, found him again flying alone at daybreak 12,000 feet over the German first lines. Craning his neck up, down, around, he caught sight of an enemy two-seater some 3000 feet above, moving slowly inside French territory. "Moving carefully," wrote Peterson, "he kept the sun at his back, and in the shade of the other fellow's tail, he started to climb. Working his way carefully, following every move of the Boche, he crept up unseen. When about 40 yards away he opened fire. After fifty cartridges the Boche slipped sideways for a thousand feet, then went into a spinning nose dive and banged into the ground about a mile and a half on the other side of the lines. Confirmation came in immediately."

Lufbery flew back to Chaudun to refuel and re-arm, pausing only long enough for his plane to be serviced and to swallow some hot coffee. He took off again and found another two-seater, this time lower down, at 6000 feet. Lufbery, who was above the German, "dived and started shooting from a very short distance. The observer crumpled up in his cockpit almost immediately; then the whole machine shivered, shook and slipped sideways into a *vrille*. It was quite foggy at the time and there were a few patches of clouds. Luf followed the plane down for 3000 feet, then it went into a cloud and was lost. We are waiting for confirmation from the infantry, as the balloons were not up at the time.

"We all made three sorties," concluded Peterson, "and everybody had three or four fights with the Boches, but no more were brought down—perhaps when we chance upon Luf's private formula, we will be a little more successful."

Part of Lufbery's "private formula" was physical: he had 20/20 vision in each eye, and the checklist filled out by the U. S. Army doctors reads "Normal" from skull to arches with monotonous regularity.

Furthermore, Lufbery worked hard to perfect his craft; he spent long hours at the target butts, practice-firing with swivel-mounted machine guns. He flew so often his Spad "was seemingly a part of himself." He never went aloft without checking each round of ammunition that would be fed into his Vickers gun. Faulty ammunition might still cost him Germans, but he had fewer stoppages than any man in the squadron.

But Lufbery's greatest secret, if it can be called that, was his endless patience when stalking the enemy; he took his time, giving himself every chance of survival. Flying skill, marksmanship, acuity of vision, coolheadedness—these qualities, shared in varying degrees by all of the great hunter-killers of the air, were of far more value than heedless courage, which usually led to the grave long before a pilot reached maturity.

Within a sixty-day period the French had twice launched offensives, and twice the weather gods smiled on their endeavors; first, in front of Verdun, and now along the flanks of the Chemin-des-Dames. During the final week in October, with the *poilus* of the French Sixth Army gaining ground every minute, the habitual early-morning ground mists were usually burned off by the mid-morning sun, and high ceilings permitted aggressive patrolling until dusk.

On the twenty-seventh, Thaw led Jim Hall and Ken Marr on a high patrol just before sunset. They discovered a flight of seven Albatros at inferior altitude, and Thaw unhesitatingly led the others down on the Germans in a hit-and-run attack Spads could usually pull off without undue risk. Thaw got off a hundred rounds into one of the enemy single-seaters and watched it "tip up sideways, sideslip for 300 feet, then tumble into a *vrille* from 12,000 feet."

Hall picked a second Albatros, and in his nervousness opened fire from the hopeless range of 1000 feet; his Vickers jammed after fifty rounds, and Hall shot past the Albatros, which fastened itself on his tail and began firing. Hall's engine began missing, and the tachometer needle dropped to only 1000 r.p.m. With his superior diving speed neutralized by the failing engine, Hall resorted to frantic acrobatics to keep the German's fire off his Spad; then he would straighten out, roll over on his back and shove the stick forward, reversing direction, "whereupon the Hun would lose me for a minute, only to find me again and come on, firing. Gee, but it was uncomfortable!"

Finally Hall ducked into a cloud at 5000 feet, circled awhile in its protective opaqueness, then came out into the clear to find the brightly painted Albatros waiting. Back into the cloud again, where he switched on the reserve tank and listened happily as his engine picked up, resuming its full-throated roar. He came out of the cloud a thousand feet over the trenches and beat it for home.

Marr had time only to warm his guns in the opening seconds of battle when a burst of lead from a sharpshooting German severed his rudder and elevator control cables. His Spad fell in a sickening dive for 3000 feet before he achieved an uncertain, jerky kind of mastery of his flight attitude by alternately reducing r.p.m. and firewalling the throttle; Marr's flight path resembled the up-and-down movements of a roller coaster as he continued to drop earthward, frantically seeking a place to land.

In the murky light of dusk, he mistook a ravine for a smooth stretch of ground and whistled in to land. The ravine was filled with shell holes, twisted strands of barbed wire and the debris of battle. Hurtling across the rugged, blasted ground, Marr had time only to realize his error before his wheels were ripped away by the lip of a shell crater and his plane was upended violently and slammed into the ground. Marr undid his safety belt and dropped head first into the center of a ruined cemetery. He was back at the field that same evening, unscratched and filled with awe that he was still alive.

Observation balloons, tethered serenely to the earth, floated over the battlefield. Fat with easily ignitable hydrogen, they offered in profile more than 1500 square feet of tender silk surface to lay sights against and were the most tempting targets imaginable. But—ringed with machine guns and 77mm batteries zeroed in at known ranges and generally protected by fighters—they were also the most dangerous. Four of these balloons had sprung up in the Group's area of responsibility, and Féquant's Group was ordered to shoot them down.

Bill Thaw could remember how, in 1916, one or two men would go it alone against a balloon in helter-skelter attack. But hard-earned experience had taught them the value of planned assault. Two pilots were assigned from each squadron as the "sausage-spearers," to be protected from above by three other Spads. The attacks were to be delivered on all four balloons simultaneously. To add to the first layer of protection, an additional ten Spads would leave the ground ten minutes prior to the departure of the assault teams and take up station over the area where the gas bags were floating, some distance behind the German third line.

Thaw designated Hall and Peterson as the "balloonatics" of the Escadrille, and their Spads were fitted with racks to carry the flaming Le Prieur rockets. They spent the day prior to the attack firing live rockets at the life-silhouette of a balloon painted on the ground, and declared themselves ready.

"Unfortunately," recounted Hall, "for Pete and I, the balloon assigned to 124 was the fartherest in of any of them. We saw two balloons go down in flames while we were still a long way from ours. And by the time we reached it, it was almost on the ground—you know how rapidly they can pull them down.

"Pete dived first, and missed. Then I went down, fired my rockets, and missed! I thought surely I had the blighter, but it was swaying from side to side. An awful disappointment.

"I came out of the dive at 1000 feet—the balloon was only 500 feet off the ground when I let go my rockets—and headed for home. We were under heavy machine gun fire from the ground, but neither Pete's machine nor mine were hit."

Two of the four German observation balloons were flamed, and those were two of only three claimed by the French during the month of October. Hall's disappointment at missing the sausage with his rockets was partly overcome a few days later when he was out with Lufbery and watched him gun down a German plane; officially confirmed, it made his fifteenth.

By the first week in November, the Escadrille roster was down to thirteen pilots, from a previous total of twenty. Masson and Johnson were gone, sent to the rear to instruct. Bigelow's face wound had become dangerously infected and he lay in a hospital, never to fight again. Campbell and MacMonagle were dead. Hewitt, unable to conquer his fear of enemy gunfire, reached the point where he could not face the ordeal of going on patrol. He was sent down from the squadron by Thénault and posted to a bomber pilot school. But airplanes were still equated with death in his mind, and he was washed out after only a few abortive flights.[1] The Escadrille lost the services of Emil Marshall, who gave up an easy job doing paper work in Thénault's office to transfer back to his old infantry regiment still in the front line. Haviland also transferred out of the Escadrille and was sent to N.102 on the Flanders front. He had written back: "They tell me the *Vaterland* arrived in England with 2000 American planes on board, and thirty-five troopships arrived in Brest in one day from the States. Not bad, what." And now Lovell was gone, sent to Chaumont to shuffle papers and wait for a commission.

One final replacement was sent to the Escadrille at the beginning of the second week of November—and he arrived without having had even one day of advanced combat flying training. Christopher W. Ford—a straight-nosed, square-jawed New Yorker—had learned to fly Wright Model B pushers at the Stinson Flying School in San Antonio, Texas, and had learned to fly all

---

[1] Hewitt returned to the United States and enlisted in an infantry regiment, but failed to get overseas. Misfortune followed him even to the grave. In 1926 he was found dead in a Washington, D. C., gutter, of complications arising from alcoholism.

over again at Avord; a clerical error resulted in posting him directly to the Escadrille without having been routed through either gunnery or acrobatics. When he confessed that he hadn't any idea how to get out of a spin, the others told him he would fall into spins during every combat and that "spins are difficult to pull out of—particularly with a German sitting on your tail."

Undaunted, Ford threw himself into combat knowing little more about flying than how to take off, turn and land. Hall reported that "during his earliest combats he practiced acrobacy of weird and unheard-of kinds." But Ford survived, and lived to paint on his upper wing a jagged red-white-and-blue lightning streak that could be seen for a thousand yards.

Although Paul Pavelka had been gone from the squadron for ten months, the band-of-brothers spirit that characterized the Lafayette Escadrille was kept alive across 2000 miles through frequent correspondence between Salonika and the Western Front, which had no monopoly on hardships.

In August, Pavelka and a driver were returning to the field from a trip to Headquarters in a light car. It was a pitch-black night, and the car was without lights. The driver ran off a narrow bridge spanning a rocky ravine and the car crashed down to the boulders below. Pavelka was propelled through the windshield. His face was slashed to ribbons, his jaw broken in two places and both knees wrenched painfully out of place. While he was sweltering in the hospital baked by 120-degree heat, a fire broke out in the main part of Salonika and nearly destroyed the city; the business and shopping district went up in flames, destroying the source of supplies the airmen had been purchasing to augment the slender, tasteless army rations.

When Pavelka was discharged from the hospital, he went to work constructing a new hut to protect himself from the onset of winter. The hut was no sooner finished when an unseasonable rain poured from the sky, rapidly flooding the area and ruining all of Pavelka's personal possessions.

Pavelka moved to higher ground.

With his jaw still wired, his knees wrapped in elastic bandages and his face still smarting painfully, Pavelka returned to duty, flying observation and bombing missions in the two-seater Nieuport. He was pleased when the French cited him in the orders of the entire *Armée de l'Orient*, and appreciative when he was given another palm to his *Croix de Guerre;* but he was in despair not to be able to return to France, even on leave, for he had been told pilots had to spend a minimum of twenty months with the Army of the Orient before transfers would be considered.

Pavelka wrote in anger concerning an American named Sims who was in the Salonika area boasting of his heroic service with the Lafayette Escadrille. "Sims," reported Pavelka, "is some sort of a social worker who goes around with U. S. A. embroidered on his shoulder straps, wearing a sort of Stetson hat, and tells everyone he is waiting to go to America to take charge of an aeroplane factory. He is a dirty skunk, and when I meet him I shall put the ki-bosh on all his yarns and make him look like thirty cents half spent." But Pavelka never had the chance to settle accounts with the fraudulent Sims.

Pavelka was visiting a British cavalry regiment encamped not far from his field when he heard his name called. He turned around to greet an Englishman whom he had known in the Foreign Legion during the early days of the war. They fell to discussing horses over lunch, and when Pavelka learned a new shipment had just arrived he asked to borrow one of the mounts to exhibit the kind of horsemanship he had learned on his father's Wisconsin farm.

Pavelka was given a horse, which was saddled with some difficulty. He heaved himself into the stirrups and immediately the large black mare began plunging and rearing, frantically trying to rid herself of the weight on her back. Pavelka kept his seat, cheered on by the ring of Britishers who had gathered to watch "the Yank bronco-buster" break the hard-mouthed mare.

Suddenly the horse fell heavily to the ground and rolled deliberately over her rider. Then she jerked herself upright and galloped back to the pen. Pavelka lay on the rocky earth, his ribs crushed, blood seeping from his mouth. He was rushed to the hospital, but died the following day from massive internal injuries.

Pavelka was buried at Zeitenlick Cemetery in Salonika at nine in the morning, November 11, 1917. His funeral was attended by a regiment of French infantry, the entire British cavalry strength and a company of Serbian infantry. There was one American pilot present, Edgar J. Bouligny, a former Legionnaire from New Orleans. Bouligny, who had arrived on the Macedonian front only a few days before, had learned of Pavelka's death only that morning. Borrowing the squadron staff car, Bouligny made the two-hour drive from his field to the cemetery just in time to see them lower the body of his friend into the rocky earth, 5000 miles from home.

By mid-November, the valley of the Aisne was in the grip of early winter. Freezing cold, unusual for that time of year, drove the men indoors and mechanics took special pains to keep the blocks of the water-cooled Hispano-Suiza engines from cracking wide open. The clear weather was broken by periods of gloomy overcast, and heavy blankets of fog rolled across northern France, wrapping aviation fields in clammy shrouds.

With activity in the air brought to a standstill, pilots began slipping away to Paris on short leaves. Jones, who had secured a forty-eight-hour pass, took part in a champagne binge before being driven to the station. He boarded the wrong train, woke up several hours later with a raging thirst to discover that he had traveled east, not south, and was stranded near Verdun. By the time he made it to Paris, his leave was up and he returned to Chaudun with nothing to show for the cherished liberty except a bad hangover and stiff muscles from the 600-mile journey.

Parsons and Billy Dugan got wind of a Y.M.C.A. "hospitality hut" being erected in the vicinity, and made their way to the first all-American establishment they had seen since leaving the States. Dugan saw a carton containing six sacks of Bull Durham tobacco on the shelf and purchased it from the "Y" man for the equivalent of three dollars—steep, Dugan told Parsons, but worth it to a man who liked to roll his own. When Dugan unloaded the carton back at the field, a slip of paper fell out. Dugan picked it up and read:

THESE FREE SMOKES FOR OUR FIGHTING MEN IN FRANCE ARE WITH THE COMPLIMENTS OF THE SUN TOBACCO FUND

From that time on the Y.M.C.A. was boycotted by the pilots of the Lafayette Escadrille.[2]

Shortly afterward, Parsons received his promotion to *Adjudant* and was given long leave in America. He left as the fog lifted over the Aisne, leaving the sky a brilliant blue and bitterly cold.

Combat patrols were resumed using more powerful engines. From an original 140 h.p., the Hispano-Suiza engines had been jumped to 150 h.p., then to 180 and finally—through gearing the propeller and increasing the compression—to 220 h.p. The 180 Hissos, as built by the parent firm in Spain, were jewels, and pilots who flew them wouldn't trade them for any 220-geared engine ever built—especially those manufactured by Peugeot, which were balky and required a complete overhaul after only fifty hours of running time.

On December 3, Thaw went up after lunch to test the trim in a new Spad just in from the depot, and to check out the engine. He stayed four miles inside his own lines, climbing steadily until he reached 16,500 feet. Then the needle on the fuel-pressure gauge began flickering back and forth. Thaw stuck his head under the cockpit rim to check the connection when "suddenly the well-known *tac-tac-tac* sounded perilously close." Thaw jerked his head up and looked behind him. An Albatros was riding his tail with both guns blazing. Thaw pushed the stick over and down, skidding out of the line of fire. Thinking to come up underneath the attacker, Thaw pulled the nose of his Spad up and was startled to find a two-seater Rumpler observation plane in his sight. Reflexively he clamped down on the trigger.

After forty rounds, flames burst from the nose of the Rumpler and it started down. The top wing ripped loose and then the big plane nose-dived toward the earth, turning in what Thaw described as a "lop-sided spin," and spewing bits of charred fabric and wood in its fiery wake. From the time Thaw had poked his head underneath the cockpit rim until the Rumpler burst into flame, perhaps twenty seconds had elapsed. He had not gone up

---

[2] When the A.E.F. arrived in France in numbers, the gouging its members received at the "hospitality huts" quickly created the legend that Y.M.C.A. stood for "You Must Come Across." Six sacks of Bull Durham were worth only thirty cents.

to seek combat at all, and it had been only good luck that the Albatros pilot hadn't gotten him first.

The following afternoon, Lufbery went out alone. He stalked two German photographic planes as they crossed the French lines. The two-seaters were flying in echelon, approximately 600 feet apart, and when Lufbery had worked himself unnoticed to the rear of the planes, at 12,000 feet, he dived and zoomed up underneath the topmost plane and opened fire from only thirty yards away. But in the sub-zero cold, the lubricants on his gun were gummy, and the Vickers stuttered to a stop. While Lufbery calmly worked at the gun to get it going again, the second German plane pulled up and got on his tail and began firing.

Lufbery automatically skidded to one side, throwing off the pilot's aim; then, with his Vickers operating again, he swung up underneath the first plane he had attacked and once more opened fire. He got off ten rounds "and the Boche just rolled over on his back with his wheels toward the sky and floated down for 3000 feet like a dead leaf; then his nose tipped a little and he plunged into a forest inside the German lines." The second German dived safely for home, but a little while later Lufbery successfully stalked another prey and sent it down for his seventeenth.

Still later in the afternoon, Peterson, Marr and Ford were ordered aloft to protect a French photographic plane sent to map terrain deep in enemy territory. They had barely crossed the lines when seven Albatros jumped the French two-seater flying at 18,000 feet. The force of Albatros slid past the three American pilots, who were occupied with trying to keep the blood circulating in their frozen hands and toes. Before they could intercept the German fighters, one had been shot down in flames by the French observer, and the other six sheered away to re-form for a second attack. The Escadrille Spads moved in on top of the French plane, and together they started working their way back to friendly territory.

Then the Germans split up into two flights of three each; one flight dropping past the Spads toward the two-seater below. But this time the Americans were ready and they bounced the Germans before they could reach the Frenchmen. But the maneuvering had left them open to attack by the other three Albatros, and they came pelting down after the Spads, leaving the two-seater alone.

"That finished it," said Peterson. "Ford caught four slugs in his engine, and I got three. We were out of the game and beat it for home. Marr stayed and kept the Boche occupied until he saw we were safe. Then the Boche left, and Marr followed us back to the field. We barely managed to glide in."

With Peterson and Ford safely home, Marr flew back alone and crossed the lines. He found a German two-seater at 6000 feet and, following the Lufbery tactic, got the sun at his back and worked his way around to the rear of the German plane and slowly closed the gap. The Germans never knew what hit them; Marr opened fire from fifty yards and the two-seater "burst into flames, dived steeply, turning sideways, and banged into the ground about three miles inside Germany."

"German aviation," commented Peterson, "is plentiful and quite strong, but it seems as if they are a trifle on the run just now."

Peterson spoke too soon.

On December 6, Peterson and Bridgman went up on voluntary patrol. They had just reached the lines when bursting white puffs of French antiaircraft shells drew their attention to the east. They banked to the right, still climbing for altitude, and above the shelling made out a German two-seater, apparently making photographs. Peterson led Bridgman around in a wide circle until the sun was at their backs, then they attacked.

"At the first volley," Peterson said later, "the Hun dropped like a shot—probably wasn't touched, only scared. Then things started happening for us.

"Seven Hun single-seaters dropped on our back out of nowhere; they, too, had evidently been using the sun. They were on top and were flying and shooting like wild men. Bridgy and I kept well together and attacked the Boche from underneath at every opportunity. About a dozen bullets had gone through my wings and Bridgy had his fuselage pumped full, but nothing serious had been done.

"After several reprisals, the Boche leader shot out a smoke bomb as some kind of signal. The Boches drew off a little towards

France. If we dove to get home, they would hop us again; if we climbed towards them, they would have us head-on—no way at all clear towards home. Then I swung around towards Bridgy and, waving towards Bridgy, started to climb for dear life. The Boche hadn't expected anything like that, and in a moment we were well above them, but quite a distance into Germany.

"When we got about 1500 feet above them, we turned towards home. We could see the Boche trying to reach us, a few of them shooting, but they were too far away to do any damage. We dove on them several times and succeeded in getting them separated; then we dropped down to their level and gave them a good broadside. By this time we were inside French territory and they were too widely scattered to make an attack, so they beat it for home. We were out of ammunition, so we came home, too.

"We had only been out half an hour, but what a lot of damage was done! Our machines were literally shot to pieces from the explosive bullets—but not a control cable or an engine was touched. Bridgy had four holes in his top plane a few inches from his head that you could stick your four fingers in."

When the holes and gashes had been patched and doped, flying wires replaced and tightened, splintered struts thrown away and new ones bolted on, the team of Peterson and Bridgman were once again ready to take their Spads into action. Joined by Hall and Jones, they went out "just pooping around" inside German territory. A French battery put up a signal in the form of a half-dozen rounds that burst at 15,000 feet three miles deeper in enemy airspace, so the four Spads quickly began racing for altitude. Peterson and Hall were flying newer engines, and as they pulled away Peterson signaled Jones and Bridgman to stay below so "they could catch the Boche as he fell."

Peterson and Hall rose smoothly upward until they were at 19,000 feet, where their breath came in short, knife-like gasps, the cold air at that altitude burning their lungs like hot iron. They craned their necks around the periphery of the pale blue sky and caught the glinting of the sun upon the wings of a pair of German reconnaissance planes a thousand feet below. They swung around to put themselves between the sun and the enemy, then dived down and opened fire on the two-seaters from less than 200 feet away. They got off a hundred rounds apiece before the surprised German pilots were able to slip out of the bullet stream and turn for home.

Hall took up position below the rearmost German plane, while Peterson chandelled and took him from the front. They opened fire once again, and Peterson saw the observer suddenly sink from view beneath the cockpit rim. After four seconds of firing, the Vickers guns on both planes slowed and stopped from the cold.

By this time, the battle had dropped to 13,000 feet, where Jones and Bridgman fell on the first two-seater and began shooting at it in rotation. The German observer stood up in the blast of cold wind and traded fire with the Americans, but then he, too, slumped down, and the Spad pilots noticed something fall over the side of the cockpit and go spinning away into space. As Jones and Bridgman closed in for the kill, their own guns jammed. "And there we were," complained Peterson later, "four against two and not a gun in the outfit."

The four Americans tried to herd the Germans back into France and there force them to land as captives, but the wind was against them, and they had to give it up and watch the two-seater pilots get safely away, taking home the two lifeless crewmen.

The frustrating combat had a curious footnote: the unknown object they had seen falling away from the German plane thudded to earth in the French lines and there was picked up by an infantryman. The rare souvenir was the German observer's rigid leather helmet, with a bullet hole square through both sides.

Later that afternoon, Lufbery, while climbing through light cloud, almost rammed a German observation plane; he swerved away, unseen, then dived down a few hundred feet and came up underneath the belly of the unsuspecting plane. He opened fire, "ripping him open from stem to stern with an awful fusillade of lead. The Boches never knew what hit them. The machine tipped up on its nose, fell for a thousand feet, then went over on its back with its wheels pointing at the sky. The observer fell out of the cockpit and went kicking through space. The plane was still falling this way when Luf lost sight of it. The infantry reported seeing the fight, but they claim the machine righted itself and landed O.K. near the German balloons. So that's another one that doesn't count.

"Perhaps someday we will manage to slip over a few official Huns when someone isn't looking. . . ."

Spad S-XIII

CHAPTER 15

PHASE OUT

There are three ways of doing a thing: the right way, the wrong way, and the Army way.

—OLD SAYING

The shifting of the Lafayette Escadrille to its ultimate duty station and its eventual breakup began with an order from Commandant Féquant saying that the lions must go. The beasts, he said, were now too large to be kept as pets on the airdrome. It was true; Whiskey was beginning to show traces of a mane, and his less-amiable mate had grown to the size of a Belgian shepherd. They were loaded into the specially fitted van for the last time and driven off to the Paris Zoo, where Thaw had arranged for lifelong care.

From Chaudun, the group itself was moved east to a disused airdrome centered around Noblette Farm, near La Cheppe. The barracks hadn't been occupied since early fall, and were open at one end. The pilots pitched in with the ground crew to erect walls and patch cracks against the freezing winds that swirled snow into drifts several feet high. It was Cachy all over again. Even with the miserable huts sealed against the wind, some nights were too cold for anybody to sleep, so the pilots made their way into Chalôns-sur-Marne, ten miles away, to put up for the night at the Hôtel de la Haute-Mère-Dieux.

The area swarmed with support troops belonging to the U. S. 1st Division, and when the word got out that the famous Lafayette Escadrille had moved into the sector, the American pilots found themselves entertaining an endless stream of curious soldiers, most of whom were disappointed not to find the lions padding around the barrack.

Although visiting American troops were welcome, there were, inevitably, the few who strained the hospitality of the Escadrille to the breaking point by acting as if the squadron bar was an open saloon and their lounge area a setting for amateur night. Not long after the Escadrille moved to Noblette Farm, a quartermaster sergeant invaded the bar and proceeded to get noisily drunk. He passed from singing ribald verses from "Mademoiselle from Armentières" to starting arguments about the qualities of the French fighting man, then to loud invitations to fight anybody who didn't agree with him. Lufbery, who had gone to bed early in case the weather should allow him to fly at dawn, listened to the caterwauling through the thinly partitioned walls as long as he could stand it, then came boiling out of bed and through the door.

Recalled a witness: "Luf's eyes were snapping like Vickers guns. He stood flat-footed on the floor, dressed in long johns and a wool sweater. He nailed the sergeant—who was several inches taller—with a look that would have frozen alcohol. 'Shut up!' he said. The sergeant looked down at Luf somewhat stupidly; he obviously didn't know who Luf was, and wasn't interested in finding out. Then he made his big mistake: he sneered and called Luf a name.

"Luf stepped forward and hit that big sonofabitch three or four times, his arms working like pistons. The sergeant flew backwards across the room and banged to the floor, out cold. When Luf saw that the loud-mouth was incapable of causing any more trouble, he turned and went back to bed to finish his sleep.

"He never looked for trouble on the ground, but when it came to him he reacted with the same speed and coordination that made him so dangerous in the air."

Solid overcast grounded the entire Group, which gave plenty of free time for the Escadrille pilots to wonder what had become of their recent offer to join the U. S. Air Service in a body. The board of examiners had come and gone two months previously, and still they had no word. *Silence absolu.*

Finally, on December 14, each pilot received a mimeographed letter from Dr. Gros, who wrote: "Knowing how impatiently you must be awaiting the time of your release, I want to tell you that everything is being done to hasten the delay, which is entirely due to the slowness of the ministerial *Bureaux*. Your papers are now going through the *Bureau* of the Ministry of War, and we expect that in a very few days your official release will be granted. At that time, you will be notified and asked to come in and take the oath as an officer in the American Expeditionary Forces."

Chiding the French for their slowness—arising, no doubt, from their almost psychopathic love for multiple forms overlaid with rubber stamps, endorsements and counter-endorsements—Gros sent a letter to the Ministry pointing out that "The Lafayette Escadrille and the members of the Lafayette Flying Corps are very much in the public eye in America . . . and at this moment American newspapers contain pointed articles, asking why we have not looked more carefully after the interests of these young men, several of whom have died for France."

An extenuating circumstance behind the delay lay in the fact that there were more than one hundred American fighter, reconnaissance and bomber pilots then active at the Front with French squadrons—including the fourteen Americans flying with the Lafayette Escadrille. The sudden release of these men would have been tantamount to pulling seven squadrons from the line all at once—a notion the French understandably had no intention of entertaining. However, the original staff at G.H.Q. (Kenly and Bolling) had so thoroughly laid the groundwork for the takeover that Chaumont had no hesitation in assuring the Ministry of

War that the American pilots released from French service would find full and active employment with the U.S.A.S. immediately upon release.

Thus, a few days before Christmas, the pilots of the Lafayette Escadrille were formally discharged from the *Service Aéronautique.* To their dismay, the pilots discovered they had been released into a vacuum—no commissions were at hand, no orders were delivered, no U. S. squadrons existed to receive them. Contrary to the promise in Major Gros's letter written only the week before, they were *not* asked to come to Paris to take the oath as officers in the A.E.F. In effect, they were civilians.

What had happened was that Foulois and the "carpetbaggers" on his staff had not finished with their re-examination of the fitness reports gathered by the examining board and approved by General Kenly. They had, in fact, written to every French commanding officer who numbered Americans in their squadrons, asking for re-evaluation. This unnecessary and time-consuming procedure was still in train at the moment of the official release, which indicates the state of liaison between Foulois and the French G.Q.G.

Although the French occasionally threaten to suffocate in their own red tape, they are quick to perceive when a bureaucratic muddle turns into a farce. The *Service Aéronautique* turned a blind eye to the technicality of continuing to use the newly created civilians in the role of combat pilots—a role they knew sooner or later the Americans would assume with legal sanction in their own army. The Escadrille pilots, therefore, continued to receive and obey orders from *Groupe* H.Q.

Paul Rockwell, who had been following "the distressing affairs *vis-à-vis* the Escadrille and the U. S. Army," drove six hours through a blizzard to reach Noblette Farm for a story for his paper.

"I was met by Dud Hill," he remembered, "bundled up like an Arctic explorer, plodding from the hangars through the deepest snow I had seen for years. We went into the mess hut and sat around a roaring fire to thaw out. Most of the boys were sore as hell at the Army, and they weren't sure whether they had made the right choice in accepting their release from the French or not. Since their allowances from the Corps had been cut off, most of them were living on the eighty cents a day paid sergeants in the French Army, and this put them in a bad fix.

"A new lot of American newspapers had arrived, and they were incensed at the number of yarns written by quitters from the training schools who returned to the States to capitalize on the name of the Lafayette Escadrille. Men who had never heard a gun fired in anger wrote outrageous stories describing the terrific combats they had been in, usually with von Richthofen, and shamelessly described what heroes they had been while flying and fighting with the Escadrille. These ludicrous articles created both amusement and indignation, as can be imagined.

"I asked where Thaw and Soubiran were, and learned they had gone out with the mechanics to cut wood for the stove; the coal supply had been quickly exhausted, and the fire had to be kept going day and night or they would all have frozen to death.

"I renewed acquaintanceship with Thaw's orderly, Robert Percy, a New Orleans Negro with whom Bill had served in the *Légion Étrangère* three years before. On one of Thaw's excursions to the trenches, he ran into Percy trembling and shaking in a dugout—not from fear, mind you, for Percy was a brave man, but from rheumatism aggravated by the incessant cold and rain of the Champagne country. Bill had Percy transferred to the Escadrille as his orderly, and Percy was as grateful as he had always been loyal.

"I returned to Paris with the impression that although the men were peeved at being left adrift by their own headquarters, they were nonetheless still eager to prosecute the war."

On New Year's Day, 1918, the pilots—"more or less unable to move"—slept late, bundled deep under mountains of cover. The morning was bitterly cold, but the skies were clearing. After lunch, Thaw and Jim Hall put on their heavy winter flying gear and shuffled through the snow to the hangar and had their Spads rolled out. They sat in the cockpits stamping their feet on the floorboards and beating their mittened hands on the tops of their thighs to keep the blood circulating while the mechanics labored to start the Hissos. Finally both engines were running, and when the tachometer needles edged reluctantly to the 1900 r.p.m.

mark, the Spads were turned into the wind and roared down the field blowing clouds of snow and ice crystals in their wake.

They climbed until they reached 14,000 feet, and although the air temperature was 20 degrees below zero, Hall was no longer conscious of the cold—it was a thing outside of himself, and his senses were numbed by the dazzling beauty through which he moved. Surrounding him were towering clouds, luminous in their whiteness, their empty canyons shaded in blues and purples. Above was the pure blue sky, open and limitless; below, where the ever-shifting layers of darker clouds parted, were patches of the earth he had so easily left behind.

At least once to all men who fly comes the feeling that they are minor gods, and it was this feeling that flooded through Hall as he sat encompassed by the finely turned wood and the tautly stretched fabric of his airplane in the heavens three miles above the earth.

He was jerked from his reverie six miles inside the German lines when it reached his mind that it was his engine alone that was sending the waves of sound against his eardrums; his eyes returned from the daydream to a point one hundred yards ahead where Thaw's airplane had been. Nothing. Only billowing clouds. Up, around and down he searched with his goggled eyes, but Thaw's Spad had vanished without a trace. He had imperceptibly but surely drifted to the east, his flight direction pushed inexorably to the right by the torque of the engine that his idle stick hand had failed to automatically correct.

He swung then to the west, scanning the area of sky and cloud in front of him, a sector at a time. There, a half mile away, he picked out a black speck against the brilliant whiteness of a cloud; perhaps Thaw had been dreaming as well, hadn't noticed that he had fallen behind. Hall opened his throttle and began climbing; he would get above Thaw, then streak down on his tail, later kid him about what an easy mark he would have been.

But when Hall drew closer, he saw that the lone airplane wasn't Thaw's at all; it was an Albatros, and the pilot was exhilarating in an endless chain of acrobatics. Hall watched the gaily painted plane pull out of a high loop and almost immediately begin a series of perfect barrel rolls. Then, the pilot began contour-chasing over the tops of the rolling clouds, making his wheels follow the now-gently, now-sharply curving tops of the cumulus. The thought passed through Hall's mind: *There is a man who loves flying as much as I do, and who has forgotten, as I sometimes do, what he's up here for.*

But the inexplicable force that had stayed his hand once before left him now. When the German passed across another brilliant cloud beneath him, Hall dived full-throttle. He fell on the unsuspecting German from 1500 feet above and opened fire from a range of a hundred yards. He put a hundred and fifty rounds through his Vickers gun and watched his tracers bouncing off the German's engine. The Albatros lurched in its flight and fell off out of control. Hall followed the stricken plane through the swirling mists of a cloud, and when it emerged momentarily in the clear he got off another hundred rounds into the vitals of the Albatros before it flopped on its back and fell into the enveloping mist. Hall pulled up, checked the time by his wristwatch, then turned and flew back to Noblette Farm.

He hurried into Verdier-Fauvety's office, but before he could open his mouth the lieutenant dressed him down for losing Thaw on the patrol; Thaw, he said, had returned twenty minutes before. When the executive officer had finished, Hall walked over to the wall map and jabbed his finger on the spot over which the battle had occurred and told him the story. Then a telephone call brought the news that the French infantry had seen the Albatros crash in no man's land, one wing having fallen inside French territory. "Congratulations!" said Verdier-Fauvety . . . "that's the way to begin the New Year."

"I suppose it was—for a pursuit pilot," Hall said later. "But I felt no elation whatsoever, only a grim kind of satisfaction that, at long last, I had avenged Doug MacMonagle's death."

Hall's first confirmed kill was the Escadrille's last. Fighting continued sporadically throughout January, with its unpredictable weather, but not even Lufbery was able to add another two-seater to his impressive log of the dead.

At last, the machinery at Chaumont began unsnarling itself, and commissions for the suffering pilots of the Lafayette Escadrille began coming through—one or two at a time, spaced more than a month apart. Lufbery's came first, and on January 7, he was feted with champagne to celebrate his right to wear a major's golden oak leaves. Unlike Lovell, whose hopes for a combat assignment had been dashed when the Army issued him a desk in the rear echelon, Lufbery looked upon his orders with a sense of deep satisfaction: he was named Commanding Officer of the U. S. 95th Pursuit Squadron and directed to take charge of the newly-created combat unit on January 16. For once, the square peg would be in the square hole, and he would be leading American pilots into action against the Germans, bestowing upon them the priceless benefit of his long combat experience. Or so he believed.

But when Lufbery arrived to take charge, he was flabbergasted to discover that the 95th existed on paper only, having neither a full quota of pilots nor any aircraft. Lufbery delivered a broadside directed toward the wingless wonders at Headquarters, and three weeks later he was removed from the fictitious squadron with a note on his dossier that said he "was not suitable for command." Lufbery was then assigned to the sprawling, primitive Aviation Instruction Center at Issoudun, where he was given a small office, but assigned no duties. Leland Rounds, from SPA.112, dropped in one day not long afterward and found his country's leading ace and one of the world's greatest combat tacticians sitting in a swivel chair with his boots and spurs on the desk, staring idly at a jar filled with sharpened pencils; in front of him was a note pad filled with aimless doodles. Rounds recalled:

"Lufbery's eyes lighted up when I walked in the door, and he swung his boots from the desk and reached down and opened a drawer and pulled out a bottle of whiskey. We had a few drinks and talked about pilots we both knew out at the Front, and what a waste our own army was making of them. Luf had no idea why he was sent down to Issoudun, and nobody there could give him the faintest notion of what his duties were.

"When I asked him about the spurs, he snorted and shrugged and said he was damned if he knew, but Air Service regulations required pilots to wear spurs everywhere except in bed.

"Seeing Luf sitting glumly in front of that useless-looking rolltop desk was one of the most depressing sights of the war."

Captain Thénault was the next man to go. On January 18, he put his bags aboard the train that would take him to Pau, where awaited him the post of Chief Pilot, School of Acrobacy. "I leave it to be imagined," he wrote later, "my sentiments and my sadness when I parted from my comrades, followed only by my inseparable companion, that good dog, Fram."

When Ted Parsons returned from leave in the States, he was shocked to discover Lufbery and Lovell holding down desk jobs far from the combat zone. Then he learned that of the surviving 152 Americans in the Lafayette Flying Corps, thirty-two had elected to remain with the French, and that twenty-six pilots—tired of waiting for the Army—had accepted commissions in the U. S. Navy and were facing the prospect of flying obsolete Hanriot fighters. Parsons promptly declined an American commission of his own. "I had a hunch," he explained, "that it would be weeks or even months before I could get into the air again; besides I felt that I still owed France something for the money they had spent on me. I had gotten only one Hun, officially, and was still on the debit side of the ledger." With the old Escadrille doomed, Parsons set about creating another.

He questioned those American pilots who were staying in the *Service Aéronautique* and learned that all of them were willing to serve in a new Lafayette Escadrille. Armed with this information, Parsons broached the matter to G.Q.G., where the idea was enthusiastically met; the French promised him support personnel and new equipment, including factory-fresh Spad XIIIs armed with twin .45 caliber Vickers guns—hinting that eventually the squadron would be supplied with 300 h.p. Spads that could outfight anything the Germans were liable to field in the foreseeable future.

"I had the financing all arranged," Parsons said, "and orders were on the point of being issued creating a second Escadrille when suddenly the boom was lowered. After nearly two months of hard organizational work, the project was scrapped. No satisfactory explanation was ever given, but I gathered that the Headquarters bunch at Chaumont had applied heavy pressure on the French to abandon the scheme as a slap in the face to the A.E.F. I often wondered if it wasn't Dr. Gros who was the snake in the woodpile—he was always prodding the boys to change over, and he certainly would have lost face with a new Escadrille he couldn't control."

The French, sympathizing with Parsons' disappointment, offered him a consolation prize: choice of French squadrons with which to serve for the remainder of the war. Parsons elected SPA. 3, escadrille of the late, great Guynemer, and the most famous outfit in the *Groupe des Cigognes*. Parsons, the only Lafayette Escadrille pilot to remain with the *Service Aéronautique*, reported for duty with that galaxy of stars on April 24, 1918.

On January 19, Bill Thaw was commissioned major in the United States Army Air Service, and directed to take command of the U. S. 103 Pursuit Squadron, to be formed of the wreckage of the Lafayette Escadrille. Three days later, a farewell dinner was given to the pilots of the 13th Combat Group that boasted such rare wartime delicacies as oysters on the half shell, jellied eggs, stuffed turkey, fruit cake and three types of wine—Chablis, Corton Clos du Roi and Champagne Dueil.

There remained only the formalities, expressed in an agreement between the *Grand Quartier Général* and Headquarters, A.E.F., in which the government of the United States agreed to vouch for all matériel taken over by the 103rd Pursuit Squadron from French inventory; further agreeing to allow the 103rd Squadron to remain attached to a French *Groupe de Combat* as needed, until such time as the U. S. Air Service could employ the squadron with a combat group of its own, under U. S. Army direction.

The Escadrille was an operational unit with the *Service Aéronautique* for a period of twenty-two months, less two days. During that time, its pilots shot down thirty-nine German aircraft confirmed, while sustaining just over 30 percent casualties. Six Escadrille pilots were killed in aerial combat, one was killed by antiaircraft fire, two died in operational accidents, and five were wounded badly enough to require hospitalization.

On February 18, 1918, the Lafayette Escadrille disappeared from the order of battle along the Western Front. Its members mourned the passing of a proud name—not knowing they were present at the birth of a legend.

EPILOGUE

The 103rd Squadron, its Spads still proudly bearing the Indian head insignia, was replenished with veterans from the Lafayette Flying Corps and with other American pilots from the training ground at Issoudun in time to meet the onrush of the great German offensive that stormed over the Western Front on March 21. In the dark days that followed, when Paris itself seemed threatened, through the summer that saw the war in the air reach new heights of fury, and to the final day of the war, the 103rd proved to be as aggressive—and as peripatetic—as its predecessor: the squadron was attached to five different French *Groupes* and *Armées,* and to the Second and Third Pursuit Groups, First Army, A.E.F.; and during that time, the squadron was credited with destroying twenty-nine German aircraft and two balloons; three of the victories belonged to Thaw, whose score had finally reached the magic number of five.

On July 26, Thaw was relieved from command of the 103rd and ordered to Vaucouleurs to organize and lead the Third Pursuit Group. This group, consisting of the 28th, 93rd, 103rd and 213th Pursuit Squadrons, began operations as a unit in mid-August, and by November 11 had accounted for eighty-seven German aircraft; its own losses amounted to twenty-nine pilots killed, wounded or missing in action.

The early fears that the long combat experience of the Lafayette Escadrille pilots would not be put to use proved largely groundless. Besides Thaw, no fewer than six of the former

SPA.124 pilots were elevated to command positions. Doc Rockwell succeeded Thaw as C.O. of the 103rd, and was in turn replaced by Soubiran, who held the post until the end of the war. Hill at first ran the 138th Pursuit Squadron, later became Commanding Officer of the Fifth Pursuit Group. Bridgman commanded the 22nd Pursuit Squadron; Peterson, the 95th. Peterson finished the war with five confirmed victories; he was killed in a crash at Daytona Beach, Florida, on March 16, 1919. Marr left the 103rd and eventually assumed command of the 94th Pursuit Squadron.

Dolan and Jones remained with the 103rd as Flight Commanders until late in the war, when they were sent back to the States to instruct; Dugan left the 103rd to act as Chief of Repair and Testing at the American Acceptance Park at Orly; and Ford learned acrobatics so well he was able to shoot down two of the new Fokker D-VIIs, but was himself shot down by machine gun fire from the ground, and remained a German prisoner from October 15 until the Armistice.

The bizarre cycle of gross misfortune, followed by incredible good luck, went with James Norman Hall throughout his combat career. On March 29, 1918, he was posted to the 94th Pursuit Squadron with the rank of captain and as Flight Commander. The Americans were flying Nieuport 28s, dragonfly-looking biplanes powered with 160 h.p. Gnôme-Rhône single-valve rotary engines. The 28 was fast—it would do nearly 130 m.p.h.—and it "flew like a dream," but it was fatally flawed: in highspeed pull-outs from dives, the fabric on the upper wing—and sometimes the leading edge itself—was prone to rip loose from the strain. The French had washed them out as first-line combat fighters, but they were all that were available when the 94th was equipped.

On May 7, Hall led American-trained Edward Vernon Rickenbacker and Edward Green across the lines; south of Metz, Hall took the others down on top of five Albatros. Hall, who was "standing on the rudder bar," had his intended victim in his sights, but before he could get within range, a ripping, cracking sound jerked his attention to his upper wing, where great shreds of fabric were tearing away from the leading edge. Hall eased out of the dive, turned the crippled Nieuport toward home. He flew through a tornado of antiaircraft shelling, afraid to take evasive action, and while still inside enemy territory he felt the airplane jump from the impact of a direct hit. He fell off out of control, his engine silenced, and with Albatros fighters circling overhead he crash-landed in an open field behind the German lines. His nose and right ankle were broken in the crash.

His wrecked Nieuport was quickly surrounded by curious Germans, and a few moments later the excited commander of the battery that had brought him down arrived, examined the Nieuport and rushed over to Hall to point out that he had been lucky, indeed: the 37mm shell fired from his battery had struck one of the heavy, whirling steel cylinders of the engine, but had failed to explode. While Hall lay on the ground drinking the water and smoking the cigarette the Germans had given him, the Albatros he had lately been engaged in attacking landed nearby, and the pilots reported that one of their number had been brought down in flames (it was Eddie Rickenbacker's second victory). Afterward, the Germans took Hall to their airdrome at Mars-le-Tour and fed him before sending him on his way to an officers' prison camp at Landshut, where he remained until the end of the war.

Not present at the fight, but learning of Hall's loss in action the moment Rickenbacker and Green landed, was Lufbery, who had finally been removed from the useless job at Issoudun to train, and later command, the 94th. Reed Chambers, one of the 94th's pilots, remembers Lufbery pacing up and down the field, muttering over and over to himself, "I *keel* the sonsabeeches! I *keel* the sonsabeeches!" Less than two weeks later, Lufbery had an opportunity for revenge almost directly over his own field.

At 10 A.M. on May 19 the French antiaircraft batteries atop Mt. St. Mihiel, north of the 94th's airdrome at Toul, opened up and began walking shrapnel across the sky. The telephone in the 94th's office rang and the voice at the other end excitedly reported a lone German two-seater headed in their direction. Lieutenant Oscar J. Gude, Jr.—fresh from the pilots' pool—took off immediately to intercept the German intruder.

Lufbery was in his quarters, a small stone hut at the far end of the field, and heard the loud, angry roar of Gude's big rotary engine as the elegant-looking Nieuport raced down the field and took to the air. Lufbery rushed from the door and watched Gude futilely fire away all of his ammunition at hopeless range; untouched, the German reconnaissance plane flew steadily on.

Lufbery jumped aboard a motorcycle standing in the middle of the road and roared up to the hangars, where a second Nieuport was warming up for takeoff. Sitting in the cockpit was another green pilot, 2nd Lieutenant Philip Davis, whom Lufbery gruffly ordered out of the cockpit. Davis propelled himself from the seat, and Lufbery jumped in, strapped on his helmet and hurriedly gunned the plane into the air.

He caught up with the slower enemy plane 6000 feet above the earth, just southwest of the field. Lufbery hurled his fighter so close to the other plane that observers on the ground caught their breaths, believing collision was inevitable. They heard the distant popping sounds of Lufbery's two Vickers guns, then saw him pull away, circling above the enemy, apparently to clear stoppages. Then Lufbery attacked again. Rickenbacker described this final assault:

"Suddenly old Luf's machine was seen to burst into roaring flames. He passed the Albatros and proceeded for three or four seconds on a straight course. Then to the horrified watchers below there appeared the figure of their gallant hero emerging headlong from the midst of a fiery furnace. . . ."

Lufbery tumbled a mile through space and plunged into the backyard of an old shoemaker's house in the tiny village of Maron, near Nancy, some twelve miles from the airdrome. One leg was impaled on a white picket fence that ran the length of the yard, his moustache and helmet were badly singed, and there was a bullet hole through his left hand—otherwise, not a mark. Lufbery died the moment his body crashed to earth. The shoemaker's daughter rushed from the house and found Lufbery lying on his back. Legend has it that she opened the top of his flying suit and, seeing the chestful of medals, "recognized him immediately." In any event, she covered his body with flowers, and afterward he was carried to the town hall by the villagers of Maron. It was there the pilots of the 94th found him.

Endless speculation has been made concerning the reason for Lufbery's fall from the cockpit of his doomed fighter. Some of his contemporaries believed he jumped out to a quick death to avoid the unbearable agony of being roasted alive; others point out he had said many times that it was best to try to sideslip down to earth—as Pavelka had done at Verdun—because at least there was a chance for life, whereas a leap into space could only mean certain death; one opinion holds that Lufbery took off in such a hurry that he forgot to fasten his safety belt, that the German bullets cut his controls and that he was flung out of the cockpit when the airplane flipped over on its back. And all of the expressed theories hint that Lufbery was trying to aim his body at the Moselle River that flows just south of Maron. But all of this is guesswork.

Lufbery was buried late the next afternoon in a small cemetery near Toul. Flights from the 94th Squadron and from *Groupe de Combat* 20 flew over the grave dropping flowers while a bugler from the 26th Division, U. S. Army, sounded Taps. One officer wrote afterward:

"The sun was sinking behind the mountain that rises so abruptly in front of Toul; the sky was a faultless blue and the air was heavy with the scent of blossoms. . . . In all my life I had never heard Taps blown so beautifully as on that afternoon. Even some of the officers joined the women there in quietly dabbing at their eyes with white handkerchiefs."

Ted Parsons never had reason to regret joining SPA.3 of the Storks Group. He finished the war with eight confirmed kills, was promoted to *sous-lieutenant* and carried the medal of the *Médaille Militaire*.[1] He was the only American to have served with both the *Escadrille Lafayette* and the *Groupe de Cigognes*, unquestionably France's two most famous fighter units.

Harold Willis broke out of prison camps on three separate occasions, but was recaptured. Willis tried again, and on the night of October 13, 1918—fourteen months after his capture—Willis and an American naval officer named Isaacs, both dressed in fake German uniforms and carrying wooden rifles, gained the

[1] In 1962, Parsons was made an officer in the *Légion d'Honneur*—forty-four years after the war.

outside of the camp at Villingen when the compound lights were short-circuited, causing the Germans to believe a mass break was in progress. In the confusion, Willis and Isaacs slipped outside the open gates with the guard sent to round up the escapees. By hiding in the woods during the daytime, and marching at night, the pair made it to the Rhine and swam across in the cover of darkness to the Swiss side of the river. Willis celebrated Armistice night in Paris, and the war was over for them all.

Considering the wartime fame of the Lafayette Escadrille, it would be surprising if at least a few men did not lay false claim to having shared in its glory. A few? By 1931, more than *four thousand* impostors had come to light, chiefly through newspaper clippings collected by the real Escadrille survivors during the thirteen years after the war. But it was October 1932 that the most macabre instance of attempting to trade on another man's record came to light.

During the World War I veterans' "Bonus March" on Washington, D. C., one of the marchers fell out on a Charlotte, North Carolina, street complaining of an injured foot. When asked his name, he replied that he was "Arthur (sic) Courtney Campbell," that he had shot down thirty-six enemy aircraft, had risen to the rank of captain, and that when he had been shot down he spent four years in a German military hospital in Düsseldorf, where he was treated for both a spinal injury and amnesia. The man claimed he had returned to America upon recovery of his memory, but could not bring himself to look up his former squadron mates because they would only stir up harrowing memories of his wartime experiences. The news was given much space in papers on both sides of the Atlantic, and Campbell's parents were at their wits' end wondering whether or not to believe the first reports.

The story was picked up in Düsseldorf, and almost immediately afterward the Paris edition of the *Tribune* received a letter from a former German pilot who expressed his indignation at the story—and in so doing also cleared up the mystery of how, exactly, Campbell met his death. The German pilot, H. Andres, wrote:

"I assume that some person is unrightfully misusing the name of the poor, brave flyer who died for his fatherland, and I cannot permit this.

"On October 1, 1917, I was ordered to accompany an artillery airplane from Laon to the Chemin-des-Dames. We left our field at Notre-Dame-de-Liesse at 11:20 A.M., the plane I was accompanying belonged to Flying Division A 265. When we had almost executed our mission, I was attacked by a single hostile single-seated sporting airplane which fired on us heavily. I succeeded, however, in shooting it down near Filain.

"A few hours later, I was at the place itself. The flyer was identified by his military papers as an American by the name of A. C. Campbell. He had a head wound and had been killed in the air.

"When a few days later the French made an attack on our positions, they won about ten kilometers of land, so the grave was then in French hands. After some time, the French dropped a message that they wanted us to give them the location of the grave of the American aviator. This request was forwarded to my division and I flew, with a detailed sketch, to the grave and threw down the desired information with a wreath for Campbell."

And from Edgar G. Hamilton, a former Lafayette Flying Corps pilot—then serving as an infantry lieutenant in the Foreign Legion in Africa—came word that he had found Campbell's grave in 1919, and while exhuming the body for reburial contracted septicemia, from which he almost died.

Faced with this evidence, the bonus marcher asked, "If I am not Campbell, who am I?" His fingerprints were taken and sent to the F.B.I., who told him quickly enough who he was: Clarence Stephen Wendler, who had deserted from the U. S. Navy on January 5, 1920, after serving less than one year of a four-year hitch.

Hollywood has had more than its share of Lafayette Escadrille impostors. In the 1930s no fewer than eight actors claimed to have flown with the Escadrille, one of whom was thirteen years old when N.124 first became operational in 1916. And as late as 1961 a Hollywood choreographer appeared on a network television program boasting of having risen from Escadrille mechanic to self-taught combat pilot.

Bert Hall's statement that the Escadrille pilots had not heard the last of him when he left the squadron in 1917 proved correct. In 1932, appeals for help were made to former Escadrille pilots on the behalf of Mme. Marcelle Hall and her two children, abandoned in Paris. At the time newspapers on both sides of the Atlantic were carrying printed pleas for help, they were also running two-column photographs of Hall with cutlines reading: *China Air Ace Ready for Battle.* Hall, who appropriately enough called himself General Chang Hooey Chang, claimed to head the Chinese air force in its unequal struggle against Japan. But Hall's only battle was in court, and it was a losing one: he was convicted in the American Court in Shanghai for swindling the Chinese government out of $10,000 in silver and sentenced by Judge Milton D. Purdy to two and a half years in the federal prison on McNeil's Island in the state of Washington.

The name *Escadrille Lafayette* was not allowed to die out in the French *Armée de l'Air.* In 1920 the name was given to the newly created 7th Squadron of the 35th Aviation Regiment, and the postwar Spad XIIIs carried the familiar Sioux Indian head insignia on the sides of the fuselage.

And in 1922, SPA.167 of the former Storks Group, was recreated as the 8th Squadron of the 35th Aviation Regiment. With the organizational change in French aviation in 1933, these two squadrons were formed into *Groupe de Chasse* 2/5. Thus constituted, the spirit of the Lafayette Escadrille and of the Storks again went to war. On September 20, 1939, *Sergent-Pilote* Legrand of the reborn Lafayette Escadrille piloted his Curtiss 75 "Hawk" to a victory over a Messerschmitt Bf-109 north of Toul for the *Groupe*'s first victory of the new war.

Early in 1940, Paul Ayres Rockwell (then a captain in the Foreign Legion reserve) and Harold Buckley Willis (a volunteer ambulance driver) effected a rendezvous in Paris in order to create a volunteer squadron of American pilots, that is, another *Escadrille Américaine.* Working with them were Lieutenant Colonel Georges Thénault and Colonel Jacques Balsan of the *Armée de l'Air,* and Dr. Edmund Gros, who was still practicing medicine in Paris. They faced almost as many difficulties as Norman Prince had nearly twenty-five years previously, and the plans were not satisfactorily completed until June. On the day that Radio Paris was to announce the formation of the American volunteer unit, the Germans marched into Paris. After incredible difficulties Rockwell and Willis made their way back to the United States, via Spain and Lisbon. Thénault stayed on in France and worked for the Underground.

Following the débâcle of 1940, the French *Escadron Lafayette* was again re-formed—this time in North Africa, and with American-built Curtiss P-40 fighter-bombers. The presentation of the P-40s on January 9, 1943, was brought about by the efforts of the French Rearmament Commission, whose members included Colonel Harold B. Willis and Colonel Paul Ayres Rockwell, U.S.A.A.F.

The new Lafayette Group, as it was then called, fought in the battle for Tunisia, then through Italy, France and Germany. At war's end, it was credited with ninety-five victories and admitted the loss of twenty-eight French pilots, killed or missing in action.

Today the seeker after the physical reminders of the war that ravaged so much of the northern face of France must reckon with the almost miraculous healing powers of Nature and Nature's handmaiden, Time. Nearly fifty years have passed since the guns were stilled along the Western Front, and two generations of Frenchmen—with time out for yet another war—have worked to bring the gutted fields back under cultivation and to rebuild the shattered villages. And they have succeeded beyond the wildest dreams of those who stood, almost a half century ago, and gazed at the wasted landscape around them.

And yet, the signs remain.

The area in front of Verdun is the most haunting. From the air, flying at the speeds and altitudes of fighters used by the pilots of the Lafayette Escadrille, you can see in all directions the overlapping shell craters, the white lips of ruined trenches, vague smears in the otherwise dense greenery that indicate the site of a town that has vanished from the earth. Returning from above the ghostly, nearly indistinct ruins of the once mighty Fort Douaumont—over which the Escadrille pilots once fought bitter battles—to trace the air route leading to the site of the field at Behonne, you get some idea of just how difficult it must have been to find landmarks in that ever-changing landscape; and when it begins to rain from a sky suddenly clouded over, you wonder that they could have found the field at Behonne at all, sitting as it did on a plateau partially hidden by the gentle hills falling off into steep valleys that appear from the rolling plain as if by magic.

On foot in front of Douaumont and Vaux, seeking for the spot where Chapman fell, you face an almost impenetrable wilderness of scrub growth and stunted trees from whose branches thorns rip and tear; this growth is so tightly woven together that, venturing off the few paths, once inside the evil woods you are plunged into gloom, for no sun comes through. The landscape inside these silent patches of woods is pocked with craters almost without end; and, knowing that the earth here abounds in unexploded shells, you go carefully enough. Through the thickets, half-obscured by coarse greenery, a small, lonesome memorial chapel rises in the wilderness; and above, surrounded by a crumbling wall, an ancient cemetery; but of the village of Beaumont itself, not a trace. And even if the spot where Chapman's Nieuport went in could be located precisely, it would require a small bulldozer to crash through the tangled underbrush to stand, at last, on the place marked with a black X on the map the Germans made showing where he fell that day in 1916.

At Luxeuil-les-Bains, the field where N.124 was twice stationed, where the bombers roared off the ground to bomb Oberndorf, now is a modern facility servicing the needs of the supersonic jets of the *Armée de l'Air*. The Hôtel Pomme d'Or, standing on the main street, retains no vestige of the charm it once held for the early Escadrille pilots; the dining room faces the open street with its noises of honking horns, and the bright pastel décor inside is an affront to the eye. Yet, to the left of the bar and standing near the opposite wall, stands the old billiard table once used by Kiffin Rockwell and Victor Chapman to while away the time waiting for the Nieuport *Bébés* to arrive. If you ask the bartenders or the current owners of the Pomme d'Or to show you the room where

Rockwell spent his last night, the request will be met with a blank, uncomprehending stare and a Gallic shrug of the shoulders; they know almost nothing of the history of the place.

But at the Luxeuil cemetery, not a five-minute walk from the hotel, the old caretaker with the scarred face will show you Rockwell's grave with its small Tricolor and Stars and Stripes fluttering from the marker; and he will tell you he remembers the old man, standing tall and proud, who comes there every few years to look for a few moments at the final resting place of his only brother; the caretaker remembers most the big man's furious white moustache, but he remembers, too, the red thread of the Legion of Honor in his lapel.

Less than half a day's drive from Luxeuil-les-Bains, Oberndorf-am-Neckar remains one of those German fairy-tale villages seen in children's picture books. Its neat store fronts gleaming with fresh plaster and paint, the steep roofs solid with shingles and chimneys, the immaculate cobbled streets twisting down to the valley—all give the impression that wars have never found their way across the ramparts of the *Schwarzwald.* The ancient cloister building that houses the administrative offices of the sprawling Mauser *Waffenfabrik* is unscarred by bombs; only time has rounded its once-angular structure. If you ask about the great raid of October 12, 1916, the company officials—all of whom are polite and seem anxious to help—will tell you that not one day's production was interfered with, not one rifle was denied the Front. One white-coated gentleman recalled that what few bombs fell that day landed only in the town—perhaps injuring women and children. He is serious, but his younger colleagues smile in embarrassment, for that is carrying a defensive love for the Fatherland too far. Gazing across the flatlands that reach from the Neckar to the steeply rising hills that surround the town, that encircle the Mauser works, you can see the long, winding stretch of valley down which the Oberndorf force must have come, and you wonder at their courage in reaching this place so far away from friendly soil, so easily defended by determined men.

Both Craonne and Craonnelle have been rebuilt from the ground up—and rebuilt just as they stood in 1914 before German shellfire smashed them to bits. Sleepy, indolent, half-deserted, both villages are rather cleaner than those French villages that were spared the ravages of war—a phenomenon noticed the length of France. Driving from Craonnelle up a clay road made slippery by rain, you reach the Château de Blanc Sablon, buried in a riot of undergrowth and second-generation trees. Rebuilt now, and on a far less pretentious scale, the white château seems somehow out of place there, like a tiny palace in a jungle nobody ever visits. But not a hundred yards from the front door you can find the vestiges of trenches, shelters and firing pits—first dug by the men of the Second Foreign Regiment, and later by the *poilus* who faced the murderous fire from the Chemin-des-Dames that rises across the valley to the north. You cannot find the spot where Rockwell and Seeger were standing guard when the grenades began to fly, but you can look at that menacing barrow across the way and can understand the terror they must have felt under its oppressive nearness, knowing that thousands of pairs of eyes could watch their every move in the open.

Nearby, you can visit the cemetery with its depressing number of weather-beaten crosses, and leafing through the fat register book you are struck with the great number of men from the 1st and 2nd Regiments of the *Légion Étrangère* who are buried there.

Throughout all of France, with its almost countless numbers of military cemeteries and innumerable monuments erected to the deeds of brave men who perished by the hundreds of thousands, the most stirring experience is to be found just outside St. Cloud, not an hour's drive from the Arc de Triomphe, in the shaded park where Corot once found inspiration.

There, at Villeneuve l'Étang, near Marnes-la-Coquette, stands the monument to the dead of the Lafayette Escadrille and their brothers-in-arms of the Lafayette Flying Corps. In the white marble crypts arranged in a serried semicircle beneath the main arch of the monument lie forty-nine of the sixty-five members of the Lafayette Flying Corps who died in the First World War. The silent interior is illuminated only by the weak sunlight that filters through a series of handsome stained-glass windows, each commemorating a phase of the war in which the American volunteers shared. The names chiseled on the plain fronts of each marble crypt read like a roll call from an American Valhalla:

McConnell, Genêt, Hoskier, MacMonagle, Campbell, Pavelka, Lufbery, Doolittle. . . .[2]

Emerging into the sunlight that bounces from the reflecting pool in front of the monument, you feel as if you have just returned from a unique and secluded world where sleep eternally the band of brothers who helped write America's first pages of combat aviation history.

---

[2] James R. Doolittle, invalided out of the Lafayette Escadrille after his wound in 1917, was later killed while instructing cadets in America; his body was returned to be buried in France next to those of his comrades.

CONFIRMED VICTORIES

Escadrille Lafayette Pilots

NAME	WITH N.124	WITH U.S.A.S. AND OTHER	TOTAL
Lufbery, G. Raoul	17	0	17
de Laage de Meux, Alfred	3	1 (C.30)	4
Prince, Norman	3	0	3
Rockwell, Kiffin Y.	2	0	2
Thaw, William	2	3	5
Hall, Weston Bert	2	1 (N.103)	3
Hall, James N.	1	2	3
Haviland, Willis B.	1	0	1
Johnson, Charles C.	1	0	1
Jones, Henry S.	1	0	1
Lovell, Walter	1	0	1
Masson, Didier	1	0	1
Marr, Kenneth	1	0	1
Nungesser, Charles *	1	44 (N.65)	45
Parsons, Edwin C.	1	7 (SPA.3)	8
Peterson, David McK.	1	4	5
Cowdin, Elliot C.	0	1 (N.65)	1
Dolan, Charles H. II	0	1	1
Ford, Christopher W.	0	2	2
Verdier-Fauvety, Louis	0	1 (N.65)	1
TOTALS	39	67	106

* Attached

American Pilots Serving with French Squadrons other than N.124 and later with the U. S. Air Service in 1918

NAME	VICTORIES	NAME	VICTORIES
Baylies, Frank L.	12	Blake, Charles R.	1
Putnam, David E.	11	Boggs, Ellison C.	1
Baer, Paul F.	9	Campbell, H. Gordon	1
Cassady, Thomas G.	9	Chapman, Charles W. Jr.	1
Larner, G. de Freest	8	Collins, Phelps	1
Biddle, Charles J.	7	Eldredge, Donald H.	1
Ponder, William T.	7	Eoff, Robert G.	1
Connelly, James A. Jr.	6	Gundelach, André	1
Grey, Charles G.	4	Guy, David W.	1
Huffer, Jean	3	Hoeber, Robert B.	1
Jacob, Sereno T.	3	Kenyon, Hugo N.	1
Sinclaire, Reginald	3	Lee, Schuyler	1
Turnure, George E. Jr.	3	Loomis, William F.	1
Veil, Charles H.	3	Nichols, Alan H.	1
Wilcox, Charles H.	3	Nordhoff, Charles B.	1
Abbott, Wainwright	2	Paden, David S.	1
Baugham, James H.	2	Reno, Leonard M.	1
Crehore, Austen B.	2	Rounds, Leland L.	1
Corsi, Edward J.	2	Sitterly, Glenn N.	1
Fairchild, Edwin B.	2	Stehlin, Joseph C.	1
Hitchcock, Thomas Jr.	2	Stickney, Henry E.	1
Rheno, Walter D.	2	Walcott, Benjamin S.	1
Saxon, Harold Y.	2	Wass, William E.	1
Shaffer, Walter J.	2	Wilson, Joseph V.	1
Stanley, Alfred H.	2	Winter, Wallace C.	1
Wellman, William A.	2	Woodward, Houston	1
Winslow, Alan F.	2	York, Walter R.	1

TOTAL 142

LAFAYETTE FLYING CORPS ROSTER

Abbreviations:

KIA = Killed in action
WIA = Wounded in action
KLD = Killed in line of duty
ILD = Injured in line of duty
POW = Prisoner of war
USAS = United States Air Service
USNAS = United States Naval Air Service
USMC = United States Marine Corps (Air)
GHQ = General Headquarters (Chaumont)
RWF = Remained with French

SOLDAT = Soldier (private)
CPL. = Corporal
SGT. = Sergeant
ADJ. = Adjudant
S/LT. = Sous-Lieutenant (2d Lieutenant)
SPA. = Spad
N. = Nieuport
BR. = Bréguet
SAL = Salmson
M.S. = Morane-Saulnier
F. = Farman
C. = Caudron

Escadrille Lafayette *Pilot Roster*

	NAME	HOME	SERVICE WITH N.124	REMARKS
1.	Thénault, Capt. Georges	Paris, France	4.18.16 to 1.18.18	INSTRUCTOR, PAU
2.	De Laage, Lt. Alfred de Meux	Clesse, France	4.18.16 to 5.23.17	KLD
3.	Chapman, Sgt. Victor E.	New York, N. Y.	4.18.16 to 6.23.16	KIA
4.	Prince, S/Lt. Norman	Prides Crossing, Mass.	4.18.16 to 10.15.16	KLD
5.	McConnell, Sgt. James R.	Carthage, N. C.	4.18.16 to 3.19.17	KIA
6.	Rockwell, S/Lt. Kiffin Y.	Asheville, N. C.	4.18.16 to 9.23.16	KIA
7.	Thaw, Lt. William	Pittsburgh, Pa.	4.18.16 to 2.18.18	USAS, C.O. 3D PURSUIT GP
8.	Hall, Adj. Weston Bert	Higginsville, Mo.	4.18.16 to 11.1.16	N.103
9.	Cowdin, Sgt. Elliot C.	New York, N. Y.	4.18.16 to 6.25.16	USAS
10.	Lufbery, S/Lt. G. Raoul	Wallingford, Conn.	5.24.16 to 1.5.18	USAS, 94TH PURSUIT SQDN, KIA 5.19.18
11.	Balsley, Sgt. H. Clyde	San Antonio, Texas	5.29.16 to 6.18.16	WIA, USAS
12.	Johnson, Adj. Charles C.	St. Louis, Mo.	5.29.16 to 10.31.17	USAS, INSTRUCTOR
13.	Rumsey, Sgt. Lawrence	Buffalo, N. Y.	6.4.16 to 11.25.16	HOSPITALIZED, RELEASED FROM DUTY
14.	Hill, Adj. Dudley L.	Peekskill, N. Y.	6.9.16 to 2.18.18	USAS, C.O. 5TH PURSUIT GP
15.	Masson, Adj. Didier	Los Angeles, Calif.	6.19.16 to 10.8.17	USAS, INSTRUCTOR
16.	Pavelka, Sgt. Paul	Madison, Conn.	8.11.16 to 1.24.17	N.391, N.507; DIED 11.12.17
17.	Rockwell, Adj. Robert L.	Cincinnati, Ohio	9.17.16 to 2.18.18	USAS, 103D PURSUIT SQDN
18.	Prince, Adj. Frederick H. Jr.	Prides Crossing, Mass.	10.22.16 to 2.15.17	U. S. ARMY, QM CORPS
19.	Soubiran, Adj. Robert	New York, N. Y.	10.22.16 to 2.18.18	USAS, 103D PURSUIT SQDN
20.	Haviland, Adj. Willis B.	St. Paul, Minn.	10.22.16 to 9.18.17	SPA.102, USNAS
21.	Hoskier, Sgt. Ronald W.	South Orange, N. J.	12.11.16 to 4.23.17	KIA
22.	Genêt, Sgt. Edmond C. C.	Ossining, N. Y.	1.19.17 to 4.16.17	KIA
23.	Parsons, S/Lt. Edwin C.	Springfield, Mass.	1.25.17 to 2.26.18	RWF, SPA.3

NAME	HOME	SERVICE WITH N.124	REMARKS
24. Bigelow, Sgt. Stephen	Boston, Mass.	2.28.17 to 9.11.17	WIA, INVALIDED OUT
25. Hinkle, Sgt. Edward F.	Cincinnati, Ohio	3.1.17 to 6.12.17	OVERAGE, DISCHARGED
26. Lovell, Adj. Walter	Concord, Mass.	3.1.17 to 10.24.17	USAS, GHQ
27. Willis, Sgt. Harold B.	Boston, Mass.	3.1.17 to 8.18.17	POW; ESCAPED 10.13.18
28. Marr, Sgt. Kenneth	San Francisco, Calif.	3.29.17 to 2.18.18	USAS, 103D AND 94TH PURSUIT SQDNS
29. Dugan, Sgt. William E. Jr.	Rochester, N. Y.	3.30.17 to 2.18.18	USAS, 103D PURSUIT SQDN
30. Hewitt, Sgt. Thomas M. Jr.	Westchester, N. Y.	3.30.17 to 9.17.17	DISCHARGED, ENLISTED U. S. ARMY
31. Campbell, Sgt. Andrew C. Jr.	Chicago, Ill.	4.15.17 to 10.1.17	KIA
32. Bridgman, Sgt. Ray C.	Lake Forest, Ill.	5.1.17 to 2.18.18	USAS, 103D AND 22D PURSUIT SQDNS
33. Jones, Sgt. Henry S.	Harford, Pa.	5.12.17 to 2.18.18	USAS, 103D PURSUIT SQDN
34. Drexel, Cpl. John A.	Philadelphia, Pa.	5.10.17 to 6.15.17	USAS, LIAISON OFFICER
35. Dolan, Sgt. Charles H. II	Boston, Mass.	5.12.17 to 2.18.18	USAS, 103D PURSUIT SQDN
36. Arnoux, Lt. Antoine de Maison-Rouge	France	5.28.17 to 10.6.17	SPA.78, KIA 5.31.18
37. Hall, Sgt. James N.	Colfax, Iowa	6.16.17 to 6.26.17	WIA
		10.3.17 to 2.18.18	USAS, 103D AND 94TH PURSUIT SQDNS; POW 5.7.18
38. MacMonagle, Sgt. Douglas	San Francisco, Calif.	6.16.17 to 9.24.17	KIA
39. Peterson, Sgt. David McK.	Honesdale, Pa.	6.16.17 to 2.18.18	USAS, 103D, 94TH, AND 95TH PURSUIT SQDNS; KLD 3.16.19
40. Doolittle, Cpl. James R.	New York, N. Y.	7.2.17 to 7.17.17	WIA, INVALIDED OUT
41. Verdier-Fauvety, Lt. Louis	Meaux, France	10.6.17 to 2.18.18	SPA.124, 163, 65; KLD 8.21.18
42. Ford, Sgt. Christopher W.	New York, N. Y.	11.8.17 to 2.18.18	USAS, 103D PURSUIT SQDN; POW 10.15.18
43. Nungesser, Lt. Charles E. M.	Paris, France	7.12.16 to 8.15.16	ATTACHED

American pilots who flew with French operational escadrilles other than l'Escadrille Lafayette, *many of whom later transferred to a U. S. branch of service*

NAME	ESCADRILLE	HOME	REMARKS
Abbott, Wainwright, Sgt.	SPA.154	Pittsburgh, Pa.	USAS
Adams, John R., Cpl.	SPA.95 SPA.81	Jersey City, N. J.	USAS
Ash, Alan N., Sgt.	BR.134	Urbana, Ill.	KIA 5.31.18
Bach, James J., Cpl.	M.S.38	Paris, France	POW 9.23.15
Baer, Paul F., Cpl.	SPA.80	Ft. Wayne, Ind.	USAS, 103 Sqdn.
Barclay, Leif N., Sgt.	N.82	New York, N. Y.	KLD 6.1.17
Batchelor, Henry A. III, Cpl.	SPA.103	Saginaw, Mich.	USNAS
Baugham, James H., Sgt.	N.157 SPA.98	Washington, N. C.	WIA, died 7.2.18
Baylies, Frank L., Sgt.	SPA.73 SPA.3	New Bedford, Mass.	KIA, 6.17.18
Bayne, James A., Cpl.	SPA.85 SPA.81	Grand Rapids, Mich.	USAS, KIA 5.8.18
Benney, Philip P., Cpl.	SPA.67	Pittsburgh, Pa.	WIA, died 1.26.18
Benoit, Leo E., Sgt.	SPA.84 SPA.228	Attelboro, Mass.	USAS, 213 Sqdn.
Biddle, Charles J., Sgt.	SPA.73	Andalusia, Pa.	USAS, WIA 5.15.18
Biddle, Julian C., Cpl.	SPA.73	Ambler, Pa.	KLD 8.18.17
Blake, Charles R., Cpl.	BR.29	Westerly, L. I., N. Y.	USAS
Bluthenthal, Arthur, Sgt.	BR.227	Wilmington, Del.	KIA 6.5.18
Boggs, Ellison C., Sgt.	SPA.81	New York, N. Y.	RWF
Booth, Vernon, Jr., Sgt.	SPA.96	New York, N. Y.	WIA, died 7.10.18
Bouligny, Edgar J., Sgt.	N.501	New Orleans, La.	USAS
Brady, Lester S., Cpl.	SPA.26	Lock Haven, Pa.	USAS, 135 Sqdn., 27 Sqdn.
Brown, Jasper C., Cpl.	SPA.67	New York, N. Y.	USAS
Buckley, Everett T., Sgt.	SPA.65	Kilbourne, Ill.	POW 9.6.17

NAME	ESCADRILLE	HOME	REMARKS
Buffum, Thomas B., Cpl.	SPA.77	New York, N. Y.	POW 5.4.18
Bullard, Eugene J., Cpl.	SPA.93 SPA.85	Columbus, Ga.	Only Negro pilot, WW I
Bullen, William G., Sgt.	N.162	Chicago, Ill.	USNAS
Bush, Philip N., Sgt.	SPA.73	Schenectady, N. Y.	USAS
Byers, Louis L., Cpl.	SPA.38	Philadelphia, Pa.	POW 7.18.18
Campbell, H. Gordon, Sgt.	Esc.St.Pol	Denver, Colo.	USNAS
Cassady, Thomas G., Sgt.	SPA.157	Spencer, Ind.	USAS, 28 Sqdn.
Chadwick, Oliver M., Cpl.	SPA.73	Lowell, Mass.	KIA 8.14.17
Chamberlain, Cyrus F., Sgt.	SPA.85 SPA.98	Minneapolis, Minn.	KIA 6.13.18
Charton, Louis, Sgt.	SPA.92	New York, N. Y.	POW 9.5.17
Chatkoff, Herman L., Sgt.	C.11	Maplewood, Mass.	ILD 6.15.17
Clapp, Roger H., Cpl.	BR.120	New York, N. Y.	USAS, 96 Sqdn. KLD 7.6.18
Caleb, James C. Jr., Sgt.	SPA.80	Buffalo, N. Y.	USNAS
Collins, Phelps, Sgt.	SPA.313 SPA.103	Detroit, Mich.	USAS, 103 Sqdn. KLD 3.12.18
Connelly, James A. Jr., Adj.	SPA.157 SPA.163	Philadelphia, Pa.	RWF
Cook, Alan A., Adj.	SPA.157 SPA.163	Canandaigua, N. Y.	RWF
Corsi, Edward J., Sgt.	SPA.77	Brooklyn, N. Y.	RWF
Cotton, John R., Cpl.	BR.120	Chicago, Ill.	USAS
Crehore, Austen B., Sgt.	SPA.94	Westfield, N. Y.	RWF
Dock, George Jr., Sgt.	SPA.12 SPA.31	St. Louis, Mo.	RWF
Donzé, Robert L., Sgt.	SPA.93 SPA.314	Santa Barbara, Calif.	USAS
Dowd, Meredith L., Cpl.	N.152	Orange, N. Y.	USAS, 147 Sqdn. KIA 10.26.18
Drew, Sidney R. Jr., Cpl.	SPA.31	New York, N. Y.	KIA 5.19.18
Duffy, Nathaniel, Sgt.	SPA.96	Buffalo, N. Y.	ILD, Rel. 8.16.18
Edgar, Stuart E., Cpl.	N.158	Nutley, N. J.	USAS, 103 Sqdn. KIA 8.17.18

NAME	ESCADRILLE	HOME	REMARKS
Eldredge, Donald H., Sgt.	SPA.76	South Bend, Ind.	USAS
Ely, Dinsmore, Sgt.	SPA.102	Winnetka, Ill.	USAS, KLD 4.21.18
Eoff, Robert G., Cpl.	N.157	Christiansburg, Va.	USAS, 95 Sqdn.
Fairchild, Edwin B., Adj.	SPA.159	Manila, P. I.	RWF
Ferguson, Fearchar I., Sgt.	SPA.96	New York, N. Y.	RWF
Forster, Henry, Sgt.	C.74 SPA.102 BR.224 SPA.15	Milton, Mass.	USNAS
Glover, Clarence M., Sgt.	SPA.78	New York, N. Y.	RWF
Grey, Charles G., Sgt.	SPA.93	Chicago, Ill.	USAS, 213 Sqdn.
Gundelach, André, Sgt.	SPA.95 SOP.111	Chicago, Ill.	USAS, 96 Sqdn. KIA 9.12.18
Guy, David W., Sgt.	SPA.155 SPA.156 SPA.38	St. Louis, Mo.	USAS
Hitchcock, Thomas Jr., S/Lt.	N.87	Westbury, N. Y.	POW 3.6.18 Escaped 8.28.18
Hobbs, Warren T., Cpl.	N.153 N.158	Worcester, Mass.	USAS, KIA 6.25.18
Hoeber, Robert B., Sgt.	SPA.103	Nutley, N. J.	RWF
Horton, Dabney D., Sgt.	C.17 SOP.255 SPA.75	Paris, France	RWF
Huffer, Jean, S/Lt.	N.95 N.62 F.36 SPA.62	Paris, France	USAS, 94 Sqdn., 93 Sqdn.
Hughes, Earl W., Sgt.	BR.66 F.110	Detroit, Mich.	RWF
Jacob, Sereno T., Sgt.	N.157	Westport, Conn.	USAS
Johnson, Harry F., Cpl.	N.85 N.98 SPA.168	South Bethlehem, Pa.	USAS, KLD 5.21.18
Johnston, Archibald, Sgt.	SPA.83	Pittsburgh, Pa.	USAS

NAME	ESCADRILLE	HOME	REMARKS
Jones, Charles M., Sgt.	SPA.73	Redbank, N. J.	USAS, 103 Sqdn., 13 Sqdn., 28 Sqdn.
Judd, David E., Sgt.	SPA.73 SPA.3	Brookline, Mass.	USNAS
Kerwood, Charles W., Sgt.	BR.117	Bryn Mawr, Pa.	POW 3.31.18
Kinsolving, Charles M., Sgt.	BR.117	Washington, D. C.	USAS, 163 Sqdn.
Kruijff, Theodore de, Cpl.	N.158	New York, N. Y.	USAS, died 11.6.18
Kyle, George M., Cpl.	BR.117	Los Angeles, Calif.	USAS
Larner, G. de Freest, Cpl.	SPA.86	Washington, D. C.	USAS, 103 Sqdn.
Lee, Schuyler, Cpl.	SPA.96	New London, Conn.	KIA 4.12.18
Lehr, Manderson, Sgt.	BR.117	Albion, Nebr.	KIA 7.15.18
Lewis, David W., Cpl.	SPA.79	Brooklyn, N. Y.	USAS
Littauer, Kenneth P., Sgt.	C.74	New York, N. Y.	USAS, 88 Sqdn. Chief of Air Service, 3rd Army Corps
Loomis, William F., Cpl.	SPA.153	Bedford, Mass.	USAS, 94 Sqdn., 213 Sqdn.
Loughran, Edward J., Sgt.	SPA.84	Desoto, Kans.	KIA 2.18.18
McAllister, Thomas F., Sgt.	SPA.285	Grand Rapids, Mich.	RWF
McCall, George A., Sgt.	SPA.23 SPA.86 SPA.48 SAL.30 SPA.103	Philadelphia, Pa.	RWF
McKee, Herschel J., Sgt.	N.314	Indianapolis, Ind.	POW 2.8.18
McKerness, William J., Sgt.	C.46	Wallingford, Conn.	KIA 8.15.18
McMillen, James H., Sgt.	SPA.38	New York, N. Y.	USAS
Molter, Bennett A., Cpl.	SPA.102	Wausau, Wis.	USAS
Moore, Robert L., Sgt.	C.305 SPA.96	Denison, Tex.	RWF
Moseley, George C., Cpl.	SPA.150	Highland Park, Ill.	USNAS

NAME	ESCADRILLE	HOME	REMARKS
Nichols, Alan H., Sgt.	SPA.85	Palo Alto, Calif.	KIA 6.2.18
Nordhoff, Charles B., Cpl.	N.99	Los Angeles, Calif.	USAS
Ovington, Carter L., Sgt.	SPA.85 SPA.98	Paris, France	USAS KIA 5.29.18
Paden, David S., Sgt.	SPA.163	Evanston, Ill.	RWF
Parker, Austin G., Sgt.	SPA.85 SPA.98	Helena, Mont.	USNAS
Pelton, Alfred D., Sgt.	N.151 N.97	Montreal, Canada	Only Canadian in LFC. KIA 5.31.18
Pollock, Granville A., Sgt.	SPA.102 SPA.65	New Orleans, La.	USAS
Ponder, William T., Cpl.	SPA.67 SPA.163	Mangum, Okla.	USAS, 103 Sqdn.
Putnam, David E., Sgt.	SPA.94 SPA.156 SPA.38	Brookline, Mass.	USAS, 134 Sqdn. KIA 9.13.18
Rand, Rufus R. Jr., Adj.	SPA.158	Minneapolis, Minn.	RWF
Randall, John F., Sgt.	SPA.158	Meriden, Conn.	USAS, 103 Sqdn. ILD 6.14.18
Reno, Leonard M., Sgt.	SPA.103 BR.134	Chicago, Ill.	USNAS
Rheno, Walter D., Sgt.	SPA.80	Vineyard Haven, Mass.	Died 10.10.18
Rocle, Marius R., Cpl.	N.84 C.46 BR.213	New York, N. Y.	USAS, 13 Sqdn., 644 Sqdn.
Rotharmel, Kenneth A., Cpl.	SPA.112	Miami, Fla.	USAS
Rounds, Leland L., Sgt.	SPA.112	New York, N. Y.	USAS
Saxon, Harold Y., Sgt.	SPA.31 SPA.12	Washington, D. C.	RWF
Shaffer, Walter J., Sgt.	SPA.156 SPA.38	Dauphin, Pa.	POW 10.3.18
Shoniger, Clarence B., Cpl.	N.99	New York, N. Y.	POW 5.29.18
Sinclaire, Reginald, Adj.	SPA.68	Corning, N. Y.	RWF
Sitterly, Glenn, Adj.	C.46 SPA.38	Spring Valley, Ill.	RWF

NAME	ESCADRILLE	HOME	REMARKS
Spencer, Dumaresq, Cpl.	N.150	Highland Park, Ill.	KLD 1.22.18
Stanley, Alfred H., Adj.	SPA.23	Elmira, N. Y.	RWF
Stearns, Russell F., Cpl.	SPA.150	Pawtucket, R. I.	USMC
Stehlin, Joseph C., Sgt.	SPA.95	Brooklyn, N. Y.	Ret. to USA, Jan. 1918
Stickney, Henry E., Sgt.	SPA.150	Rutland, Vt.	USAS
Stone, Donald E., Cpl.	SPA.12	New York, N. Y.	KIA 4.21.18
Sullivan, Upton, Sgt.	N.90	Philadelphia, Pa.	USNAS
Taber, Leslie R., Cpl.	BR.29	Auburn, N. Y.	USNAS
Tailer, William H., Sgt.	SPA.67	Roslyn, N. Y.	KLD 2.5.18
Taylor, Elmer B., Sgt.	C.74 SPA.102	Cedar Grove, N. J.	USNAS, Died 10.27.18
Thompson, Clifton B., Cpl.	SPA.99	Hyde Park, Mass.	USAS
Trinkard, Charles, Cpl.	N.68	Ozone Park, N. Y.	KLD 11.29.17
Tucker, Dudley G., Sgt.	SPA.74 SPA.15	New York, N. Y.	KIA 7.8.18
Turnure, George E. Jr., Sgt.	SPA.103	Lenox, Mass.	USAS, 103 Sqdn., 28 Sqdn.
Tyson, Stephen M., Sgt.	SPA.85	Princeton, N. J.	KIA 7.19.18
Van Fleet, William C. Jr., Sgt.	SPA.78	San Francisco, Calif.	USNAS
Veil, Charles H., Sgt.	SPA.150	East Palestine, Ohio	USAS
Walcott, Benjamin S., Cpl.	SPA.84	Washington, D. C.	KIA 12.12.17
Wass, William E., Sgt.	SPA.91	Brunswick, Maine	USAS
Wellman, William A., Sgt.	SPA.87	Cambridge, Mass.	RWF
Wells, Frank W., Sgt.	SPA.93	Syracuse, N. Y.	USAS
Whitmore, Herman, Cpl.	SPA.77	Haverhill, Mass.	POW 4.6.18
Whitmore, John J., Sgt.	SPA.315 SPA.314	New York, N. Y.	ILD, Rel. 6.19.18
Wilcox, Charles H., Sgt.	SPA.80	Pasadena, Calif.	USAS, 103 Sqdn.
Wild, Marcellus E., Sgt.	SPA.15	Rochester, N. Y.	USNAS

NAME	ESCADRILLE	HOME	REMARKS
Willard, George G., Cpl.	SPA.157	Chicago, Ill.	USAS, 147 Sqdn.
Wilson, Joseph V., Cpl.	BR.117	Wheeling, W. Va.	USAS, 163 Sqdn. KLD 10.23.18
Winslow, Alan F., Sgt.	SPA.152	River Forest, Ill.	USAS, 94 Sqdn. POW 7.31.18
Winslow, Carroll D., Sgt.	MF.44 N.112	New York, N. Y.	Rel. 4.30.17
Winter, Wallace C., Cpl.	SPA.94 SPA.156	Chicago, Ill.	KIA 3.8.18
Woodward, Houston, Cpl.	SPA.94	Philadelphia, Pa.	KIA 4.1.18
Worthington, Warwick D., Sgt.	C.53	Paris, France	USAS
Wright, Harold E., Sgt.	SPA.155	Brooklyn, N. Y.	Rel. 12.23.17
York, Walter R., S/Lt.	SPA.97	Somerville, Mass.	RWF
Zinn, Frederick W., Sgt.	F.24	Battle Creek, Mich.	USAS, GHQ

Americans in the Lafayette Flying Corps who went directly into U. S. service or whose flight instruction was halted by death or injuries

NAME	HOME	REMARKS
Baird, Benjamin H., Cpl.	New York, N. Y.	USNAS
Bassett, Charles C. Jr., Cpl.	New York, N. Y.	USNAS
Boal, Pierre, Cpl.	Boalsburg, Pa.	USAS
Bullen, Richard N., *Soldat*	Chicago, Ill.	ILD, Rel. 1.7.18
Chapman, Charles W. Jr., Cpl.	Waterloo, Iowa	USAS, 94 Sqdn. KIA 5.3.18
Cookson, Linn P., Cpl.	Carlinville, Ill.	USAS
Corey, Russell B., Cpl.	New York, N. Y.	USNAS
Cunningham, Arthur L., Cpl.	Medford, Mass.	USAS, 94 Sqdn.

NAME	HOME	REMARKS
Curtis, Frazier, *Soldat*	Boston, Mass.	ILD, Rel. 8.8.15
Cushman, Alvin A., Cpl.	Brookline, Mass.	USNAS
Davis, Philip W., Cpl.	West Newton, Mass.	USAS, 94 Sqdn. KIA 6.2.18
Faith, Clarence H., Cpl.	Nahant, Mass.	USAS, 103 Sqdn.
Faunt LeRoy, Cedric G., Cpl.	Chicago, Ill.	USAS, 94 Sqdn.
Fowler, Eric A., *Soldat*	New York, N. Y.	KLD 11.27.17
Gill, Joseph F., Cpl.	Indianapolis, Ind.	USAS
Grieb, Norman, *Soldat de deuxième classe*	Scarsdale, N. Y.	Died 8.28.17
Grier, James M., Cpl.	Philadelphia, Pa.	USNAS
Hamilton, Edgar G., S/Lt.	Newcastle, Pa.	Instructor, USAS
Hanford, Robert M., *Soldat de deuxième classe*	Brooklyn, N. Y.	KLD 10.15.17
Holden, Milton W., *Soldat*	Camden, N. J.	ILD, Rel. 1.1.18
Huger, Daniel E., Cpl.	New York, N. Y.	USNAS
Kenyon, Hugo N., Cpl.	Peacedale, R. I.	USAS, 103 Sqdn.
Kowall, John R., *Soldat*	Roxbury, Mass.	ILD, Rel. Jan. 1918
Loomis, Ralph L., Cpl.	Bedford, Mass.	USNAS
Malone, Charles T., *Soldat*	Ossining, N. Y.	ILD, Rel. 9.15.17
Meeker, William H., Cpl.	New York, N. Y.	KLD 9.11.17
Miller, Walter B., Cpl.	New York, N. Y.	USAS, 1st Obs. Gp., KIA 8.3.18
Palmer, Henry B., Cpl.	New York, N. Y.	Died 11.12.17
Read, Robert E., Cpl.	Franklin, Pa.	USNAS
Rodgers, William B. Jr., Cpl.	Pittsburgh, Pa.	USNAS
de Roode, Clifford S/Lt.		Interpreter
Scanlon, Lawrence, *Soldat de deuxième classe*	Cedarhurst, L. I., N. Y.	ILD, Rel. 9.1.17
Schreiber, Edwin B., *Soldat*	Anaconda, Mont.	USAS, KLD 8.8.18
Seaver, Horace, *Soldat*	Hartford, Conn.	ILD, Rel. 8.13.17
Skinner, Samuel W., *Soldat*	Cincinnati, Ohio	Died 10.16.17
Starrett, Frank E., *Soldat de deuxième classe*	Athol, Mass.	KLD 1.3.18
Terres, Hugh, Cpl.	London, England	USNAS, KLD 8.17.18

Americans who were released from the Service Aéronautique *while still in training due to inaptitude, physical disability or upon their own request*

Allen, Sidney T.
Appleton, Walter K. Jr.
Boyesen, Algernon
Carrère, Joseph M. Jr.
Collier, Edward M.
Court, Isidore
Dulon, Lowell R.
Eaton, Sherburne
Elliott, Chester A.
Ford, Tod
Gibson, William W.
Gouraud, Reginald G.
Guest, David P.
Harrison, John B. Jr.
Hickson, Leslie
Hough, Edwin A.
Hull, Mark L.
Kirkwood, William F.
Lee, Henry S.
Ludlam, Leslie
McCreary, James B. Jr.
McGinn, William
Macke, Gordon B.
Magley, Guy B.
Manierre, Harold L.
Miller, Alvin F.
Miller, George
Mills, Gordon R.
Mouvet, Oscar
Munson, Curtis B.
Oakes, Nathan Jr.
Potter, Thomas
Ridlon, Hugh O. J.
Rockwell, George
Rolph, John F. Jr.
Ross, Raymond T.
Shipley, Walter B.
Speers, Wallace C.
Stone, Gerald S.
Wainwright, Neal
Willoughby, Westel R.
Wilson, Pierre M.

FRENCH-ENGLISH AVIATION TERMS

A

FRENCH	ENGLISH
Abattre un avion	To shoot down an aircraft
Acajou (m.)	Mahogany
Accumulateur (m.)	Battery
Acier (m.)	Steel
Acrobatie (f.)	Stunt
Admission (f.)	Intake, inlet
Aérien	Aerial
Aéronef (m.)	Lighter-than-air craft
Aiguille de la boussole	Compass needle
Aile (f.)	Wing
Aile courbre	Cambered wing
Aile inférieure	Lower wing
Ailes (charge des)	Wing loading
Ailes en flèche	Swept-back wings
Aile souple	Wing with flexible trailing edge
Aile supérieure	Upper wing
Ailette de refroidissement	Cooling fin
Ailette de ventilateur	Fan blade
Aimant	Magnet
Ajusteur (m.)	Fitter
Alaire (surface) (f.)	Wing surface, wing area
Alcool éthylique (m.)	Ethyl alcohol
Alésage (m.)	Bore
Alésoir (m.)	Reamer
Alimentation (f.)	Feed

French	English
Alimentation sous pression	Pressure feed
Allongement d'une aile	Aspect ratio
Allonger le vol	To flatten out a glide
Allumage (m.)	Ignition
Allumage (couper l'—)	To switch off
Allumage irrégulier	Erratic ignition
Altimètre	Altimeter
Amiante (m.)	Asbestos
Ammerir	To land on water
Amortisseur (m.)	Shock absorber
Antenne (f.)	Aerial
A plein gaz	Full throttle
Appareil (m.)	Machine, aircraft
Appareil de bord	Instruments
Appareil de chasse	Fighter aircraft
Appareil monoplace	Single-seat aircraft
Arbre (m.)	Shaft
Arbre à cames	Camshaft
Atterir	To land
Atterrissage (m.)	Landing
Aurore (m.)	Dawn
Aviateur (m.)	Aviator
Avion (m.)	Aircraft

B

French	English
Balle (m.)	Bullet
Ballon (m.)	Balloon
Banc d'essais (m.)	Testing block
Baromètre métallique	Aneroid barometer
Barrette (f.) de détente	Trigger bar
Béquille (f.) arrière	Tailskid
Berceau (m.) de moteur	Engine cradle
Bielle (f.)	Connecting rod
Blindage (m.)	Armor
Bobine (f.) à trembleur	Buzzer coil
Bois (m.)	Wood
Boîte (f.) à soupape	Valve pocket
Bombe (f.)	Bomb
Bord d'attaque	Leading edge
Bord posterieur	Trailing edge
Bouchon (m.)	Plug, cap
Bougie (f.)	Spark plug
Bouleau (m.)	Birch
Boussole (f.)	Compass

French	English
Bride (f.)	Flange
Brouillard (m.)	Fog
Brume (f.)	Haze, mist
Burette à l'huile	Oil can
Buse (f.)	Venturi tube

C

French	English
Cablage des ailes	Wing rigging
Cable (m.)	Wire, cable
Cable de commande	Control cable
Cables de gauchissement	Warping wires
Cache-soupape (m.)	Valve cover
Cadran (m.)	Dial
Calage (m.)	Chock
Calamine (f.)	Carbon
Cale	Shim
Calibre (m.)	Gauge
Cambrure (f.)	Camber
Came (f.)	Cam
Cannelé	Serrated
Canon (m.)	Cannon, gun barrel
Canon anti-aérien	Antiaircraft gun
Canon de mitrailleuse	Machine gun barrel
Cap (m.)	Heading
Capot (m.)	Cowl
Capoter	To turn over
Carcasse (f.)	Framework
Carlingue (f.)	Engine bearer, cockpit
Carte (f.)	Map
Carter (m.)	Crankcase
Cartouche (f.)	Cartridge
Casque (m.)	Helmet
Cedre	Cedar
Centre de gravité (m.)	Center of gravity
Cerf-volant (m.)	Kite
Chalumeau (m.)	Blowpipe
Chambre à air	Intertube
Champ d'aviation (m.)	Airfield
Champ de tir	Firing range
Chandelle (f.)	Zoom
Charge (f.)	Stress, load
Charnière (f.)	Hinge
Charpente (f.)	Framework
Châssis d'atterrissage (m.)	Landing gear

French	English
Chemise d'eau (f.)	Water jacket
Chêne (m.)	Oak
Chute (f.)	Fall
Cible (f.)	Target
Clapet (m.)	Valve
Clé (f.)	Wrench
Cliquet (m.)	Pawl
Cogner	To knock
Coincer	To bind, to jam
Combustible (m.)	Fuel
Commande (f.)	Control
Commande de gaz	Throttle control
Commande de gouvernail	Rudder control
Commande de gouvernail de profondeur	Elevator control
Commande de mitrailleuse	Firing gear
Compte-tours (m.)	Tachometer
Cônique	Tapered
Contre-écrou (m.)	Lock nut
Contreplaque	Plywood, veneer
Correction du mélange	Mixture control
Coubure (f.)	Camber
"Coucou"	"Ship" (Aircraft)
Coup de foudre (m.)	Thunderbolt
Coup de vent (m.)	Squall, gust
Coupe (f.) droite	Cross section
Courant (m.)	Current
Course (f.)	Stroke
Court circuit (m.)	Short circuit
Coussinet (m.)	Bearing
Couvercle (m.)	Cover
Cran (m.) de sûreté	Safety catch
Cuir (m.)	Leather
Cuivre (m.)	Copper
Culasse (f.) de cylindre	Cylinder head
Cycle (m.) à deux temps	Two-stroke cycle
Cycle à quartre temps	Four-stroke cycle

D

French	English
Débit (m.)	Rate of flow
Décalage (m.) des ailes	Stagger
Déclinaison (f.) magnetique	Magnetic variation
Déclinaison occidentale	Variation to west
Déclinaison orientale	Variation to east

French	English
Décoller	To leave the ground
Démarreur (m.)	Starter
Démultiplicateur (m.)	Reduction gear
Détente (f.)	Trigger
Dièdre (m.)	Dihedral
Diffuseur (m.)	Venturi tube, choke tube
Dispositif (m.) de rupture	Contact breaker
Douille (f.)	Bushing
Dynamo (f.)	Generator

E

French	English
Échappement (m.)	Exhaust
École d'aviation	Flying school
Écrou (m.)	Nut
Égoutteur (m.)	Oil retainer
Élever (s'—)	To rise, to lift off
Emballer un moteur	To race an engine
Encrassé	Clogged up, carbonized
Enduire	To dope
Engrenage (m.)	Gear
Engrenage de distribution	Timing gear
Enrayer (s'—)	To jam
Entoilage (m.)	Covering, fabric
Enveloppe (f.)	Tire
Envergure (f.)	Span, spread
Équilibre	Balanced
Équipage (m.)	Crew
Érable (m.)	Maple
Escadrille (f.)	Squadron
Essai (m.)	Test
Essence (f.)	Gasoline
Essieu (m.)	Axle
Étain (m.)	Tin
Étanche à l'eau	Water-tight
Étouffer	To choke
Étranglé	Throttle down
Extracteur (m.)	Extractor
Extrêmité de l'aisle	Wing tip

F

French	English
Fatiguer	To strain
Fer (m.)	Iron
Fer blanc (m.)	Tin

FRENCH	ENGLISH
Fil (m.)	Wire thread
Fil d'allumage	Ignition wire
Fil de bois	Grain of the wood
Fil fouet	Whipcord
Filtre (m.)	Strainer, filter
Flotteur (m.)	Pontoon
Fondre sur	To swoop down upon
Fonte (f.)	Cast iron
Frêne (m.)	Ash (tree)
Frottement (m.)	Friction
Fuir	To leak
Fusée (f.)	Rocket
Fusil (m.)	Gun

G

Gabarit (m.) de réglage	Jig
Galvanisé	Galvanized
Gauchir	To warp
Gaz (mettre le)	To open the throttle
Geler	To freeze
Gicleur (m.)	Jet
Girouette (f.)	Weather vane
Glissade (f.)	Slip
Godet (m.)	Socket, ferrule
Gomme laque (f.)	Shellac
Gonfler	To inflate
Grain (m.)	Squall
Graisse (f.)	Lubrication
Grand Quartier Général	G.H.Q.
Grincement (m.)	Squeak
Grisard (m.)	Poplar
Guignol d'aileron	Aileron lever
Groupe moto-propulseur (m.)	Power plant

H

Hangar (m.) démontable	Portable shed
Hauban (m.)	Wire, cable
Hélice (f.)	Propeller
Hélice (pale d'—)	Propeller blade
Hélice propulsive	Pusher-type propeller
Hélice tractive	Tractor-type propeller
Hêtre	Beech
Housse (f.)	Cover

French	English
Huile (f.)	Oil
Huile de ricin	Castor oil
Hydroavion (m.)	Seaplane
Hygromètre (m.)	Hygrometer

I

French	English
Incliner sur l'aile (s'—)	To bank
Indicateur (m.) de vitesse	Airspeed indicator
Induit (m.)	Armature, rotor
Inertie (f.)	Inertia
Interrupteur (m.)	Switch
Isoler	To insulate

J

French	English
Jante (f.)	Rim
Jeu (m.)	Play, clearance
Jeu de la denture	Backlash
Joint (m.)	Gasket
Joue (f.)	Flange, cheek
Jumelle (f.)	Shackle
Jumelles (f.)	Binoculars, field glasses

K

French	English
Kilogrammètre (m.)	Kilogram-meter

L

French	English
Lâche	Slack
Laiton (m.)	Brass
Lance-bombes (m.)	Bomb-dropping gear
Levier (m.)	Lever
Ligne de vol (f.)	Line of flight
Lin (m.)	Flax
Longeur hors-tout	Overall length
"Looping" (faire le)	To loop
Lubréfiant (m.)	Lubricant
Lunettes (f.)	Goggles

M

French	English
Magneto (f.) de départ	Starting magneto
Mal des montagnes (m.)	Height sickness
"Manche à balai" (m.)	"Joystick"

French	English
Manette (f.)	Hand lever
Manomètre (m.)	Pressure gauge
Maquette (f.)	Model
Mât (m.)	Strut
Mélange (m.)	Mixture
Mettre en marche	To start up
Minium (m.)	Red lead
Mitrailleuse (f.)	Machine gun
Montant (m.)	Strut, upright
Montée (f.)	Climb
Moteur à démultiplicateur	Geared-down engine
Moteur à refroidissement par l'eau	Water-cooled engine
Moteur en étoile	Radial engine
Moteur monosoupape	Single-valve engine
Moteur rotatif	Rotary engine
Moteur surcomprimé	High-compression engine
Moyeu d'hélice	Propeller hub

N

French	English
Nervure (f.)	Rib
Nez (m.)	Nose
Niveau (de) (m.)	Level
Niveau d'huile	Oil level
Noyé	Flooded
Noyer (m.); Noyer	Walnut; to flood
Noyer le carburateur	To flood the carburetor
Nuage (m.)	Cloud

O

French	English
Observateur (m.)	Observer
Orage (m.)	Thunderstorm
Orifice (m.) d'échappement	Exhaust port
Orme (m.)	Elm
Ossature (f.)	Framework
Ouvert	Open, "on"

P

French	English
Pale d'hélice (f.)	Propeller blade
Palier (m.)	Level flight
Palonnier du gouvernail de direction	Rudder bar
Panne (f.)	Failure, breakdown

FRENCH	ENGLISH
Panne de moteur	Engine failure
Pare-brise (m.)	Windscreen
Pas (m.) d'une hélice	Propeller pitch
Percateur (m.)	Firing pin
Perdre de la vitesse	To lose speed
Pétrole (m.)	Kerosene
Peuplier (m.)	Poplar
Pièces (f.) détachées	Spare parts, components
Pilote (m.)	Airman, pilot
Piquer	To dive
Placage (m.)	Veneering
Plan (m.)	Plane, deck, airfoil
Plancher (m.)	Flooring
Planchette-support (f.) des instruments de bord	Instrument panel
Planer	To glide
Plein (faire de—)	To fill up
Pleine charge (à—)	All out
Plomb (m.)	Lead
Pneumatique (m.)	Tire
P.C.	Abbreviation of *Poids de Combustible*—fuel load
Point (m.) mort	Dead center
Pompe (f.)	Pump
Poupe (f.)	Stern
Pression (f.)	Pressure
Prévision (f.) du temps	Weather forecast
Profil (m.) de l'aile	Wing section
Profondeur de l'aile	Chord

Q

FRENCH	ENGLISH
Queue (f.)	Tail
Quille-dérive (f.)	Keel

R

FRENCH	ENGLISH
Radiateur (m.)	Radiator
Radiateur nid d'abeilles	Honeycomb radiator
Riad aérien (m.)	Air raid
Ralenti (au)	Throttled down
Raté d'allumage (m.)	Misfire
Rayon (m.)	Spoke, radius
Recul (m.)	Recoil
Redresser un appareil en vol	To flatten out an aircraft in flight

French	English
Réglable	Adjustable
Rembourré	Padded
Réservoir (m.)	Tank
Réservoir de secours	Auxiliary tank
Réservoir en charge	Gravity-feed tank
Ressort (m.)	Spring
Retour (m.)	Backfire
Révision générale (f.)	Overhaul
Robinet (m.)	Cock, tap
Rondelle (f.)	Washer
Rose des vents (f.)	Compass card
Roue (f.) de train d'atterrissage	Landing wheel
Rouille (f.)	Rust
Rouler	To roll

S

French	English
Sandow (m.)	Elastic shock cord (after the strong man)
Saucisse (f.)	Observation balloon (sausage)
Secteur (m.)	Sector, quadrant
Siège (m.)	Seat
Siège blindé	Armored seat
Soupape (f.)	Valve
Stabilisateur (m.)	Stabilizer, tail plane
Strapontin (m.)	Folding seat
Surcharger	Overload
Surface ailaire	Wing area
Sustention (f.)	Lift
Synchronisé	Synchronized

T

French	English
Tachymètre (m.)	Tachometer
Tambour (m.) de mitrailleuse Lewis	Lewis gun drum
Teck (m.)	Teak
Télégraphie sans fil (f.)	Wireless telegraphy
Télémètre (m.)	Range finder
Terrain d'atterrissage (m.)	Landing field
Tirant (m.)	Tie rod, stay
Tirer à travers l'hélice	To fire through the propeller
Tirer en chasse	To fire forward

French	English
Tissu (m.)	Fabric
Toile (f.) écrue	Unbleached linen
Tôle (f.)	Sheet iron
Tourelle (f.)	Gun rail
Traînée (f.)	Drag
Trame (f.)	Woof
Travée (f.)	Bay
Tremble (m.)	Aspen
Tribord	Starboard
Trou (m.) d'air	Air pocket
T.S.F.	Wireless telegraphy
Tuyau (m.)	Pipe

U

French	English
Usure (f.)	Wear

V

French	English
"V"	Dihedral
Vent (m.)	Wind
Vent (sous le)	Leeward
Vernis (m.)	Varnish
Vide (m.)	Vacuum, empty
Virage (m.)	Turn
Virer	To turn
Vis à tête fraisée	Countersunk screw
Vis sans fin	Worm gear
Vitesse (f.)	Speed
Vitesse à l'atterrissage	Landing speed
Vitesse en vol piquée	Diving speed
Vitesse indiquée	Indicated airspeed
Voilure (f.)	Wings
Vol (m.)	Flight
Vol de nuit	Night flight
Vol peu assuré	Unsteady flight
Vrille (f.)	Tailspin

Z

French	English
Zinc (m.)	Zinc
"Zinc" (m.)	"Ship," aircraft
Zone troublée (f.)	Disturbed area

PHILOSOPHY AND TACTICS OF AERIAL COMBAT, 1917

By late 1916, the Service Aéronautique *was able to provide the students attending the School of Combat (single-seater) at Pau a written tactical guide. This guide was constantly revised as the pattern of aerial warfare grew clearer with the passing months, and even weeks. The mimeographed sheets contained the distillate of experience of hundreds of French* chasse *pilots during two costly years of trial and error. The following translation is from an original issued to Leland L. Rounds, of New York City, in early 1917:*

Pursuit flying is a very delicate mission and the qualities required of a pursuit pilot are numerous. He must above all be animated by the highest sentiments of duty. He must be an excellent pilot and a good shot—calm and endowed with great *sang-froid.* He must go aloft with this principle: to surprise the enemy, to attack only with sure blows and with utter confidence.

Before being able to attack an enemy machine, he must above all be the complete master of his own machine, and to know how to profit from the resources it offers him. On this point, one is never strong enough, and each day, on each flight, one must perfect one's self. For this, one must work without letup while in the air. To steer an aircraft is nothing; to fly it is difficult. A good pilot must be able to do with his machine as he will, even the most difficult of acrobatic maneuvers must be executed with a complete spirit of freedom; flying must be instinctive and in no way mechanical. Such flying is not to be acquired in one day or the next, but by methodical and progressive training to which the greatest importance must be attached.

With the present system of armament, aerial combat is not only a question of maneuver; for if you are well armed, so is the enemy. To approach him at a short distance in order to deliver sure blows is a matter of great delicacy and demands much experience. The outcome of a combat always depends upon the skill displayed by one pilot or the other.

A priori, it is very difficult to indicate one method of combat for pursuit aircraft. The method, in effect, varies each day with the progress in aviation, with the perfection of armament systems, with the class of pilots. A principle which is valid today may be worthless tomorrow; a doctrine applied in one sector may be questionable in another. We will concern ourselves, then, with the study of general principles which, at the present time, pilots must respect in the preparation of combat, its execution, its breaking off.

Preparation for Combat: The flight of the hunter.

Pursuit flying is continual acrobacy. In order to protect one's self on all sides, one must never fly in a straight line. One banks gently on one wing, then the other, in such a manner so as to clearly observe what is happening on all sides. Sudden reversals of flight course and abrupt climbing turns are good in order to avoid surprises coming from the rear. ONE MUST SURPRISE AND AVOID BEING SURPRISED.

Seeking Out the Enemy:

With the great number of aircraft about, it is difficult to recognize the type or even the nationality of a machine when seen approaching from a distance. When one perceives a machine in the distance, one must proceed to examine it. The Boches have many camouflaged aircraft without crosses on their wings, others carrying cocardes with small crosses in the center. One must recognize them by their shape and by certain peculiarities which can be made out from a distance.

It is necessary, then, to be intimate with the peculiarities of all enemy aircraft and especially of the disposition of their armament.

Group Flights:

In principle, at the present time, solitary flights are prohibited. Patrols are executed by groups of two, three or more machines. Unanimity of opinion, however, has yet to be reached on this point.

The squadron leader chooses the method which seems to him the most judicious in the sector where his escadrille is operating. Discipline, whatever methods are applied, must be rigorously observed. A group must be welded together. The man flying alone is eagerly sought out by the enemy, and it is he who is first attacked. If the group is compact, even an enemy superior in numbers will hesitate to attack.

The flight leader sees a machine in the distance. He immediately shakes his wings; it is the signal to attack. If the sighted machine is alone, it is attacked by the flight leader, followed by one or two of his comrades; the remainder of the patrol stays above to protect those who are attacking. If several enemy machines are to be dealt with, the entire group attacks as a unit. If, as is often the case, the enemy is divided into separate groups, it becomes necessary for the attacking group to so separate itself and deal with the enemy on a group-to-group basis. When the combat is ended, the flight regroups itself at a predetermined point in space.

Preparation for Attack:

Preparation for attack is a primordial affair. *One must never commence firing until one is quite near.* To approach the enemy one must hurtle down from the sun, the clouds. It is very difficult to see an approaching airplane when it is falling towards one from the sun. One must then make fullest use of this aid and leap upon the enemy with the sun at one's back, diving with all possible speed.

Execution of the Combat:

Attacking a solitary *monoplace* (single-seater) is the easiest to accomplish, but this is not to say that it is not dangerous! Attacking a *monoplace* is usually done by diving straight down, then keeping always a slight altitude advantage over the enemy machine. This is the style of attack preferred by pilots of great experience in aerial combat.

Attacking a Group:

To attack a group it is necessary first to split apart the formation; for this, it is usually only necessary to maneuver in such a manner as to sow disorder. This done, the individual machines are then dealt with.

Combat:

Combat is a series of continual maneuvers. One must unnerve the enemy, to keep him continually under fire. Combats in general do not last long, the adversary retreats after several passes have been made. Never engage in combat unless all the advantages are on your side.

Defense:

If during flight you are taken by surprise, you must *not* immediately dive, but climb rapidly for altitude. If the enemy follows you, put yourself in a spiraling climb and wait for a favorable moment to attack. If, for one reason or another, you are not able to climb, it will suffice to put yourself into a circling maneuver.

Attacking a Solitary Biplace:

The *biplace* is a machine well protected from the rear, thus it is very difficult to approach. In order to get in effective bursts of fire, it is necessary to place your machine in one of the dead angles of fire—either from three-quarters in front of the enemy machine, or from directly underneath its tail. If a firing approach is made outside of these dead angles, you will find yourself under fire by the enemy observer. If he fires without letup, you have cause for rejoicing, for he will soon find himself short of ammunition. On the other hand, if he fires in short, careful bursts, take caution; he is a man with true *sang-froid.* With such an enemy, the outcome of the combat will depend largely upon the skill with which the approach is made.

Attacking an Escorted Biplace:

One often finds a *biplace* accompanied by one or two fighters. One must then attempt to maneuver in such a manner so as to lure away the escort, whereupon the *biplace* can be dealt with in the manner described above. It is folly to attack a *biplace* if the escort stays grouped in a protective position. If you miss the *biplace* on the first firing pass, you must never climb back above it but immediately break off the combat.

Attacking a Group of Biplaces:

A compact formation of *biplaces* is extremely difficult to approach and to attack, for one quickly finds himself in a cross fire from all of the machine guns. It is necessary to try to break up the formation and attack only isolated machines.

Attacking a Triplace:

The attack upon a *triplace* requires great skill and perfect knowledge of combat, as this is a machine which has but one dead angle, behind and under the tail. This angle is very narrow, only about 30 degrees.

Breaking Off Combat:

Breaking off the fight requires a delicacy of touch. If the observer has not been hit, he is waiting for the moment to fire a band of machine gun bullets at his aggressor.

The pilot must break off the battle by executing the most acrobatic maneuvers possible: spirals, wing-slips and falling-leafs.

The spiral has long been considered the most secure method. It is in effect excellent with the average opponent, but perhaps is a little dangerous when facing an enemy of quality.

Wing-slips and falling-leafs are both excellent methods of breaking off combat with a skilled enemy.

BASIC PILOTING ADVICE

A Good Pilot Must Be Adroit, Prudent, Decisive

ADROIT:

1. *Takeoff:* He leaves facing the wind, getting the tail up quickly. With vigilance in his legs, he rolls straight and long. He does not take off with his engine missing, but gets the tail down as soon as possible.

2. *In Flight:* He maintains constant speed and does not lose height in executing maneuvers around the horizontal axis of his machine.

3. *While Descending:* He cuts the engine with the throttle, at the same time diminishing the flow of fuel.

4. *The Landing:* He looks to see that other aircraft are not coming in to land at the same time as he. He lands into the wind. He proceeds for as long a time as possible in a straight line before touching down to earth. A few seconds after this moment, he cuts the ignition switch.

He diminishes his angle of descent progressively as he passes through 150 feet, in such fashion as to arrive softly on the ground. In order to touch down, he raises the nose slightly. He avoids always a too-rapid landing. He seeks to preserve his machine.

5. *While Rolling on the Ground:* He rolls softly. He avoids putting on his motor again if he is going to ground-loop, otherwise he will flip over on his back.

6. *In the Running of his Engine:* He takes care of his engine. While on the ground, he never lets it run for long periods. When he arrives at an altitude of approximately 1000 feet he throttles back so the engine is turning no more r.p.m. than necessary for the mission. While climbing, he carefully regulates his air throttle.

PRUDENT:

1. *Before Taking Off:* He examines his aircraft, tests the controls and runs up his engine for the shortest possible time that will allow him to determine that it is in perfect running order. He carefully notes the oil-pressure gauge.

2. *In Flight:* He avoids all risky maneuvers near the ground, below 1000 feet. He permits himself no liberties. He constantly scans the earth below him so as not to be caught unprepared for a sudden forced landing should his engine fail. When he decides to land he never tries to stretch his glide. He shows respect for the landing regulations of the field.

He undertakes no acrobatics unless he knows how they can be perfectly executed and unless he knows that his machine is stressed for the maneuver in question.

If his aircraft assumes a bizarre attitude which causes him momentary distress, he cuts off the fuel flow and puts all controls central; as soon as the machine has righted itself, he puts the throttle back on and resumes his flight.

He avoids entering clouds and fog banks, especially when close to the ground. Before the landing, he always switches off the ignition.

3. *In Case of Engine Failure:* If he is high, he keeps a very flat glide in order to give him the greatest amount of time to observe the terrain below and so as to conserve altitude.

If he is low, he puts his nose down and quickly seeks a place to land. If he is very low, he sets down immediately and lands directly ahead, regardless of the state of the ground.

DECISIVE:

He never loses his head. In difficult situations he faces the danger, weighs it and then makes a decision which seems to him logical. Once this decision is reached, he puts his plan into effect without the slightest hesitation.

SELECTED BIBLIOGRAPHY

Anderson, H. Graeme. *The Medical and Surgical Aspects of Aviation.* Oxford University Press, London, 1919.

Biddle, Maj. Charles J. *The Way of the Eagle.* Charles Scribner's Sons, New York, 1919.

Boraston, Lt. Col. J. H., editor. *Sir Douglas Haig's Despatches.* J. M. Dent and Sons, London, 1919.

Bordeaux, Henry. *Georges Guynemer, Knight of the Air.* Yale University Press, New Haven, Conn., 1918.

Bruce, J. M. *British Aeroplanes 1914–1918.* Putnam and Co., Ltd., London, 1957.

Buchan, John. *Nelson's History of the War.* Vol. XIII. Thomas Nelson and Sons, Ltd., London.

Carlier, *Commandant* André-H. *La Photographie Aérienne Pendant la Guerre.* Librarie Delagrave, Paris, 1921.

Channing, Grace Ellery. *War Letters of Edmond Genêt.* Charles Scribner's Sons, New York, 1918.

Chapman, John Jay. *Victor Chapman's Letters from France.* A memoir. The Macmillan Co., New York, 1917.

Chavagnes, R. de. *De Guynemer à Fonck—L'Aviation de Chasse—Le Groupe des Cigognes.* Paris, 1920.

Cheesman, E. F., editor. W. M. Lamberton's *Fighter Aircraft of the 1914–1918 War.* Harleyford Publications, Ltd., Letchworth, Hertfordshire, England, 1960.

Chinn, Lt. Col. George M. *The Machine Gun.* Vol. I. U. S. Government Printing Office, Washington, D. C., 1951.

Churchill, Winston S. *The World Crisis, 1911–1918.* Charles Scribner's Sons, New York, 1931.

Falls, Cyril. *The Great War.* G. P. Putnam's Sons, New York, 1959.

Foch, *Maréchal* Ferdinand. *Memoirs of Field Marshal Foch.* Translation by Col. T. Bentley Mott. Doubleday, Doran and Co., Garden City, N. Y., 1931.

Fokker, Anthony G. and Bruce Gould. *Flying Dutchman*. Henry Holt and Co., New York, 1931.

Fortescue, Granville. *Front Line and Deadline*. G. P. Putnam's Sons, New York, 1937.

Gibbons, Floyd. *The Red Knight of Germany*. Doubleday, Doran and Co., Garden City, N. Y., 1927.

Hall, James N. *Kitchener's Mob*. Houghton Mifflin Co., Boston, 1916.

——————. *High Adventure*. Houghton Mifflin Co., Boston, 1918.

——————, Charles B. Nordhoff and Edgar G. Hamilton, editors. *The Lafayette Flying Corps*. 2 vols. Houghton Mifflin Co., Boston, 1920. (Reprint edition: Kennikat Press, Inc., Port Washington, N.Y., 1964.)

——————. *My Island Home*. Little, Brown and Co., Boston, 1952.

Hall, Weston B. *"En l'Air!"* The New Library, New York, 1918. (largely fiction)

—————— and J. J. Niles. *One Man's War*. Henry Holt and Co., New York, 1929. (largely fiction)

Hartney, Lt. Col. Harold E. *Up and At 'Em*. Stackpole Sons, Harrisburg, Pa., 1940.

Hay, Ian (John Hay Beith). *The First Hundred Thousand*. Houghton Mifflin Co., Boston, 1916.

Horne, Alistair. *The Price of Glory; Verdun, 1916*. St. Martin's Press, New York, 1963.

Horne, Charles F., editor. *Source Records of the Great War*. Vols. I–VII. National Alumni, 1923.

Houston, David F. *Eight Years with Wilson's Cabinet, 1913–1920*. Vol. I. Doubleday, Page and Co., Garden City, N. Y., 1926.

Jauneaud, *Commandant* Marcel. *L'Aviation Militaire et la Guerre Aérienne*. Flammarion, Paris, 1923.

King, David W. *L.M. 8046*. Duffield and Co., New York, 1927.

Lycett, John. *Dictionnaire Technique de l'Aviation*. H. Dunod et E. Pinant, Paris, 1918.

McConnell, James R. *Flying for France*. Doubleday, Page and Co., New York, 1917.

Matthews, R. Borlase. *The Aviation Pocket Book for 1918*. London, 1918.

Michelin & Cie. *The Battle of Verdun—A Guide to the Battlefields*. Paris, 1920.

——————. *Ypres, and the Battles for Its Possession*. Paris, 1920.

Mitchell, Brig. Gen. William. *Memoirs of World War I*. Random House, New York, 1960.

Moore, Samuel T. *U. S. Airpower*. Greenberg, Publisher, New York, 1958.

Mortane, Jacques. *La Guerre Aérienne*. Bound editions. Paris, 1915–1918.

Mortane, Jacques. *Les As Peints par Eux-mêmes*. Librarie Alphonse Lemerre, Paris, 1917.

——— *Chasseurs de Boches*. L'Édition Française Illustrée, Paris, 1917.

——— *Carré d'As*. Éditions Baudinière. Paris, 1927.

——— *A Travers les Filets de l'Ennemi*. Éditions Baudinière, Paris, 1929.

——— *Traqués par l'Ennemi . . .* Éditions Baudinière, Paris, 1929.

Mott, Col. T. Bentley. *Myron T. Herrick: Friend of France*. Doubleday, Doran and Co., Garden City, N. Y., 1929.

Mowrer, Paul Scott. *The House of Europe*. Houghton Mifflin Co., Boston, 1945.

Palmer, Frederick, *Newton D. Baker: America at War*. Vol. II. Dodd, Mead and Co., New York, 1931.

Parsons, Edwin C. *The Great Adventure*. Doubleday, Doran and Co., Garden City, N. Y., 1937.

Prince, Norman. *A Volunteer Who Died for the Cause He Loved*. Letters. Memoir by George F. Babbitt. Houghton Mifflin Co., Boston, 1917.

Reynolds, Quentin. *They Fought for the Sky*. Rinehart and Co., New York, 1957.

Rickenbacker, Capt. Edward V. *Fighting the Flying Circus*. Frederick A. Stokes Co., New York, 1919.

Robertson, Bruce, editor. *Air Aces of the 1914–1918 War*. Harleyford Publications, Ltd., Letchworth, Hertfordshire, England, 1959.

Robertson, Bruce, Editor. *Von Richthofen and the Flying Circus*. Harleyford Publications, Ltd., Letchworth, Hertfordshire, England, 1958.

Rockwell, Col. Paul Ayres. *American Fighters in the Foreign Legion*. The Country Life Press, New York, 1925.

Rockwell, Col. Paul Ayres. *War Letters of Kiffin Yates Rockwell*. The Country Life Press, New York, 1925.

Seeger, Alan. *Letters and Diary of Alan Seeger*. Charles Scribner's Sons, New York, 1917.

Stevenson, William Y. *From Poilu to Yank*. Houghton Mifflin Co., Boston and New York, 1918.

Sweetser, Arthur. *Roadside Glimpses of the Great War*. The Macmillan Co., New York, 1916.

Thénault, Lt. Col. Georges. *L'Escadrille Lafayette*. Librarie Hachette, Paris, 1939.

The New York Times Co. *The European War*. Vols. I–XI. New York, 1916, 1917.

Toumlin, H. A. Jr. *Air Service, A.E.F.* D. van Nostrand Co., New York, 1927.

Weeks, Alice S. *Greater Love Hath No Man.* (Letters written by Americans at the Front.) Bruce Humphries, Inc., Boston, 1939.

Veil, Charles (with Howard Marsh). *Adventure's a Wench.* Grosset and Dunlap, New York, 1938.

Wharton, Edith. *Fighting France.* Charles Scribner's Sons, New York, 1915.

Winslow, Carroll Dana. *With the French Flying Corps.* Charles Scribner's Sons, New York, 1917.

PHOTO CREDITS

Air Vice-Marshall Raymond Collishaw: 17 top
David W. King: 1
National Archives: 10 top; 29 top
Edwin C. Parsons: 11 top & bottom; 26 bottom
Paul Ayres Rockwell: 2; 3; 5 top & middle; 8; 13; 14; 15 top; 16; 18-19; 20 top left; 22 top, lower left & right; 23 bottom; 24 top; 30 top; 31 top
Soubiran Collection, National Air Museum: 5 bottom; 10 bottom; 21 top & bottom; 22 top; 23 top; 25 bottom; 26 top; 27; 30 bottom; 31 bottom; 32
Robert Soubiran, U.S. Air Force Photo: 20 bottom left & right
National Air Museum: 22 bottom; 15 bottom
U. S. Air Force: 4; 7; 12; 17 bottom; 20 top right
H. Hugh Wynne: 12 top; 24 bottom; 28 top & bottom
Charles H. Dolan II: 29 bottom

NOTES AND ACKNOWLEDGMENTS

The foregoing bibliography cites only those works the author made direct use of in preparing the present volume. It does not include the hundreds of contemporary newspaper accounts and wartime magazine articles consulted in private and public collections. The most valuable works are those written by the participants, which are as factual as flight logs, combat diaries, memory and personal feelings would allow. The exceptions are the two volumes ghost-written for Weston Bert Hall; each is an imaginative blend of near-truth and outright falsehood. Indispensable to any writer on the Lafayette Escadrille and the larger organization, the Lafayette Flying Corps, is the two-volume history by Hall, Nordhoff, and Hamilton. This detailed and sometimes personal history has been consulted for nearly every chapter. Invaluable for documentation of the Americans' service with the *Légion Étrangère* is Paul Rockwell's comprehensive work that chronicles the lives of Americans in the three *Régiments de Marche* from early 1914 until the end of the war. For wit, wealth of anecdote and graphic descriptions of heroism and ludicrousness, David King's personal journal is unmatched. Ted Parsons' lively and debonair story of the Lafayette Escadrille is unique: he was the only American pilot to write a comprehensive and personal account of the Escadrille's activities to be published under a single cover. James Norman Hall wrote a very revealing and intimate story of the Escadrille while he was at the Front, but *High Adventure* contains no dates and uses fictionalized names. Of the French N.124 officers, only Georges Thénault survived the war to write his side of the story, a remarkably restrained account. The original French volume, published in 1939, is the only version worth considering. An American edition, published not long after the war, was so heavily rewritten and slanted in favor of one of the early Escadrille pilots that Thénault's own evaluation of his men has been lost. Mrs. Sarah Spencer Thénault has graciously permitted quotations from her late husband's work to appear in this volume.

Fortunately for the researcher, the Legionnaires and the Escadrille pilots were conscientious letter-writers. The published letters of Kiffin Rockwell, Alan Seeger, Victor Chapman, Norman Prince and Edmond Genêt were all consulted. Even more rewarding were the hundreds of unpublished letters made available to the author by Paul Ayres Rockwell, who corresponded regularly with nearly every American in the *Légion Étrangère* and in the various *escadrilles* of the French *Service Aéronautique*. Excerpts from these hitherto-unpublished accounts have been included in the present volume. None of the letters were written for posterity, but as spontaneous release from emotions aroused by battle, fatigue, wounds or boredom. Thus—even after fifty years—they retain an immediacy not to be found in *ex post facto* writings.

The author has made extensive use of material gathered by personal contact with the survivors of the Legion, the Escadrille and among those who flew with regular *escadrilles de chasse*. Paul Ayres Rockwell was unstinting with his time, his files, his memory and his patience during the three years this book was being prepared. The author enjoyed the hospitality of the Rockwell home, which is a veritable treasure house of memorabilia pertaining to the Escadrille. Ted Parsons has been equally as generous with personal reminiscences, photographs and tape-recorded interviews conducted in his living room and in the living room of his 1917 flying companion, Henry S. Jones. It is to Colonel Rockwell and Admiral Parsons that the author is most heavily indebted. Other N.124 survivors who have been most generous with their time are Colonel Carl Dolan, Emil Marshall and Edward Hinkle. And in the midst of a pilot's reunion in 1961, the late Colonel Harold Buckley Willis took time to steer the author toward unimpeachable sources while the initial research was under way. Many long, pleasant and profitable hours were spent in the company of the effervescent Colonel David Wooster King, to whom an introduction was arranged by Count Edward de Pianelli de la Velette, a postwar acquaintance of Lieutenant Colonel Georges Thénault.

Generous with their time and their material have been many pilots who flew with escadrilles other than N.124. The author is grateful to his literary agent, Kenneth Proctor Littauer—a pioneer reconnaissance pilot—and to Leland L. Rounds, George Dock, Jr., Charles Maury Jones, Dabney D. Horton, Herschel J. McKee, Lester S. Brady, the late Austen B. Crehore and the late Eugene Jacques Bullard, the world's first Negro military pilot. All of these men shared their experiences willingly with the author. The author is also indebted to families of the pilots, including the heirs of Frederick W. Zinn.

Corollary material was obtained first-hand from such non-Lafayette World War I pilots as Captain Edward V. Rickenbacker and Reed Chambers, of the 94th Pursuit Squadron; the late Colonel Herbert M. Mason, Sr., USAF, Ret., Clayton Knight and Lawrence Callahan, former Royal Flying Corps and U.S.A.S. pilots.

In Washington, D. C., Lieutenant Colonel James F. Sunderman and Major Gene Guerny of the U.S.A.F. Office of Information Services were most helpful, as were Philip S. Hopkins and his staff of the National Air Museum. In Dayton, Ohio, Lieutenant Colonel Kimborough S. Brown and Major Royal D. Frey put the services of the Air Force Museum at the author's disposal and personally helped track down difficult bits of information. In New York, Elizabeth Brown of the unfortunately now-defunct Institute of the Aeronautical Sciences was helpful in tracing several rare items pertaining to the visit of Thaw, Prince and Cowdin to the United States in 1916.

In Paris, the author is indebted to General Paul Stehlin, present Commander in Chief of the *Armée de l'Air,* for opening the doors to the stupendous files of the old *Service Aéronautique.* At the Caserne Denfert in Versailles, the author was ably assisted by Lieutenant Colonel Hayez, Chief of the *Service Historique,* and by M. Pierre Veujoz, *Redacteur.* Piles of dog-eared manila folders and bound operations reports covering the entire operational life of N.124 were placed at the author's disposal. It was here that many conflicts in research were clarified.

In St. Germain-en-Laye, Lieutenant Colonel Salvatore A. Pelle, Headquarters, EUCOM, was instrumental in setting up a two-hour helicopter flight over the entire Verdun battlefield. At Verdun, the author owes much to Brigadier General Donald G. Grothaus, Captain Joseph Castle and SFC Jack Coffee, all of the 4th Logistical Command, U. S. Army. Special appreciation must go to Captain George Knowles, who flew the author over the battlefields in a helicopter at altitudes and speeds common to Nieuport pilots in 1916; a simulated engine failure near the spot where Balsley must have gone down was recovered with skill that any rotary engine pilot would have found gratifying.

For specific details of the Oberndorf mission of October 12, 1916, the author is grateful for the diligent research efforts on the part of Z. H. von Herrn Flaig, of the Mauser-Werke A.G., and by Fräulein Tamara Alt, of the archival section of the Oberndorf *Schwarzwälder Bote.* A first-hand account of the raid as seen from the air was provided the author by Air Vice-Marshal Raymond Collishaw, D.S.O., M.C., D.F.C., *L.d'H., C. de G.*

Numerous personal friends contributed in various ways to the work done on this project. Among them: H. Hugh Wynne, of the *Cross & Cockade Society;* James J. Sloan, of the *American Aviation Historical Society;* J. J. Smith, who has devoted many years to tracking down the names and addresses of all U. S. pilots of First World War vintage; Cole Palen, who allowed the author to run up the engines and become familiar with the cockpit layouts of his privately-owned Spad XIII, Nieuport 28 and Fokker D VII; Martin Iger, who allowed the author to execute some of the milder combat maneuvers in his all-metal Swift; David B. Eisendrath, Jr., and Simon Nathan, who materially aided and offered sound technical advice regarding the difficult job of copying very old and faded album prints loaned by survivors.

Especial acknowledgment is made to Robert D. Loomis and Martin Caidin for valuable editorial advice given from their own extensive fund of knowledge concerning authors' problems in general and aviation in particular.

Research for this volume was conducted in New York, Washington, D. C., North Carolina, Florida, Ohio, England, France and Germany. The whole stretch of the old Western Front was covered by automobile and on foot during the summer of 1963. The route covered led from the Vosges in the east to St. Pol-sur-Mer in the west. Aerial photographs and panoramic views were made by the author of certain of the terrain features that figured largely in the lives of the Americans in the *Légion Étrangère* and in the Lafayette Escadrille. No matter how lucid a description can be found in published works, nothing can take the place of tramping over sites with your own two feet. The only out-of-the-way experience on this trip occurred near Bois Sabot, on the Souain-Tahure road—down which the First Regiment attacked on September 25, 1915. Turning east from the monument to the dead of Navarin Farm, we proceeded down this road and found it in worse repair than Genêt must have seen it forty-eight years ago. A crawling, jolting ride of five kilometers was brought to a sudden halt at the sound of artillery, crashing not too far away. Then, the sound of a light-aircraft engine. It was a bright, sunny Sunday morning with but few clouds in the sky. The guns picked up their booming—they sounded ominously like 75s—and for an instant it was easy to believe that the Champagne sector is still, as some old soldiers maintain, haunted by the ghosts of the hundreds of thousands who died there. Backing down the road, a sign (previously overlooked) was passed, the mystery solved: the huge tract of land containing the ruins of Souain, Tahure, Perthes-les-Hurlus and the Bois Sabot is today a firing range used—even on Sundays—by the French Army. The little plane buzzing low against the sky was an L-5, correcting fire.

The great majority of the photographs came from prints made from original negatives taken by Escadrille pilot Robert Soubiran and from original negatives loaned to the author by Paul Ayres Rockwell.

These negatives, averaging approximately 2½″ × 4¼″, are remarkably preserved and responded well to enlargement with routine cleaning and an occasional light application of vaseline to help subdue the inevitable scratches. Both Soubiran and Rockwell used simple folding cameras equipped with anastigmat lenses and utilizing orthochromatic roll film with a speed index of approximately ASA 8. In many cases the print quality rivals that obtainable today with the best of equipment and materials.

Where negatives were not available—as was the case with the small album prints owned by Colonel King and Admiral Parsons—copy negatives were made by the author using a 35mm reflex single-lens camera.

The same 35mm camera was used extensively in microfilming documents and even entire books, both in this country and in France. In this way, a hundred pounds of reading matter can be economically reduced to a few ounces of film and can be carried anywhere for later projection, using a portable strip-film projector with a built-in screen in a case measuring only 12″ × 14″ × 4″.

Occasional conflicts in research data were resolved by a careful check with the official records at Versailles and, wherever possible, by interview with the survivors. To cite one example: numerous written sources have it that Lieutenant de Laage was fatally injured while attempting to take off in a new Spad. But Colonel Carl Dolan, who was on the field at Ham on the day of the tragedy, clearly remembers seeing de Laage in the cockpit of a Morane. And it was Colonel Dolan who clarified the circumstances surrounding MacMonagle's last patrol.

The first draft of this book was written in New York City and in Casey Key, Florida. The final draft was completed and edited at Holleby, a farm in southern Norway.

INDEX

INDEX

About the Author

HERBERT MOLLOY MASON, JR., one of the nation's authorities on historical and contemporary airpower, is uniquely qualified through experience and his great skill as a researcher to write this book. A man who has flown in many types of aircraft at speeds from 40 to 1000 miles per hour, he has been able to blend his personal knowledge and experience in the air with his intimate story of men who many decades past blazed a path through the sky.

A native of Texas and the son of a World War I combat pilot, Mr. Mason spent his childhood in the midst of aviation activities. A United States Marine at seventeen, he served aboard heavy warships during and after World War II, and then returned to aviation. He is one of the few Americans to have attended the American University of Beirut, Lebanon; he received his degree in journalism and French from Trinity University, Texas. He has been a successful radio newsman and producer for radio and television, and for eight years was Aviation Editor of *True* magazine. He is active in many phases of aviation, and recently completed a flight to Europe in a war-weary B-17 Flying Fortress bomber. In researching this book over a period of several years, he traveled some 16,000 miles—including an extensive tour by helicopter, on foot and by automobile of the 1914–1918 Western Front.